Cult
MOVIES

PHILIP FRENCH was a senior producer with BBC Radio for thirty years and since 1978 he has been the *Observer's* film critic. Among the books he has written and edited are *Age of Austerity 1945–51*, *The Movie Moguls*, *Westerns*, *The Faber Book of Movie Verse*, and *Malle on Malle*.

KARL FRENCH is TV previewer of the *Financial Times*. He co-wrote *The French Brothers' Film Quiz Book*, edited *The Marx Brothers' Screenplays*, and *Screen Violence*. French is author of *The A–Z of Apocalypse Now* and *The A–Z of This Is Spinal Tap*.

Cult
MOVIES

Karl French and Philip French

BILLBOARD BOOKS

An imprint of Watson-Guptill Publications/New York

First published in Great Britain in 1999 by
PAVILION BOOKS LIMITED
London House, Great Eastern Wharf
Parkgate Road, London SW11 4NQ

Designed by Nigel Partridge

First published in the United States in 2000 by Billboard Books,
an imprint of Watson-Guptill Publications,
a division of BPI Communications, Inc.
at 770 Broadway, New York, New York 10003

Library of Congress Cataloging-in-Publication Data for this title can be obtained
from the Library of Congress

ISBN 0-8230-7916-3

Set in Futura
Printed in Singapore by Imago

First printing in U.S. in 2000

1 2 3 4 5 6 7 8 9 /08 07 06 05 04 03 02 01 00

CONTENTS

INTRODUCTION

Of the several dictionary definitions of a cult, the more informal ones relate to the subject of this book — i.e. 'an intense interest in and devotion to a person, idea or activity' and 'the person, idea etc. arousing such devotion'. The size of its following is not specified — the numbers can range from a handful to millions — and the object can take different forms. There is the implication, however, that a cult cannot be universal, official or orthodox. So while Christianity, for example, contains many cults, the Catholic Church and the Church of England are not cults.

The term 'cult movie' has been current for 20 years or more but the idea had been in the air since the first film was shown on the big screen to a paying audience. This was *La Sortie des Usines Lumière*, a 45-second shot of workers leaving the Lumière Brothers factory in Lyons, which was shown at the beginning of the selection of Lumière films at the Grand Café on the Boulevard des Capucines in Paris on 28th December 1895. It was followed by the more sensational *L'Arrivée d'un Train en Gare de la Ciotat,* which made nervous spectators duck for cover, and the first cinematic comedy, *L'Arroseur arrosé* (a little boy treading on a hose and causing it to spray water in a gardener's face), which made them laugh. For those Lyons labourers, the first people to see themselves up there on the screen, this film clip must have become an object of obsessive interest and they themselves would have constituted a cult drawn together by their fascination with it. Eight years later, Rudyard Kipling wrote his classic story 'Mrs Bathhurst', the first literary work of consequence about the cinema, turning upon a British soldier in South Africa who becomes obsessed with a newsreel that presented a glimpse of the eponymous New Zealand landlady. After 'The Arrival of a Train at La Ciotat', Lumière cameramen shot films of locomotive journeys around the world, and train films have been a major cult ever since. The National Film Theatre and similar cinémathèques can always fill their auditoriums with railway fans by showing programmes of vintage trains in action. Likewise *L'Arroseur arrosé*, which figured in posters all over Europe advertising the first Lumière show, became the iconic movie comedy and was re-created by François Truffaut in his feature debut, *Les Mistons*, as a homage to the Lumières and the birth of laughter on the screen.

From the 1920s to the 1960s, films played for a few weeks in the West End of London, passed on to the downtown cinemas of the big cities and then played for six days or a week in suburban cinemas (the neighbourhood movie houses that *Variety* calls 'nabes'). They might re-appear 'by public demand' but usually they went into backstreet fleapits until the prints were unshowable and then disappeared, often forever. Only a few movies were regularly reissued in new prints, and film companies didn't give a damn once a film had lost its commercial value. They did not systematically preserve their products: as late as the 1960s Warner Brothers allowed the negative of *My Fair Lady* to deteriorate, and Columbia did not keep the original negative of *Lawrence of Arabia*. Film archives were established around the world, but most of their curators saw their task as conserving films of distinction for posterity, rather than making them available for current viewing. Films of the past — a smallish canon of approved classics, mostly European — were available on 16mm from specialist distributors for film societies to show to their dedicated members who watched them from hard seats in draughty halls. At that time the passionate audience (as opposed to the casual filmgoers) was unevenly divided between serious, informed students of the cinema and dedicated, undiscriminating movie fans.

A major change came in the 1960s, brought about by the greater availability of movies through television and a radical shift in attitudes to popular culture. Commentators contrasted the older 'movie generation' of people who grew up with the cinema with the 'television generation' that was being reared in front of the small screen. But it was precisely that television generation that became steeped in, obsessed by, the movies. Seeing old movies at all times of the day and night at home, influenced by the criticism of the *Cahiers du Cinéma* critics who became fashionable directors (Truffaut, Chabrol, Godard *et al.*), they began to have a newly appreciative, less condescending attitude to Hollywood, and especially to those directors who worked in the traditionally despised or patronized genres – the Western, SF, the horror flick, and the thriller. New film magazines were started. Books on the cinema of the past and present began to appear, written in a different spirit from the few earnest volumes on film as art which had shaped the taste of cinéphiles. When the small handful of established film schools were forced to turn away thousands of prospective students, new film faculties sprang up across America, and departments of film were eventually created in conservative Britain. At the same time there occurred the so-called nostalgia boom, an American obsession with the art and artefacts of the recent past. This was partly caused, and certainly influenced, by the shock administered by the assassination of President Kennedy, an event that brought to an end his vision of a new Camelot and made the future seem less alluring. In Britain at the time there was the new hedonism that expressed itself in the phenomenon of 'Swinging London', which both embraced the new and glamorized the past, and the movies were its supreme expression.

It was in the mid-1960s that trivia quizzes became a passionate activity on US campuses, and at the Brattle Cinema in Cambridge, Mass., patronized by Harvard students, there began the cult of Bogart; which reached its apotheosis in 1969 with Woody Allen's Broadway hit *Play It Again Sam*. Walker Percy's subtle novel *The Movie-Goer*, winner of the National Book Award in 1962, assured its middle-class readers that films were not only as important as other forms of art, but as significant as life itself, and the book steadily took on classic status as the decade progressed. In 1964 Susan Sontag published her influential essay 'Notes on Camp', in which she wrote that 'movie criticism is probably the greatest popularizer of Camp taste today, because people still go to the movies in a high-spirited and unpretentious way'. In the 1960s the old-fashioned, none-too-well-informed 'film fan' was replaced by a new figure, 'the movie buff', a picturegoer steeped in popular cinema, versed in the minutiae of movie history, possessing an encyclopaedic knowledge of films. Not to be confused with the discriminating cinéphile of old, the movie buff in his or her extreme form might have been defined by Oscar Wilde as a man who knows the credits of everything and the value of nothing. The term 'buff', in this sense, had until the mid-century signified an enthusiast for fires and firefighting, the name deriving from the buff uniform once worn by New York's volunteer fire brigades.

Movie buffs saw films, wrote about films, and made films. Following the example of the French New Wave directors, young American film-makers began putting in references to the movies of the past (former critic Peter Bogdanovich led the way with *Targets* and *The Last Picture Show*). In a Hollywood picture of the 1950s, a TV set in the background invariably showed a chase from an anonymous B-feature Western. From the late 1960s, whenever a TV set is on in the background it is showing a recognizable film that comments in some way on the movie we're watching. In the 1960s your favourite movies came to reveal the sort of person you were, and choosing a film for cult status became a way of creating a personal niche of taste and identity in an amorphous mass culture and a threatening mass society. A cult movie can be a link between friends as exemplified by the group of former radicals in John Sayles's film *Return of the Secaucus Seven* (1980), who in their student days during the 1960s adopted as 'their film' Herbert Biberman's *Salt of the Earth*, the left-wing movie made by black-listed artists and shown abroad but proscribed in the US. Or, less attractively, demonstrated by the French delinquents in Bertrand Tavernier's *The Bait* who can quote (in French) every line in Brian DePalma's *Scarface*. The New York chums in *City Slickers* have chosen Howard Hawks's *Red River* as their cult movie, and John Travolta's movie buff in *Get Shorty* belongs to the cults that revere Hawks's *Rio Bravo* and Welles's *Touch of Evil*.

Some movies become cults because of difficulty of access, and in fact an astonishing number of movies that are regularly shown on TV or are available on cassette do not exist in a print fit to be projected in cinemas. Does this mean that when they become accessible, as the once elusive *Citizen Kane* now is, they are no longer cult movies? Perhaps, but not necessarily. *Casablanca*, which helped create the whole concept, remains the cornerstone of cult cinema. *Casablanca*, of course, has several of the qualities that make a cult movie – it's a picture you want to see again and again; it has unforgettable lines; and it seems to have a personal meaning for you and your friends. It was never, however, banned by the censors nor butchered by the producers, ignored by the public nor panned by the critics, a fate suffered by many cult movies. It isn't offensive, perverse, obscure, absurd, deeply flawed, ludicrous, full of preposterous dialogue or made on a shoestring – all of which are, in different combinations, the characteristics of a fair number of cult films. A good many cult pictures have the prime constituent of sad orphans – that of being abandoned and rejected; the problem is, do they retain their status as waifs after being adopted by a large, welcoming family? When Danny Peary published his three large volumes of *Cult Movies* in the 1980s, many readers felt that he was doing to their personal favourite pictures what travel writers do when they write about an idyllic, little-visited Greek island as 'the Aegean's best-kept secret'.

There are cult movies, cult directors, cult actors, and even cult film composers – Ennio Morricone, for instance, and, until they were posthumously adopted by the music critics, Erich Wolfgang Korngold and Bernard Herrmann. There are also cult posters and cult stills. Some films are local cults, some only cults outside their country of origin. Ealing comedies have always been too popular, too acceptable to polite middle-class audiences to become the subject of a cult in Britain, but among anglophiles in the States they have a cult following. Some directors who have never attained a large following or were overlooked by critics during their working lives have had cult status imposed on their whole oeuvres – Jacques Tourneur, Joseph H. Lewis, Edgar G. Ulmer, for instance. Others have produced the odd cult work, and virtually every famous filmmaker has one or two pictures, not necessarily their best, for which their admirers have a special affection. Certain actors recur in cult movies without being themselves cult figures – Jeff Bridges, for example. Jack Nicholson, an actor who has got better and better over some 40 years, is only a cult figure for his early horror films, biker movies, Westerns and early seventies road movies directed by Roger Corman, Richard Rush, Monte Hellman and Bob Rafelson. The less well-known Dick Miller, however, an amiable performer of no great distinction, is a cult actor for his 1950s Corman films like *A Bucket of Blood* and *The Little Shop of Horrors,* and because of that cult status he has been given roles in movies produced or directed by, among others, Steven Spielberg, Quentin Tarantino and Joe Dante. Vincent Price, Peter Cushing and Christopher Lee became cult actors from their appearances in horror movies, as did Boris Karloff and Bela Lugosi, who in Ulmer's *The Black Cat* were credited simply as 'Karloff and Lugosi'. The cult status of Donald Pleasence and Patrick McGoohan, on the other hand, depends less on the sort of roles they played than on the outlandish style of their performances though McGoohan is a cult TV figure for *The Prisoners*.

We decided at the outset to have only one movie per director and as this led in most cases to some argument between us over the choice of films, it is unlikely that all, or indeed most, readers will agree with our particular choices. We did not decide, however, to limit actors to one appearance each, and a good number show up two, three or four times.

In writing this book we have greatly benefited from discussions with many people, but most especially Patrick French, Sean French and Kersti French, the last named having made a major contribution to the editing of the text and the clarification of the prose.

KARL FRENCH
PHILIP FRENCH
London, February 1999

PHILIP FRENCH'S TOP 20 CULT FILMS

Atlantic City
Bad Day at Black Rock
The Bride of Frankenstein
Bring Me the Head of Alfredo Garcia
The Company of Wolves
Dead of Night
Detour
Fat City
Five Easy Pieces
Gun Crazy

The Hustler
Man of the West
The Manchurian Candidate
Once Upon a Time in the West
Pimpernel Smith
Point Blank
Se7en
Sherlock Jr
Shock Corridor
Two-Lane Blacktop

KARL FRENCH'S TOP 20 CULT FILMS

Big Wednesday
Blade Runner
Casablanca
A Clockwork Orange
Duck Soup
Eraserhead
Freaks
Get Carter
La Jetée
The Night of the Hunter

Peeping Tom
Performance
Pink Flamingos
Plan 9 from Outer Space
Reservoir Dogs
The Rocky Horror Picture Show
Some Like It Hot
The Texas Chain Saw Massacre
This is Spinal Tap
Withnail and I

ABBREVIATIONS

ADD SC	ADDITIONAL SCENES		**NARR**	NARRATION
ANIM	ANIMATION		**PH**	PHOTOGRAPHY (CINEMATOGRAPHY)
ART DIR	ART DIRECTOR		**PIC ED**	PICTURE EDITOR
BW	BLACK AND WHITE		**PR**	PRODUCER
CO-PR	CO-PRODUCER		**PR DES**	PRODUCTION DESIGN
COL	COLOUR		**PR SC**	PRODUCTION AND SCREENPLAY
COST	COSTUMES		**SC**	SCREENPLAY
D	DIRECTOR		**SD**	SOUND
DES	DESIGNER		**SD ED**	SOUND EDITOR
ED	EDITOR		**SP EFF**	SPECIAL EFFECTS
EXEC PR	EXECUTIVE PRODUCER		**SP PH**	SPECIAL EFFECTS PHOTOGRAPHY
M	MUSIC		**ST**	STORY
MD	MUSICAL DIRECTOR		★	PICTURE IN COLOUR SECTION
M SUP	MUSICAL SUPERVISOR			

AIRPLANE!

US, 1980, PARAMOUNT, 88 MINS

D JIM ABRAHAMS, DAVID ZUCKER, JERRY ZUCKER; **PR** JON DAVISON, HOWARD W. KOCH JR.; **SC** JIM ABRAHAMS, DAVID ZUCKER, JERRY ZUCKER; **PH** JOSEPH F. BIROC; **M** ELMER BERNSTEIN; **ED** PATRICK KENNEDY

CAST ROBERT HAYS (TED STRIKER), JULIE HAGERTY (ELAINE DICKINSON), LLOYD BRIDGES (MCCROSKEY), LESLIE NIELSEN (DR RUMACK), PETER GRAVES (CAPTAIN OVEUR), ROBERT STACK (KRAMER), KAREEM ABDUL JABBAR (ROGER MURDOCK), LORNA PATTERSON (RANDY), STEPHEN STUCKER (JOHNNY)

THE STORY Ted Striker boards a transcontinental flight in the hope of patching up his relationship with ex-girlfriend Elaine. Things start to go wrong when the plane hits some rough weather, and get worse when the entire flight crew bar Elaine are struck down by food poisoning. Ted is the only man qualified to land the plane, but he is still traumatized by his experiences in Nam. At last, with the help of the sage Dr Rumack and an hysterical ground crew, Ted lands the plane safely and is reconciled with Elaine.

THE FILM From its opening shot in which a plane's wing-tip is slicing through the clouds accompanied by John Williams's haunting theme from *Jaws* (1976), *Airplane!* was a winner. It created an instant adoring following. It was not merely odd, anarchic and quotable, it set up the challenge for the viewer to remember their favourite scenes and lines. This quality in turn, just before the spread of the VCR, gave it an inbuilt marketing tool. It worked not merely by word of mouth, but by encouraging the same people to see it again to catch the jokes they had missed the first time round. It made its immediate precursors,

▼ *AIRPLANE! Robert Hays (Striker) and Julie Hagerty (Elaine) betray their anxiety while the autopilot is perfectly satisfied.*

Animal House (1978), the Abrahams/Zucker brothers' own The Kentucky Fried Movie (1977), and its other antecedents – Hellzapoppin (1941), The Marx Brothers and The Three Stooges – seem restrained in comparison. It would be physically difficult and part of an exercise beyond comedy, to achieve a film with more gags, both verbal and visual. Apart from the obvious references to Airport (1969) and more specifically its sequel Airport '75 (1974), the film makes fun of The Wizard of Oz (1939), Knut Rockne – All American (1940), Pinocchio (1940), Casablanca (1942), From Here to Eternity (1953) and Saturday Night Fever (1977).

ODD/SALIENT FACTS The Abrahams/Zucker/Zucker team was formed in 1970 when the three of them made up the satirical multimedia show that they called Kentucky Fried Theater. They patented their approach to films in Kentucky Fried Movie, in which they lampooned famous films and added the essential ingredient of an occasional flash of naked breasts to complete the format that would prove irresistible to adolescents and undergraduates everywhere. While they have largely stuck to their winning formula, being variously responsible for Top Secret (1984), The Naked Gun (1988) and its sequels, Naked Gun 2½ (1991) and Naked Gun 33⅓ (1994), based on their TV show Police Squad, and Hot Shots (1991), Jerry Zucker has made a stab at legitimacy with Ghost (1990) and My Life (1993).

MEMORABLE MOMENTS The spoof of Saturday Night Fever, where Ted and Elaine dance in a dive not noticing a murder, and the two women whose fight lasts throughout the night.

The use of the very human automatic pilot, who collapses requiring manual inflation from Elaine, which leads to a broad smile and a shared post-coital smoke.

KEY LINES

Old Lady: 'Nervous?'
Ted: 'Yes.'
Old Lady: 'First time?'
Ted: 'No, I've been nervous lots of times.'

Roger Murdock: 'You have clearance, Clarence.'
Captain Oveur: 'Roger, Roger. What's our vector, Victor?'
Tower: 'Tower's radio clearance, over.'

TED: 'Surely you can't be serious'
RUMACK: 'I am serious, and don't call me Shirley.'

Oveur: 'That's Clarence Oveur. Over.'
Tower: 'Roger.'
Murdock: 'Huh?'
Tower: 'Roger, over.'
Murdock: 'Huh?'
Oveur: 'Huh?'

Oveur: 'You ever been in a cockpit before?'
Joey: 'No, sir, I've never been in a plane before.'
Oveur: 'You ever seen a grown man naked?'

Ted: 'My orders came through. My squadron ships out tomorrow. We're bombing the storage depots at Daiquiri at 1800 hours. We're coming in from the north, below their radar.'
Elaine: 'When will you be back?'
Ted: 'I can't tell you that. It's classified.'

Rumack: 'You'd better tell the Captain we've got to land as soon as we can. This woman has to be gotten to a hospital.'
Elaine: 'A hospital? What is it?'
Rumack: 'It's a big building with patients, but that's not important right now.'

Ted: 'Surely you can't be serious.'
Rumack: 'I am serious, and don't call me Shirley.'

ALL THAT HEAVEN ALLOWS

US, 1955, UNIVERSAL-INTERNATIONAL, 89 MINS

D DOUGLAS SIRK; **PR** ROSS HUNTER; **SC** PEG FENWICK (FROM A STORY BY EDNA AND HARRY LEE); **PH** (TECHNICOLOR) RUSSELL METTY; **ED** FRANK GROSS; **M** FRANK SKINNER
CAST JANE WYMAN (CARY SCOTT), ROCK HUDSON (RON KIRBY), AGNES MOORHEAD (SARA WARREN), CONRAD NAGEL (HARVEY), VIRGINIA GREY (ALIDA ANDERSON), GLORIA TALBOTT (KAY SCOTT), WILLIAM REYNOLDS (NED SCOTT), JACQUELINE DE WIT (MONA PLASH), CHARLES DRAKE (MICK ANDERSON), LEIGH SNOWDON (JO-ANN), MERRY ANDERS (MARY ANN), DONALD CURTIS (HOWARD HOFFER), ALEX GERRY (GEORGE WARREN), MANUEL (NESTA PAIVA)

▲ *ALL THAT HEAVEN ALLOWS* Rock Hudson and Jane Wyman *contemplate a sunny future together.*

THE STORY Cary Scott, a wealthy fortyish widow with two grown-up children, lives in an affluent New England dormitory town where the country club bears the sign 'For Members Exclusively'. The thirtyish Ron Kirby, an agricultural college graduate who's taken over his father's nursery business, has been tending her garden since before her husband's death, but Cary first notices him trimming her trees one day in autumn. Cary, who's being courted by a rich friend of her late husband, is impressed by Ron's indifference to social success, his love of nature and the simple life, and by his colourful rural friends.

When she falls in love with him, and he proposes marriage, her snobbish, conventional neighbours are shocked and they patronize and insult Ron at a party. Her son (a Princeton student) and daughter (a psychiatric social worker in New York) are outraged because of Ron's age and social status. In consequence, she breaks off their relationship. But at Christmas, the son and daughter announce they'll both be leaving for good and present her with a TV set to keep her company. After her doctor tells her that her recurrent headaches are psychosomatic and that she should return to Ron, she drives out to the converted mill where he lives, but he's out hunting. Trying to attract her attention as she drives away, Ron falls over a small cliff into a snow drift and suffers concussion. When he comes to in his living room, the doctor and Ron's friends have summoned Cary to his bedside, and she'll stay with him.

THE FILM In the 1950s *All That Heaven Allows* was considered a slick woman's picture, another in the glossy series directed by Douglas Sirk and produced by Ross Hunter, that turned Rock Hudson from a minor Universal contract actor into a major star. Its cult reputation stems from the 1960s when, after his retirement to Europe, its German-Danish director's reputation grew through the acclaim he received on the continent, especially in France. When Rock Hudson came out of the closet as he was dying of Aids in the late 1980s, this added to the cult status of the pictures he made at Universal, first the dramas with Sirk, then the comedies with Doris Day. Beneath its deceptively conventional surface, *All That Heaven Allows* offers a sharp critique of the suffocating conformity of the Eisenhower era. The contrast between the artificial life of Cary's middle-class circle and the honest naturalness of Ron's country friends may be none too subtle, but it is brilliantly realized through dress and decor. The film touches on issues of class, social hypocrisy, relations between parents and children, and on female sexuality, with considerable insight and without despising the conventions of its genre. And while it exposes the fissures beneath the complacency and false confidence of the 1950s, it does so in the name of Henry David Thoreau, the nineteenth-century New England dissident from whose book, *Walden*, Cary reads a famous passage. In many of his movies Sirk plays off a simple, consistent character against a complex, divided one – here the extrovert Hudson against the emotionally disturbed Wyman, though we now, of course, see in Hudson the guardian of his society's deeply buried secret.

ODD/SALIENT FACTS Henry David, Thoreau's *Walden* had been one of Sirk's favourite books in his early teenage years and helped shape his idea of what America stood for. Sirk's German disciple Rainer Werner Fassbinder used *All That Heaven Allows* as the model for one of his most popular films, *Fear Eats the Soul*, in which the mother is a white, lower middle-class widow and her young lover a North African *Gastarbeiter* in Berlin.

MEMORABLE MOMENTS Cary shocking her son by coming downstairs in a low-cut red dress ('Typical Oedipal reaction,' says daughter).

Cary in her empty house crying as she looks at carol singers in the snow.

Cary seeing her own reflection filling the television screen as the salesman says: 'All you have to do is turn that dial and you have all the company you want right there on the screen – drama, comedy, life's parade at your fingertips.'

KEY LINES

Alida, wife of Ron's best friend: 'I don't think Ron's ever read it [i.e. Thoreau's *Walden*], he just lives it.'

Ron: 'You're running away from something because you're afraid – of many things.'

Sara, Cary's best friend: 'A situation like this brings out the hateful side of human nature.'

Society matron: 'Have we ever met before?'
Ron: 'Probably in your garden. I've been pruning your trees for the last three years.'

L'ANNÉE DERNIÈRE À MARIENBAD (LAST YEAR AT MARIENBAD)

FRANCE/ITALY, 1961, TERRA FILMS ETC. (PARIS), CINERIZ (ROME), 94 MINS

D ALAIN RESNAIS; **PR** PIERRE COURAU, RAYMOND FROMENT; **SC** ALAIN ROBBE-GRILLET; **PH** (BW DYALISCOPE) SACHA VIERNY; **ED** HENRI COLPI, JASMINE CHASNEY; **M** FRANCIS SEYRIG
CAST DELPHINE SEYRIG (A), GIORGIO ALBERTAZZI (X), SACHA PITOËFF (M), FRANÇOISE BERTIN

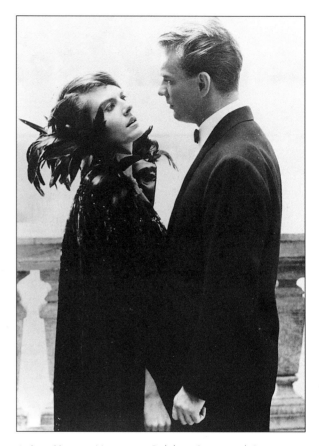

▲ *LAST YEAR AT MARIENBAD* Delphine Seyrig and Giorgio Albertazzi wondering whether Marienbad is his place or hers.

THE STORY At a large, baroque hotel standing in extensive ornamental gardens, one of the handsome guests, X, who acts as the film's narrator, claims that the previous year at Marienbad he met another guest, the beautiful young woman, A. She alleges not to have met him, nor to have agreed to leave M, 'the man who may be her husband'. X persists and enters into a series of games played with matches with M, which he always loses. But eventually X persuades A and she leaves the hotel with him.

THE FILM *L'Année dernière à Marienbad* was the third collaboration in a row between Resnais and a practitioner of the French *nouveau roman*, following the Auschwitz documentary *Nuit et Brouillard* (1956), scripted by Jean Cayrol, and *Hiroshima Mon Amour* (1959), scripted by Marguerite Duras.

Like them it is about time and memory; unlike them it is an apolitical film and a chilly, formalistic work. Audiences loved or loathed it and it excited passionate discussion. With its sweeping camera movements around the elegant hotel, the carefully arranged grouping of actors inside the hotel and in the garden, it is a beautiful film to behold, and the music, combined with the flat, almost incantatory delivery of the dialogue and the narration and the hieratic style of acting add to the mesmeric effect. What is it about? Few films have left it so open to the audience – who in fact are the movie's 'reality'. Only in the published text are the three main characters identified as A, X and M. L'Année dernière may be a mystery story. Perhaps the hotel is an asylum where X and A are patients and the commanding, unsmiling M is the chief psychiatrist. On the other hand it could be X's dream, or a collective dream. Yet again, X, A and M might be one person, or the Id, Ego and Superego. These are just a few of the explanations that were advanced in the early 1960s when the Marienbad match game (which turns on the binomial theorem) was all the fashion. But they're all reductive interpretations of a work of rare purity in which form and content are indivisible. The antecedents of L'Année dernière are Renoir's La Règle du Jeu and Sartre's Huis Clos. It came out at the same time as Antonioni's L'Avventura and La Notte, and the two directors revolutionized the way time and space were used in the cinema. The film's influence on high and low culture was shallow but widespread – immediately on Joseph Losey (The Servant) and Ingmar Bergman (The Silence), later on Dick Lester and Nicolas Roeg, and pervasively on fashion photography, TV commercials, music videos. Unlike Casablanca, which grew from its cult following into a universally adored picture, L'Année dernière went from being one of the hottest pictures of its time, an avant-garde work that broke through into the popular conscience, back to small-time cult status.

ODD/SALIENT FACTS Much was made at the time by the film's detractors of the supposed fact that Resnais thought something had happened between the couple at Marienbad and Robbe-Grillet didn't. Actually both were deliberately ambivalent. In the film's most famous scene in which characters are arranged in

> M: 'I have another game to suggest instead: I know a game I always win.'
> X: 'If you can't lose it's not a game.'
> M: I can lose. But I always win.'

the gardens like statuary, the shadows they cast were painted on the ground. Though the film was a Franco-Italian co-production and the studio work done in Paris, the location shooting was in Bavaria at various Munich palaces. When Robbe-Grillet said that the couple couldn't have met in Marienbad because it didn't exist, he made a historical point. Marienbad was the German name of Mariánskí Lázne, adopted in 1808 when it became a spa town. Goethe, Chopin, Wagner, Ibsen, Edward VII and Kafka were among its patrons. After the Communist takeover of Czechoslovakia in 1948 the old name was readopted, and the hotels steadily decayed.

MEMORABLE MOMENTS The opening tracking shots around the deserted hotel and garden.

The male guests lined up indoors for pistol shooting.

The guests seen from the hotel standing like statues.

KEY LINES

M: 'I have another game to suggest instead: I know a game I always win.'
X: 'If you can't lose it's not a game.'
M: 'I can lose. But I always win.'

X: 'You never seemed to be waiting for me – but we kept meeting at every turn of the paths – behind every bush, at the foot of each statue, near every pond. It is as if it had been only you and I in all that garden'. 'It seemed, at first glance, impossible to get lost here … at first glance … down straight paths, between the statues with frozen gestures and the granite slabs, where you were already getting lost, forever, in the calm night, alone with me.'

Unidentified guests talking on soundtrack: "I think this game's silly.' 'There's a trick you have to know.' 'All you have to do is take an uneven number.' 'There must be rules.' 'It's the one who goes first who loses.' 'I remember how Frank used to play this last year … Yes, yes, he did, I'm sure of it.' 'What you have to do is take the complement of seven each time.' 'In which row?'

APOCALYPSE NOW★

US, 1979, OMNI ZOETROPE, 153 MINS AND C. 300 MINS

D FRANCIS COPPOLA; **PR** FRANCIS COPPOLA, FRED ROOS, GRAY FREDERICKSON, TOM STERNBERG; **SC** JOHN MILIUS, COPPOLA, AND MICHAEL HERR; **PH** VITTORIO STORARO; **DES** DEAN TAVOULARIS; **M** CARMINE COPPOLA AND FRANCIS COPPOLA; **ED** RICHARD MARKS

CAST MARTIN SHEEN (CAPT. WILLARD), MARLON BRANDO (COL. KURTZ), ROBERT DUVALL (LT. COL. KILGORE), FREDERIC FORREST (CHEF), ALBERT HALL (CHIEF), SAM BOTTOMS (LANCE), LARRY FISHBURNE (CLEAN), DENNIS HOPPER (PHOTOJOURNALIST), G. D. SPRADLIN (GENERAL), HARRISON FORD (COLONEL), JERRY ZIESMER (CIVILIAN), SCOTT GLENN (COLBY)

THE STORY At the height of the Vietnam War, Willard, a US Army captain, is given his new mission. He is to head up the Nung River and terminate the command of Kurtz, a Green Beret colonel who has gone native and mad. On the journey up-river, Willard and the crew encounter an Air Cavalry platoon and their crazed leader, Kilgore; then a tiger; witness a USO show featuring Playboy bunnies; and pass through the final outpost of American military at Do Long Bridge, before reaching Cambodia. There they carry out a mini My Lai massacre on the occupants of a sampan. Clean, the youngest member of the boat's crew, is killed in a firefight. The boat's captain, Chief Phillips, is killed by a spear before the boat finally pulls into Kurtz's compound in the middle of the jungle. There Willard and the two surviving crew members are met by Kurtz's crazy sidekick, a photojournalist. Chef is decapitated, Lance is absorbed by the Montagnards and Willard finally confronts Kurtz, who tries to explain the motivation behind his murderous activities and makes Willard promise to convey these explanations and his memoirs to his son. In parallel with a ritual tribal sacrifice of an ox, Willard kills Kurtz, retrieves Lance and together they leave the compound and head back down the river.

THE FILM Coppola came to this project on the back of the enormous critical and commercial success of the two *Godfather* films. The first draft was written in 1969 by John Milius, with a little help from George Lucas. The plan was for the film to be quickly and cheaply made, employing a documentary style and unknown actors. As it evolved, eventually with script input from

'Saigon. Shit.'

Coppola himself, the film attained a level of moral ambiguity as the right-wing views of Milius were filtered through the more liberal vision of the director. The shoot began on 20 March 1976 and continued for 238 days, enduring the vagaries of both the Philippine weather and air force, the nearly fatal heart-attack and breakdown of Martin Sheen, and the problem of Marlon Brando, an overpaid, overweight and under-prepared cameo star. The film that emerged from this painful gestation succeeds for a number of reasons: the wonderful set designs by Dean Tavoularis; beautiful photography from Vittorio Storaro; an extraordinary extended editing process; great acting; a relatively honed and deceptively cohesive script; innovative sound design; and the inspired decision to commission a voiceover narration from Michael Herr, the author of the definitive Vietnam War document, *Dispatches*. It is a film that achieved widespread international success at the box office, but one that also retains an appeal in which the most fleeting reference or quotation instantly establishes a shared knowledge and obsession.

ODD/SALIENT FACTS The plot of the film is a loose transposition of Joseph Conrad's novella *Heart of Darkness* to the Vietnam War. Many incidents survive relatively unchanged in the process, and several of the characters have their source in Conrad, chiefly Kurtz, Marlow and the photojournalist. The project was conceived by Milius as a right-wing corrective to what he saw as the unfair treatment doled out to Col. Robert Rhéault, who was court-martialled for ordering the summary execution of a Vietnamese spy who he suspected – like Kurtz, and almost certainly with justification – was a double agent. Many of the more fantastical-seeming war sequences like those involving Kilgore, and the events around the Do Long Bridge, are in fact closely based on documented events of the war (with Michael Herr and the photographer Philip Jones Griffiths being particularly important source writers).

There is a cult within the cult, with some of the film's fans enthusing about the near-mythical five-hour cut of the film. This has been seen by several people in an illicit video version and includes extensions to certain scenes, such as the Air Cavalry's raid on the coastal village, a second appearance of the Playboy bunnies and an entire sequence at a French rubber plantation, including the military burial of Clean. Its ghostly existence in the minds of fans enhances the film's mythic appeal and points to its enduring cult status.

MEMORABLE MOMENTS The opening scene in which the plot is foretold and Willard's tortured state of mind is suggested.

The dawn raid which contains choreographed helicopters, planes and surfing.

The execution of Kurtz by Willard juxtaposed with the slaughter of the ox.

KEY LINES

Willard's opening line: 'Saigon. Shit.'

Kilgore's speech to Willard after the napalm drop: 'I love the smell of napalm in the morning. You know one time we had a hail bomb ... for twelve hours ... and when it was all over I walked up. We didn't find one body. Not one stinking dink body. But the smell, you know that gasoline smell ... the whole hill. It smelled like ... victory. Some day this war's gonna end.'

▲ *ASSAULT ON PRECINCT 13 Austin Stocker (Ethan Bishop), a modern day John Wayne, defends his precinct from a multi-cultural gang hell-bent on revenge.*

ASSAULT ON PRECINCT 13
US, 1976, CKK, 91 MINS

D *JOHN CARPENTER;* **PR** *IRWIN YABLANS;* **SC** *JOHN CARPENTER;* **PH** *(COL, PANAVISION) DOUGLAS KNAPP;* **M** *JOHN CARPENTER;* **ED** *JOHN T. CHANCE*

CAST *AUSTIN STOKER (BISHOP), DARWIN JOSTIN (WILSON), LAURIE ZIMMER (LEIGH), MARTIN WEST (LAWSON), TONY BURTON (WELLS), CHARLES CYPHERS (STARKER), NANCY LOOMIS (JULIE), PETER BRUNI (ICE CREAM MAN), JOHN J. FOX (WARDEN), MARC ROSS (PATROLMAN TRAMER), ALAN KOSS (PATROLMAN BAXTER), HENRY BRANDON (CHANEY), KIM RICHARDS (KATHY), FRANK DOUBLEDAY (WHITE WARLORD), GILBERT DE LA PENA (CHICANO WARLORD), PETER FRANKLAND (CAUDELL), AL NAKAUCHI (ORIENTAL WARLORD), JAMES JOHNSON (BLACK WARLORD)*

THE STORY A police ambush in which several LA gang members get killed leads to a pact between various ethnic gangs sealed with a blood oath. A middle-aged man and his young daughter are lost driving through a rough part of the city. A bus drives through the city taking three prisoners (one of them very sick) to death row. A black police lieutenant receives his first commission, to look after a precinct on the last night before it is officially closed down. The young girl is shot and killed by the White Warlord who is in turn shot and killed by her father. Suddenly catatonic, he runs into the police station. Meanwhile the young prisoner on the bus becomes so ill that the prisoners and guards also have to seek refuge in the station. The mixed group is whittled down to just four survivors as the gang cut off all communications to the precinct and launch an attack with guns fitted with silencers, but they ultimately withstand the assault.

THE FILM The film is an object lesson in narrative economy. Carpenter has spent his career in the margins between cultism and mainstream commercial cinema and glories in his role as the last great director of B-movies. His debut was the deliberately off-beat *Dark Star* (1974), which had begun as a student piece. This, his follow-up, features a cast of unknowns and blends the tautness and wit of a Hawks film with the structure and horror of a zombie movie. As a supreme auteur, Carpenter not only writes, directs and edits, but also supplies the film's haunting synthesizer score borrowed by U2 who used it for the bass-line of their hit 'New Year's Day'. For *The Thing* – (1982), like this film a Hawks update featuring a scene in which a man is chained to a dangerously, scarily sick colleague – the score was composed by Ennio Morricone, who delivered a perfect pastiche of a Carpenter soundtrack. The most inspired idea in the film is the gang's use of silencers in their attack. This enhances the tension and adds an ironic comment on urban life (borrowed in *Die Hard*, 1988) that a full-on, sustained military-style attack can take place in the middle of a city without anyone on the outside noticing.

ODD/SALIENT FACTS The movie is in part an updated urban reworking of the Howard Hawks western *Rio Bravo* (1959). This is already suggested in the opening credits with the editing attributed to John T. Chance (in fact Carpenter himself), John Wayne's character in that film. *Rio Bravo* is further quoted from

> ### 'Son, there's something about you. You got something to do with death.'

in the very brief set piece in which Bishop throws a shotgun to Wilson, who spins around, catches the gun and fires it in one movement which echoes the sequence in Hawks's film in which Nelson throws a gun to Wayne. The climax, where Bishop shoots at the flares attached to the top of the canister of explosive gas, is a version of Wayne, Nelson and Dean Martin firing at the sticks of dynamite thrown by Walter Brennan. The film also contains an unusual reference to another hero of Carpenter's, Alfred Hitchcock. Bishop is having a chat with Leigh (who herself later evokes Hawks's discovery, Lauren Bacall, in the way she lights her cigarette and extinguishes the match) about how he grew up just four blocks away. When he was about four or five his dad sent him to the police station with a note to hand to the detective. When he reads the note, the detective tells him: 'We lock up little boys who can't behave.' This is a story that Hitchcock would tell in interviews throughout his life, as an explanation of his fear of policemen which is such a feature of his films. Once he was asked what he wanted written on his tombstone and he said: 'This is what we do to bad little boys.'

MEMORABLE MOMENTS The emotionless shooting of the little girl at the ice cream van, itself including a sly reference to *The Manchurian Candidate*.

The gang's first attack on the precinct: the silenced gunshots with bullets smashing windows and the Venetian blinds and a piece of paper dancing above the desk as it is repeatedly struck.

KEY LINES

Wilson on the bus recalling what a preacher said to him as a kid: 'Son, there's something about you. You got something to do with death.' The line is a near quotation of the comment Cheyenne makes to Jill about Harmonica in *Once Upon a Time in the West*: 'People like that have something inside, something to do with death.'

While the depleted group are trying to evolve an escape strategy, Wells, the black convict says: 'In the meantime I've got a plan. It's called "Save ass".'

ATLANTIC CITY

FRANCE/CANADA, 1980, CINE-NEIGHBOUR (MONTREAL)/SELTA
FILMS-ELIE KFOURI (PARIS), 105 MINS

D *LOUIS MALLE;* **PR** *JOHN KEMENY, JOSEPH BEAUBIEN, DENIS
HEROUX;* **SC** *JOHN GUARE;* **PH** *(COL) RICHARD CIUPKA;*
ED *SUZANNE BARON*

CAST *BURT LANCASTER (LOU PASCHALL), SUSAN SARANDON
(SALLY), KATE REID (GRACE), MICHEL PICCOLI (JOSEPH), HOLLIS
MCLAREN (CHRISSIE), ROBERT JOY (DAVE), AL WAXMAN (ALFIE),
ROBERT GOULET (SINGER IN HOSPITAL), MOSES ZNAIMER (FÉLIX,
HITMAN), ANGUS MACINNES (VINNIE, HITMAN), LOUIS DEL
GRANDE (MR SHAPIRO), CEC LINDER (PRESIDENT OF HOSPITAL),
WALLACE SHAWN (WAITER), JOYCE PARKS (QUEENIE)*

THE STORY Dave, a Canadian hippie, hi-jacks a consignment
of Mafia cocaine and drives with his pregnant girlfriend,
Chrissie, to visit Sally (his estranged wife and Chrissie's sister)
in Atlantic City. Sally works at a seafood counter in a casino
but wants to become a croupier. Lou Paschall, an ageing criminal, lives in the same dilapidated apartment block and is
secretly in love with her. Lou is the kept man of Grace, a bed-
ridden, hypochondriac widow, and fears his pathetic job as a
runner for the numbers racket will be wiped out by legal gambling. Dave engages Lou to sell the cocaine. When Mafia
hitmen kill Dave, Lou is left with the drugs. He becomes Sally's
trusted friend through his handling of Dave's funeral, and they
sleep together. Sally loses her job, and when two Mafia hitmen
come for her, Lou kills both of them and drives south with Sally
to Florida. At a motel, Sally steals some of Lou's drug money to
start a new life as a croupier in Monte Carlo. Lou happily
releases her and heads back to Atlantic City. Grace leaves her
bed, helps Lou sell the remainder of the cocaine, and they prom-
enade together along the Boardwalk.

THE FILM *Atlantic City,* Louis Malle's second US picture (the
first was *Pretty Baby*), is one of the great movies about American

▼ *ATLANTIC CITY Ageing voyeur Burt Lancaster observes waitress Susan Sarandon's lemon therapy.*

19

life. It failed to reach a large public, but was a critical success. Malle's cinematic roots are in documentary, and the movie links private lives to public events as it tells a fictional story of everyday crime while documenting a city in transition. It prophesied the corruption of 1980s America, the decade in which Donald Trump, one of the creators of the new Atlantic City, would be a tarnished hero.

As Bob Rafelson had shown in *The King of Marvin Gardens* (1972), Atlantic City is a suggestive metaphor for America and the American Dream: a fashionable turn-of-the-century holiday resort; a favourite interwar playground for mobsters and adulterers; home of the Miss America pageant; the setting of the original Monopoly board; a town that, in 1980, was attempting to turn itself around as this film was being made. Burt Lancaster gives one of his very best performances, lending a comic twist to two very different kinds of roles he's played over the years: the tragic *film noir* loser of Siodmak's *The Killers*, and the detached, dignified dandy in Visconti's *The Leopard* and *Conversation Piece*.

ODD/SALIENT FACTS Malle's first choice for Lou was Robert Mitchum, but the Canadian producers thought that Lancaster would be bigger box office. Michel Legrand wrote a full score that was recorded but never used; the film has only source music. Nominated for five Oscars (best film, screenplay, director, actor and actress), the movie won nothing. When the representatives of Price, Waterhouse (the Academy's accountants) brought out the sealed envelopes, the Oscars host Johnny Carson quipped that 'They really know how to keep a secret – they also handled the distribution of *Atlantic City*'.

MEMORABLE MOMENTS Voyeur Paschall (Lancaster) looking across the ventilation shaft between his flat and Sally's (Sarandon) to watch her rubbing her breasts and arms with lemons.

Lancaster in a white slouch hat and new overcoat and Kate Reid in a veiled hat and fur coat nonchalantly walking along the Boardwalk (top property in Monopoly) at the end of the movie; in a single take they walk past the camera which pans up to a wrecker's ball smashing into an abandoned apartment block, again and again, as on the soundtrack we hear Tommy Dorsey's 'Song of India', 'Atlantic City, My Old Friend' (music and lyrics by Paul Anka), the 1945 number 'On the Boardwalk of Atlantic City', a few bars of twanging-guitar country music, and some cool jazz *à la Brubeck* played on piano with drum and bass accompaniment.

KEY LINES

Lou to Dave: 'Yes, it used to be beautiful, what with the rackets, whoring, guns. Sometimes things would happen and I'd have to kill a few people. I'd feel bad for a while. But I'd jump into the ocean and swim way out and come back feeling nice and clean and start all over again. The Atlantic Ocean was something then. Yes, you should have seen the Atlantic Ocean in those days.'

Paul Anka song, sung by Robert Goulet at the inauguration of the hospital's Sinatra Wing, while Sally arrives to identify ex-husband's body: 'I'm glad to see you born again, Atlantic City my old friend, you're back upon the map again, you sure came through.'

BAD DAY AT BLACK ROCK
USA, 1955, MGM, 81 MINS

D JOHN STURGES; **PR** DORE SCHARY; **SC** MILLARD KAUFMAN (FROM THE STORY BAD TIME AT HONDO BY HOWARD BRESLIN; **PH** (EASTMANCOLOR, CINEMASCOPE) WILLIAM C. MELLOR; **M** ANDRÉ PREVIN; **ED** NEWELL P. KIMLIN

CAST SPENCER TRACY (JOHN J. MACREEDY), ROBERT RYAN (RENO SMITH), ANNE FRANCIS (LIZ WIRTH), DEAN JAGGER (SHERIFF TIM HORN), WALTER BRENNAN (DOC VELIE), JOHN ERICSON (PETE WIRTH), ERNEST BORGNINE (COLEY TRIMBLE), LEE MARVIN (HECTOR DAVID), RUSSELL COLLINS (MR HASTINGS), WALTER SANDE (SAM)

THE STORY Late 1945, early morning, a few months after the end of the Second World War. The Super Chief locomotive stops at Black Rock, a tiny community huddled beneath the mountains of the south-western desert a couple of hundred miles east of Los Angeles. One man gets off – the one-armed John MacReedy. He becomes the subject of suspicion and hostility, especially as he wants to visit Adobe Flat, erstwhile home of a Japanese farmer called Komoko. Only Doc Velie gives MacReedy a welcome. The others in town – Hastings the telegraph clerk, Pete the hotel manager, his sister Liz who runs the local garage, Tim the drunken sheriff, Sam, owner of the town's diner, and the thuggish cowboys Hector and Coley – are all under the thumb of the racist rancher, Reno Smith. MacReedy

▲ *BAD DAY AT BLACK ROCK* One-armed stranger Spencer Tracy gets a cold Western welcome from Robert Ryan and Lee Marvin.

is told Komoko was relocated after Pearl Harbor, but at Adobe Flat he discovers a burnt-out ranch house, a well and signs of an unmarked grave. Smith, furious when Komoko discovered water on the worthless land he'd sold him, had got 'patriotic drunk' with Hector, Coley, Hastings, Sam and Pete after Pearl Harbor, and they had driven out to Komoko's ranch and killed him. MacReedy is in Black Rock to present Komoko with a medal posthumously awarded to his son after saving MacReedy's life in Italy. They intend to silence MacReedy, but

he uses his karate skills to lay out Coley, and he and Doc persuade Pete to redeem himself by helping MacReedy escape. Hector is knocked out by Doc, and Liz drives MacReedy out of town and into a trap set by Reno, whom she loves. Reno shoots her dead, and MacReedy makes a Molotov cocktail, turning Reno into a human torch. The conspirators are taken away by the state police, and Doc gets MacReedy to leave the medal to the town.

THE FILM One of the leanest thrillers ever made, *Black Rock* takes place over exactly 24 hours and was the first film to touch on a nasty American secret, i.e. the treatment of the Nisei, the American citizens of Japanese descent, robbed of their property and coralled in remote prison camps in the deserts of

California and Nevada. The film also reflected the anxieties of the McCarthy era with MacReedy an embattled representative of probity in the manner of *High Noon*'s Marshal Kane. But this picture is far more specific in its attack on the racism and xenophobia of those who purport to uphold the pioneer tradition of the West. *Black Rock* had a special appeal for embattled liberals who identified with MacReedy, the peaceful man, quite literally unarmed, who reasons until provoked beyond endurance, and wins by his superior intelligence and special skills. It's the definitive liberal revenge movie, justifying and ultimately revelling in retaliatory violence. Few movies have offered such a trio of venomous heavies as those played by Ryan, Borgnine and Marvin, and appropriately Tracy uses Eastern martial arts on the thug who calls him a 'yellow-bellied Jap lover'. The movie was among the first to use the widescreen for dramatic effect as in the anxious conference between the conspirators standing apart and straddling the railroad line, and the diner sequence where there are only three or four edits before the fight breaks out. The film made John Sturges a favourite among cinephiles, most of whom regard it as superior to more spectacular later films such as *The Magnificent Seven* and *The Great Escape*.

ODD/SALIENT FACTS *Bad Day* was the first Western shown in competition at Cannes and brought Tracy the best actor award. The film had the first important score by André Previn.

MEMORABLE MOMENTS MacReedy inspecting Adobe Flat.

Coley's provocation of MacReedy in the diner and the ensuing fight.

MacReedy, stalked by the gun-toting Reno, using guerilla tactics to make a Molotov cocktail.

KEY LINES

Train conductor: 'Man, they look woebegone and far away.'
MacReedy: 'I'll only be here 24 hours.'
Conductor: 'In a place like this that could be a lifetime.'

MacReedy to Reno: 'What did Komoko have to do with Corregidor?'

Reno to MacReedy: 'Someone is always looking for

> **Coley: 'You're a yellow-bellied Jap-lover, am I right or wrong?'**

something in this part of the West. For the historian it's the Old West. For the bookwriter it's the Wild West. For the businessman it's the undeveloped West. They say we're all poor and backward and I guess we are. We don't even have enough water. But to us it's our West, and I wish they'd leave us alone.'

Coley: 'You're a yellow-bellied Jap-lover, am I right or wrong?'
MacReedy: 'You're not only wrong, you're wrong at the top of your voice.'

BADLANDS

US, 1973, Pressman/Williams/Badlands, 94 mins
D *TERRENCE MALICK;* **PR** *TERRENCE MALICK;* **SC** *TERRENCE MALICK;* **PH** *BRIAN PROBYN, TAK FUJIMOTO, STEVAN LARNER;* **M** *GEORGE TIPTON;* **ED** *ROBERT ESTRIN*
CAST *MARTIN SHEEN (KIT), SISSY SPACEK (HOLLY), WARREN OATES (FATHER), RAMON BIERI (CATO), ALAN VINT (DEPUTY), GARY LITTLEJOHN (SHERIFF), JOHN CARTER (RICH MAN), BRYAN MONTGOMERY (BOY), GAIL THRELKELD (GIRL), CHARLES FITZPATRICK (CLERK), HOWARD RAGSDALE (BOSS), JOHN WOMACK SR. (TROOPER), DONA BALDWIN (MAID), BEN BRAVO (GAS ATTENDANT)*

THE STORY Holly, a teenager who lives in a small South Dakota town with her widowed father, begins an affair with Kit, a mentally unstable garbage collector. When Holly's dad, who strongly disapproves of the liaison, tries to stop Kit taking her away, Kit shoots him dead. Kit and Holly live a wild life hiding out in the country until they are discovered and approached by three bounty hunters, all of whom Kit kills. The couple visit Cato, Kit's friend from the garbage round, but Kit shoots him too when he suspects that he is about to betray them. Kit leads a young couple, who come to call at Cato's remote house, into a storm shelter, locks them in and fires two shots, possibly killing them. A national manhunt is launched, and Kit and Holly briefly seek refuge in the house of a rich man. They take his car and drive into the Badlands, a barren region of South Dakota and Montana where Holly begins to tire of Kit. When they are pur-

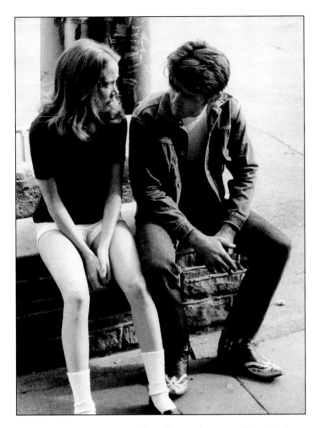

▲ **BADLANDS** *Sissy Spacek (Holly) and Martin Sheen (Kit) get to know each other before embarking on their murderous spree.*

sued by a helicopter, she refuses to go along with him, and after a final pursuit, Kit gives himself up. He becomes an instant hero to the young rangers who surround him. As they fly off, Holly reveals in her voice-over narration that Kit will be electrocuted and she will marry the son of her defence attorney.

THE FILM Kit, one of two cold killers memorably played by Sheen in the 1970s, is a cruel, wilful but sentimental child trapped in an adult body. He casually challenges his buddy to eat a dead dog they find on their round. He kills because he has a gun and: 'I always wanted to be a criminal, just not this big a one.' He wants to leave a mark, is obsessed with establishing memorials to himself and encourages his own cult status. He commemorates his and Holly's first sexual encounter with a rock, which he instantly exchanges for a smaller one. Later he sends off a time capsule dedicated to their love in a red balloon. During the climactic chase he adjusts the rear-view mirror

so he can watch himself being pursued. He then marks the spot of his own arrest with a small pile of stones and dishes out his paltry personal possessions, convinced of his status as a lasting icon. Kit and Holly are rebels without a cause who abandon their lives and adopt the personae of two icons of their time, James Dean and Priscilla Presley. Terrence Malick has ensured that he has remained the enduring cult figure of the modern Hollywood era by being its least prolific genius. After this, his debut, he waited five years before directing his next film, the beautiful *Days of Heaven* (1978). There followed a gap of twenty years before his third directorial offering, *The Thin Red Line* (1999).

ODD/SALIENT FACTS The events of the film are based on the actions of the 1950s spree killer, Charles Starkweather. On 1 December 1957, the James Dean-fixated Starkweather, along with his petite red-headed girlfriend Caril Ann Fugate, killed the first of their victims, a petrol pump attendant. They murdered another ten, including Fugate's step-parents, as they travelled across America, before being arrested in Wyoming. Fugate received a life sentence, Starkweather went to the electric chair. Malick himself makes an odd cameo appearance as the man dressed in white who comes to visit the rich man being held captive by Holly and Kit. The credits offer thanks to Arthur Penn, director of one of the seminal 'lovers on the run' movies, *Bonnie and Clyde* (1967). George Tipton's soundtrack was borrowed in Tony Scott's *True Romance* (1993).

MEMORABLE MOMENTS The burning of the house as we cut between images of a piano, a doll, a doll's house, a bed and Holly's father being consumed by the blaze as Kit's fake-suicide recording plays on the record player outside.

The final farewell dance in the car's headlights on the eve of Kit's capture.

KEY LINES

Holly in her narration: 'Little did I realize that what began in the alleys and backways of this quiet town would end in the Badlands of Montana.'

Holly: 'He wanted to die with me and I dreamed of being lost forever in his arms.'

Kit, concluding his fake-suicide record: 'I can't deny we've had fun though. That's more than I can say for some.'

Holly, after Kit has killed her father and shot Cato and his two young friends: 'Suddenly I was thrown into a state of shock. Kit was the most trigger-happy person I'd ever met.'

▲ *BARBARELLA John Philip Law as the blind Pygar and Jane Fonda as the eponymous space adventurer strive once more to banish war from the Universe.*

BARBARELLA

FRANCE/ITALY, 1968, DINO DE LAURENTIIS SP. A MARIANNE PRODUCTIONS, 98 MINS

D ROGER VADIM; **PR** DINO DE LAURENTIIS; **SC** TERRY SOUTHERN, ROGER VADIM, CLAUDE BRULE, VITTORIO BONICELLI, CLEMENT BIDDLE WOOD, BRIAN DEGAS, TUDOR GATES, JEAN-CLAUDE FOREST, BASED ON A STORY BY JEAN-CLAUDE FOREST; **PH** (COL, PANAVISION) CLAUDE RENOIR; **PR DES** MARIO GARBUGLIA; **M** BOB CREWE, CHARLES FOX; **ED** VICTORIA MERCANTON

CAST JANE FONDA (BARBARELLA), JOHN PHILIP LAW (PYGAR), UGO TOGNAZZI (MARK HAND), DAVID HEMMINGS (DILDANO), MILO O'SHEA (DURAN DURAN), ANITA PALLENBERG (THE BLACK QUEEN), MARCEL MARCEAU (PROFESSOR PING), VÉRONIQUE VENDELL (CAPTAIN MOON), SERGE MARQUAND (CAPTAIN SUN)

'Weapon? Why would anyone want to invent a weapon?'

THE STORY In the year 40,000, Barbarella, a space adventurer, receives her new mission: to discover the whereabouts of Duran Duran, the man who has invented the positronic ray gun, in a time when war has been abolished. She embarks on a series of erotic adventures in which she encounters diabolical dolls, blind angel Pygar, the rebel Dildano and the Black Queen, before saving the Universe from the megalomaniacal Duran Duran.

THE FILM You can never trust a film with eight writers credited. But even had the screenplay been coherent, there would still have been the matter of Roger Vadim's ineptitude as a filmmaker. What Vadim was competent at was spotting cult potential, as he proved when launching the Brigitte Bardot phenomenon with … *et dieu créa la femme* (… And God Created Woman, 1956). It has a kitschy feel to it from the start and is rendered watchable by Fonda's performance and the lavish production design. David Hemmings and Milo O'Shea seem to have been given little cohesive direction, and the former delivers by some distance the worst performance of his career. The camp but expensive studio sets are undermined by the deliberately bad *Flash Gordon*-style special effects. *Barbarella*, based on Jean-Claude Forest's adult comic strip, was conceived as a cult film and has duly become one.

ODD/SALIENT FACTS The film might have worked had it stuck to just one writer and become the crazed sexual satire conceived by Terry Southern. Southern was one of the key cult figures of the 1950s and '60s, contributing to the screenplays of both *Dr Strangelove* (1964) and *Easy Rider* (1969) – a project initiated by, and starring, Jane Fonda's brother Peter – as well as co-writing *Candy* and writing alone *The Magic Christian* and *Blue Movie*. Fonda herself was reluctant to do the film, but was eventually persuaded by her then husband, Vadim. In his autobiography, *Memoirs of the Devil*, he writes:

> She didn't enjoy shooting *Barbarella*. She accepted the part because I was enthusiastic about the project, but she disliked the central character for her lack of principle, her shameless exploitation of her sexuality, and her irrelevance to contemporary social and political realities. In fact Barbarella, for all its extravagant fantasy, contains a good deal of ruthless satire on the problems of our times. But humour is not one of Jane's strong points unless it is stated explicitly.

MEMORABLE MOMENTS What makes the film memorable and what surely has sealed its enduring reputation as a kitsch classic is the opening scene in which Fonda strips out of her space suit while the credits roll, teasingly hiding her nudity.

KEY LINES

The greeting: 'Love'. Then Barbarella's shock at learning that Duran Duran has devised the positronic ray: 'Weapon? Why would anyone want to invent a weapon?'

BARTON FINK

USA, 1991, CIRCLE FILMS, 116 MINS

D JOEL COEN; **PR** ETHAN COEN; **SC** ETHAN COEN, JOEL COEN; **PH** (DUART COLOR) ROGER DEAKINS; **ED** RODERICK JAMES; **M** CARTER BURWELL

CAST JOHN TURTURRO (BARTON FINK), JOHN GOODMAN (CHARLIE MEADOWS), JUDY DAVIS (AUDREY TAYLOR), MICHAEL LERNER (JACK LIPNICK), JOHN MAHONEY (W.P. MAYHEW), TONY SHALHOUB (BEN GEISLER), JON POLITO (LOU BREEZE), STEVE BUSCEMI (CHET), DAVID WARRILOW (GARLAND STANFORD), ISABELLE TOWNSEND (BATHING BEAUTY)

THE STORY Autumn 1941. Young New York Jewish playwright Barton Fink is brought to Hollywood by Jack Lipnick, head of Capitol Pictures, to write scripts. Barton's next-door neighbour at the seedy Hotel Earle is Charlie Meadows, an insurance man. Barton has writer's block and asks help from drunken novelist Bill Mayhew, whose lover eventually spends a night with Barton and is found dead in his room next morning. Charlie offers to dispose of the body, then goes off leaving Barton with a big parcel. Two cops arrive saying Charlie is serial killer Mad Man Mundt. Barton begins to write very fast, finishing a screenplay. The cops return to hotel as does Charlie. A fire breaks out and Charlie shoots the cops and retires to his room. Next day Lipnick, wearing a post-Pearl Harbor beribboned uniform run up by the studio's costume department, tells Barton his screenplay is no good and he's the property of Capitol Pictures for the time being. Barton is last seen on the beach carrying Charlie's parcel and meeting a bathing beauty who's seemingly stepped out of a picture on his hotel-room wall.

THE FILM The Coen Brothers are cult film-makers *par excellence*. All their films live in a quirky world of their own. Only their most orthodox film, *Fargo*, did notably well at the box-office. *Barton Fink* is arguably their oddest, most disturbing film and the only one to deal directly with their Jewishness and the business of movie-making. It is a black comedy, a psychological thriller, one of the cruellest of Hollywood pictures, with a succession of striking performances. Lerner's Jewish tycoon is a mixture of Louis B. Mayer, Jack Warner and Harry Cohn. Turturro's Barton is sad and touching but also a self-righteous prig. His wiry, vertically combed hair and glasses make him

▼ *BARTON FINK* John Turturro's Fink from another world gazes across the Pacific as the credits roll.

look like George S. Kaufman, but his Broadway play is in the poetic proletarian manner of Clifford Odets, and the name Fink suggests a man who, like Odets, both sold out to Hollywood and betrayed his friends to the House Un-American Activities Committee. Barton never listens to anyone and goes on about wanting to highlight the problems of 'the common man', while the perfect subject is living next door in the form of Charlie Meadows. America's entry into the war has no impact on him.

The atmosphere of the film is increasingly nightmarish, but is it a dream or something going on in Barton's head? If a dream, does it begin when Barton leaves New York? A slow dissolve between a wave breaking on the Pacific shore and the lobby of the Earle makes the hotel appear to be under water. Or does the nightmare begin with the virtuoso tracking shot from Barton and Audrey in bed, into the bathroom, down the sink and through a pipe into oblivion. After Audrey's death Barton takes a Gideon Bible from the desk drawer, opens it at random and reads an Old Testament verse in which Nebuchadnezzar says 'I recall not my dream; if ye will not make known unto me my dream, and its interpretation, ye shall be cut in pieces and your tents shall be made a dunghill.' The vast, decaying Hotel Earle is reminiscent of the Overlook Hotel in Kubrick's *The Shining*, home of another blocked writer. It's an evil haunted place, the wind roaring through empty corridors, the wallpaper slimy and peeling. As in hell, the fire makes the guests uncomfortably hot but does not consume them.

Among the numerous references to other movies, one of the most significant is to *Deadline at Dawn* (1946), a *film noir* thriller adapted by Clifford Odets from a novel by pulp writer William Irish (aka Cornel Woolrich), where a drunk finds that the woman he spent the night with has been murdered, and is driven around town by a kindly philosophical taxi-driver who turns out to be the real murderer.

ODD/SALIENT FACTS At the 1991 Cannes Festival the jury awarded Barton Fink the Palme d'Or and named Joel Coen best director and John Turturro best actor. The editing is credited to a non-existent Englishman, Roderick James, to whom they later attributed a highly critical introduction to the published screenplays of *Barton Fink* and *Miller's Crossing*.

MEMORABLE MOMENTS Jack Lipnick getting on his knees to kiss Barton's feet.

Charlie Meadows charging down the blazing corridor shouting 'Look upon me! I'll show you the life of the mind.'

Barton on the beach with the parcel and the dream girl.

KEY LINES

Lipnick: 'The writer is king here at Capitol Pictures.'

Barton: 'I guess I write about people like you. The average working stiff. The common man.'

Barton: 'But Charlie, why me?'
Charlie: 'Because you DON'T LISTEN … You're a tourist with a typewriter. I live here.'

> **'I guess I write about people like you. The average working stiff. The common man.'**

THE BATTLESHIP POTEMKIN
USSR, 1925, FIRST GOSKINO PRODUCTION, MOSCOW, 1,740 METRES (APPROX. 72 MINS)

D *SERGEI EISENSTEIN;* **PR** *JACOB BLIOKH;* **SC** *SERGEI EISENSTEIN (FROM A STORY BY NINA AGADJHANOVA AND SERGEI EISENSTEIN);* **PH** *(BW) EDOUARD TISSÉ;* **ED** *EISENSTEIN;* **M** *(FOR ORIGINAL SILENT PRODUCTION) EDMUND MEISEL*
CAST *A. ANTONOV (VAKULINCHUK), VLADIMIR BARSKY (COMMANDER GOLIKOV), GRIGORY ALEXANDROV (SENIOR OFFICER GILYAROVSKY), M. GOMOROV (SAILOR MATYUSHENKO), ANONYMOUS WORKMAN (SHIP'S SURGEON SMIRNOV), ANONYMOUS GARDENER FROM SEVASTOPOL (PRIEST), LEVCHENKO (BOSUN), REPNIKOVA (WOMAN ON THE STEPS), MARUSOV (OFFICER), SAILORS OF THE RED NAVY, CITIZENS OF ODESSA, MEMBERS OF THE PROLETCULT THEATRE (VARIOUS PARTS)*

THE STORY Set during the short-lived Russian revolution of 1905, the film unfolds in five parts, which Eisenstein saw as corresponding to the five-act structure of tragedy.

1. MEN AND MAGGOTS The revolutionary seamen Vakulinchuk and Matyushenko, serving on the Imperial Navy's *Battleship Potemkin* in the Black Sea, discuss the need to join the revolutionary workers on the mainland. Mutiny looms when sailors reject their maggot-ridden food.

▲ *THE BATTLESHIP POTEMKIN The grieving mother confronts the relentless military executioners as they descend the Odessa Steps.*

2. DRAMA ON THE QUARTER-DECK The marines are called on deck to execute some scapegoats. They refuse to fire, the sailors rebel, and the officers are killed or thrown overboard, but not before the sadistic Commander Golikov has shot Vakulinchuk.

3. AN APPEAL FROM THE DEAD (aka *The Dead Man Cries Out For Vengeance*) Vakulinchuk's body is taken ashore and laid out as a revolutionary martyr on the dock at Odessa. The citizens of the town pay their respects and express solidarity with the sailors of the *Potemkin*. The Red Flag is raised on the battleship.

4. THE ODESSA STEPS The people of Odessa rejoice and fraternize with the sailors. Suddenly the army descend on the town,

a row of soldiers in white tunics advance steadily down the wide Odessa Steps in the centre of town, methodically shooting unarmed civilians, while at the bottom of the steps a troupe of Cossack cavalry attack the crowd with sabres. The battleship retaliates by turning its guns on the Odessa Theatre, headquarters of the military commanders.

5. MEETING THE SQUADRON The *Potemkin* puts to sea, expecting to do battle with the other ships of the Black Sea fleet. But their fellow sailors refuse to fire on them and the *Potemkin* sails by, its crew cheering.

THE FILM The work of the most powerful mind ever to be actively engaged in film-making, *The Battleship Potemkin* is in every sense a revolutionary movie – a picture that employs innovatory techiques to excite its audience to rebel. Using 1,400 separate shots in seventy minutes, the film keeps up an extraordinary pace and is a great piece of graphic story-telling. Banned as inflammatory in many countries for years, it has lost little of its power and is an angry picture, demonizing the officer class while making a collective hero of the ship's crew, whose muscular bodies are admiringly observed and lovingly photographed in the below-deck scenes, given a homoerotic quality by the gay Sergei Eisenstein. The citizens of Odessa have a formidable unity taking in all classes; an anti-semite who shouts 'Down with the Jews' is turned upon and beaten. But they are also characterized so that when the massacre takes place identifiable individuals are being killed. Oddly the movie has never been widely popular in the USSR or elsewhere, and has been most keenly appreciated by art-house audiences, film-makers and students of cinema. Probably no sequence in the history of the movies has had such a hold over people as the Odessa Steps massacre, influencing artists as different as Francis Bacon, Sam Peckinpah and Brian De Palma. The use of a non-professional cast helped inspire the neo-realist movement.

ODD/SALIENT FACTS The film was intended as part of a larger work on the 1905 Revolution and was completed just in time for the twentieth anniversary celebrations. The final reel was being edited while the first one was being shown at the Bolshoi Theatre in Moscow on 21 December 1925. There was a mutiny on the *Potemkin*, the navy's largest battleship, in 1905, and the mutineers put in to Odessa, but the massacre is the invention of Eisenstein and his co-writer. Although it wasn't given a certificate for public exhibition in Britain until the 1960s, it slipped past the censor's net during the Second World War when, under the title *Seeds of Freedom*, it was presented as an inspirational story told by an ageing *Potemkin* mutineer to encourage flagging Soviet soldiers to go back into battle against the Nazis. (The additional material was filmed in New York in English.)

MEMORABLE MOMENTS A sailor working in the officers' mess angrily smashing a plate bearing the words 'Give us this day our daily bread.'

The ten *Potemkin* sailors covered in a tarpaulin on the quarterdeck waiting to be executed by a firing squad.

Commander Golikov's apoplectic expression when the marines refuse to fire.

Vakulinchuk's dead body cradled by ropes hanging beside the ship.

The Odessa Steps sequence.

KEY LINES

Lenin, the film's epigraph: 'Revolution is the only lawful, equal, effectual war. It was in Russia that this war was declared and won.'

Vakulinchuk: 'Comrades, the time has come to act. What are we waiting for? All Russia is rising. Are we to be the last?'

The Potemkin's *priest:* 'Lord, reveal Thyself to the unruly.'

Matyushenko: 'Ring up the signal – don't fight us, join us.'

A BETTER TOMORROW

HONG KONG, 1986, CINEMA CITY/FILM WORKSHOP, 95 MINS
D/SC JOHN WOO; *CO-PR* TSUI HARK; *PH* WONG WING HUNG; *M* JOSEPH KOO
CAST CHOW YUN FAT (MARK), TI LUNG (HO), LESLIE CHEUNG (KIT), EMILY CHU (JACKIE), LE CHE HUNG (SHING)

THE STORY Mark and Ho, close friends and gangsters, execute assignments for the Hong Kong syndicate around the Pacific Rim. Ho's younger brother Kit, unaware of his brother's profession, has joined the Hong Kong police and developed an attachment to Jackie, the classical musician who cares for their sick father. Accompanied by the ambitious Shing, Ho delivers a case of counterfeit money in Taiwan but is double-crossed and a bloody shoot-out ensues. Trapped by the police he lets Shing escape and serves three years in jail. Meanwhile in Hong Kong Ho's father is killed by a Taiwanese gangster sent to kidnap him, and Mark is shot in the leg while seeking revenge on those said to have betrayed Ho. Returning from jail, Ho decides to go straight, becoming a taxi driver for a firm that employs ex-convicts. But his brother holds him responsible for their father's death and his own failure to secure promotion. The crippled Mark works as an odd-job man for Shing, now deputy

28

'Comrades, the time has come to act. What are we waiting for?'

▲ *A Better Tomorrow* Chow Yun Fat, both guns blazing in a show of selfless bravery, a typical Woo combination of piety and pyrotechnics.

head of the syndicate, and is ritually humiliated. Eventually Mark and Ho are reunited against Shing, who is attempting to frame Ho and take over the whole organization. In a final gunfight on the docks, Mark gives his life to save his friend and Ho convinces his brother that he is going straight. In the final shot Ho puts the handcuffs around his own wrist and allows Kit to take him in.

THE FILM In the 1980s, Chinese and Taiwanese films stormed into European and American art-house cinemas while for less fastidious audiences Hong Kong provided cult action films, first Kung Fu pictures then gangster flicks. John Woo became the Crown Colony's hottest director through his kinetic crime pictures that filtered the lyrical violence of Sergio Leone, Sam Peckinpah and Walter Hill through an Asian sensibility and re-exported it to the States where Quentin Tarantino became a major admirer. Woo's trademarks are the stand-off, where two

or more gunmen hold each other at bay, and the ferocious gunfight in which dozens of people are killed and restaurants blown apart as the hero pirouettes and somersaults while blasting away with two automatic pistols to throbbing, synthesized Western music. *A Better Tomorrow* is a characteristic fable of male friendship, stoicism, courage, and men living by a personal code, in which women are marginalized. It made an overnight star of Chow Yun Fat, who appeared in most of Woo's pictures. The handsome, reserved, athletic Chow is the epitome of Hong Kong movie cool, a moral man in an amoral world, his character much the same whatever side of the law he is on. The movie also introduced Leslie Cheung, who was to become an iconic figure in mainland Chinese movies.

ODD/SALIENT FACTS Woo made his Hollywood debut in 1993 with *Hard Target* and went on to direct John Travolta in *Broken Arrow* and *Face/Off*. Chow Yun Fat's first American film was *Replacement Assassin* (1997), in which he played a hitman who develops a conscience. *A Better Tomorrow* is one of the favourite movies of the video-store hero of *True Romance* (1993), scripted by Tarantino.

Dimas, California, in 1988 to give them the time machine with which they can gather famous figures from the past so as to score an A+ in the following day's history presentation. This they do, collecting Napoleon, Socrates (pronounced So-crates throughout), Sigmund Freud (pronounced Frood), Beethoven, Joan of Arc and Genghis Khan. After some time-travel conundrums, a sequence in which the historical figures experience mall life and Napoleon goes to a waterworld, the greatest-ever oral history presentation is given and the future of the world ensured.

In the sequel, the future is once again threatened, this time by De Homolus who, resentful of the insidious influence of Bill and Ted, sends robot versions of them back in time to kill and discredit them. The androids take the time-travelling telephone box back to San Dimas, kill Bill and Ted, wreck their apartment, and threaten to kill their girlfriends, the medieval princesses, at the battle of the bands at which they will destroy the potential musical heritage of the Wyld Stallyns. Meanwhile the dead Bill and Ted are met by Death. They are

'Party on, dude.'

▲ *BILL & TED'S BOGUS JOURNEY The good, dead Bill and Ted briefly find they have a lot in common with their alter egos. Excellent.*

shown a glimpse of their own private hells, but get another shot at life after defeating the Grim Reaper in a series of contests. Returning to the present, with the help of Death, a couple of Martians and good robot versions of themselves, Bill and Ted defeat the bad robots, rescue the princesses and send their music around the world in a global broadcast.

THE FILMS Bill & Ted emerged at roughly the same time as Wayne & Garth and cover almost identical territory, being dorky teenage friends whose world views do not extend much beyond babes, cheesy TV and, most important of all, heavy rock. They share similar, sometimes identical jargon ('Excellent', 'Party on' , 'No way', 'Yes way' etc.) but what makes Bill & Ted cults and Wayne & Garth mainstream? Both Wayne's World films were more financially successful for a start, and this points at the smoother, more conventional approach of these projects. The Bill & Ted films are arguably funnier and more intelligent, certainly more complex and with a sharper satirical content. They are characters who think that Joan of Arc is Noah's wife and that her surname is 'Of Ark' in the same way that they address Billy the Kid as 'Mr The Kid'. They inhabit a world in which the meaning of life is to be found within the lyrics of a soft rock anthem. Somewhere not too deep below the surface is the suggestion that although the two are likeable and sympathetic, they represent the shallowness of modern American media, which is in danger of becoming the planet's lasting, dominant cultural legacy. Above all, the films succeed because they are funny in a quirky way, and they are well acted. Alex Winter simply looks very odd, but more important is the presence of Keanu Reeves. Reeves is a little like his generation's equivalent of John Travolta, who makes a succession of peculiar career choices, suggesting that he is unsure whether or not he wants to be mainstream. As a person, like Travolta, he projects an odd mixture of intuitive smartness and an ingenuousness that borders on the stupid. Not much is known of Alex Winter except that he has gone on to direct some pop videos (for heavy rock bands we hope) but you suspect, and even hope a little, that Keanu who has his own, reputedly lousy, rock band is in real life rather like Ted.

MEMORABLE MOMENTS

Excellent Adventure: The scenes in the mall in which Billy the Kid and Socrates try to chat up a couple of babes.
Bogus Journey: Death informs the recently deceased duo that they can return to life if they defeat him in a contest, so they challenge and beat him in games of Battleships, Cluedo, table football and Twister. This is a variation on Woody Allen's own variation on the Knight's game of chess against death in *The Seventh Seal* (1957). In Allen's short story *Death Knocks*, the protagonist challenges Death to a game of gin rummy and, as here, the Grim Reaper turns out to be a very bad loser.

KEY LINES

Excellent Adventure. The farewell of the future inspired by Bill & Ted's own brief awkward visit is: 'Be excellent to each other.' *To which the response is:* 'Party on, dude.'

Bill, reading Socrates: 'The only wisdom consists in knowing that you know nothing.'
Ted: 'That's us, dude.'

Bogus Journey:
Bad robot Ted on seeing a photograph of the princesses: 'I've got a full-on robot chubby.'

BLADE RUNNER – THE DIRECTOR'S CUT

US, 1982, THE LADD COMPANY, 112 MINS (ORIG, 117 MINS)
D *RIDLEY SCOTT;* **PR** *MICHAEL DEELEY;* **SC** *HAMPTON FANCHER, DAVID PEOPLES, BASED ON THE NOVEL* DO ANDROIDS DREAM OF ELECTRIC SHEEP? *BY PHILIP K. DICK;* **PH** *(COL, PANAVISION) JORDAN CRONENWETH;* **M** *VANGELIS;* **ART DIR** *DAVID SNYDER;* **ED** *TERRY RAWLINGS*
CAST *HARRISON FORD (DECKARD), RUTGER HAUER (BATTY), SEAN YOUNG (RACHAEL), EDWARD JAMES OLMOS (GAFF), M. EMMET WALSH (BRYANT), DARYL HANNAH (PRIS), WILLIAM SANDERSON (SEBASTIAN), BRION JAMES (LEON), JOE TURKEL (TYRELL), JOANNA CASSIDY (ZHORA), JAMES HONG (CHEW), MORGAN PAULL (HOLDEN), KEVIN THOMPSON (BEAR), JOHN EDWARD ALLEN (KAISER), HY PYKE (TAFFEY LEWIS)*

33

THE STORY Los Angeles, 2019. Deckard, a blade runner, is brought into the police department and forced out of retirement to kill four escaped androids, advanced Nexus 6 replicants: Leon, Roy Batty (their leader), Zhora and Pris. At the Tyrell corporation (where they were made), Deckard discovers that Tyrell's assistant, Rachael, is herself an android. Deckard finds some photographs and a single scale from a snakeskin in Leon's flat. Leon and Batty visit Chew, the designer of their eyes, who advises them to visit their maker, Tyrell, via the genetic designer, J. S. Sebastian. Pris befriends Sebastian. Deckard, sitting at his piano, dreams of a unicorn. By studying Leon's photographs and the scale, Deckard tracks down Zhora. He kills her, and his life is saved when Rachael kills Leon, who was about to kill him. Sebastian takes Batty to see Tyrell who tells him he can't extend his four-year life-span. Batty kills him. Deckard tracks Pris down to Sebastian's apartment and kills her. Batty returns and fights with Deckard. Climbing around the tops of the city's buildings, Batty saves Deckard's life before suddenly dying. Deckard returns to his apartment to escape with Rachael. On the way out he finds an origami figure, a unicorn, and, suddenly disturbed, leaves.

THE FILM This was Ridley Scott's follow-up to the remarkable, and commercially successful *Alien* (1979). It was a box-office failure, but its brilliant creation of a dystopian future LA in which an old-fashioned, arcane, psychologically and philosophically complex *film noir* thriller is played out, made it an instant cult film. The *noir* style of the film was enhanced in the release version by the addition, against the wishes of Scott and Harrison Ford, of a hard-boiled and explicatory voice-over. This device was insisted on by a studio who feared that an audience would become lost in the opaque plot. In fact the story line is rather simple. Bounty hunter comes out of retirement to track down and kill four outlaws. This is overlaid by the love interest being unmasked herself as an android and so being added to the hit-list. There is also the understated suggestion that Deckard himself may be an android. Having accomplished his task, Deckard leaves with Rachael and, picking up Gaff's origami figure, he hears once again Gaff's parting words: 'It's too bad she won't live, but then again who does?' As he and Rachael escape (incidentally the scenery that they fly over is made up of out-takes from the opening sequence of Stanley Kubrick's *The Shining*, 1980), his voice-over explains that Gaff had been there but let

▲ *BLADE RUNNER Harrison Ford (Deckard) travels down LA's futuristic mean streets aiming to retire a bunch of replicants.*

Rachael live. Deckard reassures the audience that Rachael, unlike the other androids, has no inbuilt death date, so he doesn't know how much time they have together, 'but who does?'

In *The Director's Cut*, the film is shorter than the original, and the narration has been removed. What has been restored is Deckard's dream of a unicorn which is crucial to the real end of the film. As Deckard picks up Gaff's origami unicorn and recalls his words, he is horrified because it confirms his suspicions. Gaff was there thinking of a unicorn, a recurring dream of Deckard's. The dream may even be borrowed from Gaff's own mind. After this bleak punchline there is no need for any further coda.

ODD/SALIENT FACTS The end of the chess game in which Sebastian, with help from Batty, defeats Tyrell, is inspired by the endgame of 'The Immortal Game' in which Adolf Andersson beat Lionel Kieseritzky in London in 1851. *Blade Runner* is based on a novel by Philip K. Dick, *Do Androids Dream of Electric Sheep?* The story is much altered although many of the names and characters remain (Roy Baty becomes Roy Batty) as do certain key details such as hover cars, videophones and androids being detected by empathy tests and the specific example of asking a question about boiled dog. Dick was a much married science-fiction visionary who, having consumed large quantities of LSD, believed that he was, for an extended period of time, in regular direct contact with God. He died in March 1982 shortly before the release of *Blade Runner*.

MEMORABLE MOMENTS Deckard's brief dream of the unicorn. The view of LA night life. Hover cars fly through the air, adverts are on massive electronic billboards and floating space craft, people mill around in the drizzle clutching umbrellas with luminous handles. The camera zooms in on a man sitting outside a garishly lit window reading a newspaper, and we catch a first glimpse of Deckard.

KEY LINES

Tyrell: 'What seems to be the problem?'
Batty: 'Death.'
Tyrell: 'Death, well, I'm afraid that's a little out of my league.'
Batty: 'I want more life, fucker!'

Batty: 'I've seen things you people wouldn't believe. Attack ships on fire off the shoulder of Orion. I watched C-beams glitter in the dark near the Tannhauser Gate. All those moments will be lost in time like tears in rain. Time to die.'

THE BLOB

US, 1958, PARAMOUNT/TONYLYN, 86 MINS

D IRVIN S. YEAWORTH; **PR** JACK H. HARRIS; **SC** THEODORE SIMONSON, KATE PHILLIPS, FROM AN ORIGINAL IDEA BY IRVINE H. HILLGATE; **PH** (COL) THOMAS SPALDING; **M** RALPH CARMICHAEL; **ED** ALFRED HILLMAN

CAST STEVEN MCQUEEN (STEVE ANDREWS), ANETA CORSEAUT (JANE MARTIN), EARL ROWE (LT. DAVE), OLIN HOWLIN (OLD MAN), STEVEN CHASE (DR T. HALLEN), JOHN BENSON (SGT. JIM BEST), GEORGE KARAS (OFFICER RITCHIE), ELBERT SMITH (HENRY MARTIN), VINCENT BARBI (GEORGE, THE CAFÉ OWNER), AUDREY METCALF (ELIZABETH MARTIN)

THE STORY It is night-time on the outskirts of a small town. Steve and Jane are necking in his car, watching the shooting stars, when they see one com e really close. The meteorite lands and the red goo it contains attacks an old man. Steve and Jane nearly collide with him and take him to Dr Hallen for some tests. The doctor asks the two kids to drive up to the old man's place to see what they can find out. While Steve and Jane are away, the Blob consumes the old man, then a nurse and finally the doctor. When Steve returns he catches a glimpse of the doctor being attacked. He goes to the police, who don't believe him but are convinced that it is a juvenile prank. Meanwhile the Blob, on the loose, eats a car mechanic. Steve and Jane, out to find proof, notice that Steve's dad's shop is open in the middle of the night. They are menaced by the Blob, and when they take refuge in the store's deep-freeze room notice that the Blob retreats. Finally Steve and his buddies use the air-raid siren to alert the town's citizens. The Blob attacks a movie projectionist and finally engulfs the diner in which are Steve, Jane, Jane's brother, the café owner and his wife. As the monster slithers towards them in the basement, Steve attacks it with a carbon-dioxide extinguisher and once more it retreats. Just in time, the Blob is frozen and air-lifted to the Arctic.

▼ *THE BLOB Steve McQueen, the oldest teenager in town, his girl and the local doctor examine the first victim of the hideous, gelatinous alien.*

THE FILM Several major stars and directors began their film careers in the mass of sci-fi and horror B-movies churned out in the 1950s and early '60s. Clint Eastwood featured as a lab technician in *Revenge of the Creature* (1955) and as one of the pilots zapping the vast spider with napalm in *Tarantula* (1955). Jack Nicholson's early credits include *The Little Shop of Horrors* (1961), *The Raven* (1962) and *The Terror* (1962). Early appearances of cinematic icons are always fascinating, but *The Blob* – whose opening was one of the key influences on *Alien* (1979) – not only features Steve McQueen's third screen role, and second as a star, but remains one of the great cheap horror films. The small-ness of the budget is betrayed by the few special-effects sequences and their basicness when they do come, featuring an amor-phous mass of red jelly. It is a horror film of enduring charm, and one which almost entirely neglects to be horrifying. McQueen's own, quiet, slow-burn per-sona is already formed here, but he is also clearly mimicking the screen techniques of his late contemporary, James Dean.

'It's the most horrible thing I've ever seen in my life.'

ODD/SALIENT FACTS The cult, camp status of the film is con-firmed by its appearance in *Grease* (1978). The kitschy, unscary title song is an early Burt Bacharach composition, co-written with Mack David. Steve McQueen was offered profit points in the film in lieu of his $3,000 fee. He turned it down, and it went on to return $4,000,000 on a budget of $150,000. He was already on the way to stardom and later that year he made his first appearances on TV in *Wanted: Dead or Alive*. The film also sees the last time he was billed as Steven.

MEMORABLE MOMENTS *The Blob* marks an early use of the device, later used in *Targets* (1968) and *Scream 2* (1998) – with perhaps the earliest being Hitchcock's *Saboteur* (1942), of having a horror scene in a cinema showing a horror film. Here a late-night bill of cheap horror movies is interrupted when the Blob oozes through the vent in the projection box and absorbs the projectionist. The monster then seeps through the windows and vents into the auditorium. The effect of this is undermined by the bizarrely tame scenes of the terrified audi-ence fleeing the cinema, with the extras either laughing or looking very obviously bored.

KEY LINES

The nurse, having thrown some acid over the Blob, to no avail: 'Doctor, nothing will stop it.'

Dave, on his superior officer's unfair dislike for Steve: 'Just because some kid smashes into his wife on the turnpike doesn't make it a crime to be 17.' (McQueen at 28, making an unconvincing 17-year-old.)

Dave: 'It's the most horrible thing I've ever seen in my life.'

Dave, on the radio to an Air Force officer: 'I think you should send us the biggest transport plane you have, and take this thing to the Arctic or somewhere and drop it where it'll never thaw out.'

… and with a prescient, ecologically minded final thought:
Dave: 'At least we've got it stopped.'
Steve: 'Yeah, as long as the Arctic stays cold.'

BLOW OUT
US, 1981, FILMWAYS/CINEMA 77/GERIA, 108 MINS
D BRIAN DE PALMA; **PR** PAUL DYLBERT; **SC** BRIAN DE PALMA; **PH** (COL PANAVISION) VILMOS ZSIGMOND; **M** PINO DONAGGIO; **ED** PAUL HIRSCH

CAST JOHN TRAVOLTA (JACK), NANCY ALLEN (SALLY), JOHN LITHGOW (BURKE), DENNIS FRANZ (MANNY KARP), PETER BOWDEN (SAM), CURT MAY (DONAHUE), JOHN AQUINO (DETECTIVE MACKEY), JOHN MCMARTIN (LAWRENCE HENRY), DEBORAH EVERTON (HOOKER)

THE STORY Jack Terry is a movie sound man who is out one night gathering new effects for his library. As he is recording, a passing car suffers a blow-out and plunges into the river run-ning alongside the road. Jack rescues Sally from the back of the car, but the driver, senator MacRyan, is killed. Convinced that the tyre was shot out, Jack studies the tape he made which con-firms this, and further backs this up by matching it up with film made from the photographs of the accident taken by Manny Karp. Karp and Sally had been planning to blackmail the sen-ator. Meanwhile, Burke who fired the shot, wanting to kill Sally to tie up the loose ends of the plot, accidentally kills the wrong

▲ *BLOW OUT John Travolta as sound man Jack, searching for the perfect scream and the truth behind a mysterious crash.*

woman and disguises this mistake by making it the first in a killing spree themed around Philadelphia's imminent Liberty Day celebrations. Burke poses as a TV reporter in order to get hold of the incriminating tape and kill Sally. Wired by Jack, Sally walks into the trap. Jack, who is trailing her, catches up too late to save her but does kill Burke. Jack dubs Sally's bloodcurdling death scream into the latest slasher movie he is working on.

THE FILM This flashy thriller managed to be a flop despite starring Travolta near the peak of his first period of stardom. De Palma, who started out as a satirical political film-maker before making a detour into the slasher genre, tosses everything into the mix. Inspired by Chappaquiddick and the Zapruder film as well as borrowing from several other

'It's a good scream.'

films, most obviously Antonioni's *Blow-Up* (1966), and Coppola's *The Conversation* (1974), De Palma steals from not one but two of his old movie buddies. The sudden appearance of the senator's head in the submerged car is a clear homage to the great shock moment in *Jaws* (1975). But De Palma's hero has always been Hitchcock, and he is barely able to make any film without quoting from the shower sequence in *Psycho* (1960), which he does here in the opening scene. Hitchcock always considered it a big mistake that the suspense sequence in *Sabotage* (1936) should end with the bomb going off, killing the boy. He understood that with this decision the film lost the audience's sympathy. De Palma rejoices in playing with unwritten narrative rules. He invented the shock second ending in *Carrie* (1976), repeated *Psycho's* surprise killing off of the leading lady in *Dressed to Kill* and continually confounds audience's expectations. What effectively marginalizes *Blow*

Out is the decision to have a lengthy climactic pursuit end in the violent death of the film's co-star, all to provide a little punch-line. Despite some narrative laxity, it is a dazzling and dark film that, in its mixture of stunning camera work and nastiness, offers an effective look at the haphazardness of a nascent conspiracy.

ODD/SALIENT FACTS During the editing process two reels of footage from the Liberty Parade sequence were stolen and were never to be seen again. This meant that the scenes had to be reshot at a cost of $750,000. Vilmos Zsigmond was no longer available so for these reshoots he was replaced by his compatriot Laszlo Kovacs, who was the cinematographer on *Easy Rider* (1969) and *Five Easy Pieces* (1970). Like Hitchcock, De Palma bases his most famous cinematic predilection, in his case voyeurism, on a specific childhood incident. When he was a child his parents split up, his mother accusing his father of infidelity. The young De Palma spent several days stalking his dad with recording equipment, hoping to find evidence to confirm his mother's suspicions.

In the partly improvised restaurant sequence where Jack and Sally get to know one another, she asks him how he became a soundman. Jack explains: 'It all started in school. I was the kind of kid who fixed radios, made my own stereos, won all the science fairs. You know the type.' In 1998, responding to Mark Cousins's question about his early cinematic inspiration, De Palma recalls: 'I was more of a kind of computer nerd at high school, built computers, won science fairs.'

MEMORABLE MOMENTS Jack tells Sally about a traumatic incident from the time when he was investigating police corruption. There is a flashback to when he rigged up a wire on his colleague to trap a crooked police captain. He taped the device to the man's chest and waist and followed him in a car. In time there is strong static coming across the line. It transpires that the man is so nervous, he is sweating profusely and this is shorting the circuit and burning the man's stomach. Realizing the danger, Jack follows him into a garage toilet only to find him already dead, having been found out and hanged with remarkable alacrity.

KEY LINES

Jack's final assessment of Sally's audio legacy: 'It's a good scream.'

BLOW-UP
UK, 1966, MGM, 111 MINS

D MICHELANGELO ANTONIONI; **PR** CARLO PONTI; **SC** MICHELANGELO ANTONIONI, TONINO GUERRA, FROM A SHORT STORY BY JULIO CORTAZAR (ENGLISH DIALOGUE BY EDWARD BOND); **PH** (METROCOLOR) CARLO DI PALMA; **ED** FRANK CLARKE; **M** HERBIE HANCOCK

CAST DAVID HEMMINGS (THOMAS), VANESSA REDGRAVE (THE WOMAN IN THE PARK), RONAN O'RAHILLY (MAN IN THE PARK), PETER BOWLES (RON), SARAH MILES (PATRICIA), JOHN CASTLE (BILL, THE PAINTER), JANE BIRKIN AND GILLIAN HILLS (TEENAGE GIRLS AT STUDIO), VERUSHKA (FIRST MODEL), HARRY HUTCHINSON (MAN AT ANTIQUES SHOP)

THE STORY Early on a Saturday morning Thomas, a baby-faced fashion photographer, leaves a London doss-house where he has been posing as a tramp to gather pictures for a book. Returning to his studio in his Rolls-Royce convertible, he conducts a fashion shoot, visits the abstract painter who works next door, and drives to a suburban antiques shop he's thinking of buying. Killing time before the owner returns, he walks into a park and takes some photographs of a young woman he sees embracing a middle-aged man. The woman demands that he gives her the negatives, but he refuses and, meeting his manager Ron for lunch, he decides that the peaceful park pictures would be the perfect closing images for his gritty book. The woman tracks him to his studio and after she's attempted to seduce him, he gives her a false roll of film. Developing the pictures and blowing up certain features, Thomas comes to believe that, far from an idyllic scene, he has recorded a killing. He goes back to the park after dark and discovers the man's corpse, but returning home he finds the blow-ups and negatives have been stolen. Thomas seeks help from Ron, who's stoned at a party and unable to assist. Next morning he visits the park again but the body is no longer there. Some students wearing clowns' make-up, first seen at the opening of the film, turn up and two of them begin to mime a game on the park's tennis court. When the

> 'I've gone off London this week. It doesn't do anything for me.'

▲ *BLOW-UP David Hemmings (Thomas) finds there is more in the park than meets the eye when he snaps Vanessa Redgrave at play.*

non-existent ball is struck out of the court Thomas throws it back and walks away.

THE FILM A mystery without a solution, a paranoid thriller made in Britain by Italians and based on a story set in Paris by an Argentinian, *Blow-Up* is one of the great movies about the illusory nature of reality, alienation and existential dread. This characteristic Antonioni movie, his first full-length work in English, has always divided audiences into those who think it pretentious tosh and those who love even its most portentous moments. Antonioni's combination of fastidious Marxist contempt for contemporary society and a fascination with fashion, eroticism and the high life found a happy focus in the shallow world of Swinging London, which for a few years in the mid-1960s was a centre of international attention. One of the dominant social heroes of the time was the classless photographer — Armstrong Jones, Bailey, Duffy et al. — the cool observer whose camera is

the extension of his eye, played here by an iconic figure of the period, David Hemmings. Two other icons of the time, Vanessa Redgrave and Sarah Miles, the one upper-class, the other lower, are on hand. What makes *Blow-Up* survive where most of the other Swinging London films (e.g. *A Hard Day's Night*, *Darling*, *Morgan*) seem extremely dated, is the stylized quality (including the painting red of whole suburban streets) and the discreet use of Herbie Hancock's jazz score.

ODD/SALIENT FACTS Despite the customary spelling of the title as *Blow-Up*, the print itself at the beginning and end bears the title BLOWUP. The enormous neon sign that provides the light source for the night scene in the park was created by designer Assheton Gorton and has no meaning, though if it reads TOA (rather than FOA) it might come from Antonioni's name. The street number of Thomas's studio — 39 — clearly alludes to Hitchcock and the MacGuffin of the traditional thriller.

MEMORABLE MOMENTS Thomas's first sight of the couple in the park.

The developing, printing and enlargement of the roll of pictures from the park.

terribles (1950) and *Bob le fambeur* (1955), and one of the heroes of the *nouvelle vague*.

MEMORABLE MOMENTS The almost perfunctory shooting of the policeman: he is seen approaching on his motorbike, then there is a close-up of Michel's gun; a gunshot; the policeman falls off the side of the road; then a long shot of Michel running across a field; then cut to the city.

The two-minute take, shortly before Michel is killed, as he and Patricia walk in circles around the apartment, occasionally talking over one another, pondering love and betrayal.

44

▼ *BREATHLESS Jean-Paul Belmondo and Jean Seberg enjoy some peace before their brief affair ends in betrayal and death.*

Michel to Patricia: 'It's silly, but I love you. I wanted to see you, to see if I'd want to see you.'

Patricia: 'I don't know if I'm unhappy because I'm not free, or if I'm not free because I'm unhappy.'

Patricia: 'Are you afraid of getting old? I am.'

Parvulesco: 'Two things are important in life. For men, women. For women, money.'

Michel: 'I'm tired. I'm going to die.'

Parvulesco, asked what his ambition is: 'To become
immortal, and then die.'

Michel's dying words: 'It's a bitch.' (The policeman tells
her he said: 'You're a bitch.')

THE BRIBE

USA, 1949, MGM, 98 MINS

D ROBERT Z. LEONARD; **SC** MARGUERITE ROBERTS (FROM A STORY
BY FREDERICK NEBEL); **PH** (BW) JOSEPH RUTTENBERG; **M** MIKLOS
ROZSA; **ED** GENE RUGGIERO

CAST ROBERT TAYLOR (RIGBY), AVA GARDNER (ELIZABETH
HINTTEN), JOHN HODIAK (TUGWELL HINTTEN), CHARLES
LAUGHTON (J. J. BEALER), VINCENT PRICE (CARWOOD)

THE STORY Federal agent Rigby is dispatched to Carlota,
main town of a small island off the coast of Latin America, to
investigate a gang dealing in contraband war-surplus aero-
engines. He falls in love with Elizabeth Hintten, wife of Tug
Hintten, a drunken ex-US Air Force pilot with a bad heart who
works for the gang. The racketeers' ringleader Carwood
arranges for his obese henchman Bealer to offer Rigby a bribe
and then attempts to murder him during a fishing expedition.
Carwood has Bealer blackmail Elizabeth into drugging Rigby
so the gang can escape, and subsequently kills the dying
Hintten. But Rigby recovers in time to inform the mainland police
and to kill Carwood, and while Carlota celebrates a fiesta, he's
re-united with Elizabeth.

THE FILM In classic *noir* style, the chain-smoking Rigby (he has
no Christian name) tells most of the story in flashbacks that begin
as visions he sees on the rain-lashed window of his hotel room.
His voiceover narration continues throughout as he battles with
his conscience and tries to retain his honour in a world reeking
of corruption. Laughton and Price are splendidly hammy villains
and Gardner's nightclub singer is an innocent *femme fatale* in
the manner of Rita Hayworth's Gilda.

ODD/SALIENT FACTS Robert Z. Leonard, prolific MGM contract director, is best known for musicals and the 1939 *Pride
and Prejudice*. The carefully choreographed final gunfight illuminated by fireworks was shot several weeks after the
production wrapped and was directed by Vincente Minnelli.
Marguerite Roberts, one of MGM's leading scriptwriters, was

▲ *THE BRIBE Procine conspirator Charles Laughton sets up
Robert Taylor, as femme fatale Ava Gardner looks on.*

blacklisted two years after *The Bribe*, and MGM removed her
name from *Ivanhoe* (1952), another Robert Taylor film. She
didn't work again until the 1960s when her credits, mostly on
Westerns, included *True Grit*. Carl Reiner's *Dead Men Don't
Wear Plaid* draws heavily on *The Bribe* and heads towards a
climax on Carlota.

MEMORABLE MOMENTS Carwood accelerates the fishing-
boat engine so that Rigby, strapped to his fishing rod, is pulled
overboard by a hefty marlin and the young lad rescuing him is
killed by a shark.

A passionate scene of Rigby and Elizabeth kissing on the
beach after a moonlight swim (reminiscent of *The Postman
Always Rings Twice* and *From Here to Eternity*).

The drugged Rigby deliberately trapping his hand in a door
to wake himself up.

The climactic shoot-out between Carwood and Rigby staged
in the middle of a spectacular firework display.

KEY LINES

Bealer: 'Who are you protecting? A bunch of taxpayers
who'll get it in the neck anyway. Everyone's grafting
nowadays, that's how people operate.'

BRING ME THE HEAD OF ALFREDO GARCIA

USA–MEXICO, 1974, UNITED ARTISTS/OPTIMUS PRODUCTIONS (HOLLYWOOD), ESTUDIOS CHURUBUSCO (MEXICO CITY), 112 MINS

D *SAM PECKINPAH;* **PR** *MARTIN BAUM;* **SC** *GORDON DAWSON, SAM PECKINPAH (FROM A STORY BY PECKINPAH, FRANK KOWALSKI);* **PH** *(DE LUXE COL) ALEX PHILLIPS JR.;* **ED** *GARTH CRAVEN;* **M** *JERRY FIELDING*

CAST *WARREN OATES (BENNIE), ISELA VEGA (ELITA), GIG YOUNG (QUILL), ROBERT WEBBER (SAPPENSLY), HELMUT DANTINE (MAX), EMILIO FERNANDEZ (EL JEFE), DON LEVY (FRANK), JANINE MALDONADO (THERESA), KRIS KRISTOFFERSON (PACO), DONNY FRITTS (JOHN), JORGE RUSSEK (CUETO)*

THE STORY Discovering that his daughter Theresa is pregnant, El Jefe, the rich, ruthless head of a feudal Mexican family, tortures her into confessing that the father is the womanizing Alfredo Garcia, then offers a million dollars to the person who brings him the miscreant's head. Max, head of an American business cartel, sets two gangsters, Quill and Sappensly, on Garcia's trail. They question Bennie, a penniless American pianist, who learns from his prostitute lover Elita that Garcia has been killed in a road accident and buried in his native village. Bennie sets off with a disgusted Elita to retrieve Garcia's head. He kills two bikers who attempt to rape Elita, but at the graveyard she is murdered and Bennie almost buried alive by two Mexicans who make off with the head. Bennie pursues and kills them, recovers the head, and has a shoot-out with Garcia's kinfolk, in which they and the double-crossing Quill and Sappensly end up dead. Bennie kills Max and his bodyguards, discovers El Jefe's identity and arrives at his hacienda as Theresa's son is being christened. He takes the reward, but doesn't hand over the head, kills El Jefe's lieutenants, and at Theresa's command shoots her father. Fleeing with Alfredo's head, Bennie is shot to pieces by the guards at the gate.

THE FILM *Alfredo Garcia* is Peckinpah's most complex, personal and controversial picture, a savage fable that never found a public following and divided critics into a large majority that hated it, and a small minority that loved it. It is located in the Mexico of Malcolm Lowry, Graham Greene and B. Traven (to

▲ *BRING ME THE HEAD OF ALFREDO GARCIA Gun in hand, cigarette in mouth, Warren Oates (Bennie) dispenses some rough justice South of the Rio Grande.*

whose *Treasure of the Sierra Madre* it alludes). It's an eclectic combination of existential quest, gothic tale, a political critique of US involvement in Latin America (the smooth capitalist reads *Time* with a Watergate cover story) and a love story about two losers challenging destiny. The ultimate terror resides in the central image of a low-life character transporting a decomposing head across Mexico for a reward. It's all drawn together by Peckinpah's grand vision of a doomed, dangerous world spiralling towards destruction, and two dozen or more killings are presented with Peckinpah's customary slow-motion lyricism. Warren Oates, a great character actor and member of the Peckinpah rep company, had top starring roles in only three movies – *Two Lane Blacktop, Dillinger* and *Alfredo Garcia*, all cult masterworks – and they will ensure him immortality.

> **'Nobody loses all the time.'**

ODD/SALIENT FACTS *Alfredo Garcia* was Peckinpah's challenge to Hollywood and Nixon's America: 'I'm an American resident. When Nixon was elected president, I said "I'm getting the fuck out, this cocksucker is going to ruin this country."' Pauline Kael said: 'I think Warren was imitating Sam in the picture because that was his idea of how to become a star.' Emilio Fernandez (1904–86), who plays El Jefe (and also appeared in Peckinpah's *Wild Bunch* and *Pat Garrett*) is the greatest figure in Mexican cinema as actor/writer/producer, and his bizarre career clearly appealed to Peckinpah. He was sentenced to twenty years in 1923 for revolutionary activities, jailed in the 1950s for shooting a film critic, and served time in 1976 for killing a troublesome farm labourer while on location. Helmut Dantine, the film's executive producer and chief American heavy, came to Hollywood in the late 1930s as an Austrian refugee, making memorable appearances in *Mrs Miniver* and *Casablanca*.

MEMORABLE MOMENTS Bennie in opaque shades at his bar piano.

Bennie, after a night with Elita, plucking crabs from his pubic hair and pouring tequila over his groin.

Bennie knocked out over Garcia's grave and waking to find himself buried beside his dead lover.

Bennie's intimate conversations with Alfredo Garcia's head in its burlap bag.

Bennie turning on El Jefe and his household.

KEY LINES

Bennie (to the head in the sack): 'Come on Al, we're going home.'

Bennie (to Elita): 'You pack the lunch – because we're going on a picnic, we're going to find the golden fleece, baby.'

Bennie: 'Listen, the church cuts off the feet, fingers and any other thing from a dead saint. What the hell. Alfredo's our saint, he's the saint of our money and I'm going to borrow a piece of him.'

Bennie (standing gun in hand, about to kill the man who murdered his lover): 'Why? Because it feels so goddam good.'

Bennie: 'Nobody loses all the time.'

Bennie (giving locket containing Garcia's photograph to Theresa): 'Listen, take this, you take care of the boy, I'll take care of the father.'

BRINGING UP BABY
US, 1938, RKO PICTURES, 102 MINS
D HOWARD HAWKS; **PR** CLIFF REID; **SC** DUDLEY NICHOLS, HAGAR WILDE, FROM A STORY BY HAGAR WILDE; **PH** (BW) RUSSELL METTY; **M** ROY WEBB; **ED** GEORGE HIVELY
CAST CARY GRANT (DAVID HUXLEY), KATHARINE HEPBURN (SUSAN VANCE), MAY ROBSON (AUNT ELIZABETH), CHARLES RUGGLES (MAJOR APPLEGATE), FRITZ FIELD (DR LEHMANN), GEORGE IRVING (ALEXANDER PEABODY), VIRGINIA WALKER (ALICE SWALLOW), BARRY FITZGERALD (ALOYSIUS GOGARTY), WALTER CATLETT (CONSTABLE SLOCUM), LEONA ROBERTS (HANNAH GOGARTY), TALA BIRRELL (MRS LEHMANN)

THE STORY David Huxley is a starchy paleontologist who is eagerly awaiting three significant events in his life: the arrival of the recently unearthed fossil of a brontosaurus's intercostal clavicle, the final bone in the enormous skeleton he is assembling in the Stuyvesant Museum of Natural History; the confirmation of a grant of $1 million for the museum; and his marriage the following day to his co-worker, the equally stiff Alice. While on the golf course trying to seal the grant from the donor's attorney, Mr Peabody, David has a fateful encounter with the eccentric Susan Vance. Their frantic adventures over the next several days result in a stolen golf ball, two stolen cars, a flattened top hat, ripped tails, a torn dress, the arrival of a tame leopard called Baby, the knocking unconscious of Mr Peabody, the eating of two swans valued at $150, the loss of the crucial bone, the arrival on the scene of a second wild and dangerous leopard, the incarceration of David, Susan, the inebriate gardener Gogarty, Susan's aunt Elizabeth and her aunt's big-game hunter gentleman friend, Major Applegate, before everything ends happily with the collapse of the brontosaurus skeleton.

THE FILM Howard Hawks, the man who made *Rio Bravo* (1957), which John Carpenter loosely reworked as *Assault on Precinct 13*, was arguably the most versatile director in the

▲ *BRINGING UP BABY* Cary Grant (in glasses), Katharine Hepburn (in the hat), and the crucial intercostal clavicle (in the box).

history of Hollywood, achieving noted successes in every genre he essayed: war, musical, western, gangster, historical, comedy. The second of four films co-starring Grant and Hepburn – *Sylvia Scarlett* (1936), *Holiday* (1938) and *The Philadelphia Story* (1941) – this is one of the best of the screwball comedies. A variation on 'the comedy of remarriage' a sub-genre with which Grant had several successes, this is, like *Holiday*, a comedy of premarriage. Remarkably the film was a box-office flop. This financial underperformance further damaged Hepburn's reputation which had been seriously dented by her topping the Independent Theatre Owners Association list of performers judged 'box-office poison'. It is unaccountable as

'Your golf ball! Your car! Is there anything in the world that doesn't belong to you.'

Hepburn and Grant make an hilarious couple, each playing rather against type. Grant is a stuffy, intellectual nerd, equally repelled by and attracted to Hepburn's Susan, with her harebrained schemes pursued with unshakeable upper-class confidence, throughout the action teetering on the brink of hysteria.

ODD/SALIENT FACTS Everyone involved in the project was petrified at the sight of Nissa, the leopard who played Baby, except Katharine Hepburn who claims to have found her playful. Olga Celeste, the animal's trainer told a reporter: 'If Miss Hepburn should ever decide to leave the screen, she could make a very good animal trainer.'

Peter Bogdanovich, the critic-briefly-turned-boy wonder director chose to remake and update *Bringing Up Baby* as his third feature film *What's Up Doc* (1971) in which the Hepburn and Grant roles were taken by Barbra Streisand and Ryan O'Neill. This was, along with the Coen Brothers' *The Hudsucker Proxy* (1994), the most successful of the modern attempts to recreate the screwball comedy.

Cary Grant was a bisexual icon of the golden age of Hollywood, whose affair with Randolph Scott endured as a friendship until Grant's death in 1986. In 1935 Grant, Hepburn and Howard Hughes all met one another for the first times and so began an odd troilistic relationship in which Grant and Hepburn became friends while both had on-off affairs with Hughes (see *Key lines* below).

MEMORABLE MOMENTS The meeting between Susan and David on the golf course predicts the way their relationship will progress. She is the eccentric, possibly insane predatory woman who falls almost instantly in love with David who is desperately clinging on to his dignity and eager to gain the grant to further his scientific work. The scene ends with Susan getting into David's car by mistake and crashing it in the parking lot (see *Key lines* below).

Grant and Hepburn performing a cross between a 'goose-step' and a pre-war lambada as David walks tightly behind Susan after her evening dress rips off, to conceal her underwear and protect her reputation.

KEY LINES

When David protests about Susan's crashing his car, she cries out: 'Your golf ball! Your car! Is there anything in the world that doesn't belong to you?'

Forced by circumstances and Susan's crazed plotting to wear a woman's flimsy fur-trimmed dressing gown, an extremely agitated David is confronted by a bewildered Aunt Elizabeth. She asks why he is dressed in this way. He responds: 'Because I just went gay all of a sudden.' The word 'gay' is applied here in the sense of giddy, but this possibly marks the first known use of it with its modern meaning.

THE BROOD

CANADA, 1979, LES PRODUCTIONS MUTUELLES/ELGIN INTERNATIONAL, 91 MINS

D DAVID CRONENBERG; **PR** CLAUDE HÉROUX; **SC** DAVID CRONENBERG; **PH** (COL) MARK IRWIN; **M** HOWARD SHORE; **ED** ALLAN COLLINS

CAST OLIVER REED (DR HAL RAGLAN), SAMANTHA EGGAR (NOLA CARVETH), ART HINDLE (FRANK CARVETH), CINDY HINDS (CANDICE CARVETH), HENRY BECKMAN (BARTON KELLY), NUALA FITZGERALD (JULIANA KELLY), SUSAN HOGAN (RUTH MAYER), MICHAEL MAGEE (INSPECTOR MRAZEK), JOSEPH SHAW (DR DESBOROUGH) GARY MCKEEHAN (MIKE TRELLAN)

51

THE STORY Dr Raglan runs the Somafree clinic in which he works on his theory of psychoplasmics, his study of the physical manifestations of mental illness. One of his patients is Nola Carveth who was abused as a child by her mother Juliana and has in turn abused her own daughter, Candice. When Candice returns from a visit to the clinic with a bruised back her father, Nola's estranged husband Frank becomes worried. Juliana, while looking after Candice, is attacked and killed in her kitchen by a bizarre-looking dwarf. Juliana's estranged husband Barton comes to town and is himself killed by one of these dwarfs. Candice's teacher, on whom Frank is keen, is killed by two of the dwarfs who abduct Candice. At Somafree Frank learns from

▼ **THE BROOD** *Candice Carveth (Cindy Hinds) is menaced by the brood – mutant dwarfs born of her mother's rage.*

respectively by a whining bottomless waitress, her buttocks on a table dominating the left half of the screen, and a row between a foul-mouthed hooker and a client. One of the great gambling movies, the film is a meditation on the psychology of winning, losing, and playing games. Apart from being very funny, it comments laconically on the casual acceptance of violence in everyday American life and shows its painful aftermath.

ODD/SALIENT FACTS Jeff Goldblum (who made his screen debut as an uncredited mugger in Michael Winner's *Death Wish* (1974), got his first movie credit delivering a single line as George Segal's boss. *California Split* is dedicated 'For Barbara 1933–1973'. She's Barbara Ruick, the bubbly 1950s actress (she was Carrie in the 1956 film of *Carousel*), who died before the film was released.

MEMORABLE MOMENTS Bill staggering out of the poker casino on his knees after one terrible punch.

Bill and Charlie's first bet – naming the Seven Dwarfs.

Charlie amusing Bill with his one-armed piccolo-player routine.

Charlie with a mugger's gun at his head only agreeing to give him half of the $1460 he and Bill have won that day.

Charlie sticking toilet paper up his bleeding nostrils as he straddles Lew's recumbent body retrieving cash from his wallet.

Charlie going round the Reno poker table characterizing the players for Bill based on their appearance and body language – and winning the approval of the barmaid in a white stetson.

KEY LINES

Promotional film behind credits: 'Acquiring the skills for a game like poker is a social asset … Sit erect, maintain a quiet bearing, avoid nervous habits. During the game avoid conversation on matters not related to poker.'

Charlie: 'I feel like a winner, but I know I look like a loser.'

Bill: 'You get out of here. You're gonna kill the streak.'

Charlie: 'Do you always take a big win this hard?'
Bill: 'Charlie there was no special feeling.'

Bill: 'I have to go home.'
Charlie: 'Where do you think that is?'

CARRY ON CLEO

UK, 1965, ANGLO AMALGAMATED/INSIGNIA, 92 MINS
D GERALD THOMAS; **PR** PETER ROGERS; **SC** TALBOT ROTHWELL, FROM AN ORIGINAL IDEA BY WILLIAM SHAKESPEARE; **PH** (COL) ALAN HUME; **M** ERIC ROGERS; **ED** ARCHIE LUDSKI
CAST KENNETH WILLIAMS (JULIUS CAESAR), SID JAMES (MARK ANTHONY), KENNETH CONNOR (HENGIST POD), CHARLES HAWTREY (SENECA), JOAN SIMS (CALPURNIA), JIM DALE (HORSA), AMANDA BARRIE (CLEOPATRA), JULIE STEPHENS (GLORIA), SHEILA HANCOCK (SENNA POD), VICTOR MADDERN (SERGEANT MAJOR), JON PERTWEE (SOOTHSAYER), FRANCIS DE WOLFF (AGRIPPA), MICHAEL WARD (ARCHIMEDES), BRIAN OULTON (BRUTUS), TOM CLEGG (SOSAGES), TANYA BINNING (VIRGINIA), DAVID DAVENPORT (BILIUS), PETER GILMORE (GALLEY MASTER), WARREN MITCHELL (SPENCIUS), GERTAN KLAUBER (MARCUS), WANDA VENTHAM (PRETTY BIDDER), E. V. H. EMMETT (NARRATOR)

THE STORY Hengist Pod, the British inventor of the square wheel, and his neighbour Horsa are captured by the invading Roman army. Sold into slavery, the two escape by disguising themselves as Vestal Virgins and, with Hengist unconscious, Horsa foils a plot to assassinate Julius Caesar. Horsa flees and Hengist takes the credit, and a post as Caesar's bodyguard. Anthony travels to Egypt where he falls in love with Cleopatra and the two conspire against Caesar. Anthony returns to Rome and extends Cleopatra's invitation to visit her in Egypt. On the boat journey a second assassination attempt is foiled by Horsa, now an escaped galley slave, and again Hengist takes the credit. In Egypt Hengist and Horsa save Caesar's life one more time, but Caesar is finally killed in the senate. Hengist and Horsa return to Britain and Anthony and Cleopatra end up in a bath of ass's milk together.

THE FILM For over a quarter of a century, the *Carry On* films appeared at the rate of at least one a year and brought the humour of Donald McGill cartoons to celluloid life. It is a world where men are effete or lecherous, women either fat battleaxes or scrubbers. The productions were notorious for their cheapness, but *Carry On Cleo* is the one film that can be called relatively sumptuous because of its access to the Pinewood sets used for the lavish flop *Cleopatra* (1963). The film opens in characteristic *Carry On* form with credits rolling over simple Egyptian style cartoons including a phallic Cleopatra's Needle and two very breastlike pyramids, before the opening caption: 'Whilst the characters and events in this story are based on actual characters and events, certain liberties have been taken with Cleopatra.' The punch line is emphasized with a 'whooop' whistling sound effect lest the joke be missed. One of the series' better scripts with references to Churchill and Macmillan is of course stuffed with childish humour and the essential *doubles entendres*. Kenneth Williams was outspoken in his contempt for the intellectual depths of the films but nevertheless agreed to speak his first line, while suffering from a British cold: 'Ooh, I do feel queer.' Again it is hard to

▼ *CARRY ON CLEO* Sid James (Mark Antony) seems disappointed when at last he gets a glimpse of Cleopatra's famous asp.

see beyond the *single entendre* of the exchange between Williams (Caesar) and Hawtrey (Seneca): 'Beware the Ides of March.' Caesar: 'Oh, shut up, you silly old faggot.' The screenplay is a pretty basic mix of schoolboy jokes on Latin and history (an exhausted Sid James emerging from Cleopatra's bedchamber, sighing: 'Puer, o puer, o puer!') together with the more risqué material of sexual jokes (Caesar, about to meet Cleopatra: 'Tony, I am undone. My end is in sight.' Anthony: 'Well, you better do yourself up again quick. You can't meet her like that.') and lavatorial character names (Senna Pod). In spite or because of this parochial, typically English humour that marks the series, like that of the other icon of bawdy English humour, Benny Hill, the films have gained a cult status on American TV.

55

ODD/SALIENT FACTS Beneath the surface misanthropy of the series lay undercurrents of gloom, depression and misery. Williams and James disliked one another. James, a boozer and womanizer, would die on stage in 1976. Hawtrey was a depressive alcoholic who drank himself to death, but was at least relatively comfortable with his homosexuality. Williams was a deeply confused man, never at ease in his own skin, wanting to be recognized as an erudite man, a classical actor famous for and trapped by his awkward persona that was tailor-made for the *Carry On* films. He was himself obsessed with lavatorial humour and one of his japes was what he called 'the vag trick' in which he would flash people with his genitals tucked between his closed legs. His favourite joke on the set of *Carry On Cleo* was just a touch more conventional in that he liked to lift up his toga and expose himself to the cast and crew. The film's narration was recorded by E. V. H. Emmett, whose voice was instantly familiar to the film's original audience as that of Gaumont-British and Universal news.

MEMORABLE MOMENTS Horsa and Hengist flee the slave market and seek refuge in the Palace of Vesta where only Vestal Virgins and eunuchs are allowed to enter. Seeing no option but to enter, Hengist says: 'Oh yeah, what have we got to lose?'

KEY LINES

The most famous line from all the Carry Ons *comes when Caesar's life is threatened by Bilius and the other guards. He also seeks refuge in the Palace of Vesta, where he exclaims:* 'Infamy! Infamy! They've all got it in for me.'

CASABLANCA

USA, 1943, Warner Brothers, 102 mins

D MICHAEL CURTIZ; **PR** HAL B. WALLIS; **SC** JULIUS J. EPSTEIN, PHILIP G. EPSTEIN, HOWARD KOCH (BASED ON THE UNPERFORMED PLAY EVERYONE COMES TO RICK'S BY MURRAY BURNETT AND JOAN ALLISON); **PH** ARTHUR EDESON; **M** MAX STEINER; **ED** OWEN MARKS

CAST HUMPHREY BOGART (RICK), INGRID BERGMAN (ILSA), PAUL HENREID (VICTOR LASZLO), CLAUDE RAINS (CAPTAIN LOUIS RENAULT), CONRAD VEIDT (MAJOR STRASSER), SYDNEY GREENSTREET (SEÑOR FERRARI), PETER LORRE (UGARTE), S. Z. SAKALL (CARL), MADELEINE LEBEAU (YVONNE), DOOLEY WILSON (SAM), MARCEL DALIO(CROUPIER), CURT BOIS (PICKPOCKET), HELMUT DANTINE (JAN BRANDEL)

THE STORY In 1941, after the German occupation of France and before the United States have entered the Second World War, Rick, an American adventurer, is running a nightclub in Casablanca, where European refugees get exit visas to take them via Lisbon to America. Rick has run guns in Abyssinia and fought in the Spanish Civil War, but professes neutrality when the German Major Strasser comes seeking the killer of two German couriers bearing letters of transit. Working with Strasser is Captain Renault, the cynical French prefect of police who represents Pétain's Vichy government. In fact Rick got the letters from the thief Ugarte before police shot him. Into this nest of intrigue comes charismatic resistance leader, Victor Laszlo, and his Norwegian wife Ilsa, who need exit visas for the States. Rick and Ilsa had an affair in Paris when she believed Victor had been killed by the Nazis. Discovering Victor was alive, she abandoned Rick, and black pianist Sam, without any explanation. Rick and Ilsa are still in love, and Ilsa is prepared to do anything to get Victor a permit. So Rick takes charge, ditches Ilsa gently for the greater cause and gets the Laszlos on the plane to Lisbon so that Victor can get to America and continue his resistance activities. Strasser tries to stop the plane, so Rick kills him. Renault and Rick walk off to join the Free French army in West Africa.

THE FILM Popular from the start, never out of distribution, *Casablanca* helped create the idea of the cult movie. Of all propaganda films made during the Second World War, this is the one that captures what the war was about – a conflict between democracy and totalitarianism – and expresses it through attractive characters whose style embodies their politics and morality. Rick and Ilsa sacrifice themselves to the general good, putting duty before love, which results in the immediate death of the rigid Nazi Strasser and the pricking of Renault's conscience. In a fascinating sexual transference, Ilsa and the cool, smug Victor Laszlo heading off across the Atlantic are replaced on screen, and in the audience's hearts, by the jocu-

> **'Of all the gin joints in all the towns in all the world, she walks into mine.'**

▲ *CASABLANCA In one of the world's great gin joints, Rick, Louis, Victor and Ilsa prepare to ascend a hill of beans.*

lar, homo-erotic buddy relationship between Rick and Louis.

Casablanca turned Bogart into a major romantic star and confirmed the status of Ingrid Bergman. It was the perfect expression of the cosmopolitan, polyglot culture of Hollywood in its heyday with an expatriate cast drawn from all over Europe, no fake accents and great actors like Marcel Dalio, Peter Lorre and Curt Bois in walk-on roles. For the first time a black actor, Dooley Wilson, played the hero's sidekick without any explicit reference to the colour of his skin. The movie is an object lesson in perfection arising from confusion with endless discussion over the casting, the script being constantly rewritten and the actors not knowing how the film would end. The screenwriters made different contributions – the wit and irony came from the Epstein brothers, the radical politics from Howard Koch, and the sophisticated romance from the uncredited Casey Robinson.

ODD/SALIENT FACTS The release of the movie coincided with Operation Torch, the January 1943 allied invasion of Morocco and Tunisia and the secret meeting at Casablanca between Franklin Roosevelt and Winston Churchill. Producer Hal Wallis wrote and directed the final scene between Bogart and Rains, and when, on Oscar night in 1943, he began his stately walk to pick up the Award for Best Picture, the head of the studio, Jack Warner, darted ahead of him and grabbed the statuette. A few months later Wallis left Warner to set up his own unit at Paramount.

MEMORABLE MOMENTS Ilsa's entry into Rick's Café Américain.

Rick nodding to the band leader, permitting him to play 'La Marseillaise' (a homage to Jean Renoir's *La Grande Illusion*).

Ilsa asking Sam to play 'As Time Goes By'.

Rick's speech of abnegation at the airport.

Rick and Louis striding down the tarmac en route to political commitment.

57

KEY LINES

Rick: 'You'll excuse me gentlemen, your business is politics, mine is running a saloon.'

Rick: 'Of all the gin joints in all the towns in all the world, she walks into mine.'

Rick: 'Here's looking at you kid.'

Ilsa: 'Play it Sam, play "As Time Goes By".'

Rick: 'We'll always have Paris.'

Rick: 'The Germans wore grey, you wore blue.'

Rick: 'Ilsa, I'm no good at being noble but it doesn't take much to see that the problems of three little people don't amount to a hill of beans in this crazy world. Someday you'll understand that.'

Louis: 'Round up the usual suspects.'

Rick: 'Louis, I think this is the beginning of a beautiful friendship.'

As someone once said of *Hamlet*, it's just full of quotations.

▼ *UN CHIEN ANDALOU* The squirm-in-your-seat eye-opening, razor-edged shot that launched one of the most controversial films ever made.

UN CHIEN ANDALOU ('THE ANDALUSIAN DOG')

FRANCE, 1929, 17 MINS

D *LUIS BUÑUEL;* **PR** *LUIS BUÑUEL;* **SC** *LUIS BUÑUEL, SALVADOR DALÍ;* **PH** *(BW) ALBERT DUVERGER;* **ED** *LUIS BUÑUEL*
CAST *SIMONE MAREUIL (THE YOUNG WOMAN), PIERRE BATCHEFF (THE YOUNG MAN), JAIME MITRATVILLES, SALVADOR DALÍ, LUIS BUÑUEL*

AND

L'AGE D'OR ('THE GOLDEN AGE')

FRANCE, 1930, 63 MINS

D *LUIS BUÑUEL;* **PR** *LE VICOMTE DE NOAILLES;* **SC** *LUIS BUÑUEL, SALVADOR DALÍ;* **PH** *(BW) ALBERT DUVERGER;* **ED** *LUIS BUÑUEL;* **M** *SELECTIONS BY BUÑUEL FROM MENDELSSOHN, MOZART, BEETHOVEN, DEBUSSY, WAGNER, GEORGE VAN PARYS*
CAST *GASTON MODOT (THE MAN), LYA LYS (THE WOMAN), GERMAINE NOIZET (THE WOMAN'S MOTHER, THE MARQUESS OF X), BONAVENTURA IBAÑEZ (THE WOMAN'S FATHER, THE MARQUIS OF X), LIONEL SALEM (THE DUC DE BLANGIS), MAX ERNST (THE BANDIT LEADER)*

THE STORIES Although they have narratives these films can be described shot by shot, but are beyond summary or synopsis. In the silent *Un Chien Andalou* a woman sees a man on a bicycle wearing a Dutch maid's headdress fall from his bike and apparently die. The man subsequently appears in her apartment and attempts to make love to her, before he is attacked by, and kills, his doppelgänger. The woman runs out and appears on a rocky beach to greet another man. There are no dialogue titles and in the brief final scenes, announced as 'In the Spring', the woman and the man from the beach are buried up to their waists, apparently blind and deaf.

After its prologue, a lecture on scorpions, *L'Age d'Or* shows some bandits on a seashore, apparently standing up against an invasion force of civic dignitaries, officers and church leaders. A young man and a beautiful woman make love in the mud and are separated by guards. He is appointed representative of the Assembly of Goodwill and is reunited with his lover at a party given by her aristocrat parents at their mansion outside Rome. There's a row with the Marquess, the Man and Woman make love in the garden, and the Man gets a phone call from the President of the Assembly of Goodwill, who commits suicide after accusing the Man of causing riots and massacres. The Man throws a burning tree, a bishop, plough and wooden giraffe through the window. The film ends with an allusion to the Marquis de Sade's *20 Days in Sodom*, with the Duke of Blangis, dressed as the biblical Christ, accompanied by three debauched aristocrats, and a wooden cross embellished by hanks of hair blowing in the breeze.

THE FILMS These movies belong together as the most abiding achievement of the cinematic avant-garde of the late 1920s, as collaborations between Buñuel and Dalí, and as the debut of one of the greatest of cult directors. The films were the first to be accepted by the leaders of the Surrealism movement as truly surreal and they have lost none of their power to shock, mystify, infuriate and offend. They are intended to be waking dreams that dip into the subconscious, and are not intended to make rational sense. Critics and historians invariably arrive at differing interpretations of individual scenes. In the opening sequence of *Un Chien Andalou*, one of the most disturbing in the cinema, a man (Buñuel himself) slices a woman's eye in half with a cut-throat razor. Buñuel himself said: To produce in the spectator a state which could permit the free association of ideas, it was necessary to produce a near-traumatic shock at the very beginning of the film; hence we began it with a shot of an eye being very efficiently cut open. The spectator enters into the cathartic state necessary to accept the subsequent events of the film.

ODD/SALIENT FACTS The small budget for *Un Chien Andalou* was provided by Buñuel's Spanish mother; the more expensive *L'Age d'Or* was financed by the French aristocrat Le Vicomte de Noailles and his wife. Right-wing groups wrecked the Paris cinema where *L'Age d'Or* was showing, and the police intervened preventing further screenings. Both films were subject to bans in most countries and were only seen at clubs or privately. When Dalí was reconciled to General Franco and the Catholic church in the 1940s, he dissociated himself from *L'Age d'Or*, claiming Buñuel had betrayed his ideas. The eye cut in the opening of *Un Chien Andalou* is that of a dead donkey. The film's title comes from Buñuel's first collection of poems and was his nickname for a group of aesthetic Spanish poets he disliked.

MEMORABLE MOMENTS Almost every scene, but especially: In *Un Chien Andalou*: the sliced eye; the hands coming through holes in the door holding a cocktail shaker; the books turning into pistols.

In *L'Age d'Or*: the civic dignatories raising their hats to the skeletons dressed in bishops' clothes; a maid emerging in flames from the kitchen and being ignored by the Count and Countess's guest; the Woman sucking the toe of the statue; the body of the suicide lying on the ceiling after he's shot himself.

A CLOCKWORK ORANGE ★
UK, 1971, WARNER BROS, 136 MINS

D STANLEY KUBRICK; **PR** STANLEY KUBRICK; **SC** STANLEY KUBRICK, BASED ON THE NOVEL BY ANTHONY BURGESS; **PH** (COL) JOHN ALCOTT; **M** WALTER CARLOS PLUS VARIOUS; **ED** BILL BUTLER
CAST MALCOLM MCDOWELL (ALEX), PATRICK MAGEE (MR ALEXANDER), MICHAEL BATES (CHIEF GUARD), WARREN CLARKE (DIM), JOHN CLIVE (STAGE ACTOR), ADRIENNE CORRI (MRS ALEXANDER), CARL DUERING (DR BRODSKY), PAUL FARRELL (TRAMP), CLIVE FRANCIS (LODGER), MICHAEL GOVER (PRISON GOVERNOR), MIRIAM KARLIN (CATLADY), JAMES MARCUS (GEORGIE), AUBREY MORRIS (DELTOID), GODFREY QUIGLEY (PRISON CHAPLAIN), SHEILA RAYNOR (MUM), MADGE RYAN (DR BRANOM), JOHN SAVIDENT (CONSPIRATOR), ANTHONY SHARP (MINISTER), PHILIP STONE (DAD), PAULINE TAYLOR (PSYCHIATRIST), MARGARET TYZACK (CONSPIRATOR), STEVEN BERKOFF (TOM), DAVID PROWSE (JULIAN)

THE STORY Alex and his droogs relish their violent sprees of raping and fighting. After a violent assault on a Catlady, Alex is betrayed by his droogs and arrested. In prison, he is selected for revolutionary, fast-acting corrective treatment. Over two weeks of aversion therapy, he is drugged to induce extreme sensations of nausea and is forced to watch scenes of violence in films, while listening to his beloved Beethoven. On release he is rejected by his parents, beaten up by a tramp he previously attacked, and then picked up by Dim and George, his droogs, now policemen, who beat him up. He arrives by chance at the home of Mr Alexander, whose wife died after the rape committed by Alex and his gang. When Alexander recognizes him, he and his friends, opponents of the government who sanctioned Alex's treatment, drug him, lock him in a garret room and pump Beethoven's music through the floor. Driven to despair Alex jumps out of the window. Recovering in hospital, he is treated to counter the effects of the aversion therapy, reconciled with his parents and set up with a soft job by the panicking government, while Alexander is condemned and imprisoned.

Demi Moore). *The Company of Wolves* is one of the great second films (to rank beside *The Magnificent Ambersons*, *Jaws* and *The Driver*). It has an uncompromising boldness in its approach to screen fantasy and has come as near as the screen ever did to capturing the violence, surrealism and moral force of Hans Christian Andersen and the Brothers Grimm. This is an English *Wizard of Oz* without the songs, the projection of a pubescent girl's anxieties about her sexuality and impending womanhood, and the sexual conduct of her parents, into the form of a dream. The film constructs and deconstructs traditional fairy stories, particularly 'Little Red Riding Hood', showing how such tales embody both truths and old wives' tales, and act as conduits of knowledge and counsel, and sources of experience. As the film progresses, Rosaleen grows and matures from a child who secretly wishes to kill her older sister to someone with an understanding of love and desire, who in her subconscious has come to recognize the beast in man, and that the handsome huntsman and the predatory wolf are the same person.

In addition to a fine cast, Jordan is especially endebted to two key collaborators. One is the novelist Angela Carter, a feminist with a leaning towards magic realism. The other is the production designer, Anton Furst, who conjured up the fairy-tale world of menace and wonder. He went on to work with Kubrick on *Full Metal Jacket* and with Tim Burton on *Batman*, for which he won an Oscar. Carter died of cancer in 1992 at the age of 52; Furst committed suicide in 1991 at the age of 47.

Odd/salient facts This was the second of Stephen Rea's six appearances in Jordan films.

Memorable moments/iconic scenes
The wolves surrounding the heroine's sister in the forest.

The Travelling Man coming back to his wife, turning into a wolf and being decapitated by her second husband.

Rosaleen climbing a tree to find a bird's nest with eggs that open to reveal small ceramic dolls.

Key lines
Granny: 'Never stray from the path, never eat a windfall apple, and never trust a man whose eyebrows meet.'

Granny: 'The worst kind of wolf is hairy on the inside.'

Rosaleen: 'I'm sorry, I never knew a wolf could cry. I'll tell you a story of a wounded wolf.'

THE COOK, THE THIEF, HIS WIFE, HER LOVER
UK/FRANCE, 1989, PALACE/ALLARTS COOK/ERATO FILMS, 124 MINS

D PETER GREENAWAY; **PR** KEES KASANDER; **SC** PETER GREENAWAY; **PH** (COL) SACHA VIERNY; **PR DES** BEN VAN OS, JAN ROELFS; **COST** JEAN PAUL GAULTIER; **M** MICHAEL NYMAN; **ED** JOHN WILSON

CAST RICHARD BOHRINGER (RICHARD), MICHAEL GAMBON (ALBERT), HELEN MIRREN (GEORGINA), ALAN HOWARD (MICHAEL), TIM ROTH (MITCHELL), LIZ SMITH (GRACE), CIARAN HINDS (CORY), GARY OLSEN (SPANGLER), EWAN STEWART (HARRIS), ROGER ASHTON GRIFFITH (TURPIN), RON COOK (MEWS), EMER GILLESPIE (PATRICIA), JANET HENFREY (ALICE), ANNIE BREEVELEY (EDEN), TONY ALLEFF (TROY), PAUL RUSSELL (PUP), ALEX KINGSTON (ADELE), IAN SEARS (PHILIPPE), WILLIE ROSS (ROY), IAN DURY (FITCH), DIANE LANGTON (MAY FITCH), PRUDENCE OLIVER (CORETTE FITCH), ROGER LLOYD PACK (GEOFF), BOB GOODIE (STARKIE), PETER RUSH (MELTER)

The story Within the restaurant he owns, over several days, Albert holds court around the table with his wife Georgina, various cronies and rival gangsters, discussing food and sex. Georgina starts an affair with Michael, a regular of the restaurant. Albert finds out about the affair and goes berserk. Helped to escape by Richard, the cook, Michael and Georgina spend a brief idyll out in a book depository. Albert and his gang discover the hiding place and kill Michael, by force-feeding him with a book. Georgina begs Richard to cook Michael and serve him up to Albert. So, a procession of people who have been injured and humiliated by Albert brings in the cooked body of Michael. Georgina forces Albert at gunpoint to eat. He takes a mouthful, then she shoots him dead.

The film This film is a distillation of all Greenaway's obsessions and all the recurrent themes in his work, chiefly art, decay and death. Albert is a violent philistine, unable to pronounce the names of the dishes served in his own restaurant. Treating the place like his personal salon, he beats, bullies and humiliates all around him, and expounds crudely on a variety of subjects. A deeply vulgar man, he is also the alter ego of the director, as he shares his thoughts on the vital connections between sex, food and excrement. The film is a mournful look at the fleeting nature of romantic love. Greenaway is obsessed with structure in his work. Here the story unfolds as a number of menus, over nine evenings from a Thursday to the following Friday. Perhaps Greenaway's central concern is his presentation of man as aspiring to order, beauty and understanding through the constructs of art, books, costume and architecture, while being frustrated and disgusted by the constraints and ugliness of the body and its functions. Tim Roth has spoken of how the only direction he received on the film was to move fractionally to one side or the other to enhance the symmetrical composition of the shot. This essay on food and sex, decay and death and art takes place on dazzling sound-stages. The gangsters are dressed in clothes designed by Jean Paul Gaultier in an echo of Frans Hals's painting of Dutch burghers, an enlarged

▼ *THE COOK, THE THIEF, HIS WIFE, HER LOVER (Foreground l-r) The lover (Alan Howard), the cook (Richard Bohringer), the wife (Helen Mirren), the thief (Michael Gambon) and his henchman (Tim Roth).*

reproduction of which hangs on the wall of the restaurant. It presents the notion that merely to patronize, and consume great art does not rid one of crassness and vulgarity. The arenas in which the action takes place are colour-coded: dark exteriors, green kitchen and storage area, red restaurant and white lavatories. In the impressive, fake pans between these rooms, Georgina's costumes change colour to fit the surroundings.

ODD/SALIENT FACTS The four central characters are named after the actors that Greenaway originally had in mind to play them: Albert Finney; Georgina Hale; he had initially wanted Michael Gambon to play the sensitive bibliophile; Richard Bohringer was Greenaway's first choice for the cook. Sacha Vierny, Greenaway's regular cinematographer since *A Zed and Two Noughts* (1985), has worked with Chris Marker and Alan Resnais, notably on *Last Year at Marienbad* (1961), Greenaway's favourite film.

MEMORABLE MOMENTS The final sequence. It is Friday, and Georgina heads a procession bringing the veiled, cooked body of Michael into the restaurant. When the glazed, steaming cadaver on a bed of vegetables is revealed, Albert is stunned. At gunpoint, he takes a forkful and vomits. Georgina encourages him, he eats. She says: 'Bon appetit. It's French.' She shoots him and concludes, 'Cannibal.' The curtains close.

KEY LINES

Albert: 'What you've gotta realize is that a clever cook puts unlikely things together, like duck and orange, like pineapple and ham. It's called artistry. You know, I'm an artist in the way I combine my business and my pleasure. Money's my business, eating's my pleasure, and Georgie's my pleasure too. Though in a more private kind of way than stuffing the face and feeding the sewers. Though the pleasures are related, because the naughty bits and the dirty bits are so close together that it just goes to show how eating and sex are related.'

Georgina: 'If you don't read does that make you safe?'
Michael: 'Only from bad books.'

Albert: 'How do I care what he ate? It all comes out as shit in the end.'

Richard: 'Eating black food is like eating death.'

▬

CUL-DE-SAC

UK, 1966, COMPTON-TEKLI, 111 MINS

D ROMAN POLANSKI; **PR** GENE GUTOWSKI; **SC** POLANSKI AND GÉRARD BRACH; **PH** (BW) GILBERT TAYLOR; **M** KRZYSZTOF KOMEDA; **ED** ALASTAIR MCINTYRE

CAST DONALD PLEASENCE (GEORGE), FRANÇOISE DORLÉAC (TERESA), LIONEL STANDER (RICHARD), JACK MACGOWRAN (ALBERT), WILLIAM FRANKLYN (CECIL YORK), ROBERT DORNING (PHILIP FAIRWEATHER), MARIE KEANE (MARION FAIRWEATHER), IAIN QUARRIER (CHRISTOPHER), GEOFFREY SUMNER (CHRISTOPHER'S FATHER), RENEE HOUSTON (CHRISTOPHER'S MOTHER), JACQUELINE BISSET (JACKIE), TREVOR DELANEY (HORACE)

> ' How do I care what he ate? It all comes out as shit in the end.'

THE STORY Two wounded, fugitive criminals are stranded on the causeway leading to a small island off the Northumberland Coast when their stolen car runs out of petrol. Richard, a boorish American, leaves his dying Irish comrade, Albert, in the car, and goes to the island's eleventh-century castle to call his boss, Mr Katelbach, for assistance, and takes prisoner its only occupants – the middle-aged retired businessman, George, made-up and dressed in a nightie by Teresa, his young wife. Richard has them push the stalled car up the flooded causeway to the house. When Albert dies they are made to dig a grave. George's oldest friend Philip drops in, meeting Teresa for the first time. He's accompanied by his wife and Horace, their obnoxious little boy, and a local couple, Cecil and his trendy girlfriend. Teresa pretends that Richard is a servant and gets him to serve lunch, and she flirts with Cecil. To drive away the guests George insults them and they leave after Horace has used Cecil's shotgun to smash a medieval stained-glass window in the room where Scott is said to have written Rob Roy. Teresa plays a vicious practical joke on the sleeping Richard inserting a lighted match between his toes and when he hits her she tells George he tried to kiss her. Giving George Cecil's gun, she provokes him into shooting Richard, who as he dies fires a Tommy gun, setting George's white Jaguar alight. Cecil returns to retrieve his shot-gun, Teresa drives off with him, and the bereft George sits on a rock in the sea, shouting the name of Agnes, his first wife.

THE FILM *Cul-de-Sac* was Polanski's third feature film, and like the Polish psychological drama, *Knife in the Water* (1962), and the British psychiatric horror story, *Repulsion* (1965), the characters play deadly games with a cruelty ranging from the mischievous to the calculatedly sadistic. As black comedy, or comedy of menace, the film has affinities with Beckett, Albee and Pinter; Richard and Albert descend on the disturbed, fugitive George like Goldberg and McCann pursuing Stanley in *The Birthday Party*. Pleasence, before he became a cult movie actor, was a celebrated stage exponent of Pinter, while MacGowran was one of Samuel Beckett's favourite actors. *Cul-de-sac* is a wonderfully perverse picture – it is Richard's persecution and humiliation of his reluctant host that releases George from his inhibitions, enabling him to insult his so-called friends, and killing Richard empowers him to triumph over his

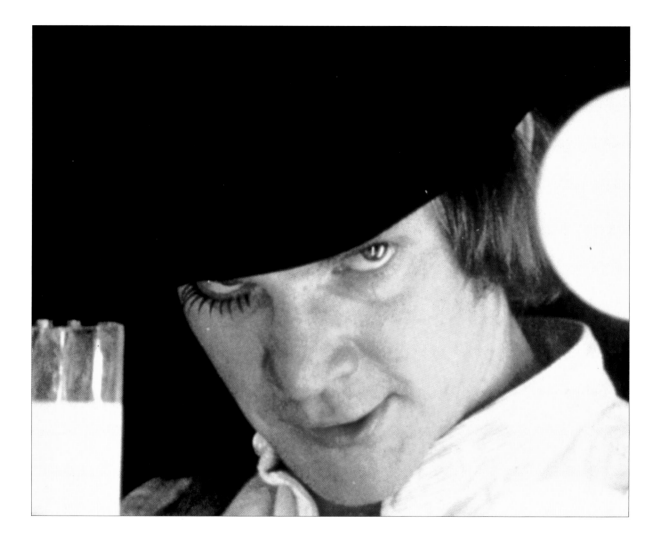

A CLOCKWORK ORANGE

*Alex (Malcolm McDowell) in the Korova Milkbar, viddies the
audience and enjoys a quick glass of milk plus vellocet in
preparation for setting out with his droogs for a bit of the old
ultra-violence.*

BIG WEDNESDAY

ABOVE: Tubular beaux Leroy (Gary Busey), Jack (William Katt) and Matt (Jan Michael-Vincent) head off to face the awe-inspiring wave of the title.

APOCALYPSE NOW

LEFT: Willard's predecessor Colby (Scott Glenn) and his band have gone native and stand in front of a plinth bearing their motto and the film's title.

THE BLUES BROTHERS

*Joliet Jake (John Belushi) and Elwood (Dan Aykroyd) are on a
mission from God to re-form their band, save an orphanage
and restore the reputation of black American music.*

GET CARTER

LEFT: London gangster Jack Carter (Michael Caine) brings hot coals to Newcastle when he returns to avenge his brother's death at the hands of local thugs.

EASY RIDER

BELOW: Billy (Dennis Hopper), Wyatt (Peter Fonda) and alcoholic lawyer George Hanson (Jack Nicholson) are yet to discover that they blew it.

MONTY PYTHON'S LIFE OF BRIAN

A lisping Pontius Pilate (Michael Palin) introduces Biggus Dickus (Graham Chapman) to the Jerusalem mob as 'the highest wanking Woman'.

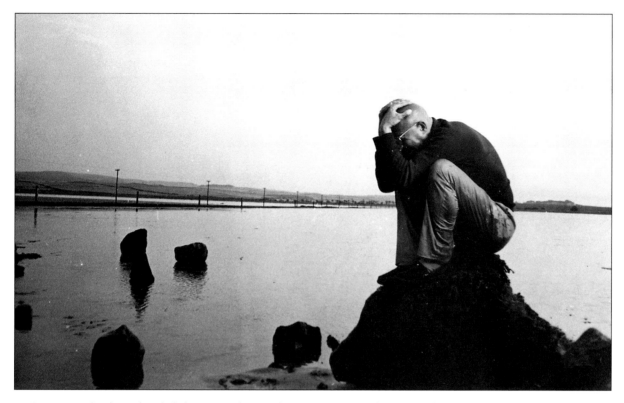

▲ *CUL-DE-SAC* *The shaven-headed Pleasence, alone and at the end of his tether, as day breaks on his remote Northumberland retreat.*

treacherous wife. The film has its roots in both Polanski's, and his co-author Gérard Brach's, wishing to exact dramatic revenge on the women who had recently deserted them when they wrote the first draft in 1963.

ODD/SALIENT FACTS Polanski and Brach wrote the exploitation horror flick *Repulsion* in 17 days, hoping that if it succeeded, the producers, Compton-Tekli, would finance *Cul-de-sac*, which they'd been trying to set up in France for two years. *Repulsion* won the Silver Bear in Berlin and was a big box-office success; *Cul-de-Sac* won the Golden Bear the following year but was liked by only a small number of critics and puzzled most audiences. For *Repulsion*, Polanski, Brach and the producer, Gene Gutowski, split $5,000. The superbly atmospheric monochrome photography is by the British cinematographer Gilbert Taylor, who had just lit

'Here we are, in the shit.'

Dr Strangelove, *A Hard Day's Night* and *Repulsion*, and went on to light Hitchcock's *Frenzy* and *Star Wars*. Originally intended to be made in Britanny (as *If Katelbach Comes*), the picture was shot entirely on location at Holy Island (aka Lindisfarne) three miles off the Northumbrian coast. Two hundred actresses were tested for the role of Teresa before Catherine Deneuve, the star of *Repulsion*, recommended her sister, Françoise Dorléac, for the part. Dorléac was killed the following year in a car crash. The gravel-voiced Lionel Stander, an established Hollywood character actor, was blacklisted after appearing before the House Un-American Activities Committee in the early 1950s and didn't work again in Hollywood for nearly twenty years.

MEMORABLE MOMENTS Françoise Dorléac first seen frolicking half-naked in the sand dunes with the teenage son of her husband's friends.

The dying Albert looking through his pebble-spectacles at the sea water rising around his car.

The virtuoso eight-minute take on the beach as Richard and

George talk, Teresa goes down to bathe and returns, a plane flies over and Richard fires off his gun.

KEY LINES

Albert: 'Here we are, in the shit.'

Richard: 'You've got to be out of your skull to live in a place like this.'

George, to his guests: 'Take your bloody filthy insinuations and get out of my fortress.'

CUTTER'S WAY

US, 1981, UNITED ARTISTS/GURIAN ENTERTAINMENT, 109 MINS
D IVAN PASSER; **PR** PAUL R. GURIAN; **SC** JEFFREY ALAN FISKIN
(FROM THE NOVEL CUTTER AND BONE BY NEWTON THORNBURG);
PH (TECHNICOLOR) JORDAN CRONENWETH; **M** JACK NITZSCHE;
ED CAROLINE FERRIOL
CAST JEFF BRIDGES (RICHARD BONE), JOHN HEARD (ALEX CUTTER),
LISA EICHHORN (MAUREEN 'MO' CUTTER), ANN DUSENBERRY
(VALERIE DURAN), STEPHEN ELLIOTT (J. J. CORD), PATRICIA
DONAHUE (MRS CORD), ARTHUR ROSENBERG (GEORGE
SWANSON), NINA VAN PALLANDT (WOMAN IN HOTEL), JON
TERRY (POLICE CAPTAIN)

THE STORY Upper-class beach bum, boat salesman and part-time gigolo Richard Bone is sitting in his car in a deserted side street in Santa Barbara, when the driver of a limousine deposits something in a trash can and speeds off. Next morning garbage collectors discover the mutilated body of a seventeen-year-old girl. Bone cannot identify the man in the alleyway and is arrested as a suspect. The following day he's at the Fiesta parade with his friend Alex Cutter, a one-eyed, one-legged, one-armed Vietnam veteran, and Cutter's alcoholic wife, Mo. As a middle-aged man rides by on a white stallion, Bone recognizes him as the man by the trash can. This man is J. J. Cord, an oil tycoon and member of a prominent family. The embittered, aggressive, hard-drinking Cutter becomes obsessed with building up a case against Cord. It gives a purpose to his life, and he draws the victim's sister Valerie into his scheme, as well as a reluctant Bone, though his wife Mo opposes it. Bone goes to bed with the vulnerable, rejected Mo, but then slips away and spends the rest of the night on a boat. Next morning the Cutters' house is found burnt down with Mo inside. Cutter believes it was Cord's doing and that the intended victim was Bone, and he persuades Bone to join him in gatecrashing a party at Cord's mansion. Security men drag Bone into Cord's study, Cutter mounts a white stallion in the stables, and is fatally wounded by guards as he rides towards the house. Crashing through the window he says 'It was him,' and dies. 'It was you,' Bone says. 'What if it were?' says Cord, as he puts his dark glasses on. Raising the gun, still clutched in Cutter's hand, Bone fires at Cord as the screen fades to black.

THE FILM *Cutter's Way* is one of the most powerful works from a cycle of post-Vietnam pictures where the moral poison of the war is seen working itself into the body politic through the failure of America to assimilate returning veterans. The film is also a fine example of the paranoid political thriller of a kind made by Frankenheimer and Pakula. The cinematographer Jordan Cornenweth gives the picture a sickly hue; the characters seem afflicted by some malaise; little is explained about their backgrounds; the plot remains unresolved.

Ivan Passer made his name in the 1960s with the Czech New Wave, writing screenplays for Milos Forman and like Forman he went into American exile after the Russian invasion

▼ *CUTTER'S WAY* Crippled one-eyed Vietnam veteran John Heard pursues his paranoid campaign against corporate turpitude.

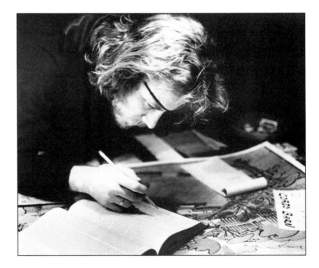

of 1968, but never enjoyed anything like Forman's success. Of his eight American films, only *Cutter's Way* is of real interest, but it is enough to ensure a cult reputation. The unusual music by Jack Nitzsche, who composed the scores for *Performance* and *One Flew Over the Cuckoo's Next*, is performed on a zither, glass harmonica and electric strings.

ODD/SALIENT FACTS United Artists initially released the film in the States as *Cutter and Bone*, but after unfavourable reviews it was withdrawn and put out as *Cutter's Way* by United Artists Classics and had a considerable success at festivals and on the art-house circuit.

MEMORABLE MOMENTS Cutter deliberately insulting blacks in a bar to bring about a confrontation.

Bone relaxing at sea with the murdered girl's sister, an emblematic oil-rig in the background.

Bone, a small, nervous presence in the imposing entrance hall of Cord Consolidated Oil.

Cutter pulling out a pistol to blast the target at a shooting gallery, and then smashing up the doll he's won and blasting it apart.

KEY LINES

Cutter: 'Richard Bone, doing what he does best – walking away.'

Cutter: 'When you were getting laid in the Ivy League, I was getting my ass shot off.'

Cutter: 'I watched the war on TV just like everybody else. Oh, I thought the same damn things, you know. What you thought when you saw a picture of a young woman with a baby lying face down in a ditch. Two gooks. You had three reactions, Rich. The same as anyone else. First one, real easy. I hate the United States of America. Yeah. You see the same thing next day and you move up a notch. There *is no God*. But you know what you finally say, what everybody finally says, no matter what? I'm hungry. He's responsible, because it's never their ass on the line, never theirs.'

Cutter: 'The routine grind drives me to drink. Tragedy I take straight.'

DEAD OF NIGHT
UK, 1945, EALING STUDIOS, 104 MINS

D ALBERTO CAVALCANTI, CHARLES CRICHTON, BASIL DEARDEN, ROBERT HAMER; **PR** MICHAEL BALCON; **SC** JOHN V. BAINES, ANGUS MACPHAIL (BASED ON STORIES BY BAINES, MACPHAIL, E. F. BENSON, H. G. WELLS), ADDITIONAL DIALOGUE T. E. B. CLARKE; **ED** CHARLES HASSE; **PH** (BW) STAN PAVEY, DOUGLAS SLOCOMBE; **M** GEORGES AURIC

CAST MERVYN JOHNS (WALTER CRAIG), ROLAND CULVER (ELIOT FOLEY), MARY MERRALL (MRS FOLEY), GOOGIE WITHERS (JOAN CORTLAND), FREDERICK VALK (DR VAN STRAATEN), ANTONY BAIRD (HUGH GRAINGER), SALLY ANN HOWES (SALLY O'HARA), RICHARD WYNDHAM (DR ALBURY), JUDY KELLY (JOYCE GRAINGER), MILES MALLESON (HEARSE DRIVER), MICHAEL ALLAN (JIMMY WATSON), BARBARA LEAKE (MRS O'HARA), RALPH MICHAEL (PETER CORTLAND), ESMÉ PERCY (MR RUTHERFORD, THE ANTIQUE DEALER), BASIL RADFORD (GEORGE PARRATT), NAUNTON WAYNE (LARRY POTTER), PEGGY BRYAN (MARY LEE), PETER JONES (GOLF CLUB BARMAN), ALLAN JEAYES (MAURICE OLCOTT), MICHAEL REDGRAVE (MAXWELL FRERE), ELIZABETH WELCH (BEULAH), HARTLEY POWER (SYLVESTER REE), MAGDA KUHN (MITZI)

THE STORY Architect Walter Craig arrives at Eliot Foley's country house. Meeting the other guests he recognizes them from a dream and predicts certain events, which do occur. The psychiatrist Van Straaten provides rational explanations but the others reveal they have had similar experiences, and five main guests tell their tales.

1. Hugh, the racing driver, dreamt he heard the driver of an old-fashioned hearse say to him 'Just room for one more, sir.' Those words spoken by a bus conductor stopped him from boarding the bus that plunged over an embankment.

2. Sally recalls a children's Christmas party at a country house, a game of hide-and-seek and her comforting a little boy who turned out to be the ghost of a child killed 80 years before by a jealous older sister.

3. Joan describes how she gave her fiancé Peter a Victorian triple mirror, in which he sees the reflection of a room where a jealous husband strangles his wife. The mirror comes to dominate Peter, and Joan narrowly escapes being murdered by smashing the glass.

4. Eliot breaks the tension with a comic tale. Two obsessive golfers in love with the same woman, decide to settle the dis-

▲ *DEAD OF NIGHT Schizophrenic ventriloquist Michael Redgrave in jail with Hugo, his manipulative dummy.*

pute through an 18-hole match. George wins by cheating, and Larry's ghost returns to torment him.

5. The ventriloquist Maxwell Frere has been charged with the attempted murder of an American ventriloquist he believed tried to steal his dummy, Hugo. Dr Van Straaten as expert witness, concludes the ventriloquist is a schizophrenic whose mind has been possessed by his creation.

After this story the mood darkens. Craig attempts to strangle Van Straaten, and experiences a surreal nightmare in which he meets the characters of the various stories, and awakes as Hugo the dummy is strangling him in a police cell. A phone call from Eliot Foley brings him back to where the film began.

THE FILM Not the first of horror/supernatural portmanteau movies, but arguably the best. People telling ghost stories around a fire is as cosy and traditional as Christmas, but the movie is taking place in the mind of Craig, an ordinary man in whose subconscious the images and incidents from all the films he sees coalesce into one great nightmare.

Dead of Night stands alongside the classic Ealing comedies that followed on, as a peak in the Ealing Studios postwar achievement. It went into production before the war ended, yet it never refers to it, and its social ambience is clearly the 1930s.

The shaggy-dog golfing story reunited the British cinema's greatest cult duo, Basil Radford and Naunton Wayne, who first appeared as the insouciant Charters and Caldicott, upper-middle-class cricket fans in Alfred Hitchcock's *The Lady Vanishes* (1938).

The co-author of the screenplay, Angus Macphail, was one of Hitchcock's influential friends, providing him with the anecdote about (and concept of) the MacGuffin, and it is inconceivable that *Psycho* wasn't influenced by the ventriloquist sequence in *Dead of Night*. Anthony Perkins's gestures and body movements reflect those of his fellow bi-sexual Michael Redgrave.

ODD/SALIENT FACTS For *Dead of Night* the great French composer Georges Auric wrote his first postwar score. Charles Barr, author of *Ealing Studios* (1977), has suggested that the film is an image of Ealing at work with the Czech actor Frederick Valk as the rational shrink standing in for the Studio's common-sensical Jewish boss, Michael Balcon.

MEMORABLE MOMENTS Joan Cortland dispelling the evil images in the mirror by the act of will of clutching her fiancé's hand.

Maxwell slapping his dummy's face.

Craig waking from his nightmare and driving out in his little sports car to re-start his dream.

KEY LINES

Craig: 'Everyone in this room is part of my dream.'

Eliot: 'So we're all powerless in the grip of Craig's dreams. That's a solemn thought.'

Peter: 'The trouble's not in the mirror, it's in my mind.'

Craig: 'Hamlet was right doctor, there are more things in heaven and earth than are dreamed of in your philosophy.'

Maxwell: 'Hugo is the only one who can help me. You see, he's more to blame than I am.'

DETOUR

USA, 1945, PRC, 68 MINS

D EDGAR G. ULMER; **PR** LEON FROMKESS; **SC** MARTIN
GOLDSMITH (FROM HIS OWN NOVEL); **PH** BENJAMIN H. KLINE;
M LEON ERDODY; **ED** GEORGE McGUIRE

CAST TOM NEAL (AL ROBERTS), ANN SAVAGE (VERA), CLAUDIA
DRAKE (SUE HARVEY), EDMUND MACDONALD (CHARLES HASKELL
JR.) TIM RYAN (GUS, DINER MANAGER), ROGER CLARK (DILLON)

THE STORY The unshaven, self-pitying Al Roberts is hitchhiking
to Los Angeles to join his girlfriend Sue, a singer in the third-rate
New York nightclub where he played piano in the band. Sue
wants a career in Hollywood. In Arizona he is picked up by
Charles Haskell, a smooth gambler with a bad heart who has

▼ *DETOUR Doomed anti-hero Tom Neal discovers he's dialled
M for murder by accidentally strangling sad pick-up Vera with
a telephone cord.*

scratches on his hand from a woman he gave a lift to. While
Al drives, Haskell falls into a deep sleep and when Al opens
the car door Haskell falls out, hitting a rock. Fearing that he'll
be suspected of murder, Al leaves the corpse in the desert, takes
the car and Haskell's identity paper, and the following day picks
up Vera, a female hitchhiker who proves to be the woman
Haskell had assaulted. The vicious, consumptive Vera blackmails Al, first into taking her to LA to sell the car, then into
impersonating Haskell to inherit the fortune of Haskell's dying
father from whom he was estranged. One night at their rented
apartment, Vera gets drunk and threatens to call the police, and
Al tugs at the cord running under her locked bedroom door and
she's strangled. Al goes on the run, expecting to be picked up
at any time for two murders.

THE FILM *Detour* is the ultimate in cult movies, an ultra-low bud-
get *film noir* by the strange Viennese intellectual, Edgar G.
Ulmer (1904–72). Having been assistant to the great Max
Reinhardt and designer for F. W. Murnau, Ulmer co-directed

Menschen am Sonntag (People on Sunday, 1929), the seminal German precursor of neo-realism, before devoting his life to endless low-budget pictures in Europe and America, mostly genre films, but also comedies and musicals in Yiddish and Ukrainian or aimed at American black audiences. These modest projects offered him considerable creative freedom, and his usually bleak pictures are an astonishing mixture of artistic sophistication and slapdash execution. His two finest achievements are The Black Cat (1934), a demented Karloff-Lugosi horror flick set in a disturbed postwar Europe, and Detour, set in a tawdry America of diners, cheap hotels, seedy nightclubs and desert roads. The self-despising, deeply unsympathetic Al is an all-American fall guy, accidentally killing a worthless, dying conman, and a ferocious, blackmailing harpie. The film's overwrought script, with its almost non-stop voice-over narration, is in a hard-boiled, epigrammatic pulp vein.

ODD/SALIENT FACTS The film was shot in six days on a budget of under $20,000 for the PRC (Producers Releasing Corporation), a small company on Poverty Row specializing in double-bills for back-street cinemas. Ulmer is the principal model for Max Castle, the mysterious director whose career obsesses the hero of Theodore Roszak's Flickers (1991), one of the best novels about movie-making. Actor Tom Neal's life is even sadder than Al Roberts's. The son of a wealthy banker, Neal (1914–72) graduated from Harvard Law School before being signed by Hollywood where virtually all his pictures were second features. After injuring Franchot Tone during a brawl over actress Barbara Payton, Neal was shunned by the industry. He married Payton, started a gardening business and went bankrupt. In 1965 he was charged with murdering his third wife and spent six years in jail for involuntary manslaughter, dying of a heart attack eight months after his release.

MEMORABLE MOMENTS Al and Sue walking through the fog of New York discussing their bleak future.

The depressed Al playing a crazed boogie-woogie version of Brahms in the New York nightclub.

Al's erotic vision of Sue while he's on the road – she's singing 'I Can't Believe That You're in Love With Me' with the shadows of a clarinettist, a saxophonist and a trumpeter on the wall beside her.

> **'That's life – whatever way you turn fate sticks out a foot to trip you up.'**

The final scene of the abject Al imagining himself being arrested by highway patrolmen.

KEY LINES

Al: 'Don't you know that a million people go out there [Hollywood] every year and end up polishing cuspidors?'

Al: 'I was tussling with the most dangerous animal in the world – a woman.'

Al: 'That's life – whatever way you turn fate sticks out a foot to trip you up.'

Al: 'Life's like a ball game, you've got to take a swing at whatever comes along before you wake up and find it's the ninth inning.'

Al: 'I know that someday a car will pick me up that I never thumbed. Yes, fate or some mysterious force can put the finger on you or me for no good reason at all.'

THE DEVILS

UK, 1970, WARNER BROTHERS, 111 MINS

D KEN RUSSELL; **PR** RUSSELL AND ROBERT SOLO; **SC** RUSSELL, BASED ON THE PLAY BY JOHN WHITING AND THE DEVILS OF LOUDUN BY ALDOUS HUXLEY; **PH** (COL, PANAVISION) DAVID WATKIN; **M** PETER MAXWELL DAVIES; **ED** MICHAEL BRADSELL **CAST** VANESSA REDGRAVE (JEANNE, MOTHER SUPERIOR), OLIVER REED (GRANDIER), DUDLEY SUTTON (BARON DE LAUBARDEMONT), MAX ADRIAN (SURGEON), GEMMA JONES (MADELEINE), MURRAY MELVIN (MIGNON), MICHAEL GOTHARD (BARRÉ)

THE STORY 1634 in the fortified city of Loudun, 150 miles south-west of Paris. The handsome, well-born, Jesuit-educated Father Grandier has created many enemies through his libertine life (a love-child, a secret marriage to a young woman), his liberal views and his support of the Huguenots. Cardinal Richelieu's people and local landowners vow the destruction of Grandier, taking advantage of the terror of the plague and Jeanne's warped love for Grandier. Jeanne, the hunchbacked Mother Superior of an Ursuline convent, and other hysterical

▲ *THE DEVILS Director Ken Russell (left) looks on encouragingly as Oliver Reed's libidinous Father Grandier examines a possessed Vanessa Redgrave.*

nuns are encouraged by the witchhunter Father Barré to testify that they have been possessed by devils working for Grandier, and he is put on trial for obscenity, blasphemy and sacrilege. After being tortured, Grandier is burnt at the stake and the walls of Loudun are torn down.

THE FILM The artistic credentials of *The Devils* are impeccable. Commissioned by the Royal Shakespeare Company in 1961 from a highly regarded playwright with a coterie reputation, it was based on a celebrated study of a real-life case of mass hysteria by one of the century's most respected literary intellectuals. The stage presentation with Richard Johnson as Grandier and Virginia McKenna as Jeanne was a restrained, if harrowing affair, as was the 1961.Polish film on the same subject, Jerzy Kawalerowicz's *Mother Joan of the Angels*, which

was an allegory about the false accusations and show trials in Eastern Europe. The film is something else again with Ken Russell, the *enfant terrible* of British film-making, upping the ante after his wild Tchaikovsky flick, *The Music Lovers*, to make a truly demented picture, a weird mixture of sado-masochistic melodrama and camp comedy, reflecting the hysteria of the nuns. Anti-clerical movies centring on the sexual shenanigans between nuns and priests had been a staple of continental movies for decades (frequently in hard and soft-core melodrama). In *The Devils*, Ken Russell (himself raised as a Catholic) brought this European tradition into a mainstream Anglo-American cinema where nuns were usually genteel creatures played by the likes of Ingrid Bergman, Deborah Kerr and Audrey Hepburn. Devoid of spirituality or thoughtfulness, the film sets out to shock and offend with scenes of a priest bedding his confessees; a Mother Superior fantasizing herself as the lover of Christ; orgies involving dozens of incensed nuns frolicking in the nude; torture; exorcism with hideous instruments;

the King shooting Huguenots for sport; and a final execution in which you can almost smell the burning flesh. As the obsessed Mother Superior, Vanessa Redgrave goes over the top, quite literally chewing her rosary, but Oliver Reed and Gemma Jones as his 'wife', providing a still centre of rationality, seem oblivious to the madness around them. The film is given a curious appearance by the gleaming black-and-white sets, theatrical and unconvincingly pristine. The jarring, atonal score is by the British avant-garde composer Peter Maxwell Davies. Brutal cross-cutting emphasizes thematic points, and dramatic elisions result in scenes that begin near their climax – as when Barré gathers the nuns in the woods and gives them the choice of being shot or accusing Grandier. This all contributes to the frenzied atmosphere and the calculated bad taste that Russell, for all his efforts, hasn't subsequently matched.

ODD/SALIENT FACTS The making of the picture was attended by stories of extras (especially those playing nuns) complaining of being assaulted and walking off the set, though these were very likely the concoctions of publicists. The censorship problems the film raised (exacerbated by a scandal-mongering tabloid press and not helped by hostile critics) prepared the way for attacks some months later on two other cult British productions, that dealt with sex and violence: Peckinpah's *Straw Dogs* and Kubrick's *A Clockwork Orange*. The sets for *The Devils* were designed by Derek Jarman who was to become one of the cult directors of the 1970s and '80s.

MEMORABLE MOMENTS/ICONIC SCENES The Mother Superior reaching out through a grill to attack Grandier's lover.

The Mother Superior engaged in self-flagellation.

The gleeful Surgeon and Chemist going about their business of purging with gigantic syringes.

The Duc presenting the Mother Superior with a charred bone as a souvenir.

KEY LINES

Peasant woman of Grandier: 'Now there's a man worth going to hell for.'

Louis XIV after shooting down a Huguenot who has run the gauntlet dressed in a blackbird costume: 'Bye bye blackbird.'

Grandier: 'Secluded women have given themselves to God, but something within them cries out to be given to man.'

Barré: 'Sin can be caught as easily as the plague.'

Grandier: 'You have turned the house of the Lord into a circus and its people into clowns.'

DIAL M FOR MURDER
USA, 1954, WARNER, 105 MINS
D *ALFRED HITCHCOCK;* **SC** *HITCHCOCK (FROM THE PLAY BY FREDERICK KNOTT);* **PH** *(3-D) ROBERT BURKS;* **M** *DIMITRI TIOMKIN;* **ED** *RUDI FEHR*
CAST *RAY MILLAND (TONY WENDICE), GRACE KELLY (MARGOT WENDICE), ROBERT CUMMINGS (MARK HALLIDAY), JOHN WILLIAMS (CHIEF INSPECTOR HUBBARD), ANTHONY DAWSON (CAPTAIN LESGATE)*

THE STORY Tony Wendice, a former tennis star now in his forties, has an indifferently paid job selling sports equipment and lives in central London with his wife Margot, whom he has married for her money. Suspecting her of an affair with Mark Halliday, an American writer of crime novels and television scripts, he blackmails a shady conman, Captain Lesgate, into agreeing to murder her at the Wendices' flat while Tony is attending a dinner, but during the ensuing struggle Margot kills Lesgate with a pair of scissors. Tony then frames her for murder, planting evidence on Lesgate to prove that he was blackmailing Margot over the affair with Mark. Chief Inspector Hubbard's investigations lead to Margot's being sentenced to death for murder. But on the eve of her execution, Hubbard the cop and Mark the crime writer, working on the case from different angles, put Tony on the spot, the crucial piece of evidence being the key stolen from Margot's purse that enabled Lesgate to enter the flat.

THE FILM *Dial M for Murder*, based on a successful, conventional stage thriller, is the only film made by a director of the first rank during the Hollywood majors' brief flirtation with stereo-scopic cinema in 1953 following the surprise success of the low-budget *Bwana Devil* the previous year. But it was shown in 3-D in only a few American cinemas and Europe had to wait for thirty years to see it as originally conceived. This virtuoso film takes its place alongside another filmed play, *Rope*, in Hitchcock's canon. Whereas other 3-D films used the process for shock effects (e.g. an arrow flying off the screen past the spectator's ear in *Hondo*), there is no aggression in *Dial M for Murder*. Hitchcock appreciated that, far from contributing to the illusion of cinematic realism, 3-D increased the artificiality. People and objects are equalized through the flatness in depth, an effect suited to a play dealing in human cyphers and phys-ical clues. The film rarely moves out of the spacious living room of the Wendices' flat and the screen is often used like a prosce-nium arch so that the audience seems to be watching from the

▼ *DIAL M FOR MURDER Grace Kelly answers the phone before plunging the scissors into would-be assassin Anthony Dawson.*

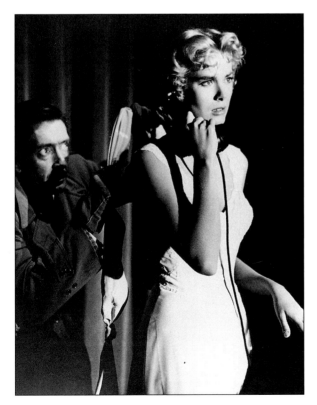

front stalls or occasionally from the circle. The theatricality of performance, dialogue, decor and lighting is emphasized, and when Margot kills Lesgate she reaches out for the scissors which appear to be a few inches from the spectators' eyes and we find ourselves willing her to seize them, though in the two-dimensional prints of the film we can hardly see the scissors until she picks them up. There are no close-ups or subjective shots of the stabbing.

ODD/SALIENT FACTS Hitchcock shot the film in 36 days and had a pit built so that the camera could be used at floor level to simulate the view from the orchestra stalls. For the disturbing close-up of Tony phoning Margot (to lure her from the bedroom to be killed by Lesgate), a giant telephone was built with a King Kong-size finger to work the dial. *Dial M for Murder* (which was originally written for TV) has been remade as *A Perfect Murder* (Andrew Davis, 1998).

MEMORABLE MOMENTS Tony manipulating the crooked Lesgate.

Margot reaching out for the scissors.

The use of theatrical space to focus our attention on the door at the rear of the stage, the opening of which provides the final climax.

Hitchcock's signature appearance on a college reunion pho-tograph which identifies him as an old friend of the two crooks Lesgate and Tony Wendice.

KEY LINES

Inspector Hubbard: 'They talk about flat-footed policemen, may the saints protect us from the gifted amateur.'

Hubbard to a policeman carrying Margot's handbag: 'You can't walk down the streets like that or you'll be arrested.'

DIVA
FRANCE, 1981, LES FILMS GALAXIE/GREENWICH FILM PRODUCTIONS , 123 MINS
D JEAN-JACQUES BEINEIX; **PR** IRENE SILBERMAN; **SC** JEAN-JACQUES BEINEIX, JEAN VAN HAMME, DIALOGUE BY JEAN-JACQUES BEINEIX, BASED ON THE BOOK BY DELACORTA; **PH** (COL) PHILIPPE ROUSSELOT; **M** VLADIMIR COSMA; **ED** MARIE-JOSEPHE YOYOTTE, MONIQUE PRIM

74

CAST *Frédéric Andréï (Jules), Roland Bertin (Simon Weinstadt), Richard Bohringer (Gorodish), Gérard Darmon (Spic), Chantal Deruaz (Nadia Kalonsky), Jacques Fabbri (Inspector Jean Saporta), Patrick Floersheim (Mortier), Thuy An Luu (Alba), Jean-Jacques Moreau (Krantz), Dominique Pinon (Le Curé), Anny Romand (Paula), Wilhelmenia Wiggins Fernandez (Cynthia Hawkins, the Diva)*

THE STORY Jules, a mobilette courier, makes a bootleg recording of a Cynthia Hawkins recital. After the concert he goes backstage to meet the Diva, and as he leaves her dressing room, steals one of her dresses. The following day outside a Parisian station, a woman, Nadia, pursued by men posing as policemen, secretes a tape cassette in Jules's panier. Jules leaves not knowing that the woman is about to be killed by Le Curé, one of the men. Jules meets up with Alba, a young oriental model, and visits the flat she shares with Gorodish, a mystic/wheeler-dealer. It turns out that the tape contains Nadia's revelations of the prostitution and drugs ring with which she was involved. Jules spends a night with a prostitute and gets her to wear the Diva's dress. He is being pursued by two men who

▼ *DIVA Deaf psycho Spic (Gérard Darmon) and his sidekick Le Curé (Dominique Pinon) in hot pursuit of Jules and the incriminating tape.*

are working for the corrupt Inspector Saporta. Jules returns the dress to Cynthia and they begin an affair. Meanwhile Cynthia, who has never released a recording, is being held to ransom by Taiwanese gangsters over the bootleg tape, which is worth a fortune. Jean takes refuge in the prostitute's flat where he listens to the beginning of Nadia's tape. It instantly reveals that Saporta is a crook and then that the prostitute is probably working for Saporta. He rushes out of the flat and is pursued through Paris by Spic and Le Curé. Having been shot, and about to be killed, Jules is rescued by Gorodish. In a fiendishly clever plot by Gorodish, blackmail money is extorted from Saporta. Then the Taiwanese, Le Curé, Spic and finally Saporta are killed. Jules returns the tape to Cynthia who hears herself sing for the first time.

THE FILM *Diva* marked the debut as feature director of the unprolific Jean-Jacques Beineix. He and his co-writer Jean Van Hamme adapted a cultish crime novel by Delacorta, the pen name of Swiss poet and novelist Daniel Odier. The source novel has the basic elements of the film but the adaptors improved on it, stripped it down and enhanced it brilliantly. There is one neat touch in the book that they don't use, in that Gorodish knew Saporta, having started out as his chauffeur, but otherwise the film is slicker and smarter, with Saporta becoming a bent copper rather than just a criminal, and the addition of the comically sinister double act in pursuit of Jules. Their most striking amendment is in the conclusion where the decent Zen-crook Gorodish effortlessly comes up with a succession of ingenious set-pieces to outwit the criminals. The film set the tone for cool cult crime films, with Beineix creating a clean, ridiculously flashy surface for a devious plot. With its operatic soundtrack, slick camerawork and studied hipness, it influenced a generation of commercial directors. *Diva* is a Hitchcockian thriller stripped of all psychological depth. It is a film about sound, where the characters struggle to control and own other people's voices and the psycho-killer is instantly recognizable by his hearing aid.

ODD/SALIENT FACTS Beineix followed the cult success of *Diva* with the ludicrous *The Moon in the Gutter* (1983) before rediscovering his touch with *Betty Blue* (1986), which became an instant cult hit and launched the career of Béatrice Dalle. Beineix seemed to have shifted into retirement after *Roselyne and the Lions* (1989), but was reinvigorated by his experiences producing a short documentary film on Jean-Dominique Bauby. Bauby, a French journalist who suffered a stroke and subsequent paralysis, termed 'locked-in syndrome', wrote his account of these experiences in *The Diving Bell and the Butterfly*, which he dictated via blinks. The author died shortly after the publication of this memoir and Beineix has suggested he may be tempted to direct the film of the book.

MEMORABLE MOMENTS The ingenious climax which begins with Saporta getting into the assigned car and playing the tape, on which Gorodish says: 'You're on board an 11 horsepower Citroën, a bit of history. This model was once favoured by the police but also by gangsters. It seemed very appropriate for you.'

KEY LINES

Gorodish to Jules, on the philosophy of the baguette:
'Some people get high on airplane glue, detergents, all sorts of fancy gimmicks. Me, my satori is this – the Zen of buttering bread.'

> 'Some people get high on airplane glue, detergents, all sorts of fancy gimmicks. Me, my satori is this – the Zen of buttering bread.'

LA DOLCE VITA

ITALY/FRANCE, 1960, RIAMA FILM/GRAY FILMS/PATHÉ CINÉMA, 178 MINS

D FEDERICO FELLINI; **PR** GIUSEPPI AMATO; **SC** FEDERICO FELLINI, ENNIO FLAIANO, TULLIO PINELLI, BRUNELLO RONDI; **PH** (BW, SCOPE) OTELLO MARTELLI; **ED** LEO CATTOZZO; **M** NINO ROTA **CAST** MARCELLO MASTROIANNI (MARCELLO RUBINI), ANOUK AIMÉE (MADDALENA), ANITA EKBERG (SYLVIA), YVONNE FURNEAUX (EMMA), ALAIN CUNY (STEINER), LEX BARKER (ROBERT), ANNIBALE NICHI (MARCELLO'S FATHER), MAGALI NOËL (FANNY), NADIA GRAY (NADIA), WALTER SANTESSO (PAPARAZZO)

THE STORY Marcello, a gossip columnist from a middle-class provincial family, works for what his mentor, the illustrious author Steiner, calls 'the semi-fascist press', reporting on the scandalous activities of Rome's fashionable café society along the Via Veneto, accompanied by the photographer Paparazzo. Callously ignoring his neurotic mistress Emma, he has an affair with the rich heiress Maddalena, becomes obsessed with the Swedish movie star Sylvia, and reports on sensational events like the two children who claim to have seen the Madonna. Marcello's father

(by implication a fascist supporter before the war) comes to Rome and collapses while attempting to have sex with Fanny, a French dancer to whom Marcello has introduced him. Steiner, the despairing intellectual, kills his two children and commits suicide. Before and after Steiner's death, Marcello attends extended parties at aristocratic homes. Soon he has not only given up the possibility of being a serious writer, but also become a drunken publicity agent and a self-despising leader of the revels at an orgy. At dawn when the partygoers come to inspect a strange fish stranded on the beach, he sees in the distance an innocent young woman he has previously encountered at a seaside café, only now he cannot hear what she is saying.

THE FILM *La Dolce Vita* ended postwar Italian cinema, bringing down the curtain on neo-realism, the movement that Fellini helped create, and opening up a new phase of expansive movie-making. The film identified and criticized a new world of media-created celebrity, a corrupt international culture where journalists, plutocrats, aristocrats, show-biz folk, film-makers and politicians meet and merge. It is a world that has banished or been deserted by God, a place where all values have been abandoned, all personal relations severed, and the goal of life reduced to the fulfilment of desire. As several references to Dante confirm, it is a form of hell, and it consumes Marcello, its observer and participant. A good deal of the film's appeal, as with all late Fellini, is the way it relishes that which it condemns. Fellini found in the minor Italian movie star Mastroianni his cinematic alter ego who was to feature thus in a succession of films (most notable *8½*), and would become one of European cinema's most prolific stars. When Fellini re-created the neon-lit, traffic-choked Via Veneto at Cinecittà, he brought the movies back from the streets and into the studio, challenging the polarization of reality and artifice. His film has a vibrancy and sadness that keeps it alive.

ODD/SALIENT FACTS Producer Dino de Laurentiis left the project when Fellini refused to cast Paul Newman as the gossip columnist. In the final sequence Marcello is attacked for publicizing a client in a fan magazine as an actor with 'a Greek profile and modern acting style that equates him with Paul Newman'.

'You are the first woman on the first day of creation. You are mother, sister, lover, friend, angel, devil, earth, home.'

The film contributed to the language its ironic title 'La Dolce Vita', and the collective term 'paparazzi' (from Marcello's photographer friend) for the hordes of celebrity-chasing photographers. Paparazzo's name was borrowed from a hotelier in *By the Ionian Sea* (1901), a travel book by George Gissing. Alain Cuny, the French actor who played the unctuous Steiner, was the European cinema's all-purpose intellectual, and in 1974 he played a suave philosopher of sex in *Emmanuelle*.

MEMORABLE MOMENTS The helicopter carrying a statue of Christ with outstretched arms away from Rome across the Vatican.

Anita Ekberg dressed as a Catholic priest in St Peter's and later wading through the Trevi Fountain at night with the besotted Marcello.

The climactic encounter with the weird beached creature reminiscent of the mysterious female body washed ashore in the early 1950s, which launched the Montesi Scandal that was to shake Italy.

KEY LINES

Sylvia (masquerading as a priest in the Vatican): 'I must remember to tell Marilyn.'

Marcello (to Sylvia): 'You are the first woman on the first day of creation. You are mother, sister, lover, friend, angel, devil, earth, home.'

Steiner (to Marcello): 'Don't be like me. Salvation doesn't lie within four walls. I'm too serious to be a dilettante and too much a dabbler to be a professional. Even the most miserable life is better than a sheltered existence in an organized society where everything is calculated and perfected.'

Transvestite (at the final party): 'By 1965 there'll be total depravity. How squalid everything will be.'

DUCK SOUP

US, 1933, PARAMOUNT PICTURES, 72 MINS

D *LEO MCCAREY;* **PR SC** *STORY, MUSIC AND LYRICS BY BERT KALMAR AND HARRY RUBY, ADDITIONAL DIALOGUE BY ARTHUR SHEEKMAN AND NAT PERRIN;* **MD** *ARTHUR JOHNSTON;* **PH** *HENRY SHARP;* **ED** *LEROY STONE*

CAST *GROUCHO MARX (RUFUS T. FIREFLY), HARPO MARX (PINKY), CHICO MARX (CHICOLINI), ZEPPO MARX (BOB ROLAND), MARGARET DUMONT (MRS TEASDALE), RAQUEL TORRES (VERA MARCAL), LOUIS CALHERN (TRENTINO), EDMUND BREESE (ZANDER), LEONID KINSKY (AGITATOR), CHARLES B. MIDDLETON (PROSECUTOR), EDGAR KENNEDY (STREET VENDOR)*

THE STORY The land of Freedonia is on the verge of war with neighbouring Sylvania. Rufus T. Firefly is appointed leader with the support of the country's chief benefactor, Mrs Teasdale. In his embassy, Sylvanian ambassador Trentino learns that revolution in Freedonia has been averted by Firefly's popularity. His spies Pinky and Chicolini gain positions in Firefly's government. With war seemingly inevitable, Trentino sends Pinky and Chicolini to steal Freedonia's battle plans from Mrs Teasdale's. Chicolini is arrested and charged with treason. His show trial is interrupted by the news that the Sylvanian troops are advancing. When a last-minute attempt to secure peace fails, war is declared. In the conflict Firefly, his secretary Bob Roland, Chicolini, Pinky and Mrs Teasdale are holed up in a small house near the front. Eventually Trentino is captured and victory is Freedonia's.

THE FILM *Duck Soup* is the last film the Marx Brothers made for Paramount and the last featuring Zeppo. When they came to negotiate a new contract with MGM, it was initially suggested that they should be paid less since there were now fewer of them. Groucho is said to have remarked: 'Without Zeppo we're worth twice as much.' Following the success of *Horse Feathers* in 1932, this film was initially to have been directed by Ernst Lubitsch. The script went through various titles (*Oo La La, Cracked Ice* and *Grasshoppers*) before settling on its final form. It was ultimately assigned to director Leo McCarey, who had experience working with Laurel & Hardy (whose trademark style is noticeable in the peanut-stand sequence with Edgar Kennedy) and Eddie Cantor, and would go on to work with W. C. Fields

▶ *LA DOLCE VITA* Sex symbol Anita Ekberg lights up the Roman night as she treads on all those coins in the Trevi Fountain.

▲ **DUCK SOUP** *Enemy spies Pinky (Harpo) and Chicolini (Chico) find gainful employment in the office of Freedonia's new leader Rufus T. Firefly (Groucho).*

and Harold Lloyd among others. Although less successful than its predecessor and the first two MGM films that followed it, it was far from a financial disaster. The film was technically – in terms of production design, direction and writing – the most accomplished the brothers had appeared in up to that point and was improved by the absence of harp and piano sequences. It is in every respect the Marx Brothers' finest hour and ten minutes and remains among the greatest comedy films ever made.

ODD/SALIENT FACTS When Mickey Sacks, the Woody Allen character, is at his lowest point in *Hannah and Her Sisters* (1986), he wanders the streets of New York City for hours before stumbling into a cinema in which *Duck Soup* is showing. The scene on the screen is the elaborate *Freedonia's Going to War* musical number, and Mickey feels instantly better, saying: 'And I started to feel how can you even think of killing yourself? I mean, isn't it so stupid? I mean, I – look at the people up there on the screen. You know, they're real funny, and, and what if the worst is true? What if there's no God ...?'

MEMORABLE MOMENTS The film's enduringly great sequence comes when Chicolini and Pinky have broken into Mrs Teasdale's house to steal the battle plans. Chicolini is upstairs

while Pinky is downstairs trying to unlock the safe. Both are disguised as Firefly. When the safe turns out to be a radio, which blares uncontrollably, Firefly comes down to see what is going on. Panicked, Pinky runs into a mirror which smashes, so when Firefly approaches him he pretends to be Firefly's mirror image in a ludicrously protracted sequence. The fake mirror routine was a stock sketch in music hall revues and had been used on screen by Charlie Chaplin and Max Linder.

KEY LINES

Firefly to Mrs Teasdale: 'Can't you see what I'm trying to
    tell you. I love you.'
Mrs Teasdale, bashfully: 'Oh, Your Excellency!'
Firefly: 'You're not so bad, yourself.'

Vera Marcal, to Firefly: 'Perhaps we get a chance to
    dance together.'

Firefly: 'I could dance with you till the cows come home.'
Vera: 'Yes?'
Firefly: 'On second thoughts I'd rather dance with the cows till you come home.'

Chicolini, reporting his and Pinky's espionage activities to Trentino: 'All right, I tell you. Monday we watch Firefly's house, but he no come out. He wasn't home. Tuesday, we go to the ball game, but he fool us. He no show up. Wednesday he go to the ball game, but we fool him. We no show up. Thursday was a double header. Nobody show up. Friday it rained all day. There was no ball game so we stayed home and we listened to it on the radio.'
Trentino: 'Then you didn't shadow Firefly?'
Chicolini: 'Sure we shadow Firefly. We shadow him all day.'
Trentino: 'What day was that?'
Chicolini: 'Shadderday.'

EASY RIDER ★

US, 1969, RAYBERT/PANDO, 94 MINS

D DENNIS HOPPER; **PR** PETER FONDA, BERT SCHNEIDER, WILLIAM L. HAYWARD; **SC** PETER FONDA, DENNIS HOPPER, TERRY SOUTHERN; **PH** (COL) LASZLO KOVACS; **ED** DONN CAMBERN **CAST** PETER FONDA (WYATT), DENNIS HOPPER (BILLY), ANTONIO MENDOZA (JESUS), PHIL SPECTOR (CONNECTION), MAC MASHOURIAN (BODYGUARD), WARREN FINNERTY (RANCHER), TITA COLORADO (RANCHER'S WIFE), LUKE ASKEW (STRANGER ON HIGHWAY), LUANA ANDERS (LISA), SABRINA SCHARF (SARAH), SANDY WYETH (JOANNE), ROBERT WALKER JR. (JACK), ROBERT BALL, CARMEN PHILLIPS, ELLIE WALKER AND MICHAEL PATAKI (MIMES), JACK NICHOLSON (GEORGE HANSON), GEORGE FOWLER JR. (GUARD), KEITH GREEN (SHERIFF), HAYWARD ROBILLARD (CAT MAN), ARNOLD HESS JR. (DEPUTY), BUDDY CAUSEY JR., DUFFY LAMONT, BLASE M.DAWSON AND PAUL GUEDRY (CUSTOMERS IN CAFE), TONI BASIL (MARY), KAREN BLACK (KAREN), LEA MARMER (MADAME), CATHI COZZI (DANCING GIRL), THEA SALERNO, ANNE MCCLAIN, BEATRIZ MONTELLI AND MARCIA BOWMAN (HOOKERS), DAVID C. BILLODEAU AND JOHNNY DAVID (MEN IN PICKUP TRUCK)

THE STORY Wyatt and Billy pull off a coke deal, hide the money in the petrol tank of Wyatt's bike and drive across country. Having spent some time in a hippie commune, they are arrested and jailed for a minor offence in a small town. In jail they meet drunken lawyer George Hanson, who pays for their release and joins them on their journey. The three of them sit around a camp-fire getting stoned. The following night having been threatened by a group of local rednecks, they are violently attacked in their sleep and Hanson is killed. Wyatt and Billy head off to New Orleans and the whorehouse recommended by Hanson. Together with Mary and Karen, they wander around the Mardi Gras and drop acid. They ride out of New Orleans and are shot dead by two rednecks in a pick-up truck.

> 'They're not scared of you, they're scared of what you represent ... What you represent to them is freedom.'

THE FILM Wyatt and Billy are modern cowboys who ride their bikes across the Monument Valley of John Ford Westerns, and in a sequence of heavy-handed symbolism, tend to a flat tyre as old-timers nearby shoe a horse. In the entry on Dennis Hopper in his *Biographical Dictionary of Cinema*, David Thomson writes: 'Then came *Easy Rider*, a disaster in the history of film to set beside the early loss of Technicolor, the invention of gross participation, the early death of Murnau, and the longevity of Richard Attenborough.' The film is continually re-examined and discussed to discover why such an obviously if inarticulately cultish, anti-establishment film should not merely make all those involved in its creation rich, but also help to change the make-up of Hollywood. There is in fact very little to the film and it is easy to see how the project could have been pitched in a couple of sentences and all the details be ironed out in one short session on Peter Fonda's tennis court. This oblique if loud statement of intent from the new generation is presented in a film conceived, written, produced, acted and eventually seen by stoned people. Editorial consultant Henry Jaglom recalls being present at an early screening when the film ran for around four hours. He was the only person not to appreciate the lengthy sequences in which the two bikers travelled through endless beautiful landscapes to the backing of endless hippie songs. As he says: 'I wasn't high. I was in real time.' The film retains some power, making its impact from just a few key ingredients, such as its attitude of defiance, the notion that somehow the heroes blew it, and the still shockingly sudden and pessimistic end.

ODD/SALIENT FACTS The authorship of the film is still disputed. What is acknowledged is that Terry Southern was an enthusiast for the project and was keen to help in any way he could. This eagerness led an already successful novelist and screenwriter of the counter-culture to perform the mundane task of rendering the work-in-progress of Hopper and Fonda into the recognizable shape of a movie script. With his name attached to the project it helped to raise the meagre $360,000 budget. His primary achievement, beyond fleshing out the character of Hanson, was to supply the film's title. In production Hopper became predictably crazed, but with the help of the dedicated cast and crew managed to deliver usable footage which was ultimately worked into the relatively coherent finished form. At the height of the production chaos, Hopper complained that everyone was conspiring to ruin his movie. As Fonda recalls still annoyed: 'His movie? I thought it was supposed to be ours.'

MEMORABLE MOMENTS The scenes which most symbolize the tension between old and new are those in which they are treated to what Hanson characterizes as 'country witticisms' in the café and the final sequence in which they are blown away by the forces unable to understand or accept the new frontier spirit of the modern rebels.

KEY LINES

As they are about to leave the hippie commune, Wyatt turns to Billy and says approvingly: 'They're gonna make it. Dig, man, they're gonna make it.'

Around the camp-fire Hanson remarks: 'You know, this used to be a hell of a country... They're not scared of you, they're scared of what you represent... What you represent to them is freedom.'

Wyatt: 'You know, Billy, we blew it.'
Billy: 'You go for the big money, you're free, dig.'
Wyatt: 'We blew it.'

ENTER THE DRAGON
US/HONG KONG, 1973, WARNER/CONCORD, 99 MINS

D ROBERT CLOUSE; **PR** FRED WEINTRAUB, PAUL HELLER, RAYMOND CHOW; **SC** MICHAEL ALLIN; **PH** (COL, PANAVISION) GILBERT HUBBS; FIGHT SEQUENCES STAGED BY BRUCE LEE; **ED** KURT KIRSCHLER, GEORGE WATTERS

CAST BRUCE LEE (LEE), JOHN SAXON (ROPER), JIM KELLY (WILLIAMS), AHNA CAPRI (TANIA), SHIEH KIEN (HAN), BOB WALL (OHARRA), ANGELA MAO YING (SU LIN), BETTY CHUNG (MEI LING), GEOFFREY WEEKS (BRAITHWAITE), YAN SZE BOLO (PETER ARCHER)

THE STORY Lee, Roper and Williams are invited to attend a martial arts competition on the private island of Han. Lee has been asked by the British secret service to investigate Han's drugs and prostitution racket. As they approach the island the story of each of the three leading characters is fleshed out in flashbacks. Lee is out to avenge the murder of his sister by Han's sidekick Oharra. Roper is facing a massive personal debt. Williams, a black man, has encountered violent harassment from the American police. On the island each man fights successfully in the early bouts, Lee killing Oharra. Williams and Roper enjoy the women supplied by Han. Lee makes a nocturnal excursion to investigate the dark secrets of Han's island complex, an outing for which Williams is erroneously blamed and savagely beaten by Han. Roper is taken around Han's underground opium factory and asked to become an American representative. He seems tempted before he sees the beaten body of his Vietnam vet buddy Williams. With Lee releasing the peasants held captive by Han, there is a great climactic fight in which Han is killed and his men defeated.

THE FILM *Enter the Dragon* is a crudely plotted and poorly edited film. It is a lame pastiche of the James Bond movies complete with snarling villain with pussy cat and fake claw, underground complex, torture museum and vat whose sole purpose seems to be for lowering rivals into. It is enlivened and made intermittently extraordinary by the presence of Lee. Pauline Kael has described him as the Fred Astaire of martial arts movies and his talents are what made this film, Hollywood's first mainstream chop-socky movie, a success. He has an odd, geekish hairstyle and is given to making peculiar howling noises but his graceful movements and sheer, taut physical presence are captivating. A philosophy graduate born in San Francisco, Lee

▲ *ENTER THE DRAGON* Bruce Lee (Lee) sporting designer scars is lost in a hall of mirrors in the climactic mortal combat.

combat. Lee was always painfully aware of this limitation in the genre's appeal and the writers make a perfunctory stab at dismissing this narrative niggle. When Lee is first approached by Braithwaite with the commission, he suggests, naturally: 'Guns. Now why doesn't somebody pull a 45 and settle it?' Braithwaite explains that Han has a great fear of guns, guns are an offence, guns are not allowed. The basic objection is: 'Any bloody fool can pull a trigger.'

ODD/SALIENT FACTS Lee died, supposedly as the result of a brain oedema just weeks before the release of *Enter the Dragon*. He was 32 years old. The rumours that always circulate around the early deaths of the beautiful and famous began almost at once. They suggested that he was murdered by Triads or tongs or perhaps died of a drug overdose. In a grim irony, his son Brandon, also apparently on the verge of becoming a Hollywood action star, died in unusual circumstances, killed by the residual powder in a blank cartridge fired at him at close range on the set of the film *The Crow* (1994). The film, like his father's *The Game of Death* (1979), was completed with added footage and a stand-in and released posthumously.

MEMORABLE MOMENTS The final confrontation between Lee and Han is staged as a knowing updated, kung fu version of the climactic duel in *Swashbucklers*, as the two fight one another in the midst of the general maul before moving to more private quarters. Han gets to use two special serrated fake hands from his Swiss-army-knife arsenal and inflicts a few photogenic slashes on Lee's torso. The finale of this scene is a borrowing from the end of *The Lady from Shanghai* (1948) as the two fight it out in a bewildering hall of mirrors, before Han is finally impaled on his own spear sticking through a mirrored door.

KEY LINES

Lee doles out some gnomic advice to his protégé: 'Don't think, feel. It is like a finger pointing away to the moon. Don't concentrate on the finger or you will miss all that heavenly glory.'

Han: 'It is defeat that you must learn to prepare for.'
Williams: 'Man, I don't waste my time. When it comes, I won't even notice it.'
Han: 'Oh? And how is that so?'
Williams: 'I'll be too busy looking good.'

had been a minor TV actor appearing in *Batman* and *The Green Hornet* before moving to Hong Kong to become an instant cult star. It is possible, given the success of this film, that Lee and the genre in which he became a success would have moved into the mainstream, at least briefly. As it is he will remain fixed in the minds of his followers as a charismatic cult icon.

In *Raiders of the Lost Ark* (1981), in a famous joke, Indie is confronted by a baddie in the market chase, who dazzles the hero with a display of threatening sword play. An unmoved Jones simply pulls his gun and shoots the man dead. The crucial problem in all martial arts films is the credibility of unarmed

ERASERHEAD

US, 1976, 89 MINS

D DAVID LYNCH; **PR** DAVID LYNCH; **SC** DAVID LYNCH; **PH** (BW) FREDERICK ELMES; **SD** ALAN R. SPLET AND DAVID LYNCH; **PIC ED** DAVID LYNCH; **SD ED** ALAN R. SPLET

CAST JACK NANCE (HENRY SPENCER), CHARLOTTE STEWART (MARY X), ALLEN JOSEPH (MR X), JEANNE BATES (MRS X), JUDITH ANN ROBERTS (BEAUTIFUL GIRL ACROSS THE HALL), LAUREL NEAR (LADY IN THE RADIATOR), JACK FISK (MAN IN THE PLANET), DARWIN JASTON (PAUL), NEIL MORAN (THE BOSS), HAL LANDON JR. (PENCIL MACHINE OPERATOR), JENNIFER LYNCH (LITTLE GIRL), PEGGY LYNCH AND DODDIE KEELER (PEOPLE DIGGING IN THE ALLEY), V. PHIPPS WILSON ('MR ROUNDHEELS', LANDLADY)

THE STORY Henry is a man with strange dreams of a celestial body, a tiny foetal creature and a man with a scarred face operating levers in a shadowy room. He has dinner with the unusual parents of his friend Mary. Mary gives birth to a mutant baby and moves into Henry's apartment. The constant whimpering of the baby drives Mary out of the flat. A woman with lumpy jowls walks on to the stage behind Henry's radiator, and treads on stringy foetuses thrown onstage. Mary returns and as she sleeps, Henry retrieves stringy foetuses that she is exuding and tosses them against the wall. Henry meets the woman from across the hall. They embrace and descend into a milky liquid. The woman on the stage sings a song. Henry imagines his head being detached and made into pencil-top rubbers. Back in the apartment Henry removes the bandages which had covered the baby below the neck, and plunges a pair of scissors into its neck. Thick effluent pours from the wound and the baby's neck stretches out. A hole is blown in the planet, the man in the shadowy room pulls on his levers and Henry hugs the jowly woman behind the radiator.

THE FILM David Lynch is a cult director. He is a true auteur with a cinematic vision inspired by the workings of his own bleakly fecund imagination. His films are characterized by a prevailing mood of moral confusion and darkness, urban alienation and disconcerting noises. Lynch created his darkest and most fully realized film with *Eraserhead*. Like all his best work it has a strongly autobiographical basis with Lynch coming up with the notion of the hideous mutant baby from his own experience of his daughter Jennifer, who suffered from club feet as a child. The film is in part an extended and deeply unsettling essay on

▲ *ERASERHEAD* Jack Nance (Henry) trapped in Lynch's nightmarish fable of fatherhood amid a bleak industrial landscape.

the nightmare of fatherhood, or at least a specific experience of fatherhood, and a revulsion at the anatomy of sex and procreation. Henry is so disturbed and displaced by the bleating mutant that in his nightmare the baby grows out from his trunk, supplanting his own head, his whole identity. Lynch would continue to explore ideas of isolation, freakishness and tortured, grim sexuality in his other two masterpieces *The Elephant Man* (1980) and *Blue Velvet* (1986). He still directs films occasionally, and has ventured into the TV world with the typically cultish *Twin Peaks* series.

ODD/SALIENT FACTS The film was partly financed by Sissy Spacek. Hal Landon Jr., who plays the Pencil Machine Operator, later played Ted's father Captain Logan in both *Bill and Ted* films. Lynch is obsessively secretive about all aspects of the elongated shoot, especially the mechanics of the mutant baby. When asked about the genesis of the child, Lynch has at different times responded: 'It was born nearby' and 'Maybe it was found.' The film, shot entirely at night, was five years in the making, which should have created an impossible strain in the relationship between director and star. Luckily in Jack Nance, Lynch found someone he described as 'a zero-motivated actor'. Nance's requirements for entertainment for the hours, days and weeks between takes were nothing beyond a room and a chair. One of the defining qualities of David Lynch's work is his use of sound. *Eraserhead* is never silent, filled with the amplified noises of shrieks and moans, sinister laughing, even eye rubbing. At its quietest, the industrial vibration recedes to a background hum. In John Alexander's *The Films of David Lynch*, the director says:

> There's not one particular kind of sound that I like but if I had to pick a category it would be factory sounds. I like the power of them and it makes a picture in my mind … I like the idea of factories and factory life probably because I don't know that much about them. I can just imagine a world and it leads to a bigger place where many strange and beautiful things can happen.

MEMORABLE MOMENTS The scene in which Henry visits Mary and her parents. The salad is tossed by immobile grandma, by mother placing the bowl in her lap, the spoons in her hands, and then manipulating her hands to mix the salad. Mary's father, Mr X has bought miniature man-made chickens, the 'strangest darn things'. He advises Henry to: 'Just cut 'em up like regular chickens.' When he does they begin to ooze blood and vibrate. Mary's mother in turn starts to squeal, gets up from the table and leaves the room.

KEY LINES

Henry is accosted by Mrs X who asks him if he has had sexual intercourse with her daughter.
Mrs X: 'There's a baby at the hospital…'
Mary: 'Mom.'
Mrs X:'… and you're the father.'
Mary: 'Mother, they're still not sure it is a baby.'

THE EXORCIST
US, 1973, WARNER/HOYA, 122 MINS

D *WILLIAM FRIEDKIN;* **PR** *NOEL MARSHALL;* **SC** *WILLIAM PETER BLATTY (FROM HIS NOVEL);* **PH** *(METROCOLOR) OWEN ROIZMAN;* **M** *KRZYSZTOF PENDERECKI, HANS WERNER HENZE, GEORGE CRUMB, ANTON WEBERN, MIKE OLDFIELD, JACK NITZSCHE;* **ED** *JORDAN LEONDOPOULOS*
CAST *ELLEN BURSTYN (CHRIS MACNEILL), MAX VON SYDOW (FATHER MERRIN), LEE J.COBB (LT. WILLIAM KINDERMAN), KITTY WINN (SHARON SPENCER), JACK MACGOWRAN (BURKE DENNINGS), JASON MILLER (FATHER DAMIEN KARRAS), LINDA BLAIR (REGAN MACNEILL), WILLIAM O'MALLEY (FATHER DYER), MERCEDES MCCAMBRIDGE (VOICE OF THE DEVIL)*

THE STORY In a prologue, Jesuit archaeologist Father Damien on a dig in Northern Iraq discovers a medallion depicting Mary and the baby Jesus near a figurine of a demon. The setting swiftly cuts to Georgetown, Washington DC, where movie star Chris MacNeill lives with her twelve-year-old daughter Regan while making a film called *Crash Course* on the campus of the Catholic Georgetown University, directed by an alcoholic Englishman, Burke Dennings. Chris is soon disturbed by odd noises in the attic and Regan reveals she and an imaginary friend have played with an Ouija board. Regan's conduct deteriorates, objects fly around her room, and she utters gross obscenities in a strange voice. Doctors operate on her, but she deteriorates further. When Burke Dennings, the film director, dies on the steps outside the MacNeill home, homicide cop Lt. Kinderman enters the scene.

Meanwhile Father Karras SJ, counsellor at Georgetown, is losing his faith and is guilty about his mother dying in a paupers' hospital. Baffled doctors suggest exorcism in Regan's case, and Chris is put in touch with Karras, who is joined by Father Merrin. During nocturnal exorcism, Merrin and Karras are subjected to physical and verbal abuse and Merrin has a fatal heart attack. When the furious Karras attacks Regan, the evil spirit leaves her body for his and he leaps to his death. Regan recovers, remembers nothing, and leaves town with her mother, who presents Karras's superior with the silver medallion Father Merrin found in Iraq.

I'm telling you that that person up there isn't my daughter.'

83

THE FILM Five of the six national newspaper critics gave *The Exorcist* a black spot – 'indicates antipathy' – in *Monthly Film Bulletin*, but the public embraced it and made it a box-office success. But it was no feel-good movie. Stories appeared in the papers of people becoming obsessed with the film and others rushing from the cinema as if possessed. It had been preceded by numerous pictures involving transactions with the devil (most famously Polanski's *Rosemary's Baby*, 1958) and many others followed, among them *The Omen* trilogy. But none had, or has had, the visceral appeal of *The Exorcist*. Friedkin's picture is both obscure and up-front, its background unexplained and dramatic ellipses accompanied by gross-out scenes of Regan

▲ *THE EXORCIST The ironic surreal image of Father Merrin confronting the ultimate evil in suburban Washington DC.*

splattering her interrogators with streams of green goo and obscene abuse that would set the special effects agenda for the next two decades.

The low-key lighting makes Washington DC look sinister and menacing. This is an insecure world, between the American withdrawal from Vietnam and the fall of Saigon, and Nixon wrestling with his personal devils. Chris MacNeill is out of a bad marriage but her daughter is attached to her Rome-based, uninvolved father. Chris despises the film she's appearing in and whose director is an alcoholic. The guilt-ridden Father Karras is losing his faith while his Jesuit colleagues have made too easy an accommodation with secular society.

Crude as it often is, *The Exorcist* touched a nerve at Watergate time. It gets below our rational guard, asking us how evil might insinuate itself within the complacencies of our society. In *Eichmann in Jerusalem* (1963), Hannah Arendt coined the phrase 'the banality of evil'; *The Exorcist*, as melodramatic metaphor, suggests that in our daily lives evil may customarily propose itself in apparently banal terms.

ODD/SALIENT FACTS Blatty, hitherto author of comic works, was inspired by a newspaper item he read while at Georgetown University, about a 14-year-old boy disturbed after using a Ouija board. Max von Sydow's performance was based on the Jesuit theologian Pierre Teilhard de Chardin (1881–1955). During the filming nine people associated with the film died, among them Jack MacGowran and von Sydow's brother, and a request was made to exorcise the set. People at early screenings vomited and went into convulsions, and though the film was briefly available on video in Britain it was subsequently banned by British censors to prevent adolescent girls from seeing it alone in bed.

MEMORABLE MOMENTS Father Merrin confronting the demonic statue in the Iraqi sunset.

Regan's head twisting through 360 degrees.

The arrival of Father Merrin in Washington, silhouetted against the MacNeill's house at night, a shot influenced by a Magritte painting.

Father Karras throwing himself through Regan's bedroom window.

KEY LINES

Regan, stabbing herself in the crotch with a crucifix: 'Let Jesus fuck you.'

Chris MacNeill: 'I'm telling you that that person up there isn't my daughter.'

Father Merrin: 'The demon is a liar. He would like to confuse us, but he will also mix lies with the truth to attack us. The attack is psychological and powerful, so don't listen. Remember that, do not listen.'

FANTASIA
USA, 1940, DISNEY/RKO, 120 MINS

D (STORY) JOE GRANT, DICK HUEMER, (INDIVIDUAL MUSIC NUMBERS) SAMUEL ARMSTRONG, JAMES ALGAR, BILL ROBERTS, PAUL SATTERFIELD, HAMILTON LUSKE, JIM HANDLEY, FORD BEEBE, T. HEE, NORM FERGUSON, WILFRED JACKSON; **MD** EDWARD H. PLUMB **D** BEN SHARPSTEEN
CAST DEEMS TAYLOR, LEOPOLD STOKOWSKI AND THE PHILADELPHIA SYMPHONY ORCHESTRA

SYNOPSIS Deems Taylor, musicologist and resident presenter of the New York Symphony Orchestra's network radio broadcasts, introduces the film as the musicians take their place and tune up. Stokowski mounts the podium and lifts his baton for:

1. 'Toccata and Fugue in D Minor' by J. S. Bach accompanied by abstract images influenced by Kandinsky and avant-garde cinema.

2. 'The Dance of the Sugar Plum Fairy' from Tchaikovsky's *Nutcracker Suite*, illustrated by fairies, mushrooms, flowers, fish and cutie snowflakes dancing.

3. Paul Dukas's 'The Sorcerer's Apprentice' featuring Mickey Mouse as the magician's hubristic assistant who draws on his master's powers to launch an unstoppable batallion of brooms fetching buckets of water, threatening to drown the Sorcerer's home. The Sorcerer awakes to banish the intruders and chastise Mickey. At the end of the piece Mickey climbs up to the podium and shakes hands with Stokowski.

4. Part 1 of the suite of Igor Stravinsky's ballet *The Rite of Spring*, the film's only work by a living composer. This has little to do with the sensational 1913 presentation in Paris by the Russian Ballet, when the combination of peasant fertility ceremonies and a dissonant, arhythmic score produced a near-riot. The Disney version (at the risk of offending fundamentalists) traced the geological creation of our planet, the development of life, the battles and extinction of the dinosaurs, and the resurgence of the world.

5. Beethoven's Sixth Symphony (the Pastoral) rendered as a campus picnic on Mount Olympus attended by bra-busting nymphs, preening sports-squad centaurs and a jocular Bacchus.

6. Ponchielli's 'Dance of the Hours' from the opera *Gioconda*, a ballet performed with comic grace and restrained ferocity by hippos, alligators, elephants and ostriches, animals not noted for their dexterity.

7. Moussorgsky's 'A Night on Bald Mountain', [sic] a gothic *Walpurgisnacht* in which spirits rise from the grave to make obeisance to the Black God, Tchernobog, gives way to Schubert's 'Ave Maria' as dawn breaks. Evil draws back into its lair, and trails of candles bear light out into the countryside.

THE FILM Animated films are probably the most labour-intensive activity since the Pyramids were built, and Walt Disney is one of the greatest, most complex artists of this century. *Fantasia* was its most ambitious picture. Four years in production, it was not only made for adult audiences but in a stereo-sound system for which no cinemas were equipped. *Fantasia* runs the gamut from the kitsch of the Beethoven, which Stokowski loathed, to the magnificent handling of *The Rite of Spring*, which was praised by the astronomer Edwin P. Hubble and the biologist Julian Huxley. Stravinsky held his tongue at the time but later called Stokowski's conducting 'execrable' and said of the animation: 'I will say nothing about the visual complement as I do not wish to criticize an unresisting imbecility.' The movie is, of course, locked in the visual ideas and social attitudes of its time

and has a reverential attitude towards high art. It is also sentimental and cute, especially in the traditional Disney preoccupation with maternal love. But in a disturbing and stimulating fashion the film expresses Disney's vision of a world torn between stability and chaos, the former being symbolized by home, the latter by metamorphosis. His feeling, or fear, that anything can readily become anything else varies from the playful to the terrifying. In *The Nutcracker* thistles become cossack dancers, toadstools turn into mandarins; in 'A Night on Bald Mountain' [sic] men are transformed into demons, giving this penultimate sequence a nightmare quality that the pallid 'Ave Maria' cannot obliterate.

Patronized by many critics and disappointing popular audiences that had rigid expectations of a Disney product, the film initially failed. Along with *Citizen Kane*, which opened a few months later, it was one of Hollywood's great 'flops d'estime' of

▼ *FANTASIA* The young rodent apprentice, in thrall to the Disney work ethic, tries to out-sorcer his master.

the early 1940s. Like Welles's masterpiece it became a cult movie, and it has never quite lost that status. For the drug generation of the late 1960s and '70s it was a trip film to get high on, like Kubrick's *2001*.

ODD/SALIENT FACTS Disney drifted accidentally into *Fantasia*, while planning a comic short based on Dukas's 'Sorcerer's Apprentice' to revive the flagging fortunes of Mickey Mouse. An encounter with Stokowski launched the movie. Stokowski was devoted to bringing classical music to a mass public and saw a collaboration with Disney as a great opportunity. According to one ex-employee Walt couldn't even pronounce the names of Bach ('Batch') and Beethoven ('Beath-uven'). Made at great expense with Stokowski conducting a pick-up Los Angeles band, the 'Sorcerer's Apprentice' film was too long and too expensive to be put out on its own. When the movie took off as a two-hour feature, the Philadelphia Orchestra, which he had conducted from 1912 to 1938, was brought in. The film was cut from 116 to 81 minutes in the States and released in a double-bill with a Western. In wartime Britain it fared better, though it couldn't be shown in stereo.

KEY LINES

A dialogue following *The Sorcerer's Apprentice*:
Mickey Mouse: 'Mr Stokowski. Mr Stokowski. [Whistling to attract attention] My congratulations, sir.'
Leopold Stokowski: 'Congratulations to you, Mickey.'
M.M.: 'Gee thanks. Well so long. I'll be seeing you.'
L.S.: 'Bye.'

FAREWELL MY LOVELY (AKA MURDER, MY SWEET)

US, 1944, RKO, 95 MINS

D EDWARD DMYTRYK; **PR** ADRIAN SCOTT; **SC** JOHN PAXTON (FROM RAYMOND CHANDLER'S NOVEL FAREWELL, MY LOVELY; **PH** (BW) HARRY J. WILD; **ED** JOSEPH NORIEGA; **M** ROY WEBB **CAST** DICK POWELL (PHILIP MARLOWE), MIKE MAZURKI (MOOSE MALLOY), CLAIRE TREVOR (VELMA VALENTO/HELEN GRAYLE), ANNE SHIRLEY (ANN GRAYLE), MILES MANDER (MR GRAYLE), DOUGLAS WALTON (LINDSAY MARRIOTT), OTTO KRUGER (JULES AMTHOR), DON DOUGLAS (LT. RANDALL), PAUL PHILLIPS (DET. NULTY), RALF HAROLDE (DR SONDERBORG), ESTHER HOWARD (MRS FLORIAN)

THE STORY Los Angeles private detective Philip Marlowe, his eyes bandaged, is being interrogated by Lt. Randall and others about a series of murders. In an extended flashback he explains how a recently released convict, the dim-witted giant Moose Malloy, hired him to find Velma Valento, his lover, whom he hasn't seen since he went to jail eight years back. Marlowe tracks down Jessie Florian, the alcoholic widow of the man who employed Velma as a singer. He is next hired by the prissy artist Lindsay Marriott, who's involved in the return of a stolen necklace and needs a bodyguard. Marlowe is knocked out, Marriott is murdered, and Marlowe is brought in for questioning. Ann Grayle, a millionaire's daughter, shows interest in his investigations. Visiting the Grayle mansion in Brentwood he meets Grayle and his much younger wife, Helen. He is dragged to quack psychologist Amthor's apartment, knocked out again and taken to a private hospital to be given truth drugs. Amthor is involved in blackmail and sets up rich women as targets for Marriott, a gigolo and thief. Helen Grayle is Moose's long-lost Velma, wanting to protect her new identity. In a final showdown at the Grayles' beach house, Helen is killed by her husband, who in turn kills and is killed by Moose Malloy, who's already murdered Amthor. Ann Grayle, a witness to the killings, clears Marlowe of all charges. She

'She was as cute as lace panties, a redhead.'

accompanies him home, and they kiss in the back of a taxi.

THE FILM *Farewell My Lovely* is double-distilled *film noir* set in a decadent Los Angeles of phoneys and criminals, old money protecting family skeletons. Linking high and low is Velma/Mrs Grayle, ex-mistress of a criminal, present wife of a patrician and, as played by Claire Trevor, one of the screen's greatest *femmes fatales*. Hardboiled, wise-cracking, incorruptible Philip Marlowe is played by lightweight musical comedy star Dick Powell. The role changed the direction of Powell's career, and he became one of the screen's new tough guys. 'It ended my ten-year effort to escape musical', he said. 'Offers for hardboiled roles poured in after the picture was released and a new career was opened for me.' The film also provided Edward Dmytryk with his first major opportunity as director.

The movie rights to *Farewell My Lovely* had been acquired by RKO for $2,000 and turned into the B-movie *The Falcon*

Takes Over (1942), featuring George Sanders. The success of Warner Brothers' *The Maltese Falcon* (1941) and the word that Chandler was working at Paramount on an adaptation of James M. Cain's *Double Indemnity* persuaded RKO that an A-picture of *Farewell My Lovely* might be profitable, and so Dick Powell became the screen's first Philip Marlowe. Many still think him the best, though Chandler's ideal actor for the role was Cary Grant and Humphrey Bogart was his favourite among those who played him in his lifetime.

Odd/salient facts The film was premiered in the States as *Farewell My Lovely*, but fearing audiences would think it a Powell musical, RKO at the last minute decided to release it as *Murder My Sweet*. Chandler's reputation was much greater in Britain where it was shown under the original title. Edward Dmytryk and the film's producer, Adrian Scott, were both members of the Communist Party and as two of the 'Hollywood Ten' they went to jail in the late 1940s for refusing to answer questions before Un-American Activities Committee. In 1975 there was another first-rate version of *Farewell My Lovely*, directed by Dick Richards, starring Robert Mitchum as Marlowe, Charlotte Rampling as Velma, and pulp novelist Jim Thompson as Mr Grayle. Dr Sonderberg and Jules Amthor were conflated into the lesbian brothel owner Frances Amthor.

▼ *Farewell My Lovely* Dick Powell, the screen's first Marlowe, ignites femme fatale Claire Trevor.

Memorable moments The blindfolded Marlowe being interrogated by the cops in a room illuminated by neon lights from across the street.

Dick Powell evoking his days as a hoofer with a little hopscotch dance on the chequered hall floor of the Grayle mansion.

Marlowe's expressionist nightmare in which he's pursued through a succession of identical doors by a man with a hypodermic syringe.

Key lines

Moose on Velma: 'She was as cute as lace panties, a redhead.'

Marlowe: 'I caught the blackjack behind my ear. A black pool opened up at my feet. It had no bottom.'

Ann: 'I don't think you know which side you're on.'
Marlowe: 'I don't know which side anyone's on, I don't even know who's playing today.'

Mrs Grayle: 'This will be the first time I ever killed someone I knew so little and liked so well.'

FAT CITY
US, 1972, Rastar/Columbia, 96 mins
D John Huston; **PR** Ray Stark; **SC** Leonard Gardner (from his own novel); **PH** (Eastmancolor) Conrad Hall; **ED** Margaret Booth; **M SUP** Marvin Hamlisch **CAST** Stacy Keach (Billy Tully), Jeff Bridges (Ernie Munger), Susan Tyrrell (Oma), Candy Clark (Faye), Nicholas Colosanto (Ruben), Art Aragon (Babe), Curtis Cokes (Earl), Sixto Rodriguez (Lucero), Billy Walker (Wes), Wayne Mahan (Bufford), Ruben Navarro (Fuentes)

The story Stockton, an inland town in Central California. The drunken, 29-year-old ex-boxer Billy Tully sees 18-year-old Ernie Munger punching a bag in the YMCA, spars with him and tells him to see his former manager, Ruben. Believing he might have a white heavyweight contender on his hands, Ruben arranges several amateur fights for Ernie. But Ernie marries Faye, his teenage girlfriend, and gives up boxing. Meanwhile Billy

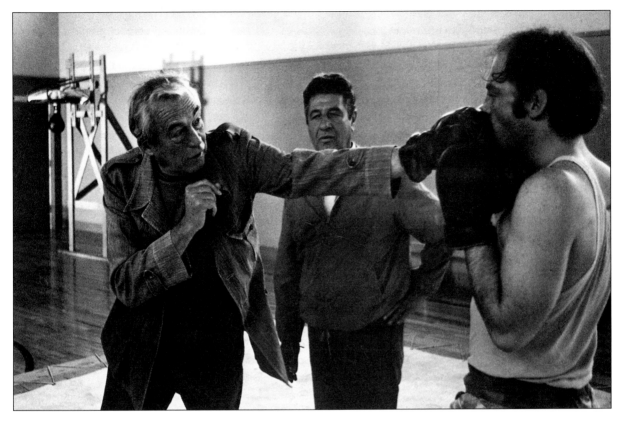

▲ *FAT CITY* Ex-champ John Huston shows Stacey Keach how to throw a straight left.

moves in with Oma, a helpless alcoholic whose black husband is doing time, and who works as a casual agricultural labourer. Ernie and Billy meet up again labouring in the fields and both decide to return to the ring. Ruben takes them both on and persuades Billy to leave Oma. Ernie wins his first professional fight in the same bill in which, as the chief attraction, Billy narrowly defeats an ailing Mexican by technical knockout. But Billy's eye is badly damaged, his cut of the purse is a mere $100, and in disgust he takes to drink and stops fighting. Some while later, a drunken bum, Billy meets Ernie who's now a father and has several minor wins to his credit. They have a cup of coffee together, sitting in silence at the counter.

THE FILM After years largely devoted to empty big-budget movies with major stars, John Huston made this small-scale, superbly acted minor masterpiece. A critical success that the general public rejected as too downbeat, *Fat City* replaced

Beat the Devil as the cult Huston movie. It's his only picture dealing with one of his great passions, prizefighting, and it examines the theme running through his best work – the pursuit of illusory dreams and the way we always finish up as losers. The film's title is a slang term for a low-life dreamer's golden paradise or the idea of having made it. Unlike most boxing pictures, *Fat City* isn't an indictment of the brutality, degradation and corruption of the fight game (though these issues are touched on); it springs from a love of boxing and a respect for its practitioners. Moreover the hopeless dreamers – Ruben the manager and Billy the fighter – are small men living in an undistinguished town with no real prospects of getting into the big time. By the end Ernie seems to have set aside his illusions to settle for points decisions in unimportant bouts. The movie has a documentary feeling in its treatment of the agri-business and of gymnasium life, and it makes great play of the contrast between the dark interiors of Stockton's seedy bars and the bright, piercing sunlight of the world outside. The film makes big, unsignalled leaps in time from sequence to sequence, and

FIVE EASY PIECES

US, 1970, BBS PRODUCTIONS, 98 MINS

D BOB RAFELSON; PR BERT SCHNEIDER; SC ADRIEN JOYCE (FROM A STORY BY RAFELSON AND JOYCE); PH (COL) LASZLO KOVACS; ED CHRISTOPHER HOLMES, GERALD SHEPPARD; M PIANO WORKS BY CHOPIN, MOZART AND BACH PLAYED BY PEARL KAUFMAN, COUNTRY AND WESTERN SONGS SUNG BY TAMMY WYNETTE CAST JACK NICHOLSON (ROBERT EROICA DUPEA), LOIS SMITH (PARTITA DUPEA), RALPH WAITE (CARL FIDELIO DUPEA), WILLIAM CHALLEE (NICHOLAS DUPEA, THEIR FATHER), KAREN BLACK (RAYETTE DIPESTO), SUSAN ANSPACH (CATHERINE VAN OST), BILLY 'GREEN' BUSH (ELTON), FANNIE FLAGG (STONEY), HELENA KALLIANIOTES (PALM APODACA), TONI BASIL (TERRY GROUSE), SALLY ANNE STRUTHERS (BETTY), MARLENE MACGUIRE (TWINKY), JOHN RYAN (SPICER), LORNA THAYER (WAITRESS)

THE STORY Bobby Dupea works as an oilrigger in Southern California and lives in a dilapidated frame house with Rayette, a good-hearted, dim-witted waitress. He spends most of his time drinking and bowling with his workmate Elton and Elton's wife Stoney. Bobby is a professional pianist in flight from his cultured family, and crisis comes when Rayette becomes pregnant, Elton is arrested for jumping bail, and Bobby learns his father has suffered two strokes and is dying. He decides to visit the family home on an island in Puget Sound in the Pacific North West and reluctantly takes Rayette with him. They give a lift to an aggressive lesbian couple heading for Alaska to escape civilization. Bobby leaves Rayette at a motel and joins his family – sister Partita, a neurotic pianist, his speechless father attended by a male nurse, his supercilious violinist brother Carl, and Carl's pianist fiancée, Catherine. While Carl is away Catherine urges Bobby to play Chopin for her, and they finish up in bed. Rayette turns up and is out of place. There is a row when some pretentious visitors annoy Catherine, patronize Rayette, and drive Bobby into a furious denunciation. The following day

▼ *FIVE EASY PIECES Impromptu concert performance by déraciné Jack Nicholson caught in a Californian tail-back.*

Bobby attempts to talk to his father about his problems, before driving off. At a filling station, Bobby slips away, leaving his car and wallet for Rayette as he hitches a lift from a truck-driver heading north into the wilds of Canada.

THE FILM *Five Easy Pieces* is the best of the six Rafelson-directed pictures Nicholson has appeared in, and his performance confirmed his star status, Bobby laying the basis for the roles of his maturity. Bobby exemplifies the rebellious mood of the Vietnam War era, but *Five Easy Pieces* transcends its times to present a superb portrait of an American malcontent. The oppressively overcultured world of the Dupea family is sharply contrasted by art director Tobe Rafelson with the garish blue-collar culture of trailer parks, bowling alleys and diners. On the soundtrack there is nothing between Bach, Chopin and Mozart on the one hand, and Tammy Wynette's declamatory C&W songs on the other. There is in fact an imbalance in the film, as in cinematic terms the world of oil rigs and trailer parks is more attractive than the claustrophobic Dupea household, and the brash, sensual Karen Black is more inviting than the repressed Susan Anspach. The classical piano pieces can't compete with the driving up-front appeal of Wynette singing about standing by your man and D-I-V-O-R-C-E. To middle-class audiences in 1970 she was a liberating force, an introduction to the hard-hat blues of Nashville. Bobby flees from the emotionally chilly family to the sentimental trailer-park ambience of Rayette and Elton, and ends up rejecting both. The ending is one of the toughest, most uncompromising in American cinema.

ODD/SALIENT FACTS The roadside diner 'No substitutions' scene was inspired by screenwriter Joyce's seeing an aggressive, young actor doing a similar routine in a Sunset Strip restaurant. She later came to know him as Jack Nicholson.

MEMORABLE MOMENTS Bobby getting mad in an early morning traffic jam, leaving his car, jumping on to a removal truck and playing Chopin on an upright piano.

Bobby's reunion with his sister in a Los Angeles recording studio.

The conversations with the two women heading for Alaska.
Bobby trying to order in the roadside diner.

The tracking shot taking in the cultural family environment during his performance of Chopin.

> **'You play that thing one more time and I'm going to melt it down into hairspray.'**

Bobby's conciliatory speech to his unresponding father on a frosty promontory.

The final long take as Bobby heads off, leaving Rayette with his wallet and the clapped-out car.

KEY LINES
Bobby to Rayette about 'Stand By Your Man': 'You play that thing one more time and I'm going to melt it down into hairspray.'

Waitress: 'I don't make the rules.'

Bobby: 'OK I'll make it as easy for you as I can. I'd like an omelette plain and a chicken salad sandwich on wheat toast. No mayonnaise, no butter, no lettuce, and a cup of coffee.'

Waitress: 'Number Two. Chicken sal san, hold the butter, the lettuce and the mayonnaise. And a cup of coffee. Anything else?'

Bobby: 'Yeah. Now all you have to do is hold the chicken, bring me the toast, and give me the check for the chicken salad sandwich, and you haven't broken any rules.'

Waitress: 'You want me to hold the chicken, huh?'

Bobby: 'I want you to hold it between your knees.'

Waitress: 'You see that sign sir? I guess you'll have to leave. I'm not going to stand any more of your smartness and sarcasm.'

Bobby: 'You see this sign?' (sweeping everything off the table)

FORBIDDEN PLANET

US, 1956, MGM, 98 MINS

D *FRED MCLEOD WILCOX;* **PR** *NICHOLAS NAYFACK;* **SC** *CYRIL HUME (BASED ON A STORY BY IRVING BLOCK AND ALLEN ADLER);* **PH** *(TECHNICOLOR, CINEMASCOPE) GEORGE J. FOLSEY;* **ED** *FERRIS WEBSTER;* **M** *('ELECTRONIC TONALITIES') LOUIS AND BEBE BARON*

CAST *WALTER PIDGEON (DOCTOR MOBIUS), ANNE FRANCIS (ALTAIRA), LESLIE NIELSEN (COMMANDER ADAMS), WARREN STEVENS (LT. 'DOC' OSTROW), JACK KELLY (LT. FAIRMAN), RICHARD ANDERSON (CHIEF QUINN), EARL HOLLIMAN (COOK)*

93

94

THE STORY 2200 AD. The US Planet Cruiser C5 7D under Commander Adams approaches the Planet Altair and lands against the protest of Doctor Mobius, who lives there with his daughter, Altaira. His spaceship, *Bellerophon*, crashed on the planet twenty years before and subsequently his wife and crew were killed. Adams and his men are met by Mobius's servant, Robbie the Robot, a multilingual genius, and they're entertained at his palatial home. They're all attracted to Mobius's beautiful daughter who has never before met any earthlings. It transpires that Altair was once occupied by the Krel, a superior race who were mysteriously wiped out, and one by one Adams's crew are killed by a strange force. It appears that this destructive enemy is a projection of the Id, first that of the Krel, now of Mobius. Only by an act of will can he confront it, killing himself, and releasing Adams to escape with Altaira from the forbidden planet before it explodes into atomic dust.

THE FILM Freud meets Shakespeare in this cunning, highly sophisticated outer-space version of *The Tempest*, in which Mobius is Prospero, Altaira a sexy 1950s Miranda, and the crucial aspects of Ariel and Caliban are divided between the loveable Robbie and the threatening Evil Force out there. Nothing dates so much as a society's idea of the future, and

▲ *FORBIDDEN PLANET Anne Francis, a young Leslie Nielsen and Walter Pidgeon attend to Robbie the Robot.*

Shakespeare's fable of a 'brave new world' here becomes frozen in a touchingly naive 1950s notion of the next millennium, and the special-effects designers draw on ideas of gracious living from *Better Homes and Gardens* and flying saucers from the covers of *Amazing Science Fiction*. But the explosion of the Id it predicted came about in the revolution of the 1960s. *Forbidden Planet* was the first time a major Hollywood studio made a movie set in outer space and it attracted an immediate cult following, paving the way for *Star Trek* and *2001*.

ODD/SALIENT FACTS Director Fred Wilcox spent his whole life working for MGM and is best-known for his first picture, *Lassie Come Home* (1943). Leslie Nielsen, the spaceship's commander, became a straight-faced figure in disaster movies (e.g. as Captain of the *USS Poseidon*) and then as star of genre send-ups (e.g. *Airplane*, *The Naked Gun*). Robbie the Robot reappeared in MGM's *Invisible Boy*. The film has one of the screen's first electronic scores, and includes one of the first scenes in which characters are 'beamed up' to their spaceship.

MEMORABLE MOMENTS Robbie's first appearance to escort the earthlings.

The cook conniving with Robbie to obtain alcohol in a similar playful way to that of the drunken butler Stephano in *The Tempest* when he goes on a spree with Caliban.

Mobius's final confrontation with the fiery Id.

KEY LINES

Mobius: 'I didn't come by him [Robbie], I created him during my first months here.'

Altaira: 'What's a bathing suit?'

Mobius: 'In times long past, this planet was the home of a mighty, noble race of beings who called themselves the Krel. Ethically and technologically they were a million years ahead of humankind. For in unlocking the meaning of nature they had conquered even their baser selves, and when in the course of eons they had abolished sickness and insanity, crime and all injustice, they turned, still in high benevolence, upwards towards space. Then having reached the heights, this all but divine race disappeared in a single night, and nothing was preserved above ground.'

Mobius: 'My evil self is at that door, and I have no power to stop it.'

Mobius, rejecting the force: 'I deny you, I give you up!'

FORCE OF EVIL

US, 1948, MGM/ENTERPRISE PRODUCTIONS, 78 MINS
D ABRAHAM POLONSKY; **PR** BOB ROBERTS; **SC** ABRAHAM POLONSKY, IRA WOLFERT (FROM WOLFERT'S NOVEL TUCKER'S PEOPLE); **PH** (BW) GEORGE BARNES; **M** DAVID RAKSIN; **ED** ART SEID

CAST JOHN GARFIELD (JOE MORSE), THOMAS GOMEZ (LEO MORSE), BEATRICE PEARSON (DORIS LOWRY), ROY ROBERTS (BEN TUCKER), MARIE WINDSOR (EDNA TUCKER), HOWLAND CHAMBERLAIN (FRED BAUER), JACK OVERMAN (JUICE), PAUL FIX (FICCO), GEORGIA BACCHUS (SYLVIA MORSE), SID TOMACK (TAYLOR), STANLEY PRAGER (WALLY)

THE STORY Ambitious young lawyer Joe Morse has risen from the New York slums to become partner in a Wall Street firm and legal adviser to gangster Ben Tucker. Morse and Tucker are planning a gambling fix forcing small-time bookies into bankruptcy so they can take over the numbers racket and turn it into a legal lottery. But Morse's elder brother Leo, who put Joe through college and runs a small illegal betting office, refuses to join. The public prosecutor is conducting a campaign to drive out the numbers racketeers, and Tucker's strong-arm partner Ficco wants a piece of the action. Joe gets Leo to work for Tucker, but then falls in love with Leo's secretary, Doris, who wants him to abandon the rackets. Joe's phone is tapped by the investigators and his partner is working against him. When Ficco's men kill Leo, Joe confronts Tucker and Ficco, kills them both, and he and Doris decide to collaborate with the crime busters.

THE FILM This quasi-biblical, quasi-Marxist movie, written in a heightened poetic manner with an anguished voice-over, was

▼ *FORCE OF EVIL* Guilt-ridden John Garfield goes 'down to the bottom of the world' to find his brother's body beneath the George Washington Bridge.

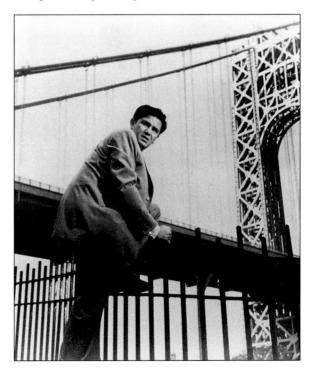

one of the first to present crime as a branch of, and metaphor for, the capitalist system. Tucker is more a ruthless tycoon than a gangster. Leo sees himself as a regular businessman and runs his set-up as if it were a family. He knows he's a crook but feels it is impossible to be honest under the present American system. Every relationship is corrupted and the film carries a terrible weight of doom. The movie gets progressively darker, David Raksin's music becomes increasingly dissonant, until the final dawn when Joe, seen from a distance, descends a great stone staircase to find his dead brother and start a new life.

Polonsky, a screenwriter and first-time director, and Garfield, a politically committed actor, both of them left-wing and Jewish, put themselves on the line with *Force of Evil*, one of the most genuinely radical pictures to come out of Hollywood. It became a cult movie after Polonsky was blacklisted for refusing to testify before HUAC in 1950 (he didn't get his name on a film again until 1968 when he scripted Don Siegel's *Madigan* and 1969 when he directed the Robert Redford Western *Tell Them Willie Boy is Here*): and Garfield, the film's moving force, died of a heart attack aged 39, his health undermined as a result of his persecution by HUAC.

ODD/SALIENT FACTS The existing copies of the film are ten minutes shorter than the director's cut to fit into a double bill. George Barnes (who won an Oscar for Hitchcock's *Rebecca*) shot the movie; to get the right look, Polonsky gave him a book of Edward Hopper's Third Avenue paintings. The film's composer David Raksin, who did the music for Chaplin's *Modern Times* and Preminger's *Laura*, requested Polonsky's permission to name him as a fellow communist before appearing as a friendly witness at a 1953 HUAC hearing. The assistant director was Robert Aldrich, one of the outstanding cult directors of the 1950s, '60s and '70s.

MEMORABLE MOMENTS Joe Morse testing his secret line to Tucker after being told it is tapped.

Morse and Doris discussing the ethics of capitalism in the back of a taxi (anticipating the taxi sequence in *On the Waterfront*).

Leo's book-keeper Bauer murdered in a café after acting as his employer's Judas.

Joe on a deserted Wall Street at twilight, walking away with a gun in his belt from a world he's renouncing.

> ## 'What do you mean, "gangsters" – it's business.'

Joe descending the steps to find his brother's body on the rock.

KEY LINES

Joe's opening statement over a high angle shot of skyscrapers dwarfing St Andrew's Church, Wall Street: 'This is Wall Street and today was important because tomorrow's July Fourth. I intended to make my first million dollars, an exciting day in any man's life. Temporarily the enterprise was slightly illegal. You see I was the lawyer to the numbers racket.'

Joe to his Harvard-educated WASP colleague who's lost everything in the Wall Street crash: 'Tucker's making me rich now, and I'm the partner that's making you rich. I wear his old school tie and you wear mine. You can buy one for yourself at lunchtime off any pushcart.'

Leo to Joe: 'All that Cain did to Abel was kill him.'

Wally, Ficco's hitman: 'What do you mean, "gangsters" – it's business.'

FREAKS

US, 1932, MGM, 90 MINS

D TOD BROWNING; **PR** IRVING THALBERG, HARRY SHAROCK; **SC** WILLIS GOLDBECK, LEON GORDON, AL BOASBERG, EDGAR ALLEN WOOLF; **PH** MERRITT B. GERSTAD; **M** GAVIN BARNS; **ED** BASIL WRANGELL

CAST OLGA BACLANOVA (CLEOPATRA), HENRY VICTOR (HERCULES), WALLACE FORD (PHROSO), HARRY EARLES (HANS), LEILA HYAMS (VENUS), ROSCOE ATES (ROSCOE), ROSE DIONE (MME TETRALINI), DAISY AND VIOLET HILTON (SIAMESE TWINS), SCHLITZE (HERSELF), PETER ROBINSON (HUMAN SKELETON), ELISABETH GREEN (BIRD WOMAN), RANDION (LARVA MAN OR LIVING TORSO), JOSEPH-JOSEPHINE (ANDROGYNE), JOHNNY ECK (TRUNK MAN), FRANCES O'CONNOR AND MARTHA MORRIS (WOMEN WITHOUT ARMS), OLGA RODERICH (BEARDED WOMAN), KOO-KOO (HERSELF), EDWARD BROPHY AND MAT-MAC HUCH (THE ROLLO BROTHERS), ANGELO ROSSITTO (ANGELENO), DAISY EARLES (FRIEDA), ZIP AND FLIP (PINHEADS)

▲ *FREAKS Director Todd Browning, the ambivalent patriarch, standing in the midst of his family of freaks.*

THE STORY The film opens as a barker tells his customers the story of his star exhibit, once a beautiful woman, known as 'the peacock of the air' . We cut to Cleopatra, a trapeze artist working in the circus of Madame Tetralini. Cleopatra is having an affair with Hercules, the strong man, but is admired by Hans, one of the dwarves, much to the annoyance of his fiancée, Frieda. When Cleo finds out that Hans has inherited a fortune she decides to seduce, marry and poison him, thus gaining possession of the money. At the wedding, the fellow freaks all sing a song and pass around a loving-cup to welcome Cleopatra to their brotherhood. A drunken Cleo is disgusted, rejects the drink and with the help of Hercules humiliates Hans. Hans falls ill, but his friends discover what is happening and decide to

save Hans and take revenge. On a stormy night as the circus caravans are on the road, the freaks pursue and kill Hercules, and then chase after Cleopatra. Cut back to the barker introducing Cleopatra, who has been transformed into a stunted human chicken.

THE FILM A lengthy prologue informs the viewer of the attitude of the film we are about to see. It talks of the historical ill-treatment of people born with physical abnormalities and makes it clear that the film wishes to avoid demonising them. This sensibility is partly a true reflection of the film's approach. We see a crude estate manager bringing the land owner along to see a group of dancing pinheads in the hope that he will share his revulsion and eject the freaks. But Madame Tetralini is there to plead their case, and the noble aristocrat is happy for them to stay on his land. The film understands that the viewer will be shocked and fascinated by the physical deformities, and shows us the human torso light and smoke a cigarette, and Johnny Eck running around on his arms. The idea is that after the shock of the difference, we get used to the humanity of the characters, the obvious sweetness of the pinheads, the romantic entanglements of the (fake) Siamese twins. We never see the characters at work in the circus, only in their normal lives. The film features some stilted performances and is slow, and crudely moralistic until the wedding feast. Here Cleopatra is given a sinister welcome into the freaks' brotherhood that clearly foreshadows the film's climax. This and the film's horrific/comic finale reverse the thrust of the film. The characters are remarginalized, given sinister powers that suggest that they live on the outside because they belong there. This dark horror that exploits the freakishness of the freaks made the film uncomfortable for audiences. It received only a limited release in the US and none at all in Britain until 1963. This delay made it seem all the more dangerous, ensuring its continuing cult status.

ODD/SALIENT FACTS In the early cuts of the film, the sequence in which Hercules is chased by the freaks ends with the clear implication that they castrate him before killing him. Browning had achieved his greatest success with *Dracula* (1931) which was filmed scene-by-scene in a Spanish-language version on the same sets and with Bela Lugosi still in the lead

▼ *FRITZ THE CAT Fritz stepping far out in one of his drug-fuelled fantasies from Ralph Bakshi's adult cartoon.*

role. Browning went on to make just three more films before retiring in 1939. He had hoped to adapt the recently published *They Shoot Horses, Don't They?*, but was frustrated. The project didn't reach the screen until Sidney Pollack's version in 1969.

MEMORABLE MOMENTS The film's two standout scenes are the menacing wedding party and the final chase in which the menace is realized. The former begins when the dwarf Angeleno stands on the table, pours a loving-cup and starts the creepy, magic song, 'Gooble-Gobble, Gooble-Gobble, We'll make her one of us.' Cleopatra reacts badly to the threat: 'You filth, make me one of you, will you?' before carrying off her diminutive husband on her shoulders while her lover joins in the fun playing a tune on the trumpet.

KEY LINES

When the circus people visit the newborn baby of the bearded woman, Phroso the clown says: 'Ain't it cute. What is it?'

With Cleopatra revealed as the mutant chicken woman, the barker concludes: 'How she got that way will never be known. Some say a jealous lover, others that it was the code of the freaks, others the storm. Believe it or not, there she is.'

FRITZ THE CAT

US, 1971, FRITZ PRODUCTIONS/AURICA, 78 MINS
D *RALPH BAKSHI;* **PR** *STEVE KRANTZ;* **SC** *RALPH BAKSHI, BASED ON CHARACTERS CREATED BY ROBERT CRUMB;* **PH** *(COL) GENA BORGHI;* **ANIM** *VIRGIL ROSS, MANUEL PEREZ, JOHN SPAREY;* **M** *ED BOGAS, RAY SHANKLIN;* **ED** *RENN REYNOLDS*
VOICES *SKIP HINNANT, ROSETTA LE NOIRE, JOHN MCCURRY, JUDY ENGLES, PHIL SEULING*

THE STORY It is the 1960s and Fritz is a horny, hippie New York City cat who plays guitar in the park with his buddies. Chatting up three women he invites them round to his apartment for an orgy. There various other friends join in a feast of sex and drugs which is interrupted by two pig cops. Fritz is chased through a synagogue before hanging out in Harlem with some black crows. He gets very stoned, has some more sex and preaches revolution before his friend gets killed in a street riot. Fritz flees with his girlfriend Winston for a journey west, but the two fall out on the road and Fritz hooks up with some revolutionary, sexually abusive types. They encourage Fritz to blow up a refinery and set him up to be killed. Finally, fully recovered in hospital he enjoys some more group sex with his girlfriends.

THE FILM Robert Crumb is a cartoonist with a bizarre talent and himself the subject of a cult documentary *Crumb* (1995). In the 1960s his already-warped visual style was forever changed by his experiments with LSD. He became the cult cartoonist of the Haight-Ashbury set with his stoner satire and strange sexual obsessions. One of his creations Fritz the Cat was taken and put into this full-length picaresque satire of the counterculture. There is the strong suspicion that those responsible for this semi-coherent if visually impressive film were taking as many drugs as the characters in the film. The satire gets rather muddled, and the humour tends to be broad at best, perhaps proving the fundamental rule that dope and humour are a bad mix. This is a period piece, something specifically of its time targeted at a very narrow audience – i.e. it barely makes any sense without drugs. It may well ultimately serve as a useful gauge. If you find the satire relevant then you know you are living in some sad hippie past and if you find it funny you are clearly far too stoned and should go straight to bed. Once a must-see for rebellious teenagers, the film now has some nostalgic appeal but is recommended for heavy-duty Cheech and Chong fans only.

ODD/SALIENT FACTS This film marked the first directorial feature for Ralph Bakshi, who had honed his skills in Terrytoons and running the New York Division of Paramount cartoons. He went on to direct the bizarre experiment in cartoon film-making, *The Lord of the Rings* (1978), in which live action was painted over for a cartoon effect, and the similar noble failure, the animation/live action fusion *Cool World* (1992).

MEMORABLE MOMENTS The opening sequence in which a passing hippie is pissed upon from a great height by a workman.

KEY LINES

One of the women patronizing the black crow on yet
   another instance of racist attitudes towards black
   people: 'Why does a great actor like James Earl Jones
   always have to play black men?'

GET CARTER★
UK, 1971, MGM, 112 MINS

D MIKE HODGES; **PR** MICHAEL KLINGER; **SC** MIKE HODGES, *BASED ON THE NOVEL* JACK'S COMING HOME *BY* TED LEWIS; **PH** (COL) WOLFGANG SUSCHITZKY; **M** ROY BUDD; **ED** JOHN TRUMPER

CAST MICHAEL CAINE (JACK CARTER), IAN HENDRY (ERIC PAICE), BRITT EKLAND (ANNA), JOHN OSBORNE (CYRIL KINNEAR), TONY BECKLEY (PETER), GEORGE SEWELL (CON MCARTY), GERALDINE MOFFATT (GLENDA), DOROTHY WHITE (MARGARET), ROSEMARIE DUNHAM (EDNA), PETRA MARKHAM (DOREAN), ALUN ARMSTRONG (KEITH), BRYAN MOSLEY (BRUMBY), GLYNN EDWARDS (ALBERT SWIFT), BERNARD HEPTON (THORPE), TERENCE RIGBY (GERALD FLETCHER), JOHN BINDON (SID FLETCHER), GODFREY QUIGLEY (EDDIE), KEVIN BRENNAN (HARRY)

THE STORY Jack Carter travels back to his native Newcastle to investigate the murder of his brother. He reimmerses himself in the city's sleazy underworld, and learns that his brother

> 'You're a big man, but you're in bad shape.'

was involved in a vice and drugs ring that was run by Kinnear and included Eric Paice, Con McArty, Brumby and Albert Swift. The sudden realization that Dorean, his niece who is also possibly his daughter, was coerced into appearing in a cheap porn film with Albert pushes Jack over the edge. He murders Albert and Brumby, watches impassively as Kinnear's girlfriend, with whom he has just slept, is drowned, sets up Kinnear to be raided by giving his brother's girlfriend a fatal overdose, and kills Paice, his brother's killer, before being shot himself by an anonymous sniper.

THE FILM This is about as bleak as the British thriller, a generally bleak genre, gets. It specifically evokes the world of Chandler, with Carter reading *Farewell My Lovely* on the train up north, but this is a parochial film. It stands alongside *Performance* as a movie that examines the brutality and darkness of the English criminal underworld and how the working and upper classes intersect. It contains the finest performance of Michael Caine's career – although you are left to wonder how a Geordie native ends up sounding like a Londoner – and shows what a powerful performer he is when he drops all

99

attempts to show any sympathetic side to his character. He is gentle only briefly to Dorean, advising her with his parting words: 'Be good and don't talk to boys.' Otherwise he kills with no sign of enjoyment or repulsion. The murder of Albert is surprisingly perfunctory and unrealistic but its drabness, ugliness and understatement fit perfectly with the general mood of the film. Carter is a 1970s man, who encourages his lover to masturbate while he talks in an early example of phone sex, and mentally undresses Kinnear's flaky girlfriend in a classically cheesy car/sex boy's fantasy montage. He is utterly ruthless in a world, and a film, that offer no escape and no hope.

ODD/SALIENT FACTS Mike Hodges has said of his film: 'The real villains come out from the cinema and say it's one of the best pictures they've ever seen. In point of fact they're proud to be portrayed accurately instead of looking like idiots.' Without *Get Carter* there would probably have been no *Long Good Friday* but even more obviously no *The Sweeney*. The two central characters of this gritty 1970s TV drama, George Carter and Jack Regan, were presumably named consciously or otherwise after Jack Carter. The film contains an odd double, with the murders of Albert and Brumby, in the violent dispatching of two men who would later emerge as TV favourites in *Minder* and *Coronation Street* respectively. In William Hall's biography, *Raising Caine*, the star discusses the importance of the film's air of authenticity: 'I modelled him on an actual hard case I once knew. I watched everything the man did. I even saw him once put someone in hospital for eighteen months. Those guys are very polite, but they act right out of the blue. They're not conversationalists about violence, they're professionals.' Michael Caine says succinctly: 'Carter was real.'

MEMORABLE MOMENTS Jack and the landlady Edna are surprised in bed by the sudden arrival of Con and Peter who have been dispatched by Gerald to bring Jack back to London. As they talk to him, Jack rolls off the bed and feels around underneath by the chamber pot and emerges with the shotgun he had hidden there. As Jack directs them out of the door, Con says with a laugh: 'Come on, Jack, put it away, you know you won't use it.' Peter adds: 'That's the gun, he means.' As they descend the stairs Con and Peter are framed by Jack's legs. The still naked Jack marches his assailants out on to the suburban street, shocking an elderly neighbour into dropping her milk bottle and provides a small distraction for a young majorette in the band practising on the street.

KEY LINES

When Jack barges into his house late at night, Brumby gets angry, but Jack puts him in his place: 'You're a big man, but you're in bad shape. With me it's a full-time job. Now behave yourself.'

THE GOLD RUSH
US, 1925, CHARLES CHAPLIN STUDIO, 74 MINS
D CHARLES CHAPLIN; **PR** CHARLES CHAPLIN; **SC** CHARLES CHAPLIN; **PH** R. H. TOTHEROE, JACK WILSON
CAST CHARLES CHAPLIN (THE LONE PROSPECTOR), MACK SWAIN (BIG JIM MCKAY), TOM MURRAY (BLACK LARSEN), GEORGIA HALE (THE GIRL), BETTY MORRISSEY (CHUM OF THE GIRL), MALCOLM WHITE (JACK CAMERON), HENRY BERGMAN (HANK CURTIS)

THE STORY It is the 1898 Klondike Gold Rush. The Lone Prospector and Big Jim McKay, a man who has discovered a fortune in gold, seek refuge in the hut occupied by Black Larsen, a violent wanted man. After drawing lots, Larsen heads off to find provisions. He stumbles upon and kills two law officers who were looking for him. Back in the hut Jim and the Prospector are reduced to eating the latter's boot. Eventually the two fight but are interrupted by the arrival of a bear which Charlie shoots, thus providing food. They go their separate ways. Jim comes across Black Larsen who has stolen his gold. The two fight, Jim is knocked out, and Larsen escapes with the gold, but falls to his death over a cliff. The Prospector arrives in the town and falls for a dance-hall girl. He invites her and her friends for New Year's Eve dinner at the shack he is looking after. He prepares an elaborate party but she forgets about him. Meanwhile a dazed Jim comes to town and recruits the Prospector to help him locate the hut and therefore the claim. This they do, narrowly avoiding death as the hut is blown to the edge of a cliff. The now rich men travel south in luxury aboard a ship on which the girl is a passenger in steerage. The Prospector poses as a tramp to be photographed for a rags-to-riches story. The girl sees him, takes him for a stowaway and protects him from the ship's officers. But the truth is revealed and all ends happily.

▶ *THE GOLD RUSH Charlie Chaplin in his iconic costume and exuding characteristic pathos as the Lone Prospector in the Klondike Gold Rush.*

THE FILM Charlie Chaplin was for a while the biggest film star and probably the most famous person in the world, yet now enjoys only minority appeal – cult status. *The Gold Rush*, his personal favourite movie, is a gem of film-making. It contains the self-pity, and sentimental, patronizing, almost masochistic attitude towards the down-trodden little man of whom he regarded himself the spokesman, that has led to him becoming a less fashionable, more marginal artist. But the simple narrative and inspired comic invention still hold an audience. With a working title of *Lucky Strike*, and then 'The Northern Story' the film entered production in early 1924 and was released in June of the following year and achieved international success.

ODD/SALIENT FACTS For the chicken sequence the special effects of Charlie becoming a chicken in Jim's eyes had to be achieved on set in the camera, using fades and Chaplin himself in the chicken costume. The original female star of the film was the 15-year-old Lita Grey. Several sequences were shot with her but soon she became pregnant by Chaplin – who reluctantly agreed to marry her – and was replaced by the little-known Georgia Hale. The film was reissued in 1942 with commentary from Chaplin. He changed the end, replacing the original climactic embrace with a fade-out as Charlie and Georgia mount the ship's stairs together.

MEMORABLE MOMENTS The Thanksgiving supper of Charlie's boot. He tends the simmering pot until he judges it perfectly cooked. He carves it, Jim getting the upper, Charlie the sole. The water is poured over the dish as gravy, the lace eaten like spaghetti and a nail offered to Jim as a wishbone.

Charlie falls instantly in love with Georgia at the saloon. She dances with him to provoke Jack. As they dance around the floor his trousers are falling down. He continually hoicks them up and then hooks them with his cane. As the two pause briefly by a table while Georgia talks to a friend, Charlie finds a piece of string which he hurriedly ties around his waist as a makeshift belt. When they recommence their dance the string turns out to be the lead of a dog, which they drag around the floor. Not realizing that they are attached to one another, Charlie repeatedly tries to kick the dog away, until a cat appears, causing the dog to chase it and pull Charlie to the floor.

As he waits pathetically for his guests to arrive on New Year's Eve, Charlie nods off and dreams of the perfect party. Instead of making a speech, he performs a little turn in which bread rolls speared with forks are used in a comical dance. At its première in Berlin, the Dance of the Rolls sequence earned the unusual accolade of a cinematic encore, with the film being rewound and replayed to rapturous applause.

KEY LINES

The hut has been blown to the edge of a precipice, and the two men inside gradually come to appreciate their perilous situation. The house is precariously balanced and the two of them are at the dangerous end when Jim says, in a line that would be adopted in the very similar scene in *The Italian Job* forty years later: 'Now listen, I've got a very good idea.'

GROUNDHOG DAY
US, 1993, COLUMBIA-TRISTAR, 101 MINS

D HAROLD RAMIS; *PR* TREVOR ALBERT, HAROLD RAMIS; *SC* DANNY RUBIN AND HAROLD RAMIS, FROM A STORY BY HAROLD RUBIN; *PH* (COL) JOHN BAILEY; *M* GEORGE FENTON; *ED* PEMBROKE J. HERRING

CAST BILL MURRAY (PHIL CONNORS), ANDIE MACDOWELL (RITA), CHRIS ELLIOTT (LARRY), STEPHEN TOBOLOWSKY (NED RYERSON), BRIAN DOYLE-MURRAY (BUSTER), MARITA GERAGHTY (NANCY), ANGELA PATON (MRS LANCASTER), RICK DUNCUMMUN (GUS), RICK OVERTON (RALPH), ROBIN DUKE (DORIS THE WAITRESS), CAROL BIVINS (ANCHORWOMAN), WILLIE GARSON (PHIL'S ASSISTANT KENNY), KEN HUDSON CAMPBELL (MAN IN HALLWAY), LES PODEWELL (OLD MAN), HAROLD RAMIS (NEUROLOGIST)

THE STORY Phil Connors, a cynical Pittsburgh weatherman, travels with his producer Rita and cameraman Larry to Punxsatawney for the annual Groundhog Day festival. There he finds himself reliving the same day, 2 February, again and again. Every day he is woken in his guesthouse room by the radio alarm playing Sonny and Cher's *I Got You Babe*. He encounters several friendly locals, including a high-school classmate, on the way to do his report from the town square. Trying to get out of town he is thwarted by a storm he failed to predict and, turning down a dinner invitation from Rita and Larry, goes to bed. He is by turns annoyed, exhilarated, bored and suicidal at the endless repetition. Then he sees the opportunity for self-improvement: he starts to help others and learns the piano as well as French and Italian and ice-sculpting. He finally lives the perfect day in which he saves at least three lives, changes

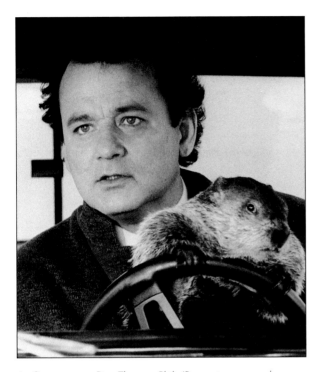

▲ *GROUNDHOG DAY* The two Phils (Punxsatawney and Connors) contemplate desperate measures to avoid the nightmare of an endlessly repeated day.

a car tyre for three old ladies, plays great jazz piano at the Groundhog Day party, becomes the most popular man in town, sleeps with Rita and wakes up redeemed on 3 February.

THE FILM Bill Murray comes from the same *Saturday Night Live* generation as Dan Aykroyd, John Belushi and Chevy Chase. Ramis, who starred alongside him in the *Ghostbusters* films, came up with the perfect vehicle for Murray's finely tuned cynical persona. It is a priceless example of a film that takes a basic premise, one idea of an endlessly repeated day, explores all its possibilities of humour and despair, and presents them in a way that is simultaneously profound and mainstream. In a sense it is a remake, or an updating of *It's a Wonderful Life* (1946) with the claustrophobia of small-town life turned into a comical nightmare. At one stage when Phil is beginning to sample the freedom and restrictions of his new life, he says to his drinking partners: 'What would you do if you were stuck in one place, and every day was exactly the same and nothing you did mattered?' One of his companions says: 'That about sums

it up for me.' Like *The Truman Show* (1998), itself a near remake of the film with spatial instead of temporal restriction, part of the idea is to suggest this plot, this extreme experience as a metaphor for everyone's life. Like those two films it is simultaneously a celebration of the simplicity and decency of small-town American life and an excoriation of its inherent claustrophobia. As in *It's a Wonderful Life* and *The Wizard of Oz* (1939) the action teeters on the edge of, and then dives straight into, the realms of nightmare only for the story to be resolved by the redemption of the cynic, the revelation that happiness is all around us and the key to finding it is mutual reliance. It is the most accomplished Hollywood comedy of the 1990s.

ODD/SALIENT FACTS *Groundhog Day* is the sixth collaboration between Murray and Ramis. Ramis attempted but failed to repeat the success of a film based on the notion of repetition with *Multiplicity* (1996), in which Michael Keaton appeared opposite Andie MacDowell and three successive clones of himself, all slightly different.

MEMORABLE MOMENTS/KEY LINES
Phil and Rita are chatting in a bar.
Rita: 'Believe it or not I studied nineteenth-century French poetry.'
Phil laughing: 'What a waste of time. (He regains his composure and improvises unsuccessfully.) I mean for someone else that would be an incredible waste of time. It's so bold of you to choose that. It's incredible, you must be a very, very strong person.'
Cut to the same scene.
Phil: 'I think people place too much emphasis on their careers. Gosh I wish we could all live in the mountains at high altitudes. That's where I see myself in five years. How about you?'
Rita: 'Oh I agree. I just like to go with the flow, see what happens.'
Phil: 'Well it's gotten you here.'
Rita: 'Uh huh. Of course it's a million miles from where I started out at college.'
Phil: 'Oh yeah? You mean you weren't in broadcasting or journalism or anything like that.'
Rita: 'Believe it or not I studied nineteenth-century French poetry.'
Phil: 'La fille qui j'aimerai / Sera comme bon vin Qui se bonifiera / Un peu chaque matin.'

103

GUN CRAZY

US, 1949, UNITED ARTISTS-KING BROTHERS, 87 MINS

D JOSEPH H. LEWIS; **PR** MAURICE KING, FRANK KING; **SC** MACKINLAY KANTOR, MILLARD KAUFMAN (FROM A SATURDAY EVENING POST STORY BY MCKINLAY KANTOR; **PH** (BW) RUSSELL HARLAN; **ED** HARRY GERSTAD; **M** VICTOR YOUNG

CAST PEGGY CUMMINS (ANNIE LAURIE STARR), JOHN DALL (BART TARE), BERRY KROEGER (PACKET), MORRIS CARNOVSKY (JUDGE WILLOUGHBY), ANABEL SHAW (RUBY TARE), HARRY LEWIS (CLYDE BOSTON), NEDRICK YOUNG (DAVE ALLISTER), RUSS TAMBLYN (BART TARE, AGED 14); DON BEDDOE (HI-JACKED CAR DRIVER), ROBERT OSTERLOH (COP OUTSIDE HAMPTON BANK), RAY TEAL (CALIFORNIA BORDER COP)

THE STORY Bart Tare, a working-class boy raised by his elder sister, has been obsessed with guns since childhood and at age fourteen is sent to reform school for stealing a revolver. Returning to his small town after four years in the school and a stretch in the army, he goes with old schoolmates to a visiting carnival where he is captivated by Annie Laurie Starr, an English sharp-shooter working for sleazy showman Packy. After he's stepped up from the audience to outshoot her, Bart joins the act, but soon Packy becomes jealous and fires them both. They marry and rapidly lose their small savings in Vegas. The ruthless, ambitious Laurie persuades the reluctant Bart, who cannot bear shooting to kill, to turn to armed robbery and they drive around America robbing banks, hotels and filling stations, becoming notorious when Packy identifies them. When the guilt-ridden Bart threatens to quit, Laurie proposes a final big job, the pay-roll from a meat-packing plant. They get away, but not before Laurie has killed two people. The FBI trace them to Los Angeles through marked notes and they go on the run, leaving the loot at a hotel. They hide out at his sister's home, where Bart's old friends, one a reporter, the other a sheriff, urge them to surrender. Instead they drive away, pursued by the police and are finally cornered in the local mountains. When Laurie is about to shoot the approaching friends, Bart kills her and is himself shot dead.

THE FILM One of a number of pictures inspired by the antics of Bonnie Parker and Clyde Barrow, *Gun Crazy* is one of the finest films of cult B-movie maverick Joseph H. Lewis. Though made on a low budget this classic *film noir* is superbly shot and edited, and in its melodramatic fashion is both blatant and subtle, involving the audience in the characters' erotic fascination with guns. This is *amour fou* American style, the sad, soft guy who expresses his manhood by carrying a gun, being dragged down a one-way road beyond the social pale by a hard-bitten *femme fatale*, old beyond her years. The 30-year-old Dall and 23-year-old Cummins were already on the way down after their early experience of stardom and this gives a sadness and desperation to their performances, which were the best either gave. The movie features a virtuoso long take from the back of the hi-jacked Cadillac, which follows in a single unbroken shot the drive up to the bank, Laurie holding a cop's attention while Bart is inside, and the getaway.

ODD/SALIENT FACTS The film was first shown in the States as *Deadlier Than the Male*, but was withdrawn a few months later and re-released as *Gun Crazy*. The script was almost entirely the work of Dalton Trumbo, one of the Hollywood Ten,

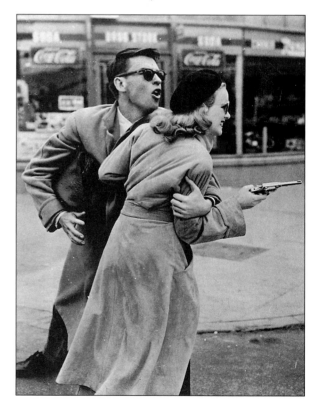

▼ *GUN CRAZY* John Dahl restrains a gun-toting Peggy Cummins after a bank hold-up.

who was cited for contempt of Congress by the House Un-American Activities in 1947 and jailed for a year. This was one of his first scripts written during his thirteen years on the blacklist, and Millard Kaufman acted as a front. In 1956, working for the same producers, Trumbo won as Oscar under the pseudonym Richard Rich.

MEMORABLE MOMENTS The fourteen-year-old Bart stealing the pearl-handled revolver from a hardware story window on a dark, rainy night and falling down in a puddle before a policeman.

Laurie and Bart shooting at matches stuck in a crown worn on their heads during their sideshow contest.

The one-shot robbery of the Hampton bank.

KEY LINES

Ruby, Bart's sister: 'It's something else about guns that gets him, it's not killing.'

Laurie: 'I told you I was no good. I didn't kid you did I? Now you know. I've been kicked about all my life. Now I'm going to kick back.'

Laurie: 'I want a guy with spirit and guts, a guy who can kick over the traces and win the world for me.'

Bart: 'We go together Laurie. I don't know why. Maybe like guns and ammunition go together.'

HARD TIMES (UK TITLE: THE STREETFIGHTER)

US, 1975, COLUMBIA, 93 MINS

D WALTER HILL; **PR** LAWRENCE GORDON; **SC** WALTER HILL, BRYAN GINDORF, BRUCE HENTSELL (FROM A STORY BY GINDORFF AND HENTSELL); **PH** (PANAVISION, METROCOLOR) PHILIP LATHROP; **ED** ROGER SPOTTISWOODE; **M** BARRY DE VORZON

CAST CHARLES BRONSON (CHANEY), JAMES COBURN (SPENCER WEED AKA 'SPEED'), JILL IRELAND (LUCY SIMPSON), STROTHER MARTIN (POE), MAGGIE BLYE (GAYLEEN SCHOONOVER), MICHAEL McGUIRE (CHICK GANDELL), ROBERT TESSIER (JIM HENRY), NICK DIMITRI (STREET), FELICE ORLANDI (LEBEAU), FRANK McRAE (HAMMERMARN), BRUCE GLOVER (DOTY), EDWARD WALSH (PETTIBON)

THE STORY During the 1930s Depression, Chaney, an unemployed man in his forties, rides a boxcar into the Deep South intending to make some money as a 'hitter' in the illegal sport of bare-knuckle boxing. He meets a charming gambler and fight promoter nicknamed Speed, who's in need of a new fighter, and they go down to New Orleans. There they meet Speed's 'permanent fiancée', Gayleen, and the middle-aged, alcoholic, Poe, a medical school dropout who's engaged to work as Chaney's second. The city's top hitter, Jim Henry, works for the wealthy businessman, Chick Gandell, who refuses a contest until Speed can put up a bet of $3,000. Speed raises the purse by borrowing at exorbitant rates from the gangster LeBeau and pitting Chaney against a Cajun champion. Meanwhile Chaney meets Lucy, whose husband is in

> **"I don't look past the next bend in the road."**

jail, and they drift into an affair. After Chaney beats Jim Henry, Speed loses most of his money in a crap game and Gandell gets a hold over him by paying the interest on his loan. Poe tells Chaney he can save Speed's life by agreeing to fight Street, the new hitter Gandell has brought from out of town. Chaney intially refuses, but at the last minute he turns up and wins a brutal contest. He gives a generous share of his winnings to Poe and Speed, and heads north on a freight train.

THE FILM *Hard Times* was the debut of writer-director Walter Hill and the first of his cult fables (others include *The Warriors*, *The Driver* and *Streets of Fire*) centring on existential heroes with no disclosed past, living by unspoken personal codes in urban (often criminal) sub-cultures. His characters reveal themselves by what they do, not what they say. Like Robert Rossen's *The Hustler* and Norman Jewison's *Cincinnati Kid*, *Hard Times* creates a private world within the interstices of American life, where hard men engage in contests and where character is as important as skill or brawn. Like Newman in *The Hustler* and McQueen is *Cincinnatti Kid* (for both of whom Hill had written screenplays), Bronson has one of his best roles: a drifting loner defined through the sport he practises and refusing to make long-term commitments. As always in Hill's movies, the tough, violent ambience is presented with considerable elegance and many of the interiors are lit to resemble paintings by Edward Hopper.

ODD/SALIENT FACTS Walter Hill's last picture as screenwriter before turning director was Sam Peckinpah's *The Getaway*, and *Hard Times* is edited by future director Roger Spottiswoode, who worked on three of Peckinpah's pictures. The film stars Peckinpah regulars Strother Martin and James Coburn. Hill's original and preferred title for the film, *The Streetfighter*, was used in Britain.

MEMORABLE MOMENTS The fights staged in deserted warehouses, empty factories and on docksides.

The lakeside Cajun party in the Bayou where Speed arranges Chaney's second fight.

Chaney breaking up a party in a pool hall as he attempts to claim the money withheld by the Cajun fighter's dishonest manager.

Chaney stretched out on his bed beneath a ceiling fan in his green-painted, ill-furnished room.

KEY LINES

Speed: 'I suppose you've been down the long hard road.'
Chaney: 'Who hasn't?'

▲ *HARD TIMES* James Coburn swallows an oyster as Charles Bronson puts his money where his fists are.

Chaney: 'I don't look past the next bend in the road.'
Speed: 'Well, you know Chick, like old momma said, next best thing to playing and winning is playing and losing.'

Chaney's exit line when asked where he's going: 'North.'

HEAT

US, 1971, SCORE/SARX, 103 MINS

D *PAUL MORRISSEY;* **PR** *ANDY WARHOL;* **SC** *PAUL MORRISSEY, BASED ON AN IDEA BY JOHN HALLOWELL;* **PH** *(COL) PAUL MORRISSEY;* **M** *JOHN CALE;* **ED** *LAN JOKEL, JED JOHNSON* **CAST** *JOE DALLESANDRO (JOE), SYLVIA MILES (SALLY), ANDREA FELDMAN (JESSIE), PAT AST (MOTEL OWNER), RAY VESTAL (PRODUCER), LESTER PERSKY (SIDNEY), ERIC EMERSON (GARY), HAROLD CHILDE, JOHN HALLOWELL, GARY KOZNOCHA, PAT PARLEMAN, BONNIE WALDER*

THE STORY Joe, a former child TV star, arrives at a Hollywood hotel. There he meets the other residents – Jessie a neurotic young woman who lives with her baby and girlfriend, two brothers who have sex with each other in their stage act – and sleeps with the motel owner to save on rent. Joe begins an affair with Jessie's mother, Sally, with whom he acted on TV. Soon Jessie, who is always demanding money from her mother, moves into Sally's mansion where Joe is already staying. Joe, who is hoping his liaison with Sally will help him professionally, begins a casual affair with Jessie. A producer friend of Sally's says he can use Joe only in the Western roles from which he is trying to break free. Joe, finding that he can't get the record deal that he was promised, is propositioned by the boyfriend of Sally's father. Declaring himself a star, Joe walks out on Sally. She follows him back to the motel, where she takes out a gun and goes to shoot him. The gun won't fire and she tosses it into the swimming pool.

THE FILM Andy Warhol's film career followed a similar, if less spectacular trajectory to his painting. He established himself as a creator of works that explored repetition and boredom as well as sexuality in the modern world, and having established a template, was able to pass the actual work on to collaborators or minions. Paul Morrissey had worked as a production assistant and camera operator on several Warhol films before working as director on *Trash* (1969). *Heat* is a camp spin on *Sunset Boulevard* (1950), complete with fading, ageing star and swimming-pool motif. The Warhol/Morrissey style as always makes it a film that is uncomfortable to watch, like a porn movie with curtailed sex scenes, or the out-takes from a substandard Cassavetes film. The camera work and lighting are equally abysmal, the editing amateurish, but somehow, something to do with the Warhol imprimatur, some genuinely off-beat humour, and the strange unreal realism make it compelling.

ODD/SALIENT FACTS Andy Warhol famously said of Sylvia Miles: 'She would attend the opening of an envelope.' The painfully stilted performance of Andrea Feldman reeks of authentic flakiness. Feldman, who also appeared in *Trash*, had been fixated on Warhol for some time and had taken to calling herself Andrea Warhola (Warhol's real surname) in the hope that he would marry her. The sequence in which she shows her cigarette burn scars to Joe is based on fact. In his definitive biography *Warhol*, Victor Bockris, the distinguished and prolific chronicler of the underground artistic elite, writes:

On one occasion she had come to the Factory, hysterical, her face covered with scabs and small round festering sores. According to one account, someone said to Warhol, 'She's very sick. Andrea should go to hospital. Did you see her face?' Warhol matter-of-factly replied, 'Well, she's putting cigarettes out on her face. She always does that.' In what had become an almost clichéd way of seeing things, Andy said she was going through a 'phase' and would get over it.

In September 1972, three weeks before the film's premiere in New York, Feldman killed herself by jumping out of a top-floor window, holding two Warhol-style icons, a rosary and a can of Coke.

▼ *HEAT Joe Dallesandro and Sylvia Miles cuddle up in this version of* Sunset Boulevard *updated and reprocessed by the Warhol factory.*

MEMORABLE MOMENTS The first sex scene between Joe and Sally in which she is continually making herself up and checking with Joe that she looks good. He is merely concerned that she will be able to help him with his career.

KEY LINES

Sally, about Bonnie: 'Do you sleep in the same room with her?'
Jessie: 'Sure, how else can I be a lesbian?'

Jessie: 'I heard you went to bed with your brother. Is that true?'
Gary: 'Yeah, but only on stage.'
Jessie: 'What do you do together?'
Gary: 'We just fool around.'
Jessie: 'Is it fun?'
Gary: 'I dunno. I guess so.'
Jessie: 'You must like it a lot, huh?'
Gary: 'Well, it's a living.'

Sally talking about Jessica: 'She can't even make a good dyke.'

Sidney, to Sally: 'You were an ageing, minor, practically unknown star … You were fantastic in every way [to Joe] but she couldn't act.'

HEAVEN'S GATE

US, 1980, UNITED ARTISTS/PARTISAN PRODUCTIONS, 219 MINS
D MICHAEL CIMINO; **PR** JOANN CARELLI; **SC** MICHAEL CIMINO; **PH** (PANAVISION/TECHNICOLOR) VILMOS ZSIGMOND; **ED** TOM ROLF; **M** DAVID MANSFIELD

CAST KRIS KRISTOFFERSON (JIM AVERILL), JOHN HURT (WILLIAM C. IRVINE), CHRISTOPHER WALKEN (NATE CHAMPION), SAM WATERSTON (FRANK CANTON), ISABELLE HUPPERT (ELLA WATSON), JOSEPH COTTEN (REVEREND DOCTOR), JEFF BRIDGES (JOHN H. BRIDGES), BRAD DOURIF (MR EGGLESTON), GEOFFREY LEWIS (WOLF TRAPPER), MICKEY ROURKE (NICK RAY), RICHARD MASUR (TULLY), TERRY O'NEILL (CAPTAIN MINARDI, US ARMY)

> 'There is only one crime in this country – to be caught.'

THE STORY In 1870 Jim Averill and Billy Irvine, sons of prominent upper-class New England families, graduate from Harvard. Twenty years later in Wyoming, Billy is a sardonic alcoholic, a member of the Stock Growers' Association that represents Eastern business interests, and Jim is US marshal of Johnson County, Wyoming, who sides with the oppressed. Infuriated by the Eastern European immigrants settling in the state and rustling their cattle with impunity, the Association, under its leader Frank Canton, draws up a death list of 125 names and hires a mercenary army of 'enforcers' to invade Johnson County. One of the people on the list is Jim's lover, the brothel owner Ella Watson, who accepts cattle in exchange for her girls' favours. Ella is also loved by Nate Champion, himself an immigrant, and one of the Association's leading hitmen. When the mercenary army arrives, Nate changes sides and is killed, Ella is raped by enforcers, and the settlers, rallied by Jim, surround the attackers. Only the arrival of the US Cavalry saves the Association's hired guns from being massacred. A little later, as they are about to marry, Jim and Ella are ambushed by gunslingers led by Canton, and Ella is killed. In an epilogue set in Newport, Rhode Island, Averill has returned to his own class and is on a luxury yacht with his upper-class wife.

THE FILM Cimino's attempt to do for the Western what his earlier populist epic, *The Deer Hunter*, had done for the war movie, went wildly over budget and is reputed to have brought down United Artists, who withdrew the 219-minute version after hostile reviews, and released it at 149 minutes to empty cinemas. It is also said to have brought an end to a period in which Hollywood auteurs prevailed over producers, and to have killed off the Western (when Costner's *Dances With Wolves* went over budget in 1990 it was dubbed 'Kevin's Gate'). The film is in fact, for all its vagueness of characterization, one of the great radical Westerns, dealing in a complex manner with the contradictions of American life and taking the conflicts in the East Coast industrial cities out into the West. Visually rich, it is a carefully patterned movie, most especially in the way it handles the so-called class traitors Averill and Champion, and like Visconti's *The Leopard*, Coppola's *The Godfather*, Leone's *Once Upon a Time in the West* and Cimino's own *The Deer Hunter*, it eschews carefully paced

▲ *HEAVEN'S GATE Brothel keeper Isabelle Huppert tries out the carriage brought to her from St Louis by Kris Kristofferson.*

narrative in favour of powerfully animated, operatic set-pieces that are often extended beyond what puritanical northern temperaments think proper.

ODD/SALIENT FACTS The film is true in spirit to the issues involved, but the actual Johnson County War of 1892 resulted in less than half a dozen deaths, one of them that of Nate Champion. John Averill, who was a rustler, and his lover Ella Watson (known as 'Cattle Kate'), were both killed by Association assassins, but in 1888. Frank Canton, was a killer turned lawman, and he lived until 1927.

In 1983, two years after the truncated *Heaven's Gate* was released, a 207-minute version appeared in cinemas, and then a 220-minute version on TV, each containing material not found in the other two.

MEMORABLE MOMENTS Averill's arrival in the bustling, smokey frontier town of Caspar, Wyoming, having delivered a convicted woman to a federal hangman in St Louis.

Canton recruiting enforcers at night from miners at a pithead. Champion executing an immigrant rustler.

The recent immigrants enjoying themselves at the Heaven's Gate roller-skating rink in Sweetwater, Wyoming.

KEY LINES

The Reverend Doctor (addressing the Harvard class of '70): 'It is the contact of the cultivated with the uncultivated. It doubly behoves us to look well to the influence we may exert of a high ideal – the education of a nation.'

Canton: 'This is no longer a poor man's country. These emigrants only pretend to be farmers. We know they are thieves, anarchists and outlaws.'

Averill: 'You're not my class, Canton, and you never will be. You'd have to die first and be born again.'

John Bridges (storekeeper/hotel owner): 'It's getting dangerous to be poor in this country.'

Capt. Minardi: 'Do you know what I really dislike about you, Jim? You're a rich man with a good name. You only pretend to be poor.'

Ella (to Jim): 'I never cheated on you. I always made Nate pay.'

A settler: 'There is only one crime in this country – to be caught'.

THE HUSTLER
US, 1961, TCF, 135 MINS

D ROBERT ROSSEN; **PR** ROBERT ROSSEN; **SC** ROBERT ROSSEN, SIDNEY CARROLL, BASED ON THE NOVEL BY WALTER TEVIS; **PH** (CINEMASCOPE BW) EUGENE SCHUFTAN; **M** KENYON HOPKINS; **ED** DEDE ALLEN

CAST PAUL NEWMAN (EDDIE FELSON), JACKIE GLEASON (MINNESOTA FATS), PIPER LAURIE (SARAH PACKARD), GEORGE C. SCOTT (BERT GORDON), MYRON MCCORMICK (CHARLIE BURNS), MURRAY HAMILTON (FINDLAY), MICHAEL CONSTANTINE (BIG JOHN), STEPHAN GIERASCH (PREACHER), VINCENT GARDENIA (BARTENDER), CLIFFORD A. PELLOW (TURK), GORDON B. CLARKE (CASHIER), ALEXANDER ROSE (SCOREKEEPER), CAROLYN COATES (WAITRESS), CARL YORK (YOUNG HUSTLER), JAKE LA MOTTA (BARTENDER)

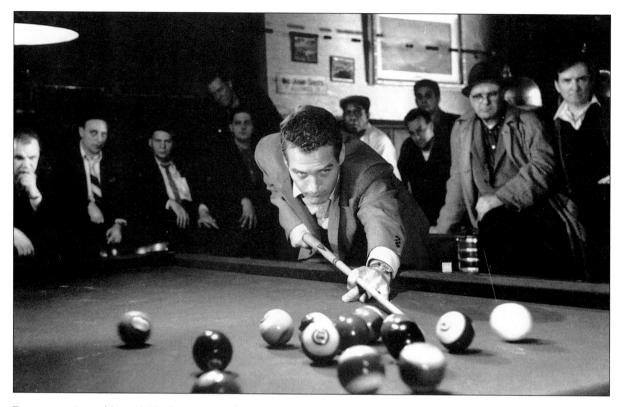

THE STORY Fast Eddie and Charlie arrive at a bar posing as a couple of travelling salesmen. They stay a while, practise a well-worked routine while playing pool and hustle the owner and the patrons. Arriving at Ames, Eddie waits for the chance to play Minnesota Fats. Fats arrives at 6 o'clock sharp, and he and Eddie play. In an epic, fluctuating 25-hour match Fats, bankrolled by Bert Gordon, triumphs. Eddie walks out on Charlie and starts a relationship with Sarah, a lame, alcoholic, part-time student. Eddie meets up with Bert Gordon who offers to become his manager but Eddie won't accept his ungenerous terms. One night the regulars in a bar break Eddie's thumbs after he has flashily hustled a young pool player. Having been nursed to recovery by Sarah, Eddie takes Bert up on his offer and the three of them go on the road. In Louisville they attend a party at the house of the wealthy Findlay where Eddie plays carom billiards and Sarah gets drunk, reacting violently to something Bert whispers in her ear. Eddie loses the money that Bert supplies and then his own, which he retrieves from Sarah's purse. When Eddie rejects Sarah, Bert bankrolls him once more and Eddie cleans up. Eddie walks back to the hotel. Sarah sleeps

▲ THE HUSTLER Paul Newman as Fast Eddie Felson lines up a shot and gets the feeling that he just can't miss.

with Bert and then kills herself. Eddie returns to Ames' pool hall, plays and beats Fats. He refuses to give Bert his share and walks out of the club knowing that he will no longer be able to play the game.

THE FILM This bleak fable of talent, compromise, doomed love, death and redemption is a profoundly autobiographical work by the director. Rossen, who had contributed to the screenplays of *The Roaring Twenties* (1939) and *The Treasure of the Sierra Madre* (1948), was badly affected by his dealings with the House Un-American Activities Committee. He had been involved with the communist party in the 1930s and at his first HUAC appearance refused to name names, but ultimately changed his mind and spilled the beans on friends and colleagues. *The Hustler* is about a man who has the talent and the passion but sells his soul and betrays the one person who really knows and loves him in a Faustian pact to gain character. Bert Gordon is specifically likened to the devil by Findlay. Eddie emerges chastened and redeemed. Some of the dialogue is a touch portentous, especially in the love scenes, but it is a wonderfully exhilarating and depressing film that blends elements of period jazzy existentialism, moody religious parable, the quality of a simply great sports movie and terrific performances from all four leads.

ODD/SALIENT FACTS Newman has been dismissive of his own performance in the film saying: 'I was just working too hard, showing too much.' Newman was nominated for an Academy Award along with Schuftan and Rossen for direction, film and screenplay (and with Carroll), Gleason, Scott and Laurie. He finally won the Oscar for best actor for his performance as Felson in Martin Scorsese's belated sequel *The Color of Money* (1986). The part of the barman in the bar where Eddie and Sarah meet for the second time is played by Jake La Motta.

MEMORABLE MOMENTS The opening sequence in which Newman plays a character playing drunk in his successful hustle of the barflies.

The scene where the reckless and unchaperoned Eddie hustles the young hustler and enrages the gang in the bar. They drag him into the adjoining room where, with Eddie's face pressed against a frosted glass window, they break his thumbs.

KEY LINES

Charlie, on entering Ames' pool hall: 'Quiet.'
Eddie: 'Yeah, like a church. The church of the good hustler.'
Charlie: 'Looks more like a morgue to me. Those tables are the slabs they lay the stiffs on.'
Eddie: 'I'll be alive when I get out, Charlie.'

Charlie, before the first game with Fats: 'How do you feel?'
Eddie: 'Fast and loose.'
Charlie: 'In the gut, I mean.'
Eddie: 'Tight, but good.'

Eddie, playing Fats: 'You know, I got a hunch, fat man. I got a hunch that it's me from here on in. "1" ball corner pocket. I mean, that ever happen to you? You know, all of a sudden you feel like you just can't miss. 'Cos I dreamed about this game, fat man. I dreamed about

this every night on the road. Five ball. You know, this is my table, man. I own it.'

Bert to Fats: 'Stick with this kid, he's a loser.'

Eddie: 'Fat man, you shoot a great game of pool.'
Fats: 'So do you, Fast Eddie.'

IF ....

UK, 1968, PARAMOUNT/MEMORIAL PRODUCTIONS, 111 MINS
D LINDSAY ANDERSON; **PR** MICHAEL MEDWIN AND ANDERSON; **SC** DAVID SHERWIN (FROM THE STORY CRUSADERS BY SHERWIN AND JOHN HOWLETT); **PH** (EASTMANCOLOR) MIROSLAV ONDRICEK; **M** MARC WILKINSON; **ED** DAVID GLADWELL **CAST** MALCOLM MCDOWELL (MICK TRAVIS), DAVID WOOD (JOHNNY KNIGHTLEY), RICHARD WARWICK (WALLACE), RUPERT WEBSTER (BOBBY PHILLIPS), ROBERT SWANN (ROWNTREE), CHRISTINE NOONAN (THE GIRL), PETER JEFFREY (HEADMASTER), ARTHUR LOWE (MR KEMP), GRAHAM CROWDEN (HISTORY MASTER), BEN ARIS (JOHN THOMAS), GEOFFREY CHATER (CHAPLAIN), MONA WASHBOURNE (MATRON)

THE STORY Set in an unnamed English public school.
1. COLLEGE HOUSE – RETURN The school assembles; prefects, 'whips', establish super-iority over new boys, 'scum'; three seniors – Travis, Knightley and Wallace – assert their uneasy independence.
2. COLLEGE: ONCE AGAIN ASSEMBLE The boys attend chapel and first lessons; the headmaster lectures sixth-formers on the role of the public school.
3. TERM TIME Travis, Wallace and Knightley discuss revolution; whip orders them to take cold baths for insolence and drinking.
4. RITUAL AND ROMANCE Phillips, a junior boy, is entranced by Wallace's gymnastic performance. Travis and Knightley go into town, steal a motorbike, pick up a girl at a café.
5. DISCIPLINE The whips administer a sadistic flogging to Travis, Wallace and Knightley.

> 'We are your new family ... help the house and you'll be helped by those in the house.'

6. RESISTANCE Travis makes a blood oath with Knightley and Wallace.

7. FORTH TO WAR The army cadet corps on manoeuvres. Travis and friends carry real ammunition and shoot the chaplain. The headmaster produces the chaplain from a drawer in his study to shake hands with the boys. The trio are assigned to clearing out the school's attics and find a cache of weapons.

8. CRUSADERS The Union Jack flies from the roof, the Establishment (a general, a bishop, a royal personage) assemble for Founder's Day ceremony in the Hall. Smoke from the floorboards creates panic, the audience flees into the quadrangle to engage in open warfare with Travis, his girlfriend, Knightley, Wallace and Phillips who target them from the roof with machine guns and grenades. The film concludes not with 'The End' but with 'If ....'

▼ *If .... Rebels Malcolm McDowell and Christine Noonan take to the school roof on Founders Day.*

THE FILM Like Eisenstein's *Battleship Potemkin*, *If ....* is a film with powerful homoerotic undertones, aiming to involve a popular audience in the visceral excitement of being a violent revolutionary. Movies like *Goodbye Mr Chips* tend to take a sentimental view of the English public school. Anderson uses it as a metaphor for a society that perpetuates snobbery, sadism and empty tradition, and functions by making people exploit each other. Although some early scenes have an almost documentary realism (Anderson made his reputation as a documentarist), the film is influenced by the surrealists and the alienation effect of Bertolt Brecht, from whom it borrows the device of the chapter headings. The switches between colour and monochrome are both Brechtian and surreal, making us aware we are watching a film, disrupting our sense of reality. Travis and company are idealistic anarchists. No mainstream film of its time took such a revolutionary position, and the film proved a rallying point for sixties rebels. It is radical rather than left-wing, directed against authority. Anderson was gay, and the film attacks the whips for their sexual exploitation of the younger boys but romanticizes the platonic relationship between Wallace and Phillips.

ODD/SALIENT FACTS The title comes from Kipling's poem, but the movie is closer to *Stalky & Co*, his novel about three rebels at an English public school. Anderson's father, like the visiting speaker in the final scene, was a general in the British army, and the movie was made at Anderson's old school, Cheltenham College. *If ....* was the first film in his trilogy about the state of Britain, and McDowell and many of the other actors appear in the two subsequent pictures, *O Lucky Man* and *Britannia Hospital*. The final scene on the roof is a homage to Jean Vigo's *Zéro de Conduite* (1933). In his 1971 film *Horizon*, Pal Gabor pays tribute to Anderson when his rebellious young hero sees *If ....* in a Budapest cinema. The 1968 Cannes Festival was abandoned out of solidarity with the protesting students in Paris. The jury of the 1969 Festival awarded the Palme d'Or to *If ....*, the film that most embodied the spirit of *les Événements* of 1968.

MEMORABLE MOMENTS Travis' first appearance, wearing a slouch hat and a scarf to conceal his new moustache.

Phillips watching Wallace perform on the parallel bars.

The sadistic punishment of Travis.

Travis firing a machine gun from the roof, echoing a magazine photograph of a black revolutionary on his wall.

KEY LINES

Housemaster: 'We are your new family ... help the house and you'll be helped by those in the house.'

Headmaster: 'Work, play, but don't mix the two.'

Headmaster: 'College is a symbol of many things. Scholarship and integrity in public office; high standards in the television and entertainment worlds. Huge sacrifice in Britain's wars. Of course some of our customs are silly; you could say that we were middle-class. But a large part of the population is in the process of becoming middle-class, and many of the middle-class's moral values are values that the country cannot do without. So we must not expect to be thanked. Education in Britain is a nubile Cinderella, sparsely clad and much interfered with.'

THE IMMORAL MR TEAS

US, 1959, PAD PRODUCTIONS, 65 MINS

D *RUSS MEYER;* **PH** *RUSS MEYER;* **PR** *PETER A. DECENZIE;*
NARR *EDWARD J. LAKSO*
CAST *BILL TEAS, ANN PETERS, MARILYN WESLEY, MISCHELE ROBERTS*

▲ *THE IMMORAL MR TEAS* Bill Teas snaps well-considered trifles on the beach to feed his fantasies.

THE STORY An unnamed Californian, around forty with a greying goatee, identified by the narrator as the typical citizen of our stressful times, emerges from his house wearing a suit and straw boater and carrying a briefcase. He passes a little girl twirling a hula-hoop who throws a stone at him. At another house he changes into orange-coloured overalls and rides around on a bicycle making deliveries. He meets a dental nurse, a secretary and a waitress in a diner, all big-breasted and apparently not wearing brassières. He visits the beach and surreptitiously photographs a photographer taking pictures of a topless model. He fantasizes about seeing the girls in the nude, and spies upon them when they frolic naked by the sea. Paying a second visit to a psychiatrist, he imagines her sitting beside the couch, pen in hand, clutching her notebook, naked except for her horn-rimmed spectacles.

THE FILM Russ Meyer (b Oakland, California 1923) began making movies as a schoolboy, was a combat cameraman with the US Signals Corps in Europe during the Second World War and is the ultimate cult film-maker . As a nudie photographer he was one of *Playboy's* first contributors (he actually married a Playmate), and for forty years he has been making self-mocking, soft-core movies about sex and violence and women with large breasts. The popularity and immense financial success of his early movies led to Hollywood invitations. But after making *Beyond the Valley of the Dolls* (1970) and *The Seven Minutes* (1971) for Twentieth Century-Fox, he retreated into idiosyncratic independent productions. The low-budget *The Immoral Mr Teas* put Meyer on the map. It has none of the violence of later Meyer pictures like *Faster Pussycat! Kill! Kill!* (1965) and it's difficult to tell whether the apparent artlessness is the product of great sophistication or of naiveté. At the time most observers thought the former, seeing the picture as a parody of Jacques Tati's Hulot films and such avant-garde American pictures as James Broughton's *Loony*

Tom. The film has no spoken dialogue, just an arch commentary about the pressures of modern society, accompanied by a tinkling jazz score.

Teas, the sad, lonely voyeur, is a hopeless innocent, anything but immoral, looking at buxom, unattainable women and feeling guilty about his obsession. At the end the film relieves him of his guilt. *The Immoral Mr Teas* is an essential link between Hollywood's post-war fetishization of the female breast and the hard-core pornography of the 1970s. In the post-war decade Jane Russell, Marilyn Monroe, Jayne Mansfield, Mamie Van Doren et al. were shown in figure-hugging clothes. Meyer removed the sweaters in 1959, leading the way to the presentation of explicit sex a dozen years later in *Deep Throat* (1972) and *The Devil in Miss Jones* (1973), hardcore pictures that became socially acceptable. His own films, by comparison, remained curiously innocuous.

ODD/SALIENT FACTS *The Immoral Mr Teas* cost under $25,000 to make and took well over a million at the box office in a year when Hitchcock's *Psycho* did well with a gross of $4m. It was the thin end of a wedge that showed there was a respectable niche audience outside the cinematic mainstream for erotic pictures with a certain wit and style. Meyer salutes the European cinema that was penetrating America without being subjected to censorship by the rigid Hays Office Code by ending his movie not with 'The End' but with a jocular 'FIN'.

MEMORABLE MOMENTS The use of the spiral device from the credits of Hitchcock's *Vertigo* to introduce Teas's fantasies.

Teas peeling a phallic banana then anxiously holding two melons to his chest as he confronts a large pair of breasts briefly exposed from a window.

Teas on a fishing expedition accidentally hooking a brassière left on the branch of a tree by one of the objects of his desire.

KEY LINES

There is no dialogue in *The Immoral Mr Teas*. The key line in the commentary comes when Teas, his voyeuristic gaze apparently liberated, observes the naked psychoanalyst in the final scene: 'on the other hand some men just enjoy being sick'.

THE INCREDIBLE SHRINKING MAN
US, 1957, U-I, 81 MINS

D *JACK ARNOLD*; **PR** *ALBERT ZUGSMITH*; **SC** *RICHARD MATHESON, FROM HIS OWN NOVEL*; **PH** *ELLIS W. CARTER*; **SP PH** *CLIFFORD STINE*; **M SUP** *JOSEPH GERSHENSON*; **ED** *AL JOSEPH*

CAST *GRANT WILLIAMS (ROBERT SCOTT CAREY), RANDY STUART (LOUISE CAREY), APRIL KENT (CLARICE), PAUL LANGTON (CHARLIE CAREY), RAYMOND BAILEY (DR THOMAS SILVER), WILLIAM SCHALLERT (DR ROBERT BRAMSON), FRANK SCANNELL (BARKER), HELENE MARSHALL (NURSE), DIANA DARRIN (NURSE), BILLY CURTIS (MIDGET)*

THE STORY Scott and Louise Carey are on a boating holiday when a cloud of dust passes over them and coats Scott's skin in its shiny residue. Some time later, Scott begins to shrink. A battery of tests reveals that his body is gradually losing its stores of nitrogen, calcium and phosphorous, apparently due to his exposure to an insecticide spray as well as the radioactive cloud. He loses his job and is forced to sell his story to a newspaper. Now only 36 inches tall he finds brief solace in a friendship with Clarice, a circus midget, and the process of shrinking is arrested. When he begins to shrink again he is forced to live in a doll's house in his own living room. One day he is attacked by his cat and seeks refuge in the cellar. In this vast landscape he must secure food from a mousetrap, battle a spider and his own existential angst before arriving at a new mystical understanding of his place within the universe.

THE FILM Though still decidedly a B-movie, this is Jack Arnold's finest film. Having directed camp classics including *It Came from Outer Space* (1953), *Creature from the Black Lagoon* (1954) and *Tarantula* (1955), he took on a project that contained elements of all of these films. The movie is roughly divided into three sections. In the first the perfect American marriage is increasingly affected by the physical practicalities of Scott's changing size. The hero's deep depression is indicative of his sense of his own emasculation. In the central section, having shrunk dramatically, Carey has to re-evaluate his world and come to terms with the change as a cellar floor becomes a vast plain, a chest of drawers a mountain and a harmless spider a

> 'Easy enough to talk of soul and spirit and essential worth but not when you're three feet tall.'

▲ *THE INCREDIBLE SHRINKING MAN* Grant Williams (Scott Carey) about to do battle with a giant spider in the hostile alien landscape that his cellar has become.

deadly predator. The story concludes with Carey's becoming suddenly verbose as he experiences his enlightenment and realizes that he does after all still exist. An effective, surprisingly intelligent film with some neat set designs and serviceable special effects.

ODD/SALIENT FACTS Screenwriter and author of the original novel *The Shrinking Man*, Richard Matheson has written widely in the science fiction and horror genres for the cinema and TV as well as novels. He wrote several screenplays for Roger Corman and, having worked on the original TV series, contributed two of the stories to the portmanteau *Twilight Zone – The Movie* (1983). Also on the credit side he wrote the novel *I Am Legend*, which has been filmed twice, notably as *The Omega Man* (1971) starring Charlton Heston, and he provided the screenplay for Steven Spielberg's breakthrough success the TV movie *Duel* (1971), later released as a feature film. On the

debit side he furnished the regrettable script for *Jaws-3D* (1983) and returned to his own source to pen the sequel *The Incredible Shrinking Woman* (1981), a lightweight vehicle for the talents of Lily Tomlin.

MEMORABLE MOMENTS We cut from Carey, distraught at the revelation that he is now shorter than Clarice and that the shrinking has started again, to him sitting in a normal living room. There is a sudden thundering sound which turns out to be Louise's footsteps descending the stairs. He is now living in a doll's house.

The various adventures he has in his new kingdom in the cellar: the epic climb up the storage unit; lighting the vast match; snatching the stale cheese from the mousetrap; his narrow escape from drowning as he tries to attract the attention of his brother and his departing wife who think him dead; the final conflict with the spider.

KEY LINES

Carey: 'Easy enough to talk of soul and spirit and essential worth but not when you're three feet tall.'

INVASION OF THE BODY SNATCHERS

US, 1956, ALLIED ARTISTS, 80 MINS

D DON SIEGEL; **P** WALTER WANGER; **SC** DANIEL MAINWARING (FROM THE NOVEL BY JACK FINNEY); **PH** (BW SUPERSCOPE) ELLSWORTH FREDERICKS; **M** CARMEN DRAGON; **ED** ROBERT S. EISEN

CAST KEVIN MCCARTHY (MILES BENNELL), DANA WYNTER (BECKY DRISCOLL), KING DONOVAN (JACK), CAROLYN JONES (THEODORA), LARRY GATES (DAN KAUFMAN), JEAN WILLES (SALLY)

AND

INVASION OF THE BODY SNATCHERS

US, 1978, UNITED ARTISTS, 115 MINS

D PHILIP KAUFMAN; **P** ROBERT H. SOLO; **SC** W. D. RICHTER; **PH** MICHAEL CHAPMAN, **M** DENNY ZEITLIN; **ED.** DOUGLAS STEWART

CAST DONALD SUTHERLAND (MATTHEW BENNELL), BROOKS ADAMS (ELIZABETH DRISCOLL), VERONICA CARTWRIGHT (NANCY BELLICEC), JEFF GOLDBLUM (JACK BELLICEC), LEONARD NIMOY (DR DAVID KIBNER)

THE STORY 1956 version: Dr Miles Bennell returns from a conference to the small Californian town of Santa Mira, where he's the local GP, to find the community both quiet and edgy, several patients suspecting relatives of having changed their identities. He and his girlfriend, Becky, gradually discover that seeds long floating in space have landed in local fields and created pods which first replicate humans, then take over their bodies while they are asleep, turning them into emotionless creatures. Eventually Miles and Becky are the only ones left and they elude their pursuers. But in an abandoned tunnel in the hills Becky falls asleep and is taken over, leaving Miles on his own to warn the world of the impending disaster.

In outline the plot of the 1978 version is similar to the earlier one, but now the setting is San Francisco and the central characters, Matthew Bennell and Elizabeth Driscoll, are colleagues at the city's Public Health department. Once again their best friends are a writer and his wife, and a psychiatrist, who initially dismisses the phenomenon as mass hysteria, and turns out to be the ringleader of the replicants. The remake, however,

'Don't be trapped by old concepts, Matthew, you're evolving into a new life form.'

ends with Bennell first attempting to destroy the factory producing the pods, then turning out to be taken over himself.

THE FILMS Siegel's low-budget classic is set in a tight, idealized community where everyone knows each other, and the tension grows as the hero notices the change in those around him, until the once familiar becomes dangerously hostile. The bodies oozing from pods are repellent, but the film uses few shock effects. Appearing at the mid-point of Eisenhower's presidency, the movie was perceived as an allegory about conformity, though it could as easily be interpreted as a warning against socialism or as an attack on the craven behaviour of the McCarthy era. The expensive 1978 film takes place in an alienated city in the wake of the Sixties' revolution and Watergate. People are high on apocalyptic science fiction, conspiracy theory, new religions and therapies, worry about the ecology, and seem ready for some takeover that would have the effect of puttng Prozac in the drinking water. Kaufman's picture accepts the cult status of Siegel's original by giving small roles to Kevin McCarthy (who throws himself on to the bonnet of Sutherland's car, shouting out a warning before being killed) and to Don Siegel (as a taxi driver who betrays the hero and heroine to the police).

ODD/SALIENT FACTS Don Siegel didn't like the script's framing device and wanted to end with Bennell standing among the passing traffic pointing at the audience and saying: 'You're next.' Sam Peckinpah worked as dialogue director, did a week-long (uncredited) polish on the script and appears as Charlie the gas-man. The film was shot in 19 days for under $300,000, and designer Ted Haworth (whose credits include Hitchcock's *Strangers on a Train* and *I Confess*) had a budget of $15,000 for special effects. In 1994 Abel Ferrara's *Body Snatchers* transposed the same story to an army base in Alabama, creating the problem of how to suggest the imposition of extraterrestrial conformity on a community of earthlings who had already surrendered their individuality to the military.

MEMORABLE MOMENTS In the 1956 film: Miles's inability to destroy his girlfriend's cloned shape.

Miles's horrified realization that Becky has become a pod person.

In both movies the sound of music (a Spanish love song in

▲ *INVASION OF THE BODY SNATCHERS* Dana Wynter, Carolyn Jones, King Donovan and Kevin McCarthy stare in horror at the pods in the greenhouse.

1956, 'Amazing Grace' in 1978), suggests on-going human life nearby, and turns out to be on a radio owned by pod people.

In the 1978 picture a street musician's dog appears with his master's bearded face after the two have fallen asleep beside a pod.

KEY LINES

Miles, 1956: 'All of us, we've … grown callous. Only when we have to fight to stay human do we realise how precious it is to us.'

Miles, 1956: 'Stop, listen to me, we're in danger, something terrible is happening, they have arrived and you're next.'

Matthew, 1978: 'Do you want to see my friend, he's a psychiatrist. He'd eliminate a lot of things – whether Geoffrey was having an affair, whether he had become gay, whether he had a social disease, whether he had become a Republican, all the alternatives that could have happened to him.'

David, the psychiatrist, 1978: 'Don't be trapped by old concepts, Matthew, you're evolving into a new life form.'

IT'S A WONDERFUL LIFE

US, 1946, LIBERTY FILMS, 129 MINS

D FRANK CAPRA; **PR** FRANK CAPRA; **SC** FRANK CAPRA, FRANCIS GOODRICH, ALBERT HACKETT; **ADD SC** JO SWERLING; **PH** (BW) JOSEPH WALKER, JOSEPH BIROC; **M** DIMITRI TIOMKIN; **ED** WILLIAM HORNBECK

CAST JAMES STEWART (GEORGE BAILEY), DONNA REED (MARY HATCH), LIONEL BARRYMORE (MR POTTER), THOMAS MITCHELL (UNCLE BILLY), BEULAH BONDI (MRS BAILEY), FRANK FAYLEN (ERNIE), WARD BOND (BERT), HENRY TRAVERS (CLARENCE), H. B. WARNER (MR GOWER), GLORIA GRAHAME (VIOLET), TODD KARNS (HARRY BAILEY), VIRGINIA PATTON (RUTH DAKEN), SAMUEL S HINDS (PA BAILEY), SHELDON LEONARD (NICK)

THE STORY It is Christmas Eve and the prayers of several residents of Bedford Falls are answered. Trainee angel Clarence is summoned to earn his wings by saving the life of the suicidal George Bailey. In a series of flashbacks Clarence is filled in on the key events of Bailey's life. As a young boy he saved the life of his kid brother Harry, and prevented his pharmacist boss from accidentally poisoning a sick child. George is prevented from leaving his small town by a succession of factors: his father's death, the needs of his family building and loan company, his brother's education and career, a run on the bank. Married with children, and in charge of the company, on the eve of his brother's heroic homecoming from war, George faces disgrace when his Uncle Billy misplaces $8,000. On the verge of suicide, George's life is saved by Clarence, who then shows him how bad things would have been had he never been born. Suddenly back in Bedford Falls after witnessing the nightmare of this parallel world, George is chastened. He returns to his family to find that all is well and that it is, after all, a wonderful life.

THE FILM *It's a Wonderful Life* was the first film that James Stewart made in nearly six years. During this 'sabbatical', he had become a decorated flying officer in the Second World War but spoke little of his wartime experiences. When Capra first brought the project to Stewart's attention, the director himself described it as: 'The lousiest piece of cheese I ever heard of.' The film was a failure at the box office and was only hailed as a classic when it became a staple of American Christmas TV from the 1960s onwards. When Capra's *Mr Deeds Goes to Town* (1936) was first shown in the Soviet Union, the censors cut the last twenty minutes so this ultimately patriotic film would instead be seen as a savage indictment of the awful-

'I wish I'd never been born.'

ness and corruption of American life. The same trick would work in *It's a Wonderful Life*. George Bailey's life is one of continual disappointment, one in which George himself comes to understand that forces are preventing him from ever leaving his claustrophobic small town. The intensity of his anguish is shocking. This is Capracorn so thoroughly disguised as unrelentingly bleak, existential gloom that it was just too much for a postwar audience. The film requires the repeated viewings allowed by TV reruns, the VCR and cinema re-releases for its

▼ *IT'S A WONDERFUL LIFE The Bailey family, their friends and creditors gather to toast George, the richest man in town.*

grimly optimistic message to be appreciated – that normal American life is awful and harrowing, built on frustration and disappointment, but it could be a lot worse, so in fact it's great after all.

ODD/SALIENT FACTS Dalton Trumbo, Dorothy Parker and Clifford Odets all did uncredited work on the script. There is a rock band called Zuzu's Petals, named after the petals that George pretends he has glued on to the flower at the bedside of his sick daughter. They disappear when Clarence eradicates all traces of George's existence and it is their return as well as his deaf ear and bleeding mouth that prove that he is alive once more. In the 1980s, a suicidal criminal in America was ordered by the judge passing sentence in his case to watch the film. The cop and cab driver buddies Ernie and Bert inspired the *Sesame Street* characters of the same names.

MEMORABLE MOMENTS George and Mary at Harry's high-school prom, dancing the Charleston wildly and oblivious to the gym floor parting to reveal the pool beneath. When they eventually fall in the pool they just carry on their delirious dancing.

Their tuneless but joyful singing of *Buffalo Girls* as they wander home in borrowed clothes, and throw stones in the ruined old house they will eventually share. Their tryst is interrupted by the news of Pa Bailey's stroke.

The scene we wait for throughout the film, the one that is instantly recognisable and that is used in *Gremlins* (1984), when the nightmare is over and George runs ecstatically through the winter wonderland of Bedford Falls.

KEY LINES

George Bailey to Potter: 'Just remember this, Mr Potter. This rabble you're talking about. They do most of the working and praying and living and dying in this community! Well, is it too much to have them work and pray and live and die in a couple of decent rooms and a bath?'

George to Clarence: 'I wish I'd never been born.'

Clarence: 'Strange, isn't it? Each man's life touches so many other lives, and when he isn't around, he leaves an awful hole, doesn't he?'

THE ITALIAN JOB
UK, 1969, PARAMOUNT/OAKHURST, 117 MINS

D PETER COLLINSON; **PR** MICHAEL DEELEY; **SC** TROY KENNEDY MARTIN; **PH** (COL) DOUGLAS SLOCOMBE; **M** QUINCY JONES; **ED** JOHN TRUMPER

CAST MICHAEL CAINE (CHARLIE CROKER), NOËL COWARD (MR BRIDGER), BENNY HILL (PROFESSOR SIMON PEACH), RAF VALLONE (ALTAHANI), TONY BECKLEY (FREDDIE), ROSSANO BRAZZI (BECKERMAN), MAGGIE BLYE (LORNA), IRENE HANDL (MISS PEACH), JOHN LE MESURIER (GOVERNOR), FRED EMNEY (BIRKINSHAW), JOHN CLIVE (GARAGE MANAGER), GRAHAM PAYN (KEATS), MICHAEL STANDING (ARTHUR), STANLEY CAINE (COCO), BARRY COX (CHRIS), HARRY BAIRD (BIG WILLIAM), GEORGE INNES (BILL BAILEY), JOHN FORGEHAM (FRANK), ROBERT POWELL (YELLOW)

THE STORY Charlie Croker is released from prison and takes on the caper of a lifetime bequeathed to him by a recently deceased fellow con. The plan is to steal a consignment of gold bullion in the centre of Turin and cre-

'Hang on a minute, lads, I've got a great idea ...'

ate a backdrop distraction of the biggest-ever traffic jam by sabotaging the computer which controls the city's traffic. Securing funding from the incarcerated criminal bigwig Mr Bridger, aided by a computer whizz-kid with a penchant for large women and with a fleet of getaway minis, the scam goes ahead. Everything goes to plan, the bullion is stolen, the minis evade the police, escape the city and load the gold on to the getaway coach heading for Switzerland. But the overzealous driver careers off the road and the coach, the gang and the gold are left in a literal cliffhanger with Charlie needing just one more great idea.

THE FILM There are some old-fashioned, unpleasant racist undertones to the film with the jingoism of the upper-class and working-class outfit taking on and beating the mafia and the Italian police. The raid is on a security van conveying money to be used in a deal between the Chinese and Fiat. Bridger is a fanatical patriot, obsessed with the Queen. The job, which coincides with a football match between England and Italy, uses three emblematically English Minis, one red, one white, one

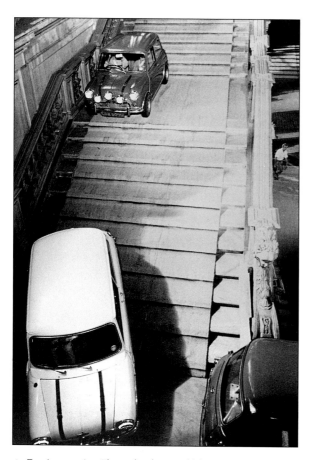

▲ *THE ITALIAN JOB The red, white and blue getaway Minis negotiate the narrow streets and stairways of Turin.*

blue, that will be driven on to a red, white and blue coach. The raid goes perfectly but is bungled only by the reckless behaviour of the black driver, 'Known as Big William for very obvious reasons.' Nevertheless this is a perennial favourite, beloved by a generation whose appreciation is instantly communicated by the exchange of a few key lines which have entered the language. Coward was encouraged out of retirement to take the role of the highly patriotic supercriminal Bridger. It was the last film he made and marked an exuberant if unsubtle swan song to the great man's career.

ODD/SALIENT FACTS The screenplay was written by Troy Kennedy Martin who became a regular writer on the TV series *The Sweeney* and also wrote the classic 1980s TV eco-thriller *Edge of Darkness*. The film is perhaps best remembered for its

bold/irritating inconclusive conclusion. This was not always how it was supposed to be as Caine recalls in William Hall's *Raising Caine*:

> There was no ending written. We figured we'd get to an ending when we got there, and that's how we left it. We were going to do a sequel: the coach is teetering on the edge of a cliff, and they have to get the weight from the back where the gold is piled. The idea is that they have to sit there for five hours with the engine running because the petrol tanks are at the back. Then the weight comes up – but as all the guys get off the gold goes over on its own ...

> At the bottom of the cliff is a Mafia leader, who makes off with the gold. He takes it across the border to the South of France, and then we were going to chase him. Instead of using Minis we were to use another British invention which was the two-seater hovercraft, with the motorcycle cops chasing us through the marshes and the roads – a real zoom-zoom ending.

MEMORABLE MOMENTS The euphoric scenes of the minis evading the Italian police, driving over the vast undulating roof, negotiating weirs, bridges, car lots and sewers, intercut with the victory parade of Bridger in prison.

Desperate to secure funding for his little job in Italy, Charlie breaks into prison for an unscheduled meeting with Mr Bridger in his toilet, thus committing the unforgivable crime of upsetting the older man's 'natural rhythm'.

KEY LINES
Peach: 'I like 'em big.'

Charlie: after a series of disastrous dummy runs in which a succession of cars are destroyed, watches his countdown lead to a van being blown to smithereens. He shouts, in Caine's inimitable crescendo: 'You're only supposed to blow the bloody doors off.'

Charlie: 'Hang on a minute, lads, I've got a great idea ... er ... er ...'

JAWS★

US, 1975, UNIVERSAL PICTURES, 124 MINS

D STEVEN SPIELBERG; **PR** RICHARD D ZANUCK, DAVID BROWN;
SC PETER BENCHLEY, CARL GOTTLIEB; **PH** BILL BUTLER; **M** JOHN
WILLIAMS; **ED** VERNA FIELDS

CAST ROY SCHEIDER (BRODY), ROBERT SHAW (QUINT), RICHARD
DREYFUSS (HOOPER), LORRAINE GRAY (ELLEN BRODY), MURRAY
HAMILTON (VAUGHAN), CARL GOTTLIEB (MEADOWS), JEFFREY C.
KRAMER (HENDRICKS), SUSAN BACKLINNIE (CHRISSIE), JONATHAN
FILLEY (CASSIDY), TED GROSSMAN (ESTUARY VICTIM), CHRIS
REBELLO (MICHAEL BRODY), JAY MELLO (SEAN BRODY), LEE KIERRO
(MRS KINTNER), JEFFREY VOORHEES (ALEX KINTNER), CRAIG
KINGSBURY (BEN GARDNER), DR ROBERT NEVIN (MEDICAL
EXAMINER), PETER BENCHLEY (INTERVIEWER)

THE STORY A woman out skinny-dipping at night is attacked
and dragged underwater by an unseen beast. Chief Brody, a
cop with a fear of water and the new chief of police in the holiday resort of Amity Island, attributes the young woman's death
to a shark attack. His attempts to close the beach are blocked
by the mayor, and after a second attack a great shark hunt
begins. On a night dive off his boat, Hooper, a wealthy ichthy-
ologist discovers that Ben Gardner, one of the fishermen, has
also fallen victim to the Great White. Brody, Quint, a local fisherman, and Hooper set out to catch and kill the Great White.
After a mighty struggle that costs Quint's life, Brody conquers
his fear of the water, blows the shark up, and paddles back to
land with Hooper.

THE FILM The film was chaotic in production, with the three
fake sharks continually malfunctioning, the project going months
behind schedule and millions of dollars over budget, and many,
including Dreyfuss, predicted it would be a dismal failure. In
post-production Spielberg and his collaborators, seeing the shots
of the cross-eyed shark, shifted the focus of the film. They
realised that what makes the film so scary is the suggestion of
danger, the delay in seeing the shark. It became the most successful film of all time and, like *Easy Rider* (1969), marked a
fundamental change in the way in which films were made in
Hollywood. Spielberg himself talks of empathizing with
Coppola over his experiences with *Apocalypse Now* (1979),
having himself courted disaster and eventually suffered panic
attacks with *Jaws*. Peter Benchley's crude best-selling novel has
been honed into a modern exploitation masterpiece with ele-

ments of the group jeopardy film, the Western and the political
conspiracy thriller.

ODD/SALIENT FACTS Richard Dreyfuss turned down the role
of Hooper three times, and as he recalls in Peter Biskind's *Easy
Riders, Raging Bulls*: 'Then I saw *The Apprenticeship of Duddy
Kravitz*, and I was just so freaked out, I thought my performance
was so terrible, that I called Steven and begged for the job. I
went with the fish movie. We started the film without a script,
without a cast, and without a shark.'

MEMORABLE MOMENTS The attack sequences – the brilliantly
constructed opening, the boy on the lilo, the fishermen on the
jetty, the man in the pond.

Roy Scheider on the beach reacting to the second attack
(achieved by the camera moving away from him on tracks while
simultaneously zooming in on his face).

The head of Ben Gardner suddenly appearing in the port-
hole of the sunken boat.

KEY LINES

The enduring cult element of the film surrounds Quint's chilling
speech at night aboard the *Orca*. He and Hooper have shown
off their scars, when Brody asks him what caused the scar on
his arm. He explains that it was a tattoo he had removed of the
USS Indianapolis. Hooper who had been laughing, falls silent,
and Quint recounts the events of the return journey of the boat
that had delivered the Hiroshima bomb. It was struck by two
Japanese torpedoes on 29 June 1945:

'11,000 men went into the water. The vessel went down
in one and a half minutes. Didn't see the first shark for
about a half an hour. Tiger. 13-footer. You know how
you know that when you're in the water, Chief? You tell
by looking from the dorsal to the tail. What we didn't
know was our bomb mission had been so secret, no dis-
tress signal had been sent. They didn't even list us
overdue for a week. Very first night, Chief, sharks came
cruising. So we formed ourselves into tight groups like
old squares in the battle, like you see in the calendar,
like in the Battle of Waterloo, and the idea was: shark
comes to the nearest man and he's pounding and hollering and screaming. Sometimes the shark'd go away,
sometimes he wouldn't go away. Sometimes that shark,
he looks right into you, right into your eyes, and you

know a thing about a shark, he's got lifeless eyes, black eyes, like a doll's eyes. When he comes at you he doesn't seem to be living until he bites you and those black eyes roll over white and then you hear that terrible, high-pitched screamin' and the ocean turns red, despite all the pounding and the hollering they all come in and they rip you to pieces …'

A brilliant piece of writing and acting that provides a depth of fear and history to the action. It suggests that sharks acted as some kind of instant divine or diabolical retribution for the Americans daring to use the bomb. The authorship of the speech was contested, with John Milius having provided an uncredited rewrite and Robert Shaw also claiming to have contributed to it.

▼ *La Jetée The beginning and the end for the unnamed hero of Chris Marker's stunning photo roman.*

LA JETÉE
France, 1962, Argos Films, 29 mins
D Chris Marker; *SC* Marker; bw
CAST Hélène Chatelain (The woman), Davos Hanich (The man), Jacques Ledoux (The scholar), André Heinrich, Jacques Branchu, Pierre Joffroy, Etienne Becker, Philbert von Lifchitz, Ligia Borowczyk, Jeannine Klein, Bill Klein, Germano Facetti, Jean Negroni (The storyteller)

THE STORY A man is chosen for a time-travel experiment in post-apocalyptic subterranean Paris because of the strength and vividness of a memory when as a boy he stood on the pier at Orly airport looking at a young woman. In these experiments, he travels back in time and meets up with this same woman on several disjointed assignations. He also travels into the future from where he receives the secret that is the salvation of life on earth. Offered the chance to live in the future, he asks instead to be sent back to the past to meet up with the woman. Back on the pier at Orly, he sees the woman and starts to run towards

124

her, but he has been followed by a man from his present who shoots him, and only then does he realize that the memory he has carried with him since childhood is a glimpse of his own death.

THE FILM This haunting, brilliant, bleak 29-minute film is told almost entirely in still photographs. Chris Marker describes it as a *photo roman*. The photographs are all in black and white, some striking and enigmatic, others banal. Sometimes the camera lingers on the image, sometimes there are quick cuts and for one sequence, the man's first journey back in time, the pictures come as a series of pulsing images that quickly fade in from black and equally quickly fade away again.

ODD/SALIENT FACTS The story, loosely of the sci-fi genre, is markedly influenced by Jorge Luis Borges. The notion of a man selected for his remarkably powerful memory brings to mind the central character in the story 'Funes the Memorious'. But the central idea of the child seeing himself die is especially reminiscent of the story 'The Other' from *The Book of Sand,* in which the narrator meets himself as an old man and converses with himself for a short while. This is Chris Marker's only fictional film. A man of mysterious origins and early life, Marker, born in 1921, has worked as a critic, poet and documentary film-maker collaborating with Alan Resnais and Walerian Borowczyk. The film inspired Terry Gilliam's *Twelve Monkeys* (1995) which (with a script by Janet and David Peoples) uses *La Jetée's* basic plot and framing device, and melds it to elements borrowed from *The Terminator* (1984) and T2 (1991) and David Cronenberg's *The Dead Zone* (1983).

MEMORABLE MOMENTS For just one sequence we see a succession of pictures of the woman lying asleep in bed, which ends with a couple of seconds of barely discernible moving film in which she opens her eyes and smiles very slightly.

KEY LINES

'He ran towards her and when he recognized the man who had been trailing him since the camp, he knew there was no way out of time, and he knew that this haunted moment he had been granted to see as a child was the moment of his own death.'

▲ *JULES ET JIM Jim (at the top), Jules and Catherine form a romantic triangle in the early Midi morning light.*

JULES ET JIM
FRANCE, 1962, LES FILMS DU CARROSSE, 105 MINS

D FRANÇOIS TRUFFAUT; **PR** MARCEL BERBERT; **SC** FRANÇOIS TRUFFAUT, JEAN GRUAULT (FROM THE NOVEL BY HENRI-PIERRE ROCHÉ); **PH** (BW, FRANSCOPE) RAOUL COUTARD; **ED** CLAUDINE BOUCHÉ; **M** GEORGES DELERUE

CAST JEANNE MOREAU (CATHERINE), OSKAR WERNER (JULES), HENRI SERRE (JIM), MARIE DUBOIS (THÉRÈSE), VANNA URBINO (GILBERTE), SABINE HAUDEPIN (SABINE), BORIS BASSIAK (ALBERT), MICHEL SUBOR (NARRATOR)

'Is her kind made for marriage? I fear she may never be happy on this earth. She is an apparition.'

THE STORY 1912, PARIS. The German writer Jules meets the French writer Jim on a visit to France; they become close friends, pursue girls together, translate each others' work. After becoming obsessed with the smile on an ancient Mediterranean sculpture, they meet Catherine, a girl with a similar smile. She's the wilful, free-spirited daughter of an aristocratic French father and a working-class English mother, and the three become inseparable. Shortly before the outbreak of the First World War, Jules and Catherine marry, and the two friends serve in the armies of their native countries, hoping never to confront each other. After the

125

war, Jim, now an established novelist, comes to Germany to write a series of articles on the country's troubles. He stays with Jules and Catherine, who now have a six-year-old daughter, and eventually becomes the lover of the sexually liberated Catherine. They break up but meet again when Jules and Catherine move back to a mill on the Seine, and finally Jim elects to marry the stable Gilberte. Some years later, after Hitler's rise to power, Jim meets Jules and Catherine at a Paris cinema showing Nazi book-burning. Re-united, Jim goes for a drive in Catherine's car and they plunge over a broken bridge to their deaths in the river beneath. Jules picks up their ashes in the crematorium.

THE FILM *Jules et Jim* was Truffaut's third feature film, one of his most loved, and possibly his greatest. Raoul Coutard's mobile camerawork gives it a restless, lyrical quality, and the black-and-white images suggest postcards and family snapshots of a bygone time. Truffaut presents an idealized form of male and female friendship, in which passionate intellectuals attempt to control their confused feelings and frustrated desires by elegant articulation and literary allusion. The film contrasts the characters' discussions and the narrator's wise certitudes. Everything centres on Moreau's commanding, destructive heroine, one of the screen's most seductive *femmes fatales*, and through her Truffaut first proposes the major theme of his work – how we confront the attractions, repulsions and inevitability of death.

ODD/SALIENT FACTS Truffaut was nicknamed 'the grave-digger of French cinema' for his critical assaults on established directors in the mid-1950s, but when he came to make movies, death scenes, funerals and cemeteries became his trademark. Roché's semi-autobiographical novel *Jules et Jim* was published in 1953 when the author was seventy-four. In 1980 writer-director Paul Mazursky made *Willie and Phil*, about three free-wheeling New Yorkers (Michael Ontkean, Ray Sharkey, Margot Kidder) who modelled their lives on the trio in *Jules et Jim*.

MEMORABLE MOMENTS Catherine's first appearance descending the outdoor staircase.

Catherine dressing as a boy and drawing a moustache on her upper lip to go out in the streets of Paris with Jules and Jim.

Jules, Jim and Catherine cycling to the beach in Provence.

Jules reciting *La Marseillaise* in perfect French to Jim over the phone on the eve of the Great War.

Catherine singing Boris Bassiak's 'Le Tourbillon' to a guitar accompaniment at the chalet in Alsace.

KEY LINES

Jim: 'Is her kind made for marriage? I fear she may never be happy on this earth. She is an apparition.'

Narrator: 'Jules' country lost the war and Jim's country won it, but the real victory was that Jules and Jim were both alive.'

Jules: 'But she is a queen. To be candid, Catherine is not particularly beautiful, intelligent or sincere – but she is a real woman, and it is this woman we love and all men desire.'

THE KING OF COMEDY★
US, 1983, 20TH CENTURY-FOX, 108 MINS

D MARTIN SCORSESE; **PR** ARNON MILCHAN; **SC** PAUL D. ZIMMERMAN; **PH** (COL) FRED SCHULER; **M** ROBBIE ROBERTSON; **ED** THELMA SCHOONMAKER

CAST ROBERT DE NIRO (RUPERT PUPKIN), JERRY LEWIS (JERRY LANGFORD), DIAHNNE ABBOT (RITA), SANDRA BERNHARD (MASHA), TONY RANDALL (HIMSELF), SHELLEY HACK (CATHY LONG), FRED DE CORDOVA (BERT THOMAS), DR JOYCE BROTHERS (HERSELF), ED HERLIHY (HIMSELF), LOU BROWN (BANDLEADER), VICTOR BORGE (HIMSELF)

THE STORY Rupert Pupkin is a fantasist fixated on Jerry Langford, one of America's leading talk-show hosts. Rupert imagines a friendship blossoming between himself and his idol. He phones and visits Jerry's office, trying to get his big break as a stand-up comic. His fantasies become more elaborate and he dreams of being invited by Jerry to spend the weekend at his country house. Rupert and his reluctant girlfriend Rita are ejected by a furious Langford. Now more determined than ever, Rupert and Masha, a fellow fan, kidnap Jerry and force the show's producers to let Rupert deliver his routine on the programme, while Masha attempts to seduce Jerry. When Jerry eventually escapes, it is too late and the show has aired. Rupert is arrested and sent to jail, but he becomes a *cause célèbre* and when he is released after nearly three years, he is rich, famous and has achieved his dream of becoming the king of comedy.

THE FILM Scorsese came to the project, which had been doing the rounds since the late Sixties, after the rigours of *Raging Bull*

(1980), before, during and after which he was seriously ill from a mixture of stress, cocaine addiction and asthma. While on a superficial level it is a lighter film, it is nevertheless essentially a reworking of the themes and plot of *Taxi Driver* (1976). Both films have central characters who are quiet sociopaths, going about their insanity anonymously in New York. Both have been driven mad by the American experience, one by the Vietnam War and the grotesque morality of urban life, the other by the obsessive cult of fame. Each woos an initially suspicious woman into agreeing to come on a date with him and each time the date ends in horrific embarrassment, one in a pornographic cinema, the other in the home of a TV star. Each is driven to exact violent revenge on an embodiment of what they despise and each film ends with the anti-hero hailed as a hero in the media. The film is pitched as a black comedy, but is in reality a comedy with no jokes and little humour. The ambiguous mood of the film was too confusing and dark for the commercial mainstream. It has, in De Niro and Lewis, two actors each arguably delivering the performance of their career. The leading character's name is so perfect for a deliberately unfunny film, and it is rendered variously Pipkin, Pumpkin, Bodkin and Crupkin. De Niro approached the role with his customary rigour, honing his skills on the stand-up circuit, having hung out with comedians Robin Williams and John Belushi. He perfected the cadence and timing of the comic, which in his climactic sequence he applies to a routine of inspired awfulness. In *Scorsese on Scorsese* (Faber & Faber) the director says of the experience of the film: 'The King of Comedy was right on the edge for us: we couldn't go any further at that time.'

ODD/SALIENT FACTS Scorsese likes to use as many members of his family in his films as possible. Having placed his parents at the centre of his documentary *Italianamerican* (1974) he casts both of them in *King of Comedy*, his mother as the nagging off-screen voice of Rupert's mother, and his father as a man in the bar when Rupert shows off his TV performance to Rita. Scorsese himself makes his Hitchcockian cameo appearance as the director of the Jerry Langford Show. Among the street scum berated by Masha are Ellen Foley and Mick Jones, Joe Strummer and Paul Simenon (credited as Paul Simmion) from The Clash. Scorsese had originally approached Johnny Carson to play the part of Langford. Carson declined, explaining that he couldn't cope with a performance that would entail more than one take, but *The Tonight Show* is given special thanks in

the credits: 'For help in researching the ambience of our film.' Other actors considered for the role were Frank Sinatra, Dean Martin and Orson Welles.

MEMORABLE MOMENTS The film's most striking scene is the embarrassing arrival of Rupert and Rita uninvited at Jerry's country home. It makes uncomfortable and disturbing viewing and leaves the audience with no one to sympathize with or root for. In *Scorsese on Scorsese*, the director recalls the shooting of this sequence as 'extremely painful. It took two weeks and it was just so painful because the scene itself was so excruciating.'

KEY LINES

In his daydream, in reply to Jerry's asking him about the secret of his talent, Rupert replies: 'I think it's that I look at my whole life and see the awful, terrible things in my life and turn it into something funny. It just happens.'

KISS ME DEADLY
US, 1955, PARK LANE PICTURES/UNITED ARTISTS, 105 MINS
D/PR ROBERT ALDRICH; **SC** A.I. BEZZERIDES (FROM THE NOVEL BY MICKEY SPILLANE); **PH** (BW) ERNEST LASZLO; **ED** MICHAEL LUCIANO; **M** FRANK DE VOL
CAST RALPH MEEKER (MIKE HAMMER), GABY RODGERS (GABRIELLE/LILY) ALBERT DEKKER (DR SOBERIN), PAUL STEWART (CARL EVELLO), JUANO HERNANDEZ (EDDIE EAGER), WESLEY ADDY (PAT CHAMBERS), MARIAN CARR (FRIDAY), MAXENE COOPER (VELDA), CLORIS LEACHMAN (CHRISTINA BAILEY), NICK DENNIS (NICK), FORTUNIO BONANOVA (TRIVAGO), JACK ELAM (CHARLIE MAX), JACK LAMBERT (SUGAR SMALLHOUSE)

THE STORY Mike Hammer, an unscrupulous Los Angeles private detective, gives a lift to Christina Bailey, a fugitive from a mental hospital. She criticizes his arrogance, he protects her at a police check point and she urges: 'Remember me!' before they are captured by thugs. She provides some information under torture before dying, and her body is placed next to Mike in his car before it goes over a cliff. Mike survives and soon discovers the FBI are interested in the case, and wants part of the action, assisted by his adoring secretary Velda. He comes up against gangsters and thugs and meets Christina's roommate Gabrielle. He is kidnapped and injected with a truth drug; his best friend Nick is murdered; and everyone is after a

▲ *KISS ME DEADLY* Gaby Rodgers recoils as she releases the nuclear horrors from the fateful box.

lead-lined box of nuclear material that contaminates all who open it. Following up the 'Remember me' clue (a reference to a Christina Rossetti poem) Hammer locates the box in the locker-room of a sports club, but it is seized by sinister Dr Soberin, kingpin of the operation, whose mistress is Gabrielle (aka Lily). Hammer tracks them down to a beach house, where they're holding Velda captive. Gabrielle/Lily kills Soberin, opens his Pandora's Box, and the house goes up in a great nuclear conflagration.

THE FILM This expressionist *film noir* masterpiece was loathed in America (where liberals despised Spillane's novels as symptoms of a culture in decline), subjected to censorship everywhere (nearly ten minutes were cut in Britain), and made Aldrich one of the cult heroes of the *Cahiers du Cinéma* critics

who nicknamed him 'Le Gros Bob'. The jagged style, the narrative short-cuts, the refusal to explain, inspired them four years later, when they became film-makers and created the *Nouvelle Vague*. Aldrich was a master of genre cinema – a great exponent of the Western, the thriller, the war movie – but this remains his wildest, least compromising picture. He was a rebel, an anarchist who never sought respectability. His heroes were outsiders embodied by stars such as Burt Lancaster, Jack Palance and Lee Marvin. In *Kiss Me Deadly* he chose to expose Spillane's right-wing, fascistic private eye Mike Hammer, by showing him going about his work beating up people, exploiting the weak. Apart from the mildly sympathetic cop, Pat Chambers, the film's only attractive characters are the poetry-loving Christina and the cheerful mechanic Nick, both of whom are killed.

The movie's violence is relentless, though most of it is implied. The dialogue (by A. I. Bezzerides, a one-time truckdriver) is stylized rather than plain demotic, and full of classical and literary allusions. In one poolside shot, three of the leading heavies in post-war Hollywood cinema are framed together – Jack Lambert, Jack Elam and Paul Stewart.

ODD/SALIENT FACTS In Spillane's original novel the box in the locker contains a consignment of heroin belonging to the Mafia. Ralph Meeker came to prominence in 1948 when he took over from Brando in A *Streetcar Named Desire* on Broadway; he rarely played sympathetic characters. Spillane apparently liked the film and in an equivocal 1955 article in the *New York Herald Tribune* Aldrich spoke of 'playing fair by Spillane fans'. Never once in the film do we hear the words bomb, thermo-nuclear or atomic.

MEMORABLE MOMENTS Christina and Mike driving through the night in his cramped sportscar.

The blonde Lily Carver sitting up in bed pointing her gun at the camera.

The spinning tapes of Mike's answering machine repeating messages.

Images of nuclear contamination concluding with Lily's final opening of the box.

KEY LINES

Velda: 'They, a wonderful word. Who are they? They are the nameless ones who kill people for the great what's it. Does it exist? Who cares?'

Dr Soberin to the drugged Hammer: 'What is it you are seeking? Diamonds, rubies, gold? Perhaps narcotics. How civilized this earth used to be. But as the world became more primitive, its treasures became more fabulous. Perhaps sentiment will succeed where greed failed. You will die Mr Hammer, but your friend, you can save her, yes you can.'

Dr Soberin to Gabrielle: 'The head of Medusa. That's what's in the box, and who looks on her will be changed not into stone but into brimstone and ashes. But of course you wouldn't believe me, you'd have to see for yourself, wouldn't you?'

LAURA

USA, 1944, TCF, 88 MINS

D/PR *OTTO PREMINGER;* **SC** *JAY DRATLER, SAMUEL HOFFENSTEIN, BETTY REINHARDT (FROM THE NOVEL BY VERA CASPARY);* **PH** *JOSEPH LASHELLE;* **M** *DAVID RAKSIN*

CAST *GENE TIERNEY (LAURA HUNT), DANA ANDREWS (MARK McPHERSON), CLIFTON WEBB (WALDO LYDECKER), VINCENT PRICE (SHELBY CARPENTER), JUDITH ANDERSON (ANN TREADWELL), DOROTHY ADAMS (BESSIE CLARY)*

THE STORY Homicide detective Mark McPherson takes over the investigation of the murder of Laura Hunt, a successful advertising executive found dead by her maid in her New York apartment, blasted in the face by a shotgun and recognizable only from her clothes. McPherson has four suspects. Waldo Lydecker, celebrated columnist and broadcaster, a waspish dandy and Laura's mentor and confidant, introducing her into society, helping her reach the top of her profession, and protecting her from unworthy suitors; Shelby Carpenter, Laura's fiancé, a charming, womanizing, irresponsible, impoverished Southern aristocrat; Ann Treadwell, Laura's rich, amoral aunt, in love with Shelby; Bessie, Laura's devoted maid, an Irish-American with a hatred for the law. Within hours of embarking on the case, McPherson falls in love with Laura's portrait hanging over the fireplace and settles in the apartment. He falls asleep and awakes to find Laura standing before him. She had been spending the weekend at her country cottage reconsidering her engagement to Carpenter. The woman killed in her

place was in fact Carpenter's mistress who answered the door while they were having an assignation. Laura senses the detective's fascination with her. It transpires that Waldo, refusing to let Laura marry Carpenter, had attempted to murder her. After McPherson has exposed him, Waldo is gunned down by the police.

THE FILM *Laura* has the contrived plot of a B-feature whodunnit, but its witty script and production values are those of an A-production, and the picture is less concerned with suspense than with exploring the perversity of the characters. Waldo, a brilliant creation, superbly played, is a Pygmalion obsessed with his Galatea, an impotent crypto-homosexual who cannot physically possess his creation and is convinced that no one else is worthy of her. Laura, the chilly career girl, has made a Faustian pact with Waldo that she attempts to break. Her aunt is drawn to the weak, epicene Shelby by their shared corruption. McPherson, who regards all women as dames or dolls, is attracted to Laura because she is unattainably dead and thus no threat to him. Like a number of 1940s movies (e.g. *Rebecca, The Woman in the Window, Portrait of Jennie*) *Laura* has as a central erotic image a painting of a woman who obsesses the characters, an effect reinforced by the repeated playing (on the

▼ *LAURA* The protective Waldo (Clifton Webb) looks on disapprovingly as Laura (Gene Tierney), cigarette in hand, is swayed by gigolo Vincent Price.

radio, phonograph and by a restaurant orchestra) of the title song by Johnny Mercer and David Raksin. Though always described as a *film noir*, the picture only occasionally goes in for expressionist effects.

ODD/SALIENT FACTS The film was begun by Rouben Mamoulian, who claimed it was essentially his work. Preminger, who initiated the project as producer and took over the direction, said that he brought in a new cameraman and scrapped all Mamoulian's footage. The film made Preminger's reputation and has his characteristic use of elaborate camera movements combined with shooting the dialogue in longish takes in which two or more characters appear together in a single shot so that none is morally favoured by the editing. The character of Waldo Lydecker appears to be based on the columnist, broadcaster and *New Yorker* theatre critic Alexander Woollcott, who was impotent, a repressed gay, a famous wit and, like Waldo, fascinated by murder. Woollcott always dined at the Algonquin Hotel, where Laura first approaches Lydecker. Darrryl F. Zanuck was opposed to casting Clifton Webb in the role because of his known homosexuality, but Preminger prevailed and the 54-year-old Webb (making his first screen appearance since the silent era) was nominated for an Oscar.

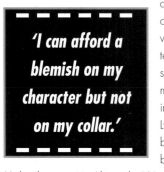

'I can afford a blemish on my character but not on my collar.'

MEMORABLE MOMENTS Waldo first seen in his bath, typing his column.

Laura's seemingly luminous portrait dominating every scene in her living room.

Mark awakening to see Laura, slightly out of focus, for the first time.

Waldo turning at the top of the staircase outside Laura's flat, his body and the banister rails casting a shadow on the wall.

KEY LINES

The opening lines: 'I Waldo Lydecker was the only man who really knew her.'

Shelby: 'I can afford a blemish on my character but not on my collar.'

Waldo: 'You'd better watch out McPherson or you'll finish up in a psychiatric ward. I doubt that they've ever had a patient who fell in love with a corpse.'

Laura: 'You forced me to give my word. I never have been nor ever will be bound by anything I don't do of my own free will.'

Waldo: 'If McPherson weren't muscular and handsome in a cheap sort of way you'd see through him in a second.'

LAWRENCE OF ARABIA
UK, 1962, COLUMBIA/HORIZON/SAM SPIEGEL, 222 MINS
D *DAVID LEAN;* **PR** *SAM SPIEGEL;* **SC** *ROBERT BOLT, ORIGINAL DRAFT BY MICHAEL WILSON;* **PH** *(COL, SUPER PANAVISION) FREDERICK A. YOUNG;* **PR DES** *JOHN BOX;* **M** *MAURICE JARRE* **CAST** *PETER O'TOOLE (LAWRENCE), ALEC GUINNESS (PRINCE FEISAL), ANTHONY QUINN (AUDA ABU TAYI), JACK HAWKINS (GENERAL ALLENBY), OMAR SHARIF (SHERIF ALI), JOSE FERRER (TURKISH BEY), ANTHONY QUAYLE (COLONEL BRIGHTON), CLAUDE RAINS (MR DRYDEN), ARTHUR KENNEDY (JACKSON BENTLEY), DONALD WOLFIT (GENERAL MURRAY), I. S. JOHAR (GASIM), GAMIL RATIB (MAJID), MICHEL RAY (FARRAJ), JOHN DIMECH (DAUD), ZIA MOHYEDDIN (TAFAS)*

THE STORY Following Lawrence's death in a motorbike accident and his memorial service, his adventures in Arabia are recounted in flashback. He was working as a military mapmaker when, with his experience of the land and the people, he was assigned to journey to the encampment of Prince Feisal and 'appreciate the situation'. En route he displays to his guide, Tafas, his strength of will and understanding of Arab ethnicity. Tafas is shot by Sherif Ali for drinking at a well owned by a rival tribe. Finding Feisal's camp under attack from the Turks, and with the British military indifferent to the needs of the Arabs, he suggests a daring attack on Aqaba. He undertakes the dangerous crossing of the Nefud desert with Ali, increasingly a friend and ally, and 50 men. Shortly before completing the journey, he risks his own life saving one of the men, Gasim. He persuades Auda, the leader of a rival tribe, to join in the raid, and shortly before the attack, Lawrence is forced to execute

▲ *LAWRENCE OF ARABIA* *Auda (Anthony Quinn) looks on as desperate Lawrence (Peter O'Toole) sees his dream of a united Arabia vanish.*

Gasim and so avert a tribal blood feud. Having taken Aqaba, Lawrence crosses the Sinai, in the process losing one of his faithful servants, to inform Allenby of the military success. Lawrence and Ali lead a campaign of sabotage against the Turkish railroad. Increasingly daring, Lawrence is arrested, and presumably raped in a Turkish garrison. Once released, Lawrence has lost heart and wants to leave the army, but is persuaded by Allenby to stay on. Before a successful raid on Damascus, he exacts a bloodthirsty revenge on the Turks. When his attempt to establish a democratic Arab council in Damascus descends into chaos, a disillusioned Lawrence returns to England.

THE FILM One of the most beautiful films ever made, this biopic of a tortured cult figure became, like *Heart of Darkness* and *Nostromo* (a long-cherished but unrealized dream of Lean's), a cult project. Many directors tried to bring the story to the screen – Lewis Milestone, Zoltan Korda, William K. Howard and Powell and Pressburger among others – with numerous stars considered for the leading role, including Robert Donat, Leslie Howard, Laurence Olivier and Cary Grant. With a cast led by the newcomer O'Toole and nearly two years spent shooting in the desert, Lean emerged with a vast and compelling study of Lawrence, an enigma driven apparently as much by his masochism and unconsummated homosexual desires, as by his passion for the land and ambition to foster a united Arabian nation. The film is remarkable for its central character's ambiguous personality, confused motivations and sexuality, his love/hate of violence, as well as its extraordinary design and cinematography. One of Lawrence's biographers said of the film: 'Perhaps this is being frivolous, but in a sense it is a picture not so much about Lawrence as about a love affair between a director, a cameraman and a desert.'

ODD/SALIENT FACTS One of the second unit directors on the film was Nicolas Roeg, co-director of *Performance* (1970). The film was restored by Robert A. Harris in 1989, with lines having to be overdubbed nearly thirty years on in reconstructed sequences in which the original soundtrack had gone missing. This is evident particularly in the sequence in which Feisal has a lengthy meeting with the American journalist Bentley. With no extant copies of the shooting script available, the restorers had to use lip-readers and guesswork to deduce what the characters were saying.

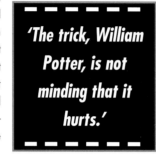

'The trick, William Potter, is not minding that it hurts.'

MEMORABLE MOMENTS Lawrence, about to leave the cartography office in Cairo, holds a match which he blows out in close-up. Cut to the desert at sunrise.

Tafas and Lawrence are at the well, Tafas drinking, Lawrence checking his compass, when he sees a speck on the horizon. The figure approaches along a demarcated path, shimmering as a mirage. As he nears the well, Ali, the rider on camel-back, shoots Tafas. The most famous entrance in cinema, Lean had intended it to be much more drawn out and regretted not sticking to his plan. According to Kevin Brownlow in his biography *David Lean*, the director turned to his designer John Box, after completing the second and final day of filming this sequence and said: 'You'll never do a better bit of design in films, ever!'

KEY LINES

Lawrence extinguishs a match with his fingertips without flinching. Potter, who has repeated this but got burnt asks: 'Well, what's the trick, then?'

Lawrence: 'The trick, William Potter, is not minding that it hurts.'

Lawrence, reporting to Allenby after the capture of Aqaba, talking of his responsibility for the deaths of Gasim and

Daud: 'There was something about it I didn't like.'
Allenby: 'Well, naturally …'
Lawrence: 'No, something else.'
Allenby: 'I see. Well, that's all right. Let it be a warning.'
Lawrence: 'No, something else.'
Allenby: 'What then?'
Lawrence: 'I enjoyed it.'

M

GERMANY, 1931, NERO-FILM, 101 MINS

D FRITZ LANG; **PR** SEMOUR NEBENZAL; **SC** LANG AND THEA VON HARBOU; **PH** FRITZ ARNO WAGNER (BW); **M** ADOLF JANSEN

CAST PETER LORRE (FRANZ BECKERT), OTTO WERNECKE (KARL LOHMAN), GUSTAV GRÜNDGENS (SCHRAENKER), THEODOR LOOS (COMMISSIONER GROEBER), ERNST STAHL-NACHBAUER (CHIEF OF POLICE), THEO LINGEN (BAURENFAENGER), ELLEN WIDMAN (MRS BECKMAN), INGE LANDGUT (ELSIE BRECKMAN), GEORG JOHN (PEDDLER)

THE STORY A psychopathic child-killer murders his ninth victim, Elsie Beckman, and writes another unsigned letter to the press about his inability to control his impulses. Terror and mutual suspicion create panic among the citizens of Düsseldorf and Inspector Lohmann, head of homicide, cracks down on the city's criminals. The threatened underworld bosses organize beggars to patrol every section of the city. Checking released mental patients the police deduce that Franz Beckert is their man, while simultaneously a blind balloon seller recognizes Beckert as the man who bought a balloon for Elsie, the clue being the same whistled tune. He alerts people and someone chalks an M (for Mörder) on the back of his coat. Beckert flees to an office block pursued by criminals who capture him and take him off to an abandoned distillery. The police arrest the single burglar left behind and trick him into revealing Beckert's whereabouts. At a kangaroo court the assembled criminals demand that the prisoner be 'put down like a mad dog', but the terrified Beckert claims they have chosen a life of crime, but he is driven by irresistible impulses. The police arrive to arrest Beckert, and the film ends with a panel of official judges assembling in court and a grieving mother saying: 'we should keep a closer watch on our children'.

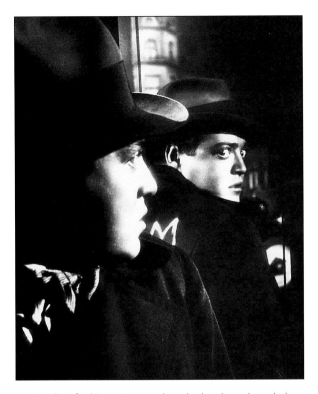

▲ *M* A horrified Peter Lorre realizes he has been branded as a murderer.

THE FILM *M* is the first sound film by Fritz Lang (1890–1976), one of the half-dozen greatest artists the cinema has produced. A pioneer of the epic, the paranoid conspiracy thriller, the SF movie, the *film noir*, and a major exponent of the Western, he produced two equally important bodies of work addressing the same theme of men struggling with fate and destiny – in the German silent cinema of the 1920s and in the American sound film of the 1930s, '40s and '50s. *M* is possibly his masterpiece, an exciting and provocative thriller, the first about a serial killer long before the term existed. It treats Beckert with sympathy without losing sight of the suffering he inflicts. It is also a seminal police-procedural thriller, with montages of cops conducting routine enquiries, blow-ups of fingerprints, the psychological interpretation of Beckert's letter by a graphologist. Lang used sound imaginatively: the children's grisly counting-out game in the opening scene anticipates the murders; Elsie's mother saying the time to worry is when you don't hear your children; a blind man hearing a whistled tune identi-

fying the killer. The film captures the Weimar Republic just before the Nazi takeover. The responses to Beckert by the angry public, a disoriented officialdom and the criminal community, constitute a paradigm of the society that sent Hitler to power. Weirdly the underworld's kangaroo court and its readiness to wipe out social undesirables anticipates the Nazi legal system and the extermination camps. The great sequence in which Lang cross-cuts between the two smoke-filled rooms where the complementary sides of society discuss their problems – a long rectangular table for the forces of law and order, a small round table for the heads of the underworld – creates a devastating image. What ultimately makes the film so compelling and gives it a deeply tragic dimension is Peter Lorre's performance. Like Shylock in *The Merchant of Venice*, he dominates the drama despite his frequent absences from the stage. Each appearance is charged by guilt, anxiety and a nervous charm, until he turns on his persecutors with his final anguished speech.

ODD/SALIENT FACTS Peter Lorre (1904–64) became a world star in *M* and worked steadily until the day he died, despite problems with drugs and alcohol. He appeared in two Hitchcock pictures, became a cult double-act with Sydney Greenstreet in the 1940s, and ended up in Roger Corman productions, and as a foil to Jerry Lewis (*The Patsy*, 1964). When Lang fled Germany after Goebbels offered him the post as head of the Nazi Film Industry, his wife, screenwriter Thea von Harbou, remained behind to serve the Nazis. Gustav Gründgens (1899–1963), the greatest German actor of his generation and Thomas Mann's son-in-law, remained in Germany and inspired Claus Mann's novel *Mephisto*, filmed in 1981 by Istvan Szabo. Lang became an iconic figure, and played himself with immense dignity as a director from the golden age in Jean-Luc Godard's *Le Mépris* (1963).

MEMORABLE MOMENTS Elsie bouncing her ball against the 'Who is the Murderer?' poster and Beckert's shadow falling upon it.

Beckert's reflection in a mirror as he discovers the letter M on the back of his overcoat.

Beckert shrinking into the corner of the attic like a trapped rat.

KEY LINES

Leading criminal: 'A non-member is ruining our respective businesses. If the situation is not restored to order we'll be ruined.'

Ditto: 'We're just doing a job but this man is beyond the pale and has no right to live.'

Beckert: 'You have chosen to be criminals, but I can't help myself. I can't control the evil within me.'

MAD MAX – THE ROAD WARRIOR★

US, 1981, KENNEDY MILLER, 96 MINS

D GEORGE MILLER; **PR** BYRON KENNEDY; **SC** GEORGE MILLER, TERRY HAYES, BRIAN HANNANT; **PH** (COL) DEAN SEMLER; **M** BRIAN MAY; **ED** DAVID STIVEN, TIM WELLBURN, MICHAEL BALSON

CAST MEL GIBSON (MAX), BRUCE SPENCE (THE GYRO CAPTAIN), PAPPAGALLO (MIKE PRESTON), MAX PHIPPS (THE TOADIE), VERNON WELLS (WEZ), KJELL NILSSON (THE HUMUNGUS), EMIL MINTY (THE FERAL KID), VIRGINIA HEY (WARRIOR WOMAN), WILLIAM ZAPPA (ZETTA), ARKIE WHITELEY (THE CAPTAIN'S GIRL), STEVE J. SPEARS (MECHANIC), HAROLD BAIGENT (VOICE OF NARRATOR)

THE STORY Having lost his wife and child in the first film, the sequel sees Max still battling road nasties and searching for fuel in the post-apocalyptic near-future. After a battle over a container truck, he escapes with a little more fuel and a music box that plays 'Happy Birthday to You'. Max encounters a comical helicopter man who shows him a compound which contains a supply of precious fuel. From their mountain view they see a rival group of thugs, including those with whom Max had the opening fight, terrorizing those leaving the compound. Max rescues one man and takes him back to the fuel depot, but the man dies before he can fulfil his promise of giving Max some petrol. Instead Max helps the people, among them a wild child, who are led by Pappagallo, withstand an attack from The Humungus and his troops. Max then offers to bring them a rig with which they can transport their stock of fuel to the coast. This he does and then takes some fuel and attempts to escape. He is pursued and driven off the road, his dog is killed and when his car blows up he is left for dead. The helicopter man rescues him

'You're a scavenger, Max, you're a maggot. D'you know that? Living off the corpse of the old world.'

and brings him back to the compound where at last he resolves to drive the rig himself. After a protracted chase in which many people are killed on both sides, the rig is crashed and is seen to be filled with sand. The surviving members of Pappagallo's community, among them the kid who will grow up to be the film's narrator, head off, leaving Max to travel the road.

THE FILM Less than twenty years after its release it is hard to see exactly why The Road Warrior caused such a stir. A loose reworking of Shane, it was influential but unlike, say, Blade Runner it is no better than many of the films it influenced. Apart from Gibson himself, the cast is pretty ordinary, but the editing is slick and the direction keeps the action ticking along at a good pace. The film ends on a high point with the protracted and chaotic climactic chase. Its big features are its star and its design. It was, like the first Mad Max film, enormously popular in Japan and in its presentation of a desolate, post-apocalyptic cartoon future world it helped shape the character of video games. It established Gibson as an international star and along with Mad Max set the template for what would become his stock role – the committed family man confronting the death of, or threat to, his family.

ODD/SALIENT FACTS In Brian Pendreigh's Mel Gibson and His Movies, the star recalls the atmosphere and the pricking of his tough guy persona on the film's New South Wales location: 'There were some pretty tough lads there but we got along very well. I used to have a pair of pinkish bedroom slippers and I wore them everywhere. They thought it was a great joke, Mad Max wearing pink bedroom slippers. One night I went into the local pub and one of the boys showed me that on the roof of the pub he had written "Mad Max drives a Mini and wears pink bedroom slippers". Well, I got on his shoulders and crossed out the word "pink" and wrote "red". That could have been a situation that got out of hand but it turned out to be good fun.'

MEMORABLE MOMENTS Apart from the lengthy chase at the end with its brilliant stunt work, the film's signature image is the iconic stance of the road warrior with which the film opens and closes.

KEY LINES

From the opening narration: 'I remember a time of chaos, ruined dreams and wasted land. But most of all I remember the road warrior, the man we called Max.'

Classic loner, light-travelling anti-hero Max, on his dog, his car and some fuel: 'I got all I need here.'

Pappagallo on Max: 'You're a scavenger, Max, you're a maggot. D'you know that? Living off the corpse of the old world.'

'Lasso's a ghost town Dock, and that's what you are Dock, a ghost.'

MAN OF THE WEST

US, 1958, UNITED ARTISTS/ASHTON PRODUCTIONS, 100 MINS

D *ANTHONY MANN;* **PR** *WALTER M. MIRISCH;* **SC** *REGINALD ROSE (FROM THE NOVEL BY WILL C. BROWN);* **PH** *(COL CINEMASCOPE), ERNEST HALLER;* **M** *LEIGH HARLINE;* **ED** *RICHARD HEERMANCE*

CAST *GARY COOPER (LINK JONES), LEE J. COBB (DOCK TOBIN), JULIE LONDON (BILLIE ELLIS), ARTHUR O'CONNELL (SAM BEASLEY), JACK LORD (COALEY), JOHN DEHNER (CLAUDE TOBIN), ROYAL DANO (TROUT), ROBERT WILKE (PONCH), JACK WILLIAMS (ALCUTT), CHUCK ROBERSON (RIFLEMAN ON TRAIN)*

THE STORY On a journey across Texas to hire a schoolteacher for Fort Worth, reformed outlaw Link Jones is stranded in the wilds with cardsharp Sam Beasley and saloon singer Billie Ellis when their train speeds off after a botched hold-up. Link leads Beasley and Billie to an abandoned farmhouse once used by Dock Tobin, who treated his mob as a family and Link as a son. There he finds the aged demented Dock surrounded by psychopaths and it transpires they are the train robbers and have Link's carpet-bag containing the money for the teacher. Link pretends to be returning to the gang, and Dock believes him, though Dock's son, Claude, is suspicious. The party set out to rob the bank at Lasso and Link creates dissension in the gang, leading to the death of Beasley, who takes a bullet intended for Link; Dock kills the man who fired the shot. Link and the vicious Trout discover Lasso is a ghost town, Trout shoots the only inhab-

itant and Link kills him. There is a shootout in which the two remaining gang members die. Returning to the camp, Link discovers that Dock has raped Billie. Link threatens to take him in, and Dock provokes a gun fight. Link discovers his township's money on Dock's corpse and rides off with Billie.

THE FILM Anthony Mann made cult classics in three genres – the *film noir T-Men* in the 1940s, a string of Westerns in the 1940s, the epic *El Cid* in the 1960s. His most celebrated Westerns are the six with James Stewart, but the one closest to the hearts of his admirers is *Man of the West*, the story of a reformed man drawn back into his past and forced to employ the violence and low cunning he has renounced to defeat his captors and confirm his redemption. It is an unromantic film – the love between Billie the saloon girl and Link, a married man with two young children, is one-sided – but there is considerable erotic tension when he attempts to prevent Billie's striptease, and pretends to be her lover to halt Dock's advances. Mann is unsurpassed in his use of the widescreen and in the way he uses the landscape. Link's journey takes him first from civilization to the wilderness, then from the verdant countryside to the parched desert around the ghost town. Although Beasley the gambler is a comic figure, his demise is sudden and tragic, and the picture is relentlessly tense, with death a constant threat. The first person to be killed (the shots heard off-stage) is a gang member wounded during the robbery and thereafter everyone dies except Link and Billie.

ODD/SALIENT FACTS This was the penultimate Western for both Mann and Cooper. The professional relationship between Mann and James Stewart came to an end when Mann refused to direct Stewart in *Night Passage* (1957) or give him the role that he coveted in *Man of the West*, and Mann died in 1967 before the friendship could be renewed. *Man of the West* is the only Western to be scripted by Reginald Rose, who wrote *Twelve Angry Men* (1957) and created the TV series *The Defenders*. Reviewing the film in *Cahiers du Cinéma* (February 1959) Jean-Luc Godard wrote: 'I have seen nothing so completely new since – why not? – Griffith. Just as the director of *Birth of a Nation* gave one the impression that he was inventing the cinema with every shot, each shot of *Man of the West* gives one the impression that Anthony

The opening titles state that this 'excerpt from the diary of a cameraman' is 'a manifesto expressed in celluloid', that it has no inter-titles or scenario, that it sets out to create an international language that owes nothing to theatre or literature. Each of the film's eight reels pursues a different theme, every single image is dense with meaning about cinema, society and the revolution, many of them (e.g. visualizations of precepts by Trotsky) in need of explication.

ODD/SALIENT FACTS Like most Soviet avant-garde films, *The Man with the Movie Camera* was not a success with popular audiences in Russia, but for 70 years it has been one of the most discussed and analysed pictures ever made, a hypnotic work to be watched again and again. The film's editor, Elizaveta Svilova, was Vertov's wife and its cinematographer, Mikhail Kaufman, was his brother. Another brother, Boris Kaufman (1906–80), emigrated to France in 1927, where he photographed Jean Vigo's *À Propos de Nice*, *Zéro de conduite* and *L'Atalante*, and then moved on to Canada and the United States, where he lit several films for Elia Kazan (winning a 1954 Oscar for *On the Waterfront*) and Sidney Lumet (including *Twelve Angry Men*).

MEMORABLE MOMENTS A couple getting a divorce followed by a split screen of trams going in different directions.

The film stopping to show strips of film that have yet to be seen being viewed by the film editor.

The cameraman in an iron foundry drawn back from the flames by a worker.

The hand-held coverage of a football match in which the cameraman appears to be taking part.

Cross-cutting between workers and machines that makes them interdependent.

THE MAN WITH TWO BRAINS
US, 1983, WARNER/ASPEN, 93 MINS

D CARL REINER; **PR** WILLIAM E. MCEUEN, DAVID V. PICKER; **SC** CARL REINER, STEVE MARTIN, GEORGE GIPE; **PH** MICHAEL CHAPMAN; **M** JOEL GOLDSMITH; **ED** BUD MOLIN

CAST STEVE MARTIN (DR MICHAEL HFUHRUHURR), KATHLEEN TURNER (DOLORES BENEDICT), DAVID WARNER (DR NECESSITER), PAUL BENEDICT (BUTLER), RICHARD BRESTOFF (DR PASTEUR), JAMES CROMWELL (REALTOR), GEORGE FURTH (TIMON), PETER HOBBS (DR BRANDON), EARL BOEN (DR CONRAD)

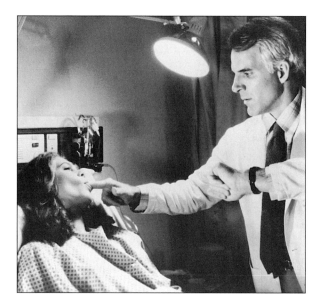

▲ *THE MAN WITH TWO BRAINS* Dr Hfuhruhurr (Steve Martin) acts as a human thermometer while he checks on Dolores (Kathleen Turner) recovering from his cranial screw-top brain surgery.

THE STORY Dr Michael Hfuhruhurr, a brilliant brain surgeon, falls in love at first sight with Dolores, a deceitful woman whom he has just knocked down and whose life he saves using his revolutionary cranial screw-top method of entry into the brain. He marries her in hospital, but she refuses to consummate the marriage. Michael accepts an invitation to lecture in Vienna, hoping that a honeymoon will inspire some marital romance. But there his work is interrupted by the activities of 'the elevator killer' who is murdering women by injecting them with window cleaner. He discovers that Dr Necessiter is keeping the brains of the killer's victims alive in jars, and falls telepathically in love with the brain of Anne Uumellmahaye. Dolores finds out that Michael has inherited $15 million and decides to stick around. Michael moves with Anne's brain and Dolores to the country, where he finally splits with Dolores. Finding that Anne's brain is starting to die, Michael returns to the city where he searches for a fresh corpse into which Dr Necessiter can transplant Anne's brain. At last he stumbles upon the body of Dolores, the most recent victim of the elevator killer, who turns out to be Merv Griffin. The operation is performed in the nick of time and Michael and Anne in Dolores's body arrive at the 'House of Hfuhruhurr'.

THE FILM *The Man With Two Brains* marks the third of the four collaborations between Steve Martin and writer/director and sometime actor Carl Reiner. The films they made together – *The Jerk* (1979), *Dead Men Don't Wear Plaid* (1982), and *All of Me* (1984) – were of consistently brilliant comic inventiveness and perfect vehicles for Martin at the height of his talent. But the middle two performed poorly at the box office to the extent that in the UK *The Man With Two Brains* was not granted a theatrical release, but instead quietly put out directly on video. Particularly compared to *Dead Men Don't Wear Plaid*, a superb, affectionate spoof on *film noir* which weaves scenes from classic movies of the 1930s and '40s into its story of Steve Martin's quest for the inventor of a dangerously potent cheese, this is not a slick piece of film-making. But although relentless and artless it is crammed with visual and verbal gags and is simply one of the funniest films of the decade. It slowly gathered a reputation as a lost gem and eventually received a limited arthouse release in the UK in 1986. By the mid-1980s Martin seems to have consciously abandoned the pure, inspired approach to comedy that had made him an enormously wealthy star of rock stadia, TV and LP recordings before he reached the big screen. He began to appear in more conventional, generally tedious, mainstream fare which allowed him, if nothing else, to add to his impressive private collection of twentieth-century art.

ODD/SALIENT FACTS The central idea of the story in which a self-centred man wants to have the perfect brain in the perfect body within a comic framework must have been unconsciously borrowed from *Stardust Memories* (1980). The voice of Anne Uumellmahaye is supplied, uncredited, by Sissy Spacek. The pop group The Pointy Birds take their name from the poem by John Lillith, Britain's greatest one-armed poet, and the first person to be hit by a car. It goes:

A pointy birds
A-pointy-pointy
Anoint my head
Anointy-nointy

MEMORABLE MOMENTS Dr Hfuhruhurr is stopped by the Austrian police and made to do some drunk tests. He has to walk along the white line in the middle of the road, then back on his hands, then on one hand, then roll over, turn over and flip, then juggle three balls, do a tap dance while singing the Catalina Magdalena, Lupensteiner, Wollendeiner

song. As he says: 'Damn, your drunk tests are hard.' He gets back into the car and Dolores's body slumps across him. The policeman shouts: 'She's not drunk, she's dead.' To which Dr Hfuhruhurr replies: 'Dead?! My God! I better get her to a cemetery right away.'

KEY LINES

Dr Hfuhruhurr, to the journalist interviewing him: 'Will you read that back to me. I'm afraid that might make me sound pompous to your readers.'

Journalist: 'My brilliant research into brain transplantation is unsurpassed and will probably make my name live beyond eternity.'

Dr Hfuhruhurr: 'No, that's fine. Take out the "probably". It makes me sound wishy-washy.'

As the newly wed Dr Hfuhruhurr and Dolores drive up to his home, Ramon and his wife are waiting on the porch, surrounded by potted plants.

Dolores: 'What are those assholes doing on the porch?'

Dr Hfuhruhurr: 'Those aren't assholes. It's pronounced azaleas.'

THE MANCHURIAN CANDIDATE

US, 1962, UNITED ARTISTS/MC PRODUCTIONS, 126 MINS

D JOHN FRANKENHEIMER; **PR** GEORGE AXELROD, JOHN FRANKENHEIMER; **ART DIR** RICHARD SYLBERT; **SC** GEORGE AXELROD, BASED ON THE NOVEL BY RICHARD CONDON; **PH** LIONEL LINDON; **M** DAVID AMRAM; **ED** FERRIS WEBSTER **CAST** FRANK SINATRA (BENNETT MARCO), LAURENCE HARVEY (RAYMOND SHAW), JANET LEIGH (ROSIE), ANGELA LANSBURY (RAYMOND'S MOTHER), HENRY SILVA (CHUNJIN), JAMES GREGORY (SENATOR JOHN ISELIN), LESLIE PARRISH (JOCIE JORDAN), JOHN MCGIVER (SENATOR THOMAS JORDAN), KHIGH DIEGH (YEN LO), JAMES EDWARDS (CORPORAL·MELVIN), DOUGLAS HENDERSON (COLONEL), ALBERT PAULSEN (ZILKOV), BARRY KELLEY (SECRETARY OF DEFENCE), LLOYD CORRIGAN (HOLBORN GAINES), MADAME SPIVY (BEREZOVO)

THE STORY Raymond Shaw, a deeply unpopular officer in Korea, is led along with his platoon into a trap. Returning to America he is granted the Congressional Medal of Honor, and takes a job as the assistant to a decent Republican journalist, Holborn Gaines, against the wishes of his scheming mother and crude, commie-baiting stepfather, Senator Iselin. Meanwhile his former fellow soldiers Bennett Marco and Al Melvin are suffering almost identical recurring nightmares in which the members of the troop are hypnotized and Shaw turned into an emotionless killer. In New York the brainwashed Shaw is activated with the use of a queen of diamonds playing card by the communist conspirators. His effectiveness as an assassin is tested by having him kill Gaines. Marco at last persuades the authorities that his dreams are flashbacks to the troop's capture in Korea, and is employed to investigate Shaw's activities. Shaw marries his old sweetheart, the daughter of a liberal senator and arch enemy of Iselin. After a brief honeymoon, Shaw is induced by the conspiracy's American chief, his mother, to kill his wife and father-in-law. Marco tracks Shaw down to an eyrie in Madison

▼ *THE MANCHURIAN CANDIDATE* *A brainwashed Raymond Shaw (Laurence Harvey) about to blow the brains of his comrade over a portrait of Stalin.*

Square Garden, where Shaw is due to kill the presidential nominee, thus dramatically advancing his stepfather's political career. At the last moment Shaw breaks the spell, shooting his mother and stepfather, then himself.

THE FILM The outstanding film of Frankenheimer's career, this faithful screen version of Richard Condon's conspiracy thriller is a remarkable prediction of the mood that would overtake the US and elsewhere in the wake of the century's most famous assassination. It is a strange thriller, one that manages to maintain its delicately balanced mood of dark political foreboding and black humour. The script is sharp, the direction taut, the production design excellent. Part of its skill is the unshowy way it presents complex visual scenes, such as the superb nightmare flashbacks and the sequence in which Iselin provokes his rival in a live TV debate. The film not only marks career highpoints for the director and Laurence Harvey, but was also the last noteworthy movie of Sinatra's career. It was made as Hollywood was recovering from the self-inflicted wounds of McCarthyism and was, unwittingly, gearing itself up for the sudden, violent end of the Kennedy presidency. In Gerald Pratley's *The Films of John Frankenheimer*, the director says: 'I wanted to do a picture that showed both how ludicrous McCarthy-style far right politics are and how dangerous the far left is also, how they were really exactly the same thing, and the idiocy of it all. I wanted to show that and I think we did.'

ODD/SALIENT FACTS President Kennedy himself played a role in the film's genesis. Arthur Krim, president of United Artists and national finance director of the Democratic Party, considered the novel too politically inflammatory. Sinatra, by this stage being forced into the background of the presidential set, took the matter directly to JFK, who liked the idea and agreed to persuade Krim to give the project the go-ahead. As Richard Condon recalled: 'That's the only way the film ever got made. It took Frank going directly to Jack Kennedy.' Later Sinatra arranged a private screening of the film for Kennedy, and after the president's assassination, denied permission for a re-release of the movie. The film contains one of the traditional Hollywood parent–child relationships in which the 37-year-old Angela Lansbury, who had appeared in Frankenheimer's *All Fall Down* (1962), played the mother of the 34-year-old Laurence Harvey.

MEMORABLE MOMENTS The nightmares of Marco and Melvin. The camera pans smoothly around the set in 360-degree shots which interchange the various versions of the audience – the black women, the white women and the communist soldiers who were really there. Having already strangled one of his men, Shaw is ordered to shoot the young soldier Bobby Limbeck. After close-ups of the barrel of the gun and Bobby smiling we see the scene from the gallery. The gun is fired, Limbeck flies back in his chair as his brains splatter over a large portrait of Stalin that forms part of the stage's back-drop.

The assassination of Senator Jordan. Shot through the carton of milk he is removing from the fridge, the liberal politician is shown to bleed milk.

KEY LINES

Yen Lo to the assembled audience: 'I'm sure you've all heard the old wives' tale that no hypnotized subject may be forced to do that which is repellent to his moral nature, whatever that may be. Nonsense of course.'

MANHUNTER

US, 1986, RECORDED RELEASING/RED DRAGON/DE LAURENTIIS ENTERTAINMENT, 120 MINS

D MICHAEL MANN; **PR** RICHARD ROTH; **SC** MICHAEL MANN, BASED ON THE NOVEL RED DRAGON BY THOMAS HARRIS; **PH** DANTE SPINOTTI; **M** THE REDS AND MICHAEL RUBINI; **ED** DOV HOENIG

CAST WILLIAM PETERSEN (WILL GRAHAM), KIM GREIST (MOLLY GRAHAM), DENNIS FARINA (JACK CRAWFORD), JOAN ALLEN (REBA), BRIAN COX (DR HANNIBAL LECTER), STEPHEN LANG (FREDDIE LOUNDS), TOM NOONAN (FRANCIS DOLLARHYDE), DAVID SEAMAN (KEVIN GRAHAM), BENJAMIN HENDRICKSON (DR CHILTON), MICHAEL TALBOT (GEEHAN), DAN E. BUTLER (JIMMY PRICE), MICHELE SHAY (BEVERLY KATZ), ROBIN MOSELEY (SARAH), PAUL PERRI (DR SIDNEY BLOOM), PATRICIA CHARBONNEAU (MRS SHERMAN)

THE STORY Will Graham is tempted out of early retirement to help catch the 'Tooth Fairy', a serial killer operating on nights of a full moon, in the southern states of America. He visits his incarcerated nemesis Dr Lecter to get some advice and refamiliarize himself with the psychotic mindset. Will also watches

> *Have you seen blood in the moonlight, Will? It appears quite black*

home movies of the two dead families, and visits the murder scenes. It is discovered that Lecter is communicating with the 'Tooth Fairy' using an indecipherable code. Graham employs Lounds, a sleazy tabloid journalist, to set himself up as human bait for the killer. But the killer, styling himself after Blake's Red Dragon, kidnaps and kills Lounds. When it emerges that Lecter has informed the killer of Graham's address, his family is moved into a safe house. Red Dragon, Francis Dollarhyde, begins an affair with Reba, a blind woman, in the film labs where they both work. It is the night of the full moon. Dollarhyde misconstrues Reba's innocently kissing a co-worker, kills the man and takes Reba back to his house. Meanwhile Graham finally realizes that the 'Tooth Fairy' must have seen the same films that he has. Flying to St Louis, they identify Dollarhyde as the killer just before landing. Dollarhyde kills two policemen before being killed himself by Graham. Graham returns to his family's peaceful beachfront home.

THE FILM The project was caught up in the producer's legal wranglings. This delay in release led it to be perceived as a problem film and it became an instant cult movie, apparently incapable of mainstream appreciation because of its uncompromising approach to its unpalatable subject matter. Yet four years later *The Silence of the Lambs* (1990), a sequel of sorts, was a smash hit. Will Graham is an older version of Clarice Starling, a dedicated professional who has risked his life and soul to track down murderous psychopaths. In both films, Lecter, played by a Celtic actor, is around to steal the show with his darkly comic cameos. Both films feature modern takes on the battle of good versus evil and the dangers of good people entering the minds of their prey. Each film has a sequence in which the net of law enforcement is apparently being tightened around the killer, only for a sudden twist to reveal that they are on the wrong track, and instead an unsuspecting party encounters the killer. Each ends with the killer attacking a woman who is actually or effectively blind. Michael Mann earlier created the mainstream TV success *Miami Vice* and went on to *The Last of the Mohicans* (1992) and *Heat* (1995). He employs his trademark slick visuals and a very eighties synth-rock soundtrack. Timing, technique and mood ensure that this remains a dark cult favourite.

▲ *MANHUNTER Brian Cox as the fiendishly clever Dr Hannibal Lecter, establishing contact from his top security cell with his newest disciple, the Red Dragon.*

ODD/SALIENT FACTS Dennis Farina, then a serving police officer, began as an advisor to Mann on police matters, before moving into acting himself on TV and in films, notably as the irascible crime boss in *Midnight Run* (1988). The notorious sequence in *Henry: Portrait of a Serial Killer* (1986), in which the killer watches his own work on a video set at a skewed angle, is based on the killer's-eye-view opening sequence of *Manhunter*.

MEMORABLE MOMENTS Graham's intuition of the killer's modus operandi leading him to instruct the forensic scientists to check for fingerprints on the victims' fingernails, toenails and their corneas.

Lecter's casual ingenuity in short-circuiting the phone and then getting hold of Graham's address.

Graham's being woken on his plane journey by the screams of the young girl sitting next to him who has caught sight of the grisly photos that have spilled out of his case file.

With time running out Graham's climactic realization that the 'Tooth Fairy' has seen the same films that he has.

KEY LINES

Lecter: 'By implication you think you're smarter than me since you caught me.'
Graham: 'No, I know that I'm not smarter than you.'

Lecter: 'Then how did you catch me?'
Graham: 'I had advantages.'
Lecter: 'What advantages?'
Graham: 'You're insane.'

Lecter: 'Have you seen blood in the moonlight, Will? It appears quite black.'

Lecter: 'Do you know how you caught me? The reason you caught me, Will, is we're just alike. You want the scent, smell yourself.'

THE MASQUE OF THE RED DEATH

UK, 1964, AMERICAN INTERNATIONAL PICTURES/ALTA VISTA, 86 MINS

D/PR *ROGER CORMAN;* **SC** *CHARLES BEAUMONT, R. WRIGHT CAMPBELL (FROM THE STORIES 'THE MASQUE OF THE RED DEATH' AND 'HOP-FROG' BY EDGAR ALLAN POE);* **PH** *(COL SCOPE) NICOLAS ROEG;* **ED** *ANN CHEGWIDDEN;* **M** *DAVID LEE*
CAST *VINCENT PRICE (PRINCE PROSPERO), HAZEL COURT (JULIANA), JANE ASHER (FRANCESCA), PATRICK MAGEE (ALFREDO), SKIP MARTIN (HOP TOAD), DAVID WESTON (GINO), NIGEL GREEN (LUDOVICO), JOHN WESTBROOK (MAN IN RED), PAUL WHITSUN-JONES (SCARLATTI), JOHN LODGE (SCARLATTI'S WIFE), VERINA GREENLAW (ESMERALDA)*

THE STORY In medieval Italy, Prince Prospero, worshipper of Satan, withdraws into his castle with his mistress Juliana, chosen friends and corrupt courtiers, as the Red Death plague sweeps his province. He takes along a peasant girl, Francesca, a virginal Christian, whose father Ludovico and fiancé Gino he has sentenced to death for their insolence. Juliana, handmaid of Satan, is jealous of Francesca and arranges for her to escape with her father and Gino, but all three are recaptured. Prospero's cruel lieutenant Alfredo has humiliated Esmeralda, a dwarf dancer, whose lover Hop Toad swears revenge. At a feast Prospero produces five knives, one of them bearing a deadly poison, and forces Ludovico and Gino to cut themselves. Ludovico attempts to stab Prospero and is killed; Gino is expelled to catch the plague but Death's emissary, the masked Man in Red, tells him to return and rescue Francesca. Juliana is punished by being ripped to death by Prospero's falcon. At the great ball the Man in Red appears, and Prospero mistakes him for Satan. In a *danse macabre*, the blood-spattered guests die of the plague, and Prospero sees that the Man in Red's face is his own. The Man in Red ensures that Francesca's and Gino's lives are spared.

THE FILM Made in England on a slightly larger budget and longer shooting schedule (25 days instead of 15) than his earlier films, *Red Death* is the seventh and best of Roger Corman's Poe movies, and sticks more closely to the two tales it draws on. It features the finest performance in a Corman movie of Vincent Price, whose Prince Prospero is a witty dandy, a thoughtful connoisseur of evil, who has found God's creation wanting and opted to serve Satan.

Less shocking than its predecessors, much influenced by Ingmar Bergman's *Seventh Seal*, using an eloquent script, *Red Death* is more poetic than horrific. Sets and costumes are more opulent than before (Corman's Hollywood designer worked on

▼ *THE MASQUE OF THE RED DEATH* Evil Prince Prospero communes with fellow predator in his somber courtyard.

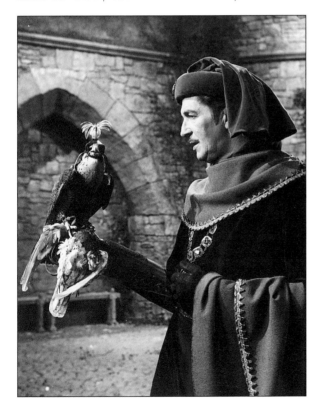

the picture uncredited): the castle's chequered floor ballroom and the suite of identical rooms Juliana walks through after meeting Satan are beautifully conceived. The dramatic lighting drew attention to the then little-known cinematographer Nicolas Roeg. Corman used some distinguished local actors, most especially the Irishman Patrick Magee as the sadistic Alfredo. He was shortly to appear as the Marquis de Sade in Peter Brook's production of *The Marat Sade* for the Royal Shakespeare Company.

The film is not without its imperfections. The hallucinatory sequence of Juliana's marriage to the Devil is arty and pretentious. The choreography is stiffly formal, tepid when it should be orgiastic, and the final dance of death fails to chill in the way intended.

ODD/SALIENT FACTS The former child actress Jane Asher, then seventeen, had her first starring role in *Red Death*; she was the girlfriend of Paul McCartney, whose first film, *A Hard Day's Night*, opened the same month. Corman, always noted for ingenious ways of squeezing his budgets, used the set of a monastery left over from the British comedy *Crooks in Cloisters*; Robert Jones is credited as designer on both pictures. John Trevelyan, the Secretary of the British Board of Film Censors, was so worried about recrudescence of devil worship in Britain that he insisted on Juliana's Satanic dream being cut from the British release print. Corman couldn't find a suitable dwarf to play Esmeralda, so he used a young girl and dubbed her with an adult voice.

MEMORABLE MOMENTS The Man in Red's presenting a white rose speckled with blood to a peasant woman at the beginning of the film, telling her: 'Take this to your village and tell the people that the day of their deliverance is at hand.'

Prospero's first appearance to sneer at the villagers.

Juliana's branding her breast with an inverted cross to become Satan's handmaiden.

Prospero's sticking five daggers into the banqueting table as he speaks to his guests.

The Man in Red's presenting a Tarot card to Gino in the forest.

Prospero's seeing his own face beneath the cowl of the Man in Red.

KEY LINES

Alfredo: 'Can such eyes ever have known sin?'

143

Prospero: 'They will, Alfredo, they will.'

Prospero: 'Not *corrupting*, Alfredo, *instructing*.'

Prospero: 'If a God of love and light did exist, he is long since dead. Someone, something rules in his place.'

Man in Red: 'There is no face of Death until the moment of your own death and I am one of many messengers.'

MONTY PYTHON'S LIFE OF BRIAN★

UK, 1979, HANDMADE FILMS, 93 MINS

D TERRY JONES; **PR** JOHN GOLDSTONE; **SC** GRAHAM CHAPMAN, JOHN CLEESE, TERRY GILLIAM, ERIC IDLE, TERRY JONES, MICHAEL PALIN; **PH** (EASTMAN COLOR) PETER BIZIOU; **M** GEOFFREY BURGON; **ED** JULIAN DOYLE

CAST TERRY JONES (MANDY, MOTHER OF BRIAN ET AL.), GRAHAM CHAPMAN (BRIAN ET AL.), MICHAEL PALIN (PONTIUS PILATE ET AL.), JOHN CLEESE (DIRK REG, LEADER OF JUDEAN PEOPLE'S FRONT ET AL.), ERIC IDLE (MR CHEEKY ET AL.), TERRY GILLIAM (REVOLUTIONARY ET AL.), KEN COLLEY (JESUS), GWEN TAYLOR (MRS BIG NOSE), CAROL CLEVELAND (MRS GREGORY), SUE JONES-DAVIES (JUDITH), SPIKE MILLIGAN (SPIKE), GEORGE HARRISON (MR PAPADOPOULIS)

THE STORY Three Wise Men bring gifts of gold, frankincense and myrrh to the stable in Bethlehem where Mandy Cohen has just given birth to her son Brian. Realizing their error, they retrieve the gifts and present them to Joseph and Mary in the manger down the road. Thirty-three years later ('Judea AD 33 – Saturday Afternoon – About Teatime') Brian and Mandy are in the crowd listening to Christ's Sermon on the Mount, though she would rather be at a stoning. Brian, who sells sweetmeats at the Jerusalem Colosseum, is shocked to learn his father was a Roman Centurion, and joins the People's Front of Judea, an anti-Roman liberation movement. Captured during an attempt to kidnap Pontius Pilate's wife, he is brought before Pilate but escapes. Posing as a speaker at Prophets Corner he attracts a following who proclaim him the Messiah.

He is recaptured and added to 139 other people sentenced to be crucified at Passover. His mother, the leaders of the People's Front, and his revolutionary girlfriend Judith all make their self-serving farewells, and he dies with his fellow victims, cheerfully singing Eric Idle's song 'Always Look on the Bright Side of Life'.

THE FILM A film of the 1970s that wittily criticizes the 1970s, *Life of Brian* gives the team a firm line on which to peg their gags and is the most sustainedly funny, the most daringly irreverent, and the most stylistically consistent of the Python movies. It sends up the pious, sadistic, bogusly uplifting tradition of run-of-DeMille religious epics from the silent era down to *Ben Hur* (whose credit titles it parodies). But it isn't truly blasphemous and lacks the bruised resignation of Jewish humour on the one hand and the Catholic fascination with the liturgical and sacerdotal on the other. It is a very C of E approach by a group of middle-class, public-school-educated agnostic rationalists who have come to find the historical context of the gospels and the theology they contain comic, ludicrous and absurd. Through the competing revolutionary movements in Judea, the film mocks the pomposity and hypocrisy of the trade unions (then exerting a stranglehold on British life) and the ineffectuality of Marxist revolutionary groups that had such an appeal for the students of the 1970s. Christ, however, in the two scenes in which he appears, is treated with respect if not reverence. One of the movie's great attractions is that between them the six members of the Monty Python team play some forty characters, populating a whole world.

'He's not the Messiah, he's a very naughty boy.'

ODD/SALIENT FACTS *Life of Brian* was largely shot on sets built in Tunisia for the reverential, star-studded Lew Grade TV production, *Jesus of Nazareth*, directed by Franco Zeffirelli. Lord Grade's brother, the impresario Sir Bernard Delfont, withdrew the support of his distribution chain from *Life of Brian* on the grounds that it would offend audiences. Fortunately George Harrison's HandMade company picked up the film.

MEMORABLE MOMENTS Brian caught by a Roman centurion daubing the graffito 'Romanes eunt domus' (Romans Go Home) on Pontius Pilate's palace and being instructed, with ear-pulling sadism as if by a traditional Latin master, to construe the language and come up with the correct 'Romani ite domum' and write it out a hundred times on Pilate's wall.

The naked Brian opening his front door to find himself confronted by a crowd of devoted followers.

Pilate confronted by a crowd mocking his speech impediment and introducing his friend Bigus Dickus as a hero who 'wanks as high as any in Wome'.

KEY LINES

Misheard beatitude passed on during the Sermon on the Mount: 'Blessed are the cheese-makers.'

Leader of Judea People's Front: 'All right. *Apart from* the aquaducts, the sanitation, the roads, the medicine, the irrigation, the education, the wine, the public order, what have the Romans ever done for us?'

Brian: 'All right, I'm the Messiah. Now fuck off!'
His followers: 'How shall we fuck off, O Lord?'

Mandy: 'He's not the Messiah, he's a very naughty boy.'

Brian: 'You don't need to follow me, you don't need to follow anyone, you've got to think for yourselves, you're all individuals.'
His followers, in unison: 'We are all individuals.'

THE MOST DANGEROUS GAME (UK TITLE: THE HOUNDS OF ZAROFF)

US, 1932, RKO, 63 MINS

D ERNEST B. SHOEDSACK, IRVING PICHEL; **PR** ERNEST B. SHOEDSACK, MERIAM B. COOPER; **SC** JAMES A. CREELMAN (FROM A STORY BY RICHARD CONNELL); **PH** (BW) HENRY GERRARD; **M** MAX STEINER; **ED** ARCHIE F. MARSHEK
CAST LESLIE BANKS (COUNT ZAROFF), JOEL MCCREA (BOB RAINSFORD), FAY WRAY (EVE), ROBERT ARMSTRONG (MARTIN) NOBLE JOHNSON (IVAN), STEVE CLEMENTO (TARTAR), WILLIAM DAVIDSON (CAPTAIN)

THE STORY Count Zaroff, a rich Cossack who escaped the Soviet Revolution with his fortune intact, has tired of hunting big game and retired to a small island in the Malayan archipelago to hunt humans. Using fake lights he lures ships to their destruc-

tion and treats survivors as guests at his castle until they are ready to become his prey as he stalks them through the jungle with a long-bow. The latest to be marooned is celebrated American big-game hunter Bob Rainsford, who has been preceded to the island by Eve and her drunken brother, Martin. Martin becomes Zaroff's next victim. Refusing Zaroff's invitation to join him in the hunt, Rainsford is given a knife and let loose in the jungle with Eve, who will go to the victor. The chase escalates from bow to telescopic rifle as the resourceful Rainsford fights back, and finally Zaroff brings out his pack of hounds. But the American turns the tables on his pursuer, and as Rainsford and the girl escape by motorboat, the fatally wounded Zaroff is savaged by his own hounds.

THE FILM This intense, economical thriller gives a principled big-game hunter a taste of his own medicine and in his fight for survival makes him as ruthless a killer as his enemy. Suave, decadent European is pitted against resourceful American and the picture pre-figures the conflict between the totalitarianism (Zaroff dresses like an Italian fascist) and democracy of the Second World War. The Count is an early example of the criminal as sadistic, world-weary aesthete, living in a private world in the manner of Dr No and other Bond villains, and the way he strokes his scarred forehead anticipates Ernst Stavro Blofeld. The film has been remade twice and much imitated, most famously in the Geoffrey Household novel *Rogue Male* that Fritz Lang adapted as *Manhunter*, and was much admired by the European surrealists, with Georges Franju evoking it in his *Les Yeux Sans Visage*.

ODD/SALIENT FACTS Many members of the production team (producer, writer, co-director, composer and several actors) were simultaneously engaged on the making of another cult movie, *King Kong*, though the latter's script was still being written. Both films concern terrible occurrences on uncharted islands, and the same jungle set was used for both. Some scenes for *Kong* involving Fay Wray and Robert Armstrong were shot between takes on *The Most Dangerous Game*. The original idea was to have Zaroff use leopards to track his prey, but when this didn't work the company borrowed a pack of Great Danes from comedy star Harold Lloyd. This was the first film of British stage star Leslie Banks who, as a result of a wound received during the Great War, had a partially paralysed face that made his right profile peculiarly sinister, producing a Jekyll and Hyde effect.

MEMORABLE MOMENTS The knocker on the door of Zaroff's castle depicting a wounded satyr clutching a maiden.

Zaroff at his grand piano in a silk dressing gown.

The mounted human heads on the walls of the Count's trophy room.

Rainsford fleeing through the jungle dragging the heroine after him à la James Bond.

KEY LINE

Zaroff: 'He talks of wine and women as a prelude to the hunt. We barbarians know that it is after the chase, and then only, that man revels. You know the saying of the Ogandi chieftains: "Hunt first the enemy, then the woman." It is the natural instinct. The blood is quickened by the kill. One passion builds upon another. Kill, then love! When you have known that, you have known ecstasy.'

▲ *THE MOST DANGEROUS GAME Fay Wray and Joel McCrea flee from Leslie Banks on the set where she and Bruce Cabot will later flee from King Kong.*

MYSTERY TRAIN

US, 1989, PALACE/VC, 110 MINS

D/SC JIM JARMUSCH; **PR** JIM STARK; **PH** ROBBIE MÜLLER (COLOUR DUART); **M** JOHN LURIE; **ED** MELODY LOUDUN

CAST MASATOSHI NAGASI (JUN), YOUKI KUDOH (MITZUKO), SCREAMIN' JAY HAWKINS (DESK CLERK), CINQUÉ LEE (BELLBOY), NICOLETTA BRASCHI (LUISA), ELIZABETH BRACCO (DEE DEE), JOE STRUMMER (JOHNNIE), STEVE BUSCEMI (CHARLIE), RICK AVILES (WILL), TOM NOONAN (CONMAN IN DINER), TOM WAITS (DISK-JOCKEY)

THE STORY Three parallel narratives centre on foreigners in Memphis, Tennessee, who spend the night at a seedy hotel away from the spruce new city centre and leave the following morning by train, plane and truck. In each story the same disk-jockey is heard playing Elvis's 'Blue Moon', the same gunshot rings out, the same train is seen passing over a bridge at night. FAR FROM YOKOHAMA: Two young Japanese rock fans, the cheerful Mitzuko and the morose Jun, make a pilgrimage to Memphis to visit Sun Studios and Graceland. They trail around town, and finally book into a cheap hotel where they talk about rock music, make love and leave the following day.

A GHOST: Luisa, an attractive Italian widow, is escorting her husband's coffin to Rome. A conman in a diner tells her Elvis's ghost wants him to give her his comb and collect a delivery fee of $20. She gives him $10 for the comb and $10 to go away, but when he menaces her she takes refuge in the same hotel as the Japanese. In the foyer she meets Dee Dee, who cannot

afford a room, but the desk clerk suggests they share one. The flighty Dee Dee tells Luisa she is quitting Memphis, leaving behind her English common-law husband Johnny and her brother Charlie, a hairdresser. Luisa tells Dee Dee the conman's story and learns he's a well-known trickster. When Dee Dee goes to sleep, Elvis's ghost appears to Luisa.

LOST IN SPACE: Dee Dee's husband, Johnnie, hates Presley since people keep calling him Elvis because of a slight resemblance. Having lost his job he sits around in a black bar with a friend, getting drunk and flashing a loaded gun. Another black friend, Will, owner of a pick-up truck, and his brother-in-law Charlie are summoned to take him away. Visiting a liquor store, the drunken Johnnie shoots the manager and the three go on the run, drinking steadily and ending up in the same seedy hotel, where the desk clerk is Will's brother-in-law. In the morning Charlie discovers that Johnnie isn't his real brother-in-law because Dee Dee never actually married him. When Johnnie attempts suicide there is a scuffle over the gun and Charlie is

▼ *MYSTERY TRAIN* Japanese Elvis fans relax in their hotel room after a day's sightseeing in Memphis.

Gus: 'Amazing, and how d'you know all this?'
Walter: 'Well, she married a hoodlum, didn't she? What kind of a dame ... would marry a hood?'
Gus: 'All kinds.'

Walter to 'Mrs Neil': 'My partner's dead and it's my fault. He's dead and you're alive. Some exchange.'

THE NIGHT OF THE HUNTER

US, 1955, UNITED ARTISTS, 93 MINS

D *CHARLES LAUGHTON;* **PR** *PAUL GREGORY;* **SC** *JAMES AGEE, CHARLES LAUGHTON, FROM THE NOVEL BY DAVIS GRUBB;* **PH** *(BW) STANLEY CORTEZ;* **M** *WALTER SCHUMANN;* **ED** *ROBERT GOLDEN;* **ART DIR** *HILYARD BROWN;* **SETS** *AL SPENCER* **CAST** *ROBERT MITCHUM (HARRY POWELL), SHELLEY WINTERS (WILLA HARPER), LILLIAN GISH (RACHEL), BILLY CHAPIN (JOHN), PEARL (SALLY JANE BRUCE), PETER GRAVES (BEN HARPER), EVELYN VARDEN (ICEY SPOON), DON BEDDOE (WALT SPOON), JAMES GLEASON (UNCLE BIRDIE), GLORIA CASTILLO (RUBY)*

THE STORY Harry Powell, a murderer and fake preacher, is jailed for the theft of a car. He shares a cell with Ben Harper, who has secreted a stolen $10,000 in his daughter Pearl's doll. Harper is executed. On his release, Powell charms his way into the life of Ben's widow, Willa. The two are soon married, and Powell tries to discover the whereabouts of the cash, but John (Ben and Willa's young son) mistrusts him and makes Pearl promise not to tell him. Powell kills Willa, but the children manage to escape down-river. Powell pursues them on horseback. John and Pearl seek refuge with Rachel who looks after other waifs and strays. Rachel sees off Powell who tries to snatch the

▼ *THE NIGHT OF THE HUNTER Robert Mitchum as preacher Harry Powell brings the wrath of God down upon his innocent wife Willa (Shelley Winters).*

children, and only when Powell is being arrested does John give him the money from the doll.

THE FILM The role of Powell is perfect for Mitchum, who imbues it with a mixture of broad humour and menace. According to Simon Callow in *Charles Laughton: A Difficult Actor*, when the director first spoke of the project to his proposed star, he explained: 'This character I want you to play is a complete shit.' Mitchum replied: 'Present.' Mitchum's phony preacher dominates the film, with his singing, his sinister presence, and humorous psychosis. He is a ruthless killer, who prays sincerely but only for personal gain and in the finest performance of his career Mitchum turns him into one of the greatest of all cinema's charismatic psychopaths. Laughton also turned his hand to writing and entirely reshaped James Agee's 350-page script. Cinematographer Stanley Cortez lends the film its distinctive look, with every shot adding to the dark fairy-tale atmosphere. Cortez himself said: 'Every day I consider something new about light, that incredible thing that can't be described. Of the directors I've worked with, only two have understood it: Orson Welles and Charles Laughton.'

The film like *The Window* (1949) skilfully derives its horror from the impotence of children in the face of violent, devious, vindictive adults. It is only John who instantly sees through the obviously phony Powell. He senses from the outset that Powell is after the money, but his mother is blinded by love, indeed the whole town is taken in. The children try to get help from their uncle Birdie, who has discovered Willa's body but he tells no one to avoid being blamed for it himself. Birdie is hopelessly drunk, and John has to look out for himself and Pearl. As they travel down the river, John has temporarily to become an adult, until he can resume his childishness in his new surrogate family. Apart from his tremendous performance, Mitchum lent Laughton further assistance, as he recalled: 'Charles loathed those children. He made *me* direct them.' Laughton briefly flirted with the idea of adapting Norman Mailer's *The Naked and the Dead* for the screen, but was so dismayed at the failure of this highly personal work that he never directed another film.

ODD/SALIENT FACTS Winters was cast as Willa by her friend Laughton. She writes in her autobiography, *Shelley*, of her problems at having to retrieve her natural Southern accent that she had so studiously lost. Laughton encouraged her: 'In this life we never forget our bad habits, Shelley. They stay around somewhere and are easily recalled when we need them.' Mitchum was unimpressed by his co-star, commenting bluntly: 'Shelley got what she deserved, lying there dead at the bottom of the river.'

MEMORABLE MOMENTS John winces as his father is arrested. He repeats the empathic gesture when Powell, his evil stepfather is in turn arrested.

Powell telling the story of the eternal battle between Love and Hate, via the tattoos on his knuckles.

The off-screen execution of Ben Harper. The camera follows the executioner as he returns home to his wife and children. Cut to John and Pearl being teased about their dead father.

Willa's body strapped into a car in the river, with her hair flowing with the tide. The body is discovered by the feckless Uncle Birdie.

As the children sleep in a barn by the side of the river, Powell is seen in silhouette passing on a nearby road, riding his stolen horse and singing.

KEY LINES

Powell, praying in prison: 'Lord, I reckon you knowed what you was doing when you put me in this very cell at this very time – a man with $10,000 hidden somewhere and a widow in the making.'

Rachel: 'It's a hard world for little things.'

NOSFERATU (EINE SYMPHONIE DES GRAUENS)

GERMANY, 1922, PRANA FILMS, APPROX. 72 MINS

D F.W. MURNAU; **SC** HENRIK GALEEN (LOOSELY BASED ON THE NOVEL DRACULA BY BRAM STOKER); **PH** (BW) FRITZ ARNO WAGNER; **DES** ALBIN GRAU; **M** (FOR ORIGINAL PRESENTATION) HANS ERDMAN

CAST MAX SCHRECK (COUNT ORLOK, NOSFERATU THE VAMPIRE), ALEXANDER GRANACH (KNOCK, AN ESTATE AGENT), GUSTAF VON WANGENHEIM (HUTTER, KNOCK'S ASSISTANT), GRETA SCHRÖDER (ELLEN, HUTTER'S WIFE), G. H. SCHNELL (HARDING, A SHIPBUILDER), RUTH LANDSHOFF (ANNE, HIS WIFE), JOHN GOTTOWT (PROFESSOR BULWER, A PARACELSAN), GUSTAV BOTZ (PROFESSOR SIEVERS, TOWN MEDICAL OFFICER), MAX NEMETZ (SHIP'S CAPTAIN), GUIDO HERZFELD (INNKEEPER) who leads him to the docks and to a ship which she hopes will take him to safety. As Johnny and Kathleen arrive at the docks in the heavy snow, the police close in on them. Kathleen fires towards the police and she and Johnny are shot dead.

THE FILM The film, based on a novel by F. L. Green, marks Reed's first collaboration with the cinematographer Robert Krasker. Krasker, born in Australia, had his view of films shaped by the German Expressionist cinema. The stylized lighting effects that would be such a feature of *The Third Man* (1948), the third of Reed's great trilogy after *The Fallen Idol* (1947), are quite evident here. The Organization and the city are never named but clearly stand for the IRA and Belfast. In *The Man Between*, Nicholas Wapshott's biography of Reed, Joseph Tomelty of the Group Theatre, Belfast, recalls the director as a stickler for the film's authentic detail, demanding of his researchers: 'Describe an armoured car. Do the letters GPO appear on Belfast pillar boxes? Is a police car a Ford, Vauxhall or Morris? What is the uniform of a prison warder in Northern Ireland?' Yet there are some obvious flaws to the film. The main one is the unevenness of the accents with most of the cast speaking in an Irish brogue which stands in stark contrast when heard against the genuine Belfast accents of the film's IRA-wor-shipping street kids. Despite the overblown eccentricities of Robert Newton's performance as the artist Lukey, the film is beautifully worked out and, in David Thomson's assessment 'one of the greatest Irish films ever made'.

ODD/SALIENT FACTS Although the chief source for *Reservoir Dogs* (1992) is *City on Fire* (1989), it must also have been partly inspired by *Odd Man Out*, with its plot of a well-planned heist going badly wrong, and one of the raiders spending the entirety of the action apparently bleeding to death before being shot at the very last. The pub, the Four Winds, in which Johnny

▼ *ODD MAN OUT Fatally wounded Johnny McQueen (James Mason) and Kathleen (Kathleen Ryan) meet up at last at Belfast's snow-covered docks.*

154

hides, was an almost exact replica of the Belfast pub The Crown. The last time the latter was all but destroyed by a terrorist attack, its interior was rebuilt using the production designs for the film.

MEMORABLE MOMENTS The various shootings – the man outside the mill and Johnny, Pat and Nolan, Kathleen and Johnny – before all of which the camera pans away.

The shots of Murphy, Pat and Nolan, and later Dennis running through the streets, filmed with a wide lens and lit from below to show them with their vast distorted shadows pursued across a menacing cityscape.

Johnny's hallucinations of the girl with the football in the shelter as a prison warder, and later seeing the faces of figures from his past in the bubbles of his spilt beer.

KEY LINES

Dennis to Kathleen on Johnny: 'As long as he lives he'll belong to the Organization.'

Shell, hoping to get a reward for Johnny from Father Tom: 'A fella was telling me, I heard tell that his Reverence the Pope is quare and rich.'

Lukey on Johnny: 'I'd paint him and it would all be there, the truth of life and death.'

Johnny, having his epiphany in Lukey's studio, on Father Tom: 'We've always drowned your voice with our shouting, haven't we, Father?'

ON THE WATERFRONT

US, 1954, COLUMBIA/HORIZON PICTURES, 108 MINS

D ELIA KAZAN; **PR** SAM SPIEGEL; **SC** BUDD SCHULBERG (BASED ON ARTICLES BY MALCOLM JOHNSON); **PH** (BW) BORIS KAUFMAN; **ED** GENE MILFORD; **M** LEONARD BERNSTEIN

CAST MARLON BRANDO (TERRY MALLOY), EVA MARIE SAINT (EDIE DOYLE), KARL MALDEN (FATHER BARRY), LEE J. COBB (MICHAEL J. SKELLY, AKA JOHNNY FRIENDLY), ROD STEIGER (CHARLEY MALLOY), PAT HENNING (KAYO DUGAN), JOHN HAMILTON (POP DOYLE), LEIF ERICKSON (GLOVER, CRIME COMMISSION AGENT), JAMES WESTERFIELD (BIG MAC), TONY GALENTO (TRUCK), TAMI MAURIELLO (TILLIO), FRED GWYNNE (SLIM)

▲ *ON THE WATERFRONT Marlon Brando as Terry Malloy seeks redemption in the arms of Eva Marie Saint.*

THE STORY Terry Malloy, a slow-witted young ex-boxer, works for racketeer Johnny Friendly who runs a branch of the Longshoremen's Union on the docks of Hoboken, New Jersey. Terry's educated older brother, Charley, is Friendly's chief lieutenant, and he and Friendly, through fixing fights, were responsible for Terry quitting the ring. Joey, a friend of Terry's and fellow pigeon-fancier, is about to appear before the Waterfront Crime Commission, when Terry unwittingly lures him to the roof of their tenement from which he is thrown to his death by Friendly's goons. Joey's sister Edie, a trainee teacher, gets

KEY LINES

Harmonica: 'No Frank?'
Knuckles: 'Frank sent us.'
Harmonica: 'Did you bring a horse for me?'
Knuckles: 'Looks like we're shy one horse.'
Harmonica: 'You brought two too many.'

Before Frank and Harmonica's final shootout.
Frank: 'Nothing matters now, not the land, not the money, not the woman. I came to see you because I know that you'll tell me what I'm after.'
Harmonica: 'Only at the point of dying.'
Frank: 'I know.'

ORPHÉE

FRANCE, 1950, LES FILMS DU PALAIS ROYAL, 112 MINS

D/SC *JEAN COCTEAU;* **PR** *ANDRÉ PAULVÉ;* **PH** *(BW) NICOLAS HAYER;* **M** *GEORGES AURIC;* **ED** *JACQUELINE SADOUL*
CAST *JEAN MARAIS (ORPHÉE), FRANÇOIS PÉRIER (HEURTEBISE), MARIA CASARÈS (THE PRINCESS), MARIE DÉA (EURYDICE), ÉDOUARD DERMITHE (CÉGISTE), JACQUES VARENNE (THE FIRST JUDGE), JULIETTE GRECO (AGLAONICE), ROGER BLIN (THE WRITER)*

THE STORY At the Café des Poètes in Paris the celebrated poet Orphée runs into fans of his young rival Cégiste, whom he despises. The Princess arrives in a Rolls-Royce driven by Heurtebise; there is a riot and Cégiste is killed by two motorcyclists.

'Mirrors are the doors by which death comes?'

The Princess drives him away, persuading Orphée to come along as a witness. She is Death, the motorcyclists are her aides, and she takes Cégiste through a mirror into the next world leaving Orphée to wake up in a sand quarry. Heurtebise drives Orphée home where his wife Eurydice is being comforted by a police inspector and Eurydice's friend Aglaonice, leader of women and owner of the nightclub Les Bacchantes. Orphée becomes obsessed by the cryptic messages coming from the car radio in the Rolls-Royce (e.g. 'The bird sings with its fingers, once', 'Silence is twice as fast backwards, three

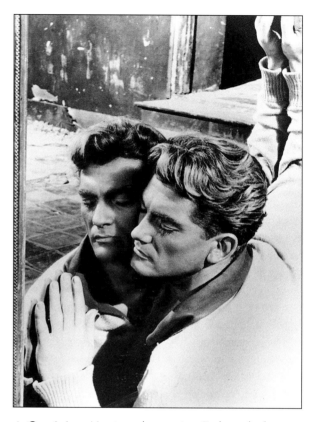

▲ *ORPHÉE Jean Marais as the questing Orpheus clutches a mirror, the gateway to the Underworld.*

times') and is indifferent to his wife. It transpires that Orphée and Death are in love with each other, and Heurtebise loves Eurydice. When Eurydice is killed while cycling, Heurtebise takes Orphée through a mirror into the Zone, an underworld of ruins, where they appear with Death before a tribunal that allows Eurydice to return to life provided Orphée doesn't look at her, but he does and she's taken away. Orphée is attacked and killed by Aglaonice's followers, who believe Orphée has stolen Cégiste's poems (the gnomic lines heard on the car radio). Death and Heurtebise decide to sacrifice themselves so that Orphée and Eurydice can be free, and are led away by the two motorcyclists.

THE FILM *Orphée* is still one of the most magical fantasy movies, despite the technical advances made in special effects. The journeys through mirrors (achieved by using doubles, vats of mercury, troughs of water and unsilvered glass) have a

dreamlike quality and the Zone beyond them has the haunted nightmare feeling of a 1940s neo-romantic painting. A versatile poet, playwright, artist, essayist and film-maker, Cocteau (1889–1963) made this, his fifth and best movie, in his sixtieth year. He identified with the egotistical, death-loving Orphée, and the hostility that people in the movie have towards the poet represents the homosexual, dilettante, politically uncommitted Cocteau's own resentment of the attacks made upon him by the Surrealists and communists in the 1920s, and after the war by younger critics. The tribunal in the underworld is a combination of wartime resistance meetings and postwar courts set up to judge collaborators The cryptic snatches of poems on the car radio were inspired by the coded messages sent by the BBC to the French Resistance. The casting of Jean Marais as the fading poet and Édouard Dermithe as the rising one reflects the position the two actors had in Cocteau's life. The film is at once timeless and a reflection of Paris in the postwar years.

Orphée has its weaknesses, but generally it has worn well and while it may seem less obscure today it has lost little of its poetic charm. Some of its particular grace comes from the performances of the handsome Marais, the striking Casarès, and François Perier.

ODD/SALIENT FACTS *Orphée* won First Prize at the 1950 Venice Festival. The request 'Astonish us', spoken to Orphée at the café, was originally addressed to the young Cocteau by Sergei Diaghilev in the form 'Étonne-moi'. Most of the underworld scenes were shot in the blitzed ruins of the St Cyr military academy. Roger Blin became famously associated with Beckett's plays. Georges Auric (whose score incorporates themes from Glück's *Orpheus and Eurydice*) composed the music for many French, American and British films, e.g. *Passport to Pimlico* (1949) and *The Lavender Hill Mob* (1951).

MEMORABLE MOMENTS The first glimpse of Death's Rolls-Royce stopping outside the café.

Orphée's opening the avant-garde magazine *Nudisme* to discover that all its pages are blank.

The handpiece of the telephone floating back into the holder after Heurtebise takes a call from the police inspector.

Heurtebise and Orphée floating along a wall in the Zone.
Death and Heurtebise being led away at the end.

KEY LINES

Man in café to Orphée: 'Your trouble is knowing just how far to go too far.'

The Princess: 'The role of the dreamer is to accept his dreams.'

The Princess: 'What are you staring at, Cégiste? Did you expect a shroud and a scythe?'

Heurtebise: 'Mirrors are the doors by which death comes?'

The Princess: 'Perhaps he sleeps and dreams us. We are his bad dreams.'

OUT OF THE PAST (UK TITLE: BUILD MY GALLOWS HIGH)
US, 1947, RKO, 96 MINS

D *JACQUES TOURNEUR;* **SC** *GEOFFREY HOMES (FROM HIS NOVEL BUILD MY GALLOWS HIGH);* **PH** *(BW) NICHOLAS MUSURACA;* **M** *ROY WEBB;* **ED** *SAMUEL E. BEETLEY*

CAST *ROBERT MITCHUM (JEFF BAILEY), JANE GREER (KATHIE MOFFETT), KIRK DOUGLAS (WHIT STERLING), RHONDA FLEMING (META CARSON), STEVE BRODIE (FISHER), VIRGINIA HUSTON (ANN)*

'You started this and you'll end it. Besides Joe couldn't find a prayer in a Bible.'

THE STORY World-weary ex-private-eye Jeff Bailey, attempting to start a new life with Ann, a small-town girlfriend in California's Sierra Nevada, is tracked down by a henchman of sadistic gambler Whit Sterling. Flashbacks reveal that Sterling had hired Bailey to trace his mistress, Kathie, who had shot him and fled with $40,000. Pursuing her to Mexico, Jeff falls for her and together they go on the run to San Francisco where the treacherous Kathie kills Jeff's crooked partner and involves Jeff in a complex intrigue that leads to the grave.

THE FILM One of the great *film noir* thrillers, it contrasts (in the manner of eighteenth-century English fiction) the wholesome, boring countryside against the wicked, alluring town; the cold, repressive United States against the torrid, liberating Mexico.

159

Insidiously presenting the world of nightclubs, irregular occupations and unsanctified relationships as more desirable than settled, middle-class family life, the movie goes to the cruel heart of American *noir*. The moral retribution demanded by Hollywood's Hays Office Code happily coincides with the film-makers' world view, leading to an ending of tragic finality far more satisfying than most American movies.

ODD/SALIENT FACTS Dick Powell was originally announced to play the leading role. Geoffrey Homes is a pseudonym for the left-wing novelist Daniel Mainwaring who wrote several screenplays under his own name, including those for *The Lawless* (Joseph Losey, 1950), *Invasion of the Bodysnatchers* (Don Siegel, 1956) and *Baby Face Nelson* (Don Siegel, 1957). Jane Greer has a cameo role in *Against the Odds* (Taylor Hackford, 1984), a remake of *Out of the Past* in which Jeff Bridges and James Woods replace Robert Mitchum and Kirk Douglas.

MEMORABLE MOMENTS Kathie's first appearance, wearing a white broad-brimmed hat, entering from the sun-drenched street into the dark Acapulco bar where Jeff awaits her.

The couple on a silvery moonlit beach, framed by fishing nets that symbolize both the trap they are in and the spider's web into which Kathie has lured Jeff.

▼ *OUT OF THE PAST* Brunette enchantress Jane Greer emerges from the shadows to re-enter private eye Mitchum's life.

KEY LINES

Jeff: 'I never saw her in the daytime. We seemed to live by night. What was left of the day went away like a pack of cigarettes you smoked.'

Whit: 'You started this and you'll end it. Besides Joe couldn't find a prayer in a Bible.'

Kathie: 'Jeff, you ought to have killed me for what I did a moment ago.'
Jeff: 'There's time.'

PANDORA'S BOX

GERMANY, 1929, NERO FILM A.G., 140 MINS (ALTERNATIVE VERSIONS 120 AND 131 MINS)

D G. W. PABST; **PR** GEORGE C. HORSETZKY; **SC** LADISLAUS VAJDA, JOSEPH R. FLIESNER FROM THE PLAYS ERDGEIST AND DIE BÜCHSE DER PANDORA BY FRANK WEDEKIND; **PH** (BW) GÜNTHER KRAMPF; **M** CURTIS IVAN SALKE; **ED** JOSEPH R. FLIESLER

CAST LOUISE BROOKS (LULU), FRITZ KORNER (DR PETER SCHÖN), FRANZ LEDERER (ALWA SCHÖN), CARL GÖTZ (SCHIGOLCH, PAPA BROMMER), ALICE ROBERTS (COUNTESS ANNA GESCHWITZ), DAISY D'ORA (MARIE DE ZARNIKO), KRAFFT RASCHIG (RODRIGO QUAST), MICHAEL VON NEWLINSKY (MARQUIS CASTI-PIANI), SIEGFRIED ARNO (STAGE MANAGER), GUSTAV DIESSL (JACK THE RIPPER)

THE STORY Lulu, a prostitute, hopes to marry the prosperous newspaper owner, Schön, and is upset by his engagement to Marie Adelaide de Zarniko. At the theatre where she is due to appear in a revue, Lulu is inflamed with jealousy and refuses to go on. Schön appeases her and the two are discovered in a passionate embrace by Marie and Alwa. Schön and Lulu marry, but on their wedding night Lulu shoots and kills Schön. The subsequent trial descends into chaos and Lulu escapes with the help of Schigolch, Rodrigo and Alwa. This mismatched quartet survive blackmail and a three-month stay on a gambling boat before ending up in a seedy garret in London. There, Lulu, working as a prostitute is killed by Jack the Ripper.

THE FILM This film, distilled from two Wedekind plays, is remarkable for several reasons, first for being the only film for which a gifted director and iconic star are widely remembered. Pabst's use of an elliptical narrative technique, brilliant lighting

▲ *PANDORA'S BOX Louise Brooks as Lulu, the role that both defined and effectively finished her career.*

and complex sight-lines create an unsettling effect but his film would hardly be talked of today were it not for an inspired piece of casting in the central role. Louise Brooks was a 23-year-old former dancer who had appeared in a handful of Hollywood films, one alongside W. C. Fields, before appearing in what she saw as an 'unimportant part' in Howard Hawks's *A Girl In Every Port* (1928). This role brought her to the attention of Pabst who saw her as perfect for the role of the destructive and self-destructive prostitute, Lulu. Her performance retains its erotic charge and created the cult of Lulu, or Loulou. Brooks herself would work hard for the rest of her life to cultivate this enigmatic persona.

ODD/SALIENT FACTS Brooks returned to Hollywood after making one more film for Pabst and another in France but found that her status there had been harmed by her having abandoned her contract with Paramount, and she gradually withdrew from films, making her last appearance in 1938. She slipped into obscurity working as a storegirl in New York before her repu-

tation was revised and her cult status assured by the revival of several of her films in the 1950s. She studied cinema and began to publish autobiographical and critical pieces for film journals, a collection of which were published as *Lulu in Hollywood*. Louise Brooks's status as an icon was enhanced in a series of profiles, most notably by Kenneth Tynan (whose wife, the late Kathleen Tynan, wrote a screenplay about their affair, soon to be filmed), and cemented by cult director Jonathan Demme's *Something Wild* (1986). One of the best of the mid-eighties mini-genre of 'yuppie nightmare' movies, this tells the story of Jeff Daniels' urban wimp being transported on an ever more dangerous adventure by fantasist Lulu played by Melanie Griffiths, complete with Louise Brooks black bob wig.

MEMORABLE MOMENTS Backstage at the theatre, Schön and his fiancée are enjoying the frenetic action. Marie and then Schön stare at Lulu and she stares back, suddenly so upset that she refuses to go onstage: 'I'll dance for the whole world, but not in front of that woman.' Pabst ignores the grammar of film here to have the characters captured from different angles making it appear as if they are all three staring in the same direction.

When Marie finds her fiancé kissing in the back room, Lulu can't suppress her delighted smile and Schön declares: 'This is my execution.'

The murder scene itself is filmed with Schön's back filling almost the entire screen, so that we see Lulu's head and realize the shot has been fired only from the wisp of smoke rising between the two of them.

KEY LINES

Louise Brooks wrote: 'The finest job of casting G. W. Pabst ever did was casting himself as the director, the Animal Trainer of his adaptation of Wedekind's "tragedy of monsters".'

This insinuation of director into the story is echoed in the film. Directly after the murder scene we cut to the last words of the defence speech which suggests what the film has shown: 'Honoured Court: in a rapid series of pictures I have shown you a fearful destiny.' The prosecution responds: 'Honoured court – gentlemen of the jury. The Greek gods created a woman, Panndora. She is beautiful, enticing, well versed in the arts of flattery.'

PEEPING TOM

UK, 1960, ANGLO-AMALGAMATED, 103 MINS

D/PR MICHAEL POWELL; **SC** LEO MARKS; **PH** OTTO HELLER;
M BRIAN EASDALE; **ED** NORMAN ACKLAND

CAST CARL BOEHM (MARK LEWIS), MOIRA SHEARER (VIVIAN), ANNA MASSEY (HELEN STEPHENS), MAXINE AUDLEY (MRS STEPHENS), ESMOND KNIGHT (ARTHUR BADEN), BARTLET MULLINS (MR PETERS), BRENDA BRUCE (DORA), MARTIN MILLER (DR ROSEN), PAMELA GREEN (MILLIE), MICHAEL POWELL (PROFESSOR A. N. LEWIS), SHIRLEY ANNE FIELD (PAULINE SHIELDS), MICHAEL GOODLIFFE (DON JARVIS), JACK WATSON (CHIEF INSPECTOR GREGG), NIGEL DAVENPORT (DET. SGT. MILLER), MILES MALLESON (CUSTOMER IN NEWSAGENT'S)

THE STORY The reclusive Mark Lewis's tenants in his London house include Helen, a librarian attracted to Mark, and her blind mother, who distrusts him. Mark works at a film studio and aims to eventually direct movies, and has a projection room and laboratory at home. He has two clandestine projects: taking nude photographs in a sleazy studio above a newsagent's, and filming women at the moment of death; they see their faces in a mirror as the knife in the camera tripod plunges into their throats. The death of a prostitute in Central London, and of Vivian, a stand-in at 'Chipperfield Studios', alert Scotland Yard to the presence of a serial killer. It is revealed that Mark's father was a biologist interested in the physiology of fear. He experimented on the young Mark, observing his reactions when suddenly finding a lizard on his bed, seeing his mother's corpse, or meeting his father's new young wife. Mark is told by a psychiatrist that his father was doing research into voyeurism or scopophilia, 'the morbid desire to gaze', only curable with years of treatment. That night Mark, now under police surveillance, murders his third victim, and returning home finds Helen horrified at the film of Vivian's death. Mark tells her all and completes his film by photographing the arrival of the police and his own suicide using the method employed on his victims. The last words are from a tape-recording of Mark the child saying: 'Goodnight Daddy'.

THE FILM Peeping Tom retains its capacity to shock, disgust, slyly amuse, and to shame us, the movie audience, into recognizing that every time we enter the cinema we become voyeurs. This is Hitchcock's Rear Window with the velvet glove removed from the steel fist. It's a bizarre collaboration between one of

the great geniuses of the cinema and a British studio known for low-budget exploitation flicks, that had just launched a series of low-brow farces with Carry On Sergeant. For nearly thirty years Powell, the romantic Englishman, had collaborated with Emeric Pressburger, the ironic Mittel-European, on some of the most sophisticated pictures ever made in Britain, A Matter of Life and Death and The Red Shoes among them. The partnership was dissolved in 1956 and neither did anything of consequence in the last three decades of life apart from Peeping Tom, one of the most savage works ever made about film and the film business, by someone fascinated and disgusted by film in equal measure.

Peeping Tom is deliberately cheap-looking, glibly edited, and much of the acting is coarse-grained. It is a picture about a film company run by a cost-cutting studio boss with contempt for his own product. Mark's friend frequents the Everyman Cinema in Hampstead and reads Sight and Sound, but is also

▼ *PEEPING TOM* Duffel-coated homicidal photographer Carl Boehm returns to the scene of the crime.

a connoisseur of porn photographs. Mark's other employer, the newsagent, sells obscene pictures to respectable readers of *The Times* and *Daily Telegraph*.

The film divided critics, most of whom loathed it ('this beastly picture', C. A. Lejeune, *Observer*), some admired it ('a masterpiece', *Sunday Times*), and it rapidly developed a cult following. The idea that the vilification ended Powell's career is a myth.

ODD/SALIENT FACTS Powell put himself at the centre by playing Mark's father and using his own son as the young Mark. The screenwriter Leo Marks was apparently trying to exorcise demons from his role in wartime espionage when he had to send people to their deaths. Powell chose Newman Passage (off Upper Rathbone Place, north of Oxford Street) for the pre-credit sequence murder of the prostitute because that was where he shot the first scene on location in his directorial debut, *Two Crowded Hours* (1931). Anna Massey had her first substantial film role in *Peeping Tom*.

MEMORABLE MOMENTS The prostitute realizing that she is the cameraman's victim just as the spectator recognizes that the camera eye resembles the assassin's beady lens.

The monochrome home-movie footage of the lizard dropped on young Mark's bed like a creature in *Jurassic Park*.

The blind Mrs Stephens standing between screen and projector, sensing something evil.

Mark showing Helen his instrument of death, her face hideously distorted in the mirror.

KEY LINES

Helen: 'I like to understand what I'm shown. What was your father trying to do?'

Helen: 'Mark are you crazy?'
Mark: 'Yes, do you think they'll notice?'

Mrs Stephens: 'All this filming isn't healthy. Get some help Mark.'

Mark: 'Do you know what the most frightening thing in the world is? It's fear.'

Two cops in final sequence: 'It's only a camera.'
'Only?'

PERFORMANCE★

UK, 1970, WARNER BROS/GOODTIME ENTERPRISES, 105 MINS
D DONALD CAMMELL, NICOLAS ROEG; **PR** SANFORD LIEBERSON; **SC** DONALD CAMMELL; **PH** (COL) NICOLAS ROEG; **M** JACK NITZSCHE; **ED** ANTHONY GIBBS, BRIAN SMEDLEY-ASTON **CAST** JAMES FOX (CHAS), MICK JAGGER (TURNER), ANITA PALLENBERG (PHERBER), MICHELLE BRETON (LUCY), ANN SIDNEY (DANA), JOHN BINDON (MOODY), STANLEY MEADOWS (ROSEBLOOM), ALAN CUTHBERTSON (THE LAWYER), ANTHONY MORTON (DENNIS), JOHNNY SHANNON (HARRY FLOWERS), ANTHONY VALENTINE (JOEY MADDOCKS), KEN COLLEY (TONY FARRELL), JOHN STERLAND (THE CHAUFFEUR), LARRAINE WICKENS (LARRAINE)

THE STORY Chas is an enforcer working for gay gangster Harry Flowers. When Chas kills Joey, he

'I am a bullet.'

goes into hiding in the basement flat of decadent, reclusive pop star Turner. Turner, involved in a sexual *ménage à trois*, sees the violent Chas as a kind of alter ego, and sets about dismantling him with drugs and mind games. Just before Chas is taken away by his old cronies, he shoots Turner, but as the car pulls away, it is Turner's face that looks out at the camera.

THE FILM *Performance* marks the directorial debut for both Cammell and Roeg. The former was a successful painter who turned to film-making as a more vibrant art form. Roeg was a distinguished cinematographer who had shot, among others *The Masque of the Red Death* (1964), *Fahrenheit 451* (!1966) and *Far From the Madding Crowd* (1967). The background to the story is the new social fluidity of the time in England. Sex, drugs and money facilitated a coming together of the aristocracy, show business, particularly actors and rock stars, and gangsters in a hip new demi-monde. Early cuts of the film had a clear two-part structure of roughly equal weight given to the gangster material and the sex and drugs and rock 'n' roll, with the actors on either side knowing little or nothing of the rest of the film. The need to trim the first half helped reinforce a quality that was already in the later scenes and would mark the few remaining Cammell and Roeg movies of the 1970s. Cammell's belief that time itself was an illusion is conveyed by sudden jump-cuts and jarring temporal juxtapositions. The other central thrust of the film is the notion of spiritual twinning, diametrically

163

opposed characters being halves of a whole, parallel to the social mixing, a blurring of the distinctions in gender, sexuality, light and dark. The relationship between Chas and Turner is symbiotic and destructive, a dark melding of the personalities of two performers.

ODD/SALIENT FACTS During the shoot, the Notting Hill house set became a scene for the blurring of the barriers between art and life. In this closed environment, the actors were kept away from natural light and Cammell and Jagger set about the deconstruction of Fox's ego in replication of the on-screen drama. This they achieved so effectively that Fox withdrew first from their social milieu, but then from acting itself. He worked as a Christian evangelist throughout the 1970s, only returning to the screen in the mid-1980s. Off-screen tensions arose between Jagger and his own glimmer twin, Keith Richards, over the authenticity of the intimate sex scenes between Jagger and Pallenberg, Keef's then girlfriend. There was a persistent rumour that the bullet's-eye shot as Chas shoots Turner was achieved by placing a camera between Pallenberg's legs and doing a zoom shot of her vagina. The myth is apparently unfounded, although its spread was presumably encouraged by the filmmakers themselves. A further rumour has it that the shot was achieved by a zoom shot into the bullet wound of a corpse. Cammell's own post-*Performance* career was one largely of frustration, with only two completed films, *The Demon Seed* (1977) and *White of the Eye* (1987). *Performance* is the work of a man obsessed with mirrors, questions of identity and death. Cammell had always planned to end his life by suicide, unable to contemplate the randomness of a natural death. In 1995, professionally frustrated by the post-production problems with *Wild Side* (1996), Cammell shot himself in the head, and survived without pain for perhaps 45 minutes, during which time he asked for a mirror so that he could watch himself die.

MEMORABLE MOMENTS Turner, Pherber and Lucy share a bath and plaster on to one another the notes that Chas has given them.

As Pherber questions Chas about his identity she holds a mirror against his chest, so that it looks as if he has her breast, and against his face, so that he seems to have half of her face.

The climactic shooting in which the fatal bullet enters Turner's head, travelling along some apparently pre-existing tunnel before smashing through a photograph of the great Argentinian writer Jorge Luis Borges.

It is said that Cammell's dying words were: 'Did you see Borges?'

KEY LINES

Chas to Harry Flowers: 'I know who I am, Harry.'

Chas, just before killing Joey: 'I am a bullet.'

Turner to Chas: 'The only performance that makes it, that really makes it, that makes it all the way, is the one that achieves madness.'

PIMPERNEL SMITH
UK, 1941, BRITISH NATIONAL, 121 MINS

D LESLIE HOWARD; **PR** LESLIE HOWARD; **SC** ANATOLE DE GRUNWALD, ROLAND PERTWEE BASED ON A STORY BY A. G. MCDONELL AND WOLFGANG WILHELM; **PH** MUTZ GREENBAUM; **M** JOHN GREENWOOD; **ED** SIDNEY COLE
CAST LESLIE HOWARD (PROFESSOR HORATIO SMITH), MARY MORRIS (LUDMILLA KOSLOWSKI), FRANCIS L. SULLIVAN (GENERAL VON GRAUM), HUGH MCDERMOTT (DAVID MAXWELL), RAYMOND HUNTLEY (MARX), MANNING WHILEY (BERTIE GREGSON), DAVID TOMLINSON (STEVE), PETER GAWTHORNE (SIDIMIR KOSLOWSKI), ALLAN JEAYES (DR BECKENDORF), DENNIS ARUNDELL (HOFFMAN), PHILIP FRIEND (SPENCER), JOAN KEMP-WELCH (SCHOOLTEACHER), LAWRENCE KITCHIN (CLARENCE ELSTEAD), BASIL APPLEBY (JOCK MCINTYRE), PERCY WALSH (DVORAK), ROLAND PERTWEE (SIR GEORGE SMITH), CHARLES PATON (STEINHOF), AUBREY MALLALIEU (THE DEAN), GEORGE STREET (SCHMIDT), A. E. MATTHEWS (EARL OF MEADOWBROOK), BRIAN HERBERT (JAROMIR), ARTHUR HAMBLING (JORDAN)

THE STORY Berlin, spring 1939. A scientist is rescued from Nazi Germany by a mystery man who whistles 'There Is a Tavern in the Town' and carries a calling card that reads: 'The mind of man is bounded only by the universe.' Cut to Cambridge University where the dreamy, misogynist Professor Horatio Smith teaches archaeology. He takes six of his students along with him on a trip to Germany to investigate an ancient Aryan civilization. They spend a night at a chalet by the Swiss border across which another man escapes the Nazis late one night with the help of the mysterious, whistling benefactor.

▲ *PIMPERNEL SMITH Professor Smith explains the finer points of British humour to an uncomprehending General von Graum. (Francis L. Sullivan).*

Meanwhile General von Graum hatches a plot to catch him. The man disguised as a scarecrow is shot in the arm while helping a pianist escape. Smith's pupils finally realize that Smith is the hero and insist on helping him. Von Graum tries to trap the mystery man with the help of Ludmilla, the daughter of a prisoner of the Nazis. She identifies Smith, but the two fall in love and he resolves to help her father escape. This he does with the aid of his students, under the noses of the Germans and, having disproved the existence of an Aryan civilization, escapes himself.

THE FILM Leslie Howard went into acting largely as therapy to help him counter the shell shock he suffered in the First World War. Having established himself as a major star on both sides of the Atlantic, he returned to England at the outbreak of the Second World War. The character of Smith is a fusion of two of his most popular pre-war roles, Sir Percy Blakeney from *The Scarlet Pimpernel* (1935) and Professor Higgins from *Pygmalion* (1938). The heroism of the former is joined to the intellect and initial misogyny of the latter. It remains a sparklingly entertaining piece of propaganda which, apart from its influence on the mood of the audience at the time, had a major effect in shaping one of the most popular franchises of modern Hollywood. The idea of an archaeologist hero who leads a double life as a staid professor and a bold adventurer battling the Nazis

inspired George Lucas and Steven Spielberg to invent their own character, Indiana Jones.

ODD/SALIENT FACTS The impact of Howard's propaganda work in general, and particularly with *Pimpernel Smith* and his subsequent film *First of the Few* (1942), was tremendous. It remains unclear whether Howard's plane, returning from a secret mission to Lisbon on 1 June 1943, was shot down because the Nazis believed that Churchill was aboard, or simply to eradicate Howard himself, who was, according to his son Ronald 'Britain's most powerful and effective propagandist'. The film has been interpreted as a specifically Christian fable with Smith described by his students as 'the greatest man in the Universe', being identified by his wounded wrist and finally vowing to return. But its culthood lies in the iconic status and death of Howard and the striking effect the film had on the young Swedish diplomat Raoul Wallenberg, who went on to save the lives of thousands of Hungarian Jews from the Nazis (Howard's own father was a Hungarian Jew). In *Righteous Gentile*, his biography of Wallenberg, John Bierman writes of how in the winter of 1942 Wallenberg went with his half-sister to a special screening of the film at the British embassy in Stockholm: 'Wallenberg identified strongly with Howard's quiet, pipe-smoking Professor Smith, whom he physically resembled. "On the way home he told me that was just the kind of thing he would like to do," Nina Lagergren recalls. By an astonishing twist of fate, Wallenberg was to get his chance.'

MEMORABLE MOMENTS The shooting of the scarecrow followed by silence and the discreet trickle of blood from its wrist.

Smith's final escape from under the spotlight at the station, gone with a wisp of smoke.

KEY LINES

Smith: 'No I hate violence. It seems such a paradox to kill a man before you can persuade him what's right.'

Smith, explaining his reasons for helping others escape: 'You see, when a man holds the view that progress and civilization depend in every age upon the hands and brains of a few exceptional spirits, it's rather hard to stand by and see them destroyed.'

Smith's final assurance to von Graum: 'Don't worry. I'll be back. We'll all be back.'

PINK FLAMINGOS★

US, 1972, SALIVA FILMS, 95 MINS

D JOHN WATERS; **PR** JOHN WATERS; **SC** JOHN WATERS;
PH JOHN WATERS; **M** VARIOUS; **ED** JOHN WATERS
CAST DIVINE (DIVINE/BABS JOHNSON), DAVID LOCHARY
(RAYMOND MARVEL), MINK STOLE (CONNIE MARVEL), MARY
VIVIAN PEARCE (COTTON), EDITH MASSEY (MAMA EDIE), DANNY
MILLS (CRACKERS), CHANNING WILROY (CHANNING), COOKIE
MUELLER (COOKIE), PAUL SWIFT (EGGMAN), SUSAN WALSH (FIRST
KIDNAPPED WOMAN), LINDA OLGEIRSON (SECOND KIDNAPPED
WOMAN)

THE STORY Divine/Babs Johnson, lives with her super-trailer-trash family – the relatively normal Cotton (her egg-obsessed mother) and mentally retarded son Crackers – and rejoices in her reputation as the filthiest person alive. This title is challenged by her rivals, the homicidal, drug and porn-peddling Marvels. They track down Divine by arranging for Cookie to have sex with Crackers and a live chicken. They send Divine a turd as a birthday gift. At the party, Mama Edie marries the eggman, and when the police, who have been called by the Marvels, arrive, they are killed and eaten. Divine and Crackers get revenge on the Marvels by licking their furniture, and release Channing, who had been locked in a closet for spying on the Marvels having sex. Channing is in turn castrated by the two pregnant women who had been locked in the Marvels' basement. When she finds that the Marvels have burnt down the family's trailer, Divine tars and feathers them and, in front of journalists, shoots them. Moving to Boise, Idaho, Divine cements her reputation as the filthiest person in the world by eating dog shit.

THE FILM John Waters was born in Baltimore and dropped out of NYU's film school to begin his career as a genius of painstakingly tasteless low-budget film-making. He has proved himself, whatever the people behind Serial Mom (1994) may have thought, incapable of working within the mainstream. Pink Flamingos is the purest expression of his unique talents and was trumpeted by the director himself as 'the most disgusting picture of all time'. The film's and the director's desire to appal with every scene is somehow infantile, but the film has an undeniable potency and a unique brand of humour. The final sequence is still genuinely disgusting, as is the perverse chicken-fucking scene. Pink Flamingos is the film that launched Waters and Divine as major cult figures. It remains a kind of masterpiece of

schlock, an essay in gross-out, an exercise in defining and then surpassing limits of tastelessness.

ODD/SALIENT FACTS Waters is Quentin Crisp's favourite current director. The mayor of Baltimore declared 7 February 1985 as 'John Waters Day'. Dedicated to trash in all its forms, Waters attempted to revive the short-lived Fifties cinematic vogue for smellovision. Polyester (1981) was released in Odorama, with a scratch and sniff card for each member of the audience with its smells including gas, smelly socks and, inevitably, a fart. In a recent questionnaire in Vanity Fair magazine, Waters' response to the question, 'If you could choose what to come back as, what would it be?', was: 'A mirror in a Douglas Sirk film.'

MEMORABLE MOMENTS The one scene for which Waters will always be remembered, and for which his and Divine's names will go down in the annals of grotesqueness, is the shit-eating climax. Divine said in an interview for Image in 1977 of having to perform for the sequence: 'Well, I thought about it and checked with doctors and things and they said it really wouldn't hurt me or do anything to me. It was strictly done for shock value. I threw up afterward, and then I used mouthwash and brushed my teeth. There was no aftertaste of anything. I just forgot about it as quickly as I could.'

KEY LINES

Connie: 'There are two kinds of people, my kind and
    assholes.'

*Divine, on discovering her birthday present from the
    Marvels:* 'Someone has sent me a bowel movement.'
Crackers: 'No one sends you a turd and expects to live.'

PLAN 9 FROM OUTER SPACE

US, 1959, WADE WILLIAMS PRODUCTIONS, 79 MINS

PR/D/SC/ED EDWARD D. WOOD JR; **PH** WILLIAM THOMPSON;
M SUPERVISOR GORDON ZAHLER
CAST TOR JOHNSON (INSPECTOR CLAY), VAMPIRA (VAMPIRE GIRL),
BELA LUGOSI (GHOUL MAN), GREGORY WALCOTT (JEFF TRENT),
MONA MCKINNON (PAULA TRENT), TOM KEENE (COL.
EDWARDS), DUKE MOORE (LT. HARPER), DUDLEY MANLOVE
(EROS), JOANNA LEE (TANNA), JOHN 'BUNNY' BRECKINRIDGE
(THE RULER), LYLE TALBOT (THE GENERAL), DAVID DEMEEERING
(DANNY, CO-PILOT), CRISWELL (HIMSELF)

THE STORY Criswell, the TV clairvoyant, tops and tails the movie, assuring the audience that 'future events like these will affect your future' and that every 'incident is based on sworn testimony'. Extraterrestrials Eros and Tanna descend on earth in their flying saucer at the behest of their Ruler to prevent the earthlings destroying the universe by harnessing sunlight. They are observed flying into Los Angeles by airline pilot Jeff Trent, but he is sworn to silence by Federal authorities, who rally the army to repel the invasion from outer space. At a San Fernando Valley cemetery, near the home of Jeff and his wife Paula, the aliens activate the bodies of a recently dead couple, who become the Vampire Girl and the Ghoul Man, and kill the detective, Inspector Clay, who is investigating the deaths of two gravediggers. Trent, a police lieutenant and an army colonel are lured into the flying saucer, debate with the visitors, and escape just before it takes off and explodes in the air over Los Angeles.

THE FILM By general agreement *Plan 9 From Outer Space* (aka *Graverobbers From Outer Space*) is the worst movie by the world's worst director, Edward D. Wood Jr. (1922–78), the cult director of all time, promoted by Harry and Michael Medved on TV and in their influential book *The Golden Turkey Awards* (1980) and apotheosized by Tim Burton in his cinebiography *Ed Wood* (1994) starring Johnny Depp as the producer/director/writer/editor. The movie has a mesmerising awfulness: wooden acting, performers bumping into the flimsy sets, incoherent plotting and ludicrous dialogue. It takes a genius of sorts to make a movie so badly and Wood's admirer Burton is incapable of matching it, just as he could only improve on the 1950s SF films he sends up in *Mars Attacks* (1996). Oddly, Depp is less attractive on screen than the conventionally good-looking Wood. Yet the issues it touches on are those of the angst-ridden SF films of the time and Wood thought of himself as an auteur, a follower of Orson Welles. An alcoholic transvestite, Wood is surrounded by a cast of similar ineptitude including the ex-wrestler Tor Johnson, the camp TV personality Criswell, and the flagrantly gay Bunny Breckinridge, who was on his way to Mexico for a sex-change operation when he was drawn into playing the extraterrestrial Ruler. The film's 'music supervisor' selected the music from available records. Every expense was spared; the same wall with different curtains was used for the cabin in an airliner and the flying saucers were painted hub-caps. Bela Lugosi, a cult figure from the moment he appeared in Tod Browning's *Dracula* (1931), was a drug addict whose career was in terminal decline when he met his admirer Wood and appeared in *Glenn or Glenda* and *Bride of the Monster*. He is billed as a Guest Star in *Plan 9* because he died after one day's shooting and only appears in two early scenes before being killed in an off-screen road accident. As a corpse resurrected by aliens he is played by a stand-in (Tom Mason, a hypnotist and chiropractor), his face covered by a cloak.

ODD/SALIENT FACTS *Plan 9* was financed by Southern Baptists in order to raise funds for a series of religious movies and at their insistence Wood and his cast were baptised by full immersion in a swimming pool. Wood ended his career making hardcore porn films and writing pornographic novels, one of them called *Captain Fellatio Hornblower*.

MEMORABLE MOMENTS Tor Johnson's arrival to investigate the killings at the cemetery, his thick accent and stiff movements matched only by the woodenness of the cops.

The effete alien Ruler in an office that resembles a fortune-teller's tent being greeted by his two followers with a cross-armed salute.

KEY LINES

Jeff Trent: 'I saw a flying saucer.'
Paula Trent: 'Saucer – you mean the kind up there?'

▼ *PLAN 9 FROM OUTER SPACE* Ed Wood regulars Tor Johnson and Vampira succumb to extra-terrestrial powers.

Lt. Harper: 'One.thing's for sure. Inspector Clay is dead. Murdered. And someone's responsible.'

The Ruler: 'Plan 9? Ah, yes. Plan 9 deals with the resurrection of the dead. Long distance electrodes shot into the pineal and pituitary gland of the recently dead.'

POINT BLANK

US, 1967, MGM, 92 MINS

D JOHN BOORMAN; **PR** JUDD BERNARD, ROBERT CHARTOFF; **SC** ALEXANDER JACOBS, DAVID NEWHOUSE, RAFE NEWHOUSE (FROM THE NOVEL THE HUNTER BY RICHARD STARK); **PH** (COL, PANAVISION) PHILIP H. LATHROP; **M** JOHNNY MANDELL; **ED** HENRY BERMAN

CAST LEE MARVIN (WALKER), ANGIE DICKINSON (CHRIS), KEENAN WYNN (YOST), CARROLL O'CONNOR (BREWSTER), LLOYD BOCHNER (CARTER), MICHAEL STRONG (STEGMAN), JOHN VERNON (MAL REESE), SHARON ACKER (LYNNE), JAMES B. SIKKING (HIRED GUN)

THE STORY Walker, a professional criminal, is double-crossed by his wife, Lynne, and his best friend, Reese, and left to die in a cell in the abandoned Alcatraz where they have hi-jacked a cash drop for the crime syndicate. But the badly wounded Walker makes his way to the sea and two years later on a tourist boat circumnavigating Alcatraz he meets Yost, a mystery man, who tells him that Reese is now working for the Organization and living with Lynne in Los Angeles. He pursues them there, and with Yost hovering in the background, he works his way up rung-by-rung through the anonymous Organization in search of the $93,000 he's owed. His wife commits suicide shortly after he's tracked her down; her sister Chris is used as bait to get to Reese, who falls naked from the balcony of his penthouse while grappling with Walker. Eventually Brewster, number two man in the Organization, leads Walker back to Alcatraz to pick up his money. But Brewster is shot, Yost reveals himself as Fairfax, head of the Organization, and Walker withdraws into an empty cell.

THE FILM This seminal thriller, one of the first to be made after Hollywood abandoned the Hays Office Code, introduced the techniques of the French New Wave to American cinema and most particularly flashback techniques associated with Alain

Resnais, who in *La Guerre est fini* used flash-forwards to suggest alternative routes the hero's life might take. It may well be that, as with Ambrose Bierce's Civil War story 'An Occurrence at Owl Creek Bridge', *Point Blank* might be going on in the mind of the dying Walker. The film is a devastating account of an angry, lone avenger up against a criminal syndicate, the Organisation, run by neatly dressed men with Waspish names who work in polished boardrooms behind the reflective facades of skyscrapers, carry credit cards, and support worthy causes. It is in fact an image of American corporate society that was prospering while an insane war was being fought in Vietnam and violence raged in the cities across the nation.

ODD/SALIENT FACTS Director John Boorman (whose only previous work for the big screen was the 1965 Dave Clark Five picture, *Catch Us If You Can*) became involved in the project while gathering material in Los Angeles for a BBC documentary on D. W. Griffith. He established immediate rapport with Lee Marvin (then making *The Dirty Dozen* in England), who used his position as number one box-office attraction to have Boorman get carte blanche to rewrite the script and direct and edit in an innovative fashion. It was Marvin's idea that in the reunion scene with his wife she alone would speak, giving answers to Walker's unspoken questions. This was the first film to use Alcatraz Island after the prison was closed in 1963 and possibly the first to

▼ *POINT BLANK*: World-weary avenger Lee Martin between worried sister-in-law Angie Dickinson and anxious gang boss Carroll O'Connor.

have a major scene (a double killing) set in the Los Angeles storm drains. Underlying much of Boorman's work is the story of the Grail legend and he saw Walker, Lynne and Reese as modern versions of Arthur, Guinevere and Lancelot. James B. Sikking, who plays a cool, pipe-smoking assassin, found fame on TV in *Hill Street Blues* and the film had a considerable influence on other moviemakers, most notably Walter Hill and Michael Mann. *The Hunter* is one of a series of books about a gangland loner called Parker, written by Donald E. Westlake under the pseudonym of Richard Stark. Jean-Luc Godard filmed Stark's *The Jugger* as *Made in U.S.A.* (1966).

MEMORABLE MOMENTS Cross-cutting between Walker striding along a corridor at Los Angeles airport and his wife visiting a beauty parlour, the only sound being his pounding footsteps.

Walker blasting away with his pistol at the empty bed his wife and best friend have shared.

Walker extracting information from a car salesman by taking him on a destructive, bone-shaking drive without a seat belt in one of his own cars.

Walker with a gun to Reese's head in the foreground as the naked Chris hastily dresses in the background.

KEY LINES

Lynne: 'How good it must be being dead. Is it?'

Chris: 'What's my last name?
Walker: 'What's my first name?'

Fairfax to the dying Brewster: 'You should have stayed an accountant.'

THE PRODUCERS

US, 1967, SPRINGTIME/MGM/CROSSBOW, 88 MINS

D MEL BROOKS; **PR** SIDNEY GLAZIER; **SC** MEL BROOKS;
PH JOSEPH COFFEY; **M** JOHN MORRIS; **ED** RALPH ROSENBLUM
CAST ZERO MOSTEL (MAX BIALYSTOCK), GENE WILDER (LEO BLOOM), KENNETH MARS (FRANS LIEBKIND), ESTELLE WINWOOD ('HOLD ME, TOUCH ME'), RENÉE TAYLOR (EVA BRAUN), CHRISTOPHER HEWETT (ROGER DEBRIS), LEE MEREDITH (ULLA), ANDREAS VOUTSINAS (CARMEN GIYA), DICK SHAWN (LORENZO ST DUBOIS), JOSEPH ELLIC (VIOLINIST), MADLYN CATES (CONCIERGE), JOHN ZOLLER (DRAMA CRITIC), BILL HICKEY (FAILURE)

THE STORY Max Bialystock is a once-successful Broadway producer fallen on hard times. Leo Bloom, a neurotic accountant doing Bialystock's books, gives him the idea of over-financing a production that would be a guaranteed flop. After an exhaustive search the new partners find their play, *Springtime for Hitler*, and secure the rights from its unreconstructed Nazi author, Franz Liebkind. Bialystock visits his many elderly girlfriends and raises 25,000% of the play's budget. They hire the inept Roger DeBris as director and cast Lorenzo St DuBois, a spaced-out hippie, to play Hitler. Despite all their careful planning the play is a surprise smash. In desperation Bialystock, Bloom and the incensed Liebkind blow up the theatre in which the play is on. They are sent to prison where they repeat their fraudulent scam for the production of *Prisoners of Love*.

THE FILM Mel Brooks launched himself from the realm of the sketch (on film, television and record) into the world of the feature film with this brilliant near disaster about a failed disaster. In *When the Shooting Stops … the Cutting Begins*, his memoirs of a life in film-editing, Ralph Rosenblum outlines the chaotic, sometimes hostile atmosphere that Brooks engendered on his first film. What emerged from this chaos was an intermittently inspired comic near-masterpiece. The central plot of the deliberate, calculated courting of failure is an old one. The film plays with tastelessness, but its satirical intent is somehow diffused. It won't quite admit that its whole point is that it is tastelessness that succeeds, that there is nothing too base to be a triumph. The audience watching the film is allowed the sophisticated pleasure of laughing at the appallingness of the idea of the musical, 'a gay romp with Adolf and Eva at Berchtesgaden'. But not the people watching the play. As the camera moves across the audience, in a recreation of the famous Charles Addams cartoon, each member is frozen in open-mouthed shock, except for Franz Liebkind who is loving every moment. The success of the play comes via a technicality, the odd fact that the audience suddenly finds funny the anachronistic, hippie presentation of a fascist fantasy that has apparently been rewritten according to the whim of Lorenzo, a man so stoned that he can't remember his own name. Brooks himself has acknowledged that the film should have ended with the 'Springtime for Hitler' number. This is a crucial, but not fatal flaw in what remains a wonderfully funny film. Zero Mostel is hammy and large and genuinely misanthropic as the desperate, unlikely gigolo Bialystock. He and Wilder are hilarious in their first scene together. In fact Gene Wilder has never been better than as Bloom, the role that made him, although his tendency towards sentimentality is already evident in the courtroom scene. With *Blazing Saddles* (1974) and *Young Frankenstein* (1974) Brooks would make slicker, smarter films but as a director he would never again come so close to genius.

ODD/SALIENT FACTS The film had the working title *Springtime for Hitler*, but Joseph E. Levine persuaded Brooks that this would mean commercial suicide. A compromise title of *Springtime for Mussolini* was rejected. The title was retained for the Swedish release and has been used for all Brooks's subsequent films (e.g. *Springtime for the Sheriff*, 1974; *Springtime for Frankenstein*, 1974). Dustin Hoffman was originally sought to play Liebkind, but instead opted to appear in *The Graduate* (1967).

MEMORABLE MOMENTS The elaborately staged Busby Berkeley-style musical number *Springtime for Hitler*. The couplet:

Don't be stupid, be a smarty
Come and join the Nazi party

is dubbed by Brooks himself. Brooks used the joke of the inappropriate musical treatment again in *History of the World – Part I*

▲ *THE PRODUCERS A chorus line of glamorous storm-troopers in full high-kicking glory for the film's musical show-stopper 'Springtime for Hitler'.*

(1981), in which he stages a musical version of the Spanish Inquisition.

KEY LINES

Bialystock soliciting Bloom's help: 'You can do it, you're in a noble profession. The word "count" is part of your title.'

Bialystock: 'What's the matter with you?'
Bloom: 'I'm hysterical. I'm having hysterics. I'm hysterical. I can't stop when I get like this. I can't stop. I'm hysterical. [Bialystock takes a glass of water and throws it at Bloom] I'm wet. I'm wet. I'm hysterical and I'm wet. [Bialystock slaps him in the face.] I'm in pain and I'm wet and I'm still hysterical.'
Liebkind: 'Hitler was a great painter. He could paint an entire apartment in one afternoon. Two coats.'

Bloom on DeBris: 'Is he good? I mean is he bad?'
Bialystock: 'He stinks. He is perhaps the worst director that ever lived. He's the only director whose plays close on the first day of rehearsals.'

Jury foreman: 'We find the defendants incredibly guilty.'

QUADROPHENIA

UK, 1979, THE WHO FILMS, 120 MINS

D *FRANC RODDAM;* **PR** *ROY BAIRD, BILL CURBISHLEY;* **EXEC PR** *THE WHO;* **SC** *DAVE HUMPHRIES, MARTIN STELLMAN, FRANC RODDAM;* **PH** *(COL) BRIAN TUFANO;* **M** *THE WHO PLUS VARIOUS ARTISTS;* **ED** *SEAN BARTON, MIKE TAYLOR*

CAST *PHIL DANIELS (JIMMY), MARK WINGETT (DAVE), PHILIP DAVIS (CHALKY), LESLIE ASH (STEPH), GARRY COOPER (PETE), TOYAH WILCOX (MONKEY), STING (ACE), TREVOR LAIRD (FERDY), KATE WILLIAMS (JIMMY'S MOTHER), MICHAEL ELPHICK (JIMMY'S FATHER), KIM NEVE (YVONNE), RAYMOND WINSTONE (KEVIN), GARY SHAIL (SPIDER)*

THE STORY By day Jimmy works as a mail boy for an advertising company, but at night and on weekends his life revolves around music, drugs, girls, his scooter and his Mod mates. He and his friends pop pills, gatecrash a party and have skirmishes with Rockers. On the Bank Holiday weekend Jimmy and his friends go to Brighton. The increasingly erratic Jimmy gets kicked out of a club. He spends the night staring at the sea. The next day everyone meets up and the gang wanders along the seafront. They set upon a gang of Rockers in a café. This leads to an all-out battle between the two groups and the police when they arrive in force. In the midst of the action, Jimmy and Mod-girl Steph sneak down an alley and have sex. Returning to the riot, Jimmy is arrested and shares a paddy wagon with Ace, the leader of the Mods. Back in London, Jimmy walks out of his job, and finds that Steph has now hooked up with Dave, one of his mates. He is kicked out of his home by his mum. Finally rejected by Steph, and having smashed up his scooter, he takes a load of pills and booze on the train to Brighton. Everything is quiet and he discovers that his idol, Ace, is working as a hotel bell-boy. He steals Ace's scooter and rides it along the chalk

▼ *QUADROPHENIA The gang's all here, l-r: Ferdy (Trevor Laird), Monkey (Toyah Wilcox), Chalky (Philip Davis), Ace (Sting), Steph (Leslie Ash), Jimmy (Phil Daniels), Spider (Gary Shail), Pete (Garry Cooper), Dave (Mark Wingett).*

cliffs. Suddenly he turns the bike and speeds towards the cliff. We see only the bike fly over the edge and land on the rocks below.

THE FILM This film came just four years after Ken Russell's dismal attempt to bring The Who's other rock opera, *Tommy* (1975), to the screen. Where that remained a musical, this is a narrative developed from the themes and central character devised by Pete Townshend. It is about growing pains and youth culture, with Jimmy an updated version of his namesake in *Rebel Without a Cause* (1955). He is torn between the need to belong and the need to establish his own identity. He seeks calm, spending much time staring into the canal or out to sea, but he is never happier than when speeding, riding his beloved Lambretta with his mates, dancing and fighting Rockers. His already split personality is further divided by drugs and his post-adolescent confusion leading to the four-way psychic split of the musically punning title. The film is an exhilarating expression of disaffection but also a touching story about the aimlessness and pointlessness of divisions among youth cults. In the scene in the baths where Jimmy and Kevin duel between 'Be-Bop-a-Lula' and 'You Really Got Me', the schism between Mods and Rockers is seen to be absurd. Kevin has been in the army, is unimpressed with artificial regimentation and is uninterested in mutually hostile cults. Jimmy tries to explain his philosophy: 'It isn't the bikes, is it? It's the people ... I don't wanna be the same as everybody else. That's why I'm a Mod, see. I mean, you gotta be somebody, ain't ya, otherwise you might as well jump in the sea and drown.' The two are essentially good friends and the revelation that Kevin is one of the Rockers being beaten up by his mates, deeply affects Jimmy. It represents the folly of a civil war with sides being allotted and families divided arbitrarily. This is another factor in Jimmy's mental ill health. Jimmy's sense of loss of identity leads him to contemplate jumping in the sea at the end, but the change of heart suggests a sudden epiphany, an optimistic turn towards adulthood.

ODD/SALIENT FACTS The alley in Brighton where Steph and Jimmy retreat for their quickie in the middle of the riot has itself become a cult place, a shrine to the film. Fans of the film have travelled from all over Europe to pay their respects and leave graffiti messages commemorating their visit.

MEMORABLE MOMENTS The film achieves a rare thing, convincing crowd sequences and even more remarkable, realistic

'Nothing seems right apart from Brighton

riots. The sense of excitement and immediacy was achieved by Roddam simply making them as real and unchoreographed as possible. The director recalls telling the actors: "Those fucking police are fucking up the scene, go for them for real." And so when they mix these people are almost fighting for their lives. Phil Daniels himself remembers laying into one of the policemen: 'It seemed as real as you can get.'

KEY LINES

Jimmy's mum, on her son's habit of riding around at night with his mates: 'It's not normal.'
Jimmy: 'Oh yeah, what's normal, then?'

Jimmy to Steph: 'Nothing seems right apart from Brighton.'

Jimmy to the van driver who has smashed his Lambretta: 'You've killed me scooter.'

THE QUIET MAN

US, 1952, REPUBLIC/ARGOSY PICTURES, 129 MINS
D JOHN FORD; **PR** JOHN FORD, MERIAN C. COOPER;
SC FRANK S. NUGENT (FROM A STORY BY MAURICE WALSH);
PH (TECHNICOLOR) WINTON C. HOCH AND (SECOND UNIT) ARCHIE STOUT; **ED** JACK MURRAY; **M** VICTOR YOUNG
CAST JOHN WAYNE (SEAN THORNTON), MAUREEN O'HARA (MARY KATE DANAHER), VICTOR MCLAGLEN (RED WILL DANAHER), BARRY FITZGERALD (MICHAELEEN OG FLYNN), WARD BOND (FATHER LONERGAN), MILDRED NATWICK (MRS SARAH TILLANE), FRANCIS FORD (DAN TOBIN), ARTHUR SHIELDS (REVD CYRIL PLAYFAIR), EILEEN CROWE (MRS ELIZABETH PLAYFAIR), SEAN MCCLORY (OWEN GLYNN), JAMES LILBURN (FATHER PAUL), JACK MCGOWRAN (FEENEY), KEN CURTIS (DERMOT FAHY)

THE STORY Irish-American boxer Sean Thornton returns to Innisfree whence his family emigrated when he was a child. Sean became the prizefighter 'Trooper Thorn', but his championship bid was cut short when he killed an opponent in the ring, and he has vowed never to fight again. Back in Innisfree he's taken under the wing of Michaeleen, the village's crafty,

▲ THE QUIET MAN *Wayne courts O'Hara in a shot reprised by Steven Spielberg in* E.T.

drunken bookie and matchmaker. He falls in love with the spirited Mary Kate Danaher, but crosses her boorish brother Will when he outbids him to buy the old family cottage from the wealthy widow Tillane. Will Danaher opposes the match, but a benign conspiracy between the Catholic priest, the vicar, and Michaeleen persuades him that giving Mary Kate to Thornton will ease his path to marrying the widow Tillane. Sean and Mary Kate cut short the elaborate courting ceremonies and marry, but when the widow rejects Danaher's proposal, he reneges on the agreement. Mary Kate, humiliated, refuses to consummate the marriage unless her dowry is paid, and they spend their wedding night in separate rooms. The Reverend Playfair, the only person to rumble Sean's identity and the reason he won't fight Danaher, encourages him to do so for Mary Kate's sake. Sean drags her over to confront Danaher, they get – and burn – the dowry, and an epic cross-country fist-fight between Sean and Danaher ensues. Followed from pub to pub by the whole village, and a visiting bishop, they arrive drunk, battered and reconciled at Mary Kate's dinner table.

THE FILM A re-working of *The Taming of the Shrew*, this is Ford's most joyous movie, a celebration of marriage and community, in which his favourite actor and actress engage in a courteous love affair between America and Ireland, and traditional preconceptions are turned on their heads. Wayne represents the search for the anti-material simple life; O'Hara is obsessed with material possessions. *The Quiet Man* is one of the most gloriously romantic pictures ever made, apparently free-wheeling but in fact carefully patterned. Its Ireland is an Irish-American idyll, but it quietly mocks the pretensions of the IRA and sees Protestants and Catholics living happily together in the unforgettable scene where Father Lonergan encourages the villagers to cheer the Church of Ireland bishop and thus ensure the tenure of the Reverend Playfair. *The Quiet Man*, once Ford's most popular film, but subsequently rejected as politically incorrect, has become the cult picture in his oeuvre. The melodies on the soundtrack and the communal singing trump most musicals.

ODD/SALIENT FACTS Maurice Walsh's story appeared in the *Saturday Evening Post* in 1933, and Ford optioned it for $10 in 1936. Many years later the British writer Richard Llewellyn, author of *How Green Was My Valley*, expanded the tale for Frank S. Nugent to write a screenplay, but didn't take a credit. The film brought Ford his fourth Oscar as Best Director. The film is a family affair that took Ford back to Ireland and gave work, behind and in front of the camera, to numerous members of his repertory company, two of his brothers, several of John Wayne's children, two of Maureen O'Hara's brothers, Victor McLaglen's son, as well as Barry Fitzgerald's brother Arthur Shields. Mae Marsh, the heroine of D. W. Griffith's *Intolerance* and several Ford pictures, appeared as the priest's housekeeper.

MEMORABLE MOMENTS Sean's first sighting of Mary Kate tending the sheep.

Sean and Mary Kate escaping on a tandem from Michaeleen, their chaperone, for a lyrical ride through the countryside.

The expressionistic flashback from Danaher's attack on Sean at the wedding breakfast to the fatal knock-out in the boxing ring.

The epic, ten-minute fight.

KEY LINES

Sean: 'I'm Sean Thornton and I was born in that little cottage over there and I'm coming home and that's where I'm going to stay.'

Michaeleen (reacting to Sean's first sight of Mary Kate): 'It's only a mirage brought on by your terrible thirst.'

Sean: 'Some things a man doesn't get over so easily – like the sight of a girl coming through the fields with the sun on her hair, and kneeling in church looking like a saint.'

Michaeleen (to Mary Kate): 'Have the good manners not to hit the man until he's your husband and entitled to hit back.'

Michaeleen (misinterpreting the collapsed bridal bed on which Sean has thrown Mary Kate): 'Impetuous! Homeric!'

Father Lonergan (rallying the villagers to impress the protestant Bishop): 'Now, when the Reverend Playfair comes down, good man that he is, I want you all to cheer like Protestants.'

RASHOMON

Japan, 1950, Daeie, 88 mins

D Akira Kurosawa; PR Jinkichi Minoura; SC Kurosawa and Shinobu Hashimoto (from two stories by Ryunosuke Akutagawa); PH Kazuo Miyagawa; M Takashi Matsuyama CAST Toshiro Mifune (Tajamuru, the bandit), Machiko Kyo (the wife), Masayuki Mori (the husband), Takashi Shimura (the woodcutter), Minoru Chiaki (the priest), Kichijiro Ueda (the commoner)

THE STORY In the countryside of war-torn medieval Japan three men – a priest, a woodcutter and a cynical traveller – shelter from the rain in the ruins of the Rashomon gate. Three days earlier the priest and the woodcutter appeared as witnesses at the trial of a notorious bandit, Tajamuru, charged with murdering a nobleman, raping his wife and stealing his horse, and they seem deeply disturbed by the experience. Questioned by the traveller, they describe the trial and in flashbacks, and flashbacks within flashbacks, the film presents the events as recounted by the woodcutter who claims to have found two hats and the dead body; by the priest who passed the married couple on the road; the bandit, who admits to rape and murder; the now-widowed wife who fled from the scene; and (through a female medium) the dead man, who says he committed suicide. The stories are in sharp conflict, and eventually under pressure from the stranger, the woodcutter admits to having spied on the events but having concealed this because he subsequently stole a valuable knife belonging to the wife. His account shows that everyone has been lying. Suddenly an

▲ *RASHOMON Bandit Toshiro Mifune gives his version of what happened in the woods.*

abandoned baby is found among the ruins and the priest's faith in humanity is restored when the woodcutter offers to take it home to be reared with his five children.

THE FILM One of the most beautifully crafted films ever made, *Rashomon* has three distinctive settings – the rain-lashed ruin of a once grand building in which the framing narrative takes place; the idyllic woods where the sun shining through the trees casts delicate shadows on the encounter between the bandit and the married couple; the courtyard with a sand-covered floor and a wall that bisects the screen laterally where the trial is held. In the court scenes, the magistrate is neither seen nor heard; the characters address the camera turning the cinema audience into judges. We are all familar with the fact that through imperfect memory, dishonesty and self-interest subjective reports on events rarely tally, and this has been the basis of such works as Browning's *The Ring and the Book* and the modest British crime movie *The Woman in Question* (1949), which was shown in the US as *Five Angles on Murder*. But none before had approached the subject with such subtle irony, psychological insight and moral force, and almost immediately the film's title entered the language in the phrase 'a *Rashomon* situation' as a dozen years later *Catch-22* did. Moviegoers would discuss the meaning of the movie and the issues it raises as earlier they talked of Rosebud in *Citizen Kane* and later whether the couple in *Last Year in Marienbad* had actually met before.

ODD/SALIENT FACTS *Rashomon* won the Gold Lion at the 1951 Venice Festival and an Oscar as the best foreign language film (it was also nominated for best art direction) and was the first Japanese movie to be shown widely in the West, opening the eyes of the West to a hitherto neglected national cinema. As such it played a key role in the healing process after the Second World War, helping citizens of the allied nations to look sympathetically on Japan, recognize the Japanese as individuals and to appreciate the country's culture. Machiko Kyo, a dancer playing her first important dramatic role, became an international star as did Toshiro Mifune, the first Japanese actors to do so since Sessue Hayakawa became a Hollywood star in 1914. *Rashomon* was presented on Broadway as a play in 1959 (starring Claire Bloom and Rod Steiger) and was re-made as the Western *The Outrage* (1964) and as *Iron Maze* (1991), a US-Japanese thriller set in Pittsburgh produced by Oliver Stone. In *Easy Riders, Raging Bulls* (1998) Peter Biskind remarks: 'Kurosawa's *Rashomon* remains one of the truest movies about the movies and people who make them.'

MEMORABLE MOMENTS The bandit seeing the wind raise the veil hanging from the wife's straw hat as she rides by on her horse.

The look of cold contempt on the husband's face as he looks at his wife after the rape in her flashback.

The wife's knife glinting at the edge of the clearing as the husband approaches it contemplating suicide.

The female medium, her hair blowing in the wind, speaking in the nobleman's voice to the court.

KEY LINES

The commoner: 'Men are only men, they can't tell the truth, not even to each other.'

The priest: 'It's because men are so weak, that's why they lie, that's why they must deceive themselves.'

REBEL WITHOUT A CAUSE
US, 1955, WARNER BROS, 111 MINS

D NICHOLAS RAY; **PR** DAVID WEISBART; **SC** STEWART STERN; **PH** (COL, CINEMASCOPE) ERNEST HALLER; **M** LEONARD ROSENMAN; **ED** WILLIAM ZIEGLER
CAST JAMES DEAN (JIM STARK), NATALIE WOOD (JUDY), JIM BACKUS (JIM'S FATHER), ANN DORAN (JIM'S MOTHER), ROCHELLE HUDSON (JUDY'S MOTHER), WILLIAM HOPPER (JUDY'S FATHER), SAL MINEO (PLATO), COREY ALLEN (BUZZ), DENNIS HOPPER (GOON), ED PLATT (RAY), STEFFI SYDNEY (MIL), MARIETTA CANTY (PLATO'S NURSE-MAID), VIRGINIA BRISSAC (JIM'S GRANDMOTHER), BEVERLEY LONG (HELEN), FRANK MAZZOLA (CRUNCH), ROBERT FOULK (GENE), JACK SIMMONS (COOKIE), NICK ADAMS (MOOSE)

THE STORY The paths of three adolescents – Jim, Judy and Plato – cross one night in a police station. Jim, newly arrived in town, has been arrested for public drunkenness, Plato for shooting some puppies, while Judy has been found wandering the streets alone late at night. At his new school Jim and Buzz, a gang leader, have a knife fight. When this is broken up they agree to settle the score with a 'Chickie run' in their cars. During this contest Buzz plunges to his death over a cliff. Misunderstood by his parents and ignored by the police, Jim gets together with Judy, who dated Buzz, and Plato at an abandoned mansion. Jim and Judy become surrogate parents to Plato. When Plato

▼ *REBEL WITHOUT A CAUSE* Rebels Judy (Natalie Wood) and Jimmy (James Dean) create their own perfect nuclear family.

175

falls asleep Judy and Jim sneak off to consummate their love. A disoriented Plato is woken by angry members of Buzz's gang. He shoots one of them and flees to a planetarium, pursued by the police. Jim and Judy follow Plato and persuade him to give himself up. But as they leave Plato, upset by the blinding lights from the police cars, makes a run for it and is fatally shot.

THE FILM The film and its central examination of the alienation of the American adolescent, is a companion piece to *The Wild One* (1953), the film that confirmed Dean's great rival Marlon Brando as the star of his generation. In that film, Brando's character responds to the question of what he is rebelling against with the famous line: 'Whatcha got?' In *Rebel Without a Cause*, the rebellion is inspired by the decline of the conventional nuclear family. All three leading characters come from conspicuously wealthy families and are driven to rebellion by specific things lacking in their domestic lives. Plato is upset because his parents have abandoned him, and replace love with a maid and cash. Judy wants her father to be physically affectionate to her, something he hasn't been since she became a woman. Jim is sent crazy by the fact that his mother is strong and confident, his father weak – given to wearing a pinny around the house. Jim is very clear about how things should change and believes that a gentle beating should get his mother back in line. Together the three teenagers improvise the perfect family. *Rebel Without a Cause* remains a cult film despite a dated and reactionary story and script. Visually it is brilliantly composed throughout. It has three fascinating and iconic leading players all of whom died prematurely (Dean, 24; Mineo, 37; Wood, 43) of unnatural causes, respectively car crash, murder and drowning. Its lingering resonance comes from Dean. This was one of only three films in which he starred – after *East of Eden* (1955) and before *Giant* (1956). The film works better in the memory or with the sound turned down and offers a tantalizing view of Dean's potential.

ODD/SALIENT FACTS In *Hollywood Babylon* Kenneth Anger claims that the odd twitchiness of Dean's performance was the result of the crabs from which he suffered through much of the production. The homoerotic overtones of the script's relationship between Plato and Jimmy were matched in real life, at least in an attraction between the two actors. When questioned on the subject by Boze Hadleigh in *Conversations With My Elders*, Mineo answered: 'I might tell you some people I had affairs with – maybe. But Jimmy was special, so I don't want to say.'

During the shoot Dean had a long-standing girlfriend, and a possibly platonic relationship with Ursula Andress, as well as a brief liaison with Natalie Wood, which was uncomfortably consummated in his Porsche. Wood was simultaneously having affairs with Dennis Hopper and Nicholas Ray. Crunch is played by Frank Mazzola, who was employed as an advisor on gang life and later worked as editor alongside Donald Cammel on the final cut of *Performance*.

MEMORABLE MOMENTS The film is memorable for its use of red in the transference of red jackets, first to Judy, then Jimmy and finally, fatally, to Plato. The film's two great scenes are the choreographed knife fight in which Jimmy is wounded and the chicken race in which Buzz is killed.

KEY LINES

Jimmy, contorted with psychic rage, to his bickering
    parents in the police station: 'You're tearing me apart.'

Jimmy to Judy: 'You live here, don't you?'
Judy: 'Who lives?'

Jim's father: 'You can't be idealistic all your life, Jim.'
Jimmy: 'Except to yourself.'

RESERVOIR DOGS ★
US, 1992, RANK/LIVE AMERICA/DOG EAT DOG, 99 MINS
D QUENTIN TARANTINO; **PR** LAWRENCE BENDER; **SC** QUENTIN TARANTINO; **PH** (COL) ANDRZEJ SEKULA; **M** VARIOUS; **ED** SALLY MENKS
CAST HARVEY KEITEL (MR WHITE, LARRY), TIM ROTH (MR ORANGE, FREDDY NEWENDYKE), MICHAEL MADSEN (MR BLONDE, VIC VEGA), CHRIS PENN (NICE GUY EDDIE), STEVE BUSCEMI (MR PINK), LAWRENCE TIERNEY (JOE CABOT), RANDY BROOKS (HOLDAWAY), KIRK BALTZ (MARVIN NASH), EDDIE BUNKER (MR BLUE), QUENTIN TARANTINO (MR BROWN), MICHAEL SOTTILE (TEDDY), ROBERT RUTH (SHOT COP), LAWRENCE BENDER (YOUNG COP)

THE STORY A diamond heist goes badly wrong. The surviving gang members make their way back to the rendezvous – Mr White, the badly wounded Mr Orange, Mr Pink, Mr Blonde and later the leaders Joe and his son Eddie. Mr Blue

PERFORMANCE

ABOVE: Decadent sixties rock 'n' roll troilism as Turner (Mick Jagger), Lucy (Michele Breton) and Pherber (Anita Pallenberg) take to the bath in the scene that really upset the suits at Warner Brothers.

ONCE UPON A TIME IN THE WEST

RIGHT: Charles Bronson as Harmonica, another mysterious Spaghetti gunfighter with no name, confronts an opponent in a characteristically striking Leone composition.

PINK FLAMINGOS

*Divine (Divine), eager to prove him/herself the filthiest
person in the world, prepares to tuck in. If you think this is
disgusting, you ain't seen nothing yet.*

RESERVOIR DOGS

Things are looking increasingly bad and bloody for
Mr Orange (Tim Roth) despite the tender ministrations of
Mr White (Harvey Keitel).

THE ROCKY HORROR PICTURE SHOW

LEFT: Tim Curry as transvestite scientist Dr Frank-N-Furter stands in front of the tower of RKO Radio Pictures, ready to celebrate the glories of classic horror films with Brad, Janet and Rocky.

SINGING IN THE RAIN

RIGHT: Cathy Selden (Debbie Reynolds) and Don Lockwood (Gene Kelly) are the new romantic team that rescues R. J. Simpson's Monumental Pictures as sound comes to Hollywood.

THIS IS SPINAL TAP

ABOVE: Nigel Tufnel (Christopher Guest) and David St Hubbins (Michael McKean) rock it on stage as 'the Tap' crank it up to eleven on their uneven American tour.

THE TERMINATOR

RIGHT: The terminator (Arnold Schwarzenegger) single-handedly takes out a police precinct, having assured the desk sergeant 'I'll be back'.

WITHNAIL AND I

ABOVE: I (Paul McGann) and Withnail (Richard E, Grant), with the rubber-boot money generously given to them by Monty (Richard Griffiths), have the means to demand the finest wines available to humanity.

THE WICKER MAN

RIGHT: Scottish copper Edward Woodward pays the ultimate price for preserving his virginity as the eponymous sacrificial pyre goes up in smoke.

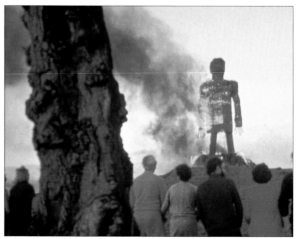

and Mr Brown are dead. In a frenzy of accusations and panic, the story unfolds at the warehouse and in flashback. We see the plans for the raid, the recruitment of the gang, and the immediate aftermath of the heist. Mr Orange is an undercover cop who kills Mr Blonde as he in turn is about to kill a cop whom he has taken hostage and is torturing. Eddie, Mr White and Mr Pink and finally Joe arrive back at the warehouse. After a brief Mexican stand-off, Joe shoots Mr Orange, Mr White shoots and kills Joe, Eddie shoots Mr White, and Mr White shoots and kills Eddie. Mr Pink, who had been hiding under a ramp, escapes with the diamonds but his exit is followed by the sound of police sirens and gunfire. Mr Orange tells Mr White that he is a cop. As the police arrive Mr White shoots Mr Orange and is himself blown off the screen.

THE FILM Quentin Tarantino, a movie obsessive, came to his feature debut, with his sum total experience being, by all accounts, a wretched short film *My Best Friend's Birthday* on his CV. He had however recently sold his script of *True Romance* (1993) to Tony Scott. The script for *Reservoir Dogs* was written in just three weeks and is a blend of originality, enthusiasm and homage. Tarantino worked in a video store and turned himself into a sponge and encyclopaedia of cult, often violent, marginal and sometimes classic cinema. The film is dedicated to, among others, the cult figures Jean-Luc Godard, Jean-Pierre Melville, Chow Yun Fat and Roger Corman. The taut screenplay is filled with references to Tarantino's favourite films: *The Killing* (1956), *White Heat* (1949), *Rififi* (1955), *Ocean's Eleven* (1960) and *Straight Time* (1977) – based on a book by Eddie Bunker, aka Mr Blue – among many, many others. The concept of a gang of mutual strangers known only by colours appears in the New York Subway train heist movie, *The Taking of Pelham 123* (1974), one of Tarantino's favourite films. A key source was another Tarantino favourite, Ringo Lam's *City on Fire* (1989), which features Chow Yun Fat as an undercover cop infiltrating a jewel gang, scenes in a café, a sequence where the cool-looking gang walk in hip, bedraggled unity towards the camera, and concludes with an identically composed Mexican stand-off. Another source was *Odd Man Out*. The film is fascinating for its complex borrowings but most admirable for the profane poetry of the dialogue, the complexity of the

'You gonna bark all day, little doggy, or are you gonna bite?'

narrative structure (itself similar to *Rashomon* [1951]), and the stylishly camp soundtrack. It is supremely cool, and gained an instantly devoted following. Everything about it was taken from somewhere else, and yet it had a style of dialogue that immediately established the Tarantino signature, and a look and sound all its own.

ODD/SALIENT FACTS The film was executive produced by cult director Monte Hellman, who had initially wanted to come out of his semi-retirement to direct the project himself. Steve Buscemi had at first wanted to play Mr Blonde. Mr Blonde, Vic Vega is the brother of Vincent Vega, the John Travolta character in *Pulp Fiction* (1994). The film created an added buzz by its narrative ambiguities. In the Mexican stand-off, which ends with four men being shot, only three guns are seen being fired. Similarly, the shot by which Mr Orange is supposedly killed is not shown on screen. Of the latter it would just seem hard for Mr White to miss. Of the end of the stand-off, if Mr White's swivel and shooting of Eddie weren't already visible, Tarantino's screenplay makes it clear that Mr White does in fact shoot Eddie after shooting Joe and being shot himself.

MEMORABLE MOMENTS The gang, plus Eddie and Joe, walking towards the camera in the credit sequence.

The torture and ear-cutting scene – 'It's amusing to me to torture a cop' – accompanied by the cheerful sounds of Stealer's Wheel playing 'Stuck in the Middle with You'.

KEY LINES

Mr White to Mr Blonde: 'You shoot me in a dream, you better wake up and apologize.'

Mr Pink, in the midst of his reasons for not tipping waitresses: 'And this non-college bullshit you're telling me. I got two words for that: "Learn to fuckin' type."'

Pink, seeing Mr Orange in a pool of his own blood: 'It's bad. It's bad. Is it bad?'
Mr White: 'As opposed to good?'

Mr Blonde to Mr White: 'You gonna bark all day, little doggy, or are you gonna bite?'

THE REVENGE OF FRANKENSTEIN

UK, 1958, HAMMER FILMS, 89 MINS

D TERENCE FISHER; *PR* ANTHONY HINDS; *SC* JIMMY SANGSTER (ADDITIONAL DIALOGUE BY HANFORD JANES); *PH* (TECHNICOLOR) JACK ASHER; *ED* ALFRED COX; *M* LEONARDO SALZEDO

CAST PETER CUSHING (DR VICTOR STEIN), FRANCIS MATTHEWS (DR HANS CLEVE), EUNICE GAYSON (MARGARET CONRAD), MICHAEL GWYNN (THE CREATURE), OSCAR QUITAK (KARL, THE DWARF), JOHN WELSH (BERGMAN), LIONEL JEFFRIES (FRITZ), RICHARD WORDSWORTH (UP PATIENT), CHARLES LLOYD PACK (PRESIDENT OF THE MEDICAL COUNCIL), JOHN STUART (INSPECTOR), MARGERY CRESLEY (COUNTESS BARSCYNSKA), ARNOLD DIAMOND (MOLKE), ANNA WARMSLEY (VERA BARSCYNSKA), GEORGE WOODBRIDGE (JANITOR), MICHAEL RIPPER (CURT), IAN WHITTAKER (BOY), AVRIL LESLIE (GERDA, THE GIRL)

THE STORY 1860: Baron Frankenstein is led to the scaffold for the murders committed by his monster. However, Frankenstein, with the assistance of his servant, the hunchback Karl, manages to have a Catholic priest executed and buried in his place. Three years later Frankenstein has established himself in Carlsbrück as Dr Victor Stein, the town's most prosperous general practitioner and devoted surgeon in charge of the workhouse hospital. Stein is invited to join Carlsbrück's medical

▼ *THE REVENGE OF FRANKENSTEIN Dr Stein instructs his new assistant Cleve in the Promethean arts.*

council, he refuses their offer, but one council member, the brilliant young Hans Cleve, recognizes Frankenstein and asks to become his assistant. Stein is determined to avenge himself on the medical establishment and his first major project is to transplant the brain of the deformed Karl into a perfect body he has cobbled together from parts taken from his indigent patients. Stein and Cleve perform the operation successfully. But Cleve reveals to the Creature that he is to be an exhibit alongside the ugly body of Karl to demonstrate Frankenstein's brilliance to medical science. While the Creature is strapped down to recover from the operation, Margaret, an altruistic aristocrat working at the hospital, unwittingly releases his bonds. He first thrusts Karl's corpse into the furnace, then kills Stein's janitor, and murders a peasant girl. Finally he crashes into an elegant party and dies at the feet of his creator. The Medical Council demands Stein's arrest, but before this can be affected, vengeful victims of Stein's experiments are alerted and inflict fatal injuries on him. Reacting rapidly, Dr Cleve shows Stein's corpse to the authorities, then transplants Frankenstein's brain into a waiting body. The film ends with Cleve and Frankenstein (moustachioed, monocled, and called Dr Franck) running a fashionable practice in London's Harley Street.

THE FILM Founded in 1948, Hammer Studios spent eight years producing B-feature schlock until establishing its identity with sexy, elegantly staged, Technicolor horror flicks that, like Roger Corman's Edgar Allan Poe movies being made in Hollywood, looked far more costly than their low budgets would have suggested. They were set in a stylized nineteenth century where graveyards loomed out of the fog and red gore flowed freely. Hammer's cult period lasted half-a-dozen years and though the studio ventured into most genres, the key works were horror movies starring Peter Cushing (1913–96) and Christopher Lee (b. 1922), minor British character actors who became international icons. Their names are forever linked as Frankenstein and the Creature, and Van Helsing and Dracula, though they played together in other movies. Whereas Karloff had dominated the 1930s James Whale movies, to the extent that the name Frankenstein became popularly associated with the monster rather than his creator, Cushing's Frankenstein is at the centre of the Hammer movies. The 1957 *Curse of Frankenstein* was generally excoriated by the critics, but this sequel, following in the wake of *Dracula*, proved that Cushing was a star and his polite, coldly fastidious, quietly sadistic

Frankenstein became a new kind of mad scientist for the second part of the twentieth century, a sort of stiff-upper-lip Anglo-Saxon brother to Dr Mengele. *Revenge* also introduced the strong element of dark humour and camp that was to be a part of the Hammer tradition. The women in the movies are invariably pallid.

ODD/SALIENT FACTS Universal Studios had copyright in the appearance of Karloff's Monster and after playing a new-style Monster in *The Curse of Frankenstein*, Christopher Lee refused to play the role again. The first British critic to recognize the merits of Hammer films was the screenwriter Paul Dehn, movie reviewer of the now defunct *News Chronicle*, who happened to be the long-time companion of James Bernard, Hammer's house composer. The American censors intervened to prevent the results of the creature's cannibalism being shown on screen.

MEMORABLE MOMENTS Frankenstein using a Bunsen burner to show Dr Cleve how eyes and hands suspended in glass tanks react to heat.

The Creature seeing himself in the mirror.

The Creature putting Karl's corpse into the furnace.

KEY LINES

Frankenstein: 'That's the arm of a pickpocket. You need sensitive fingers to be a member of that profession. It will be very useful to me.'

The Creature's last words: 'Frankenstein, help me!'

Dr Franck in his Harley Street surgery: 'You were an excellent pupil Hans. These scars will hardly show.'

RIDE LONESOME

US, 1959, RANOWN/COLUMBIA, 73 MINS

D BUDD BOETTICHER; **PR** HARRY JOE BROWN; **SC** BURT KENNEDY; **PH** (COL, CINEMASCOPE) CHARLES LAWTON JR.; **M** HEINZ ROEMHELD; **ED** JEROME THOMAS

CAST RANDOLPH SCOTT (BEN BRIGADE), KAREN STEELE (CARRIE), PERNELL ROBERTS (SAM BOONE), JAMES BEST (BILLY JOHN), LEE VAN CLEEF (FRANK), JAMES COBURN (WID), DYKE JOHNSON (CHARLIE), BOYD STOCKMAN (INDIAN CHIEF)

THE STORY Bounty hunter Ben Brigade captures fugitive killer Billy John and aims to take him to Santa Cruz to stand trial. He is joined by Carrie, whose husband has been captured by marauding Indians, and by two young outlaws, Sam and Wid, who believe they can obtain an amnesty if they turn in the wanted Billy. They can then give up their life of crime and start a new life as ranchers. At a staging post Brigade attempts to keep an Indian war party at bay by pretending to sell Carrie to them as a squaw, but she breaks down and panics when she notices that the Indians have her husband's horse. Brigade and his party head off across holy Indian land pursued by Indians and feuding among themselves. It transpires that Brigade is using Billy as bait to capture his brother Frank, a vicious outlaw who has abducted and murdered Brigade's wife. Using the same tree on which his wife was hanged, Brigade strings up Billy to draw Frank into a gunfight. Frank is killed. Brigade hands over Billy to Wid and Sam so they can obtain their amnesty, and Carrie rides off with them. Brigade sets fire to the hanging tree and rides off alone.

THE FILM Two of the screen's great collaborations between star and director took place in the 1950s. Starting with *Winchester 73* in 1950, James Stewart and Anthony Mann made eight films together, five of them Westerns. Beginning in 1956 with *Seven Men From Now*, Randolph Scott and Budd Boetticher made seven pictures together, all of them Westerns. The Scott-Boetticher pictures are taut, ironic fables either set in corrupt townships or on journeys in which the impassive Scott, his face weathered and leathery, is invariably a widowed ex-lawman, confronting or reluctantly travelling with outlaws. Andrew Sarris has called the films 'floating poker games' and they involve serious games-playing in which cards are concealed and people are invited to call their opponents' bluff. All the films last under 80 minutes (four exactly 77 minutes) and the best are the four written by Burt Kennedy (who would himself direct Westerns in the 1960s): *Seven Men From Now* (1956), *The Tall T* (1957), *Ride Lonesome* (1959) and *Comanche Station* (1960). They're shot in the same arid, rocky landscapes and not only have similar plots, but incidents and lines of dialogue recur. They are Westerns pared down to their essential moral core in the manner of Samuel Beckett's plays and it is significant that Monte Hellman's pair of spare cult Westerns of 1967, *Ride in the Whirlwind* and *The Shooting*, were influenced both by Boetticher and Beckett.

The withdrawn, slightly mysterious probity of Scott brings out the character of the outlaws, giving colour and substance to

179

▲ *RIDE LONESOME Karen Steel and Randolph Scott negotiate with hostile Indians in the Mojave Desert.*

their villainy. Mann's Westerns with James Stewart suggest that the hero will settle down in a community he has helped create. Boetticher's Westerns on the other hand imply that we are essentially isolated beings who live and die alone and that society is a sham. Thus we are faced with the certainty that the Scott character will proceed on his way unaccompanied.

ODD/SALIENT FACTS *Ride Lonesome* and most of the other Scott-Boetticher films were shot at Big Pines, a recreational area north of Los Angeles in the south-west section of the Mojave Desert. James Coburn made his screen debut as the wise-cracking outlaw in *Ride Lonesome*; Pernell Roberts, who played his partner, became famous two years later as Adam Cartwright in the long-running TV series *Bonanza*. Budd Boetticher was trained as a matador before entering the cinema as technical adviser on *Blood and Sand*, and there is a resemblance between his films and the rituals of bullfighting. After their final collaboration on *Comanche Station* (1960), Scott and Boetticher made a single feature film each, Scott

appearing in Peckinpah's *Ride the High Country* (1962) and Boetticher directing the Audie Murphy Western *A Time For Dying* (1969).

MEMORABLE MOMENTS Scott emerging through the rocks to corner his prey in the opening shot.

The widescreen image of the five travellers being followed by an Indian war party across medicine country.

The shootout with Indians at an abandoned coach station.

KEY LINES

Brigade, after the burial of a stagecoach driver: 'Hang on to that shovel because likely enough you're going to be needing it again, soon.'

Sam: 'The way I look at it, it's half so hard if a man knows the way he's going to die.'

Frank: 'There's no hurry, he'll be waiting.'

Sam (a line also spoken by Scott as Pat Brennan in The Tall T*):* 'There are some things a man can't ride around.'

THE ROCKY HORROR PICTURE SHOW★

US, 1975, TCF, 100 MINS

D JIM SHARMAN; **PR** MICHAEL WHITE; **SC** JIM SHARMAN, RICHARD O'BRIEN FROM RICHARD O'BRIEN'S PLAY THE ROCKY HORROR SHOW; **PH** PETER SUSCHITZKY; **M** RICHARD O'BRIEN; **ED** GRAEME CLIFFORD

CAST TIM CURRY (DR FRANK N. FURTER), BARRY BOSTWICK (BRAD MAJORS), SUSAN SARANDON (JANET WEISS), RICHARD O'BRIEN (RIFF RAFF), JONATHAN ADAMS (DR EVERETT MAJORS), NELL CAMPBELL (COLUMBIA), PETER HINWOOD (ROCKY), MEATLOAF (EDDIE), PATRICIA QUINN (MAGENTA), CHARLES GRAY (NARRATOR/THE CRIMINOLOGIST), HILARY LABOW (BETTY MUNROE), JEREMY NEWSON (RALPH HAPSCHATT)

THE STORY Brad and Janet, travelling from a wedding to seek the blessing for their own marriage from their favourite professor, Dr Scott, stumble upon a big creepy house. They meet the inhabitants, the butler Riff Raff, the maid Magenta, the owner Frank N. Furter and their party guests. Their host shows them his latest creation, a man called Rocky whom he has created as a prospective lover for himself. But Rocky is scared and hides. Eddie, who is adored by another maid, Columbia, arrives but is brutally murdered by Frank. That night Frank seduces first Janet and then Brad. Janet who sees Brad and Frank on a TV monitor, makes love to Rocky. Dr Scott arrives at the castle having been alerted to strange goings-on by his nephew, Eddie. Everyone sits down to a feast, the meat course of which turns out to be Eddie. Frank turns Brad, Janet, Dr Scott, Columbia and Rocky to stone and brings them back to life for a stage performance. Riff Raff and Magenta turn on and kill Frank. Janet, Brad and the doctor escape the house which flies as a massive spacecraft back to the planet Transylvania.

THE FILM Watched coldly it is easy to see why *The Rocky Horror Picture Show* was a commercial flop when it first opened. A confused musical pastiche of horror and sci-fi movies in an atmosphere of sexual ambiguity, it is approximately half an entertaining film that goes badly out of control in its later stages. There are some very catchy tunes and a spectacular performance from Curry. In the many revivals of the stage show, the central role has become irresistible to a succession of actors and pop stars who want to show that they have an edge and a sense of humour. But there is no point in watching the film in other than ideal circumstances, that is in a late-night screening with an audience of aficionados who know the routine. The year after its disappointing opening it was given a tactical re-release at strictly targeted venues as a late-night event movie. It began to attract a devoted following of fans who developed a set of responses to the actions on screen. This phenomenon that began in New York City spread across the US and eventually to Britain. The audience arrive in costume, and throughout the film comment on the events of the movie. The lines are spoken simultaneously with the characters, or mocked, or treated to prepared or improvised responses. Water pistols are fired, toast, loo rolls and playing cards thrown at the screen. The audience response has turned each screening into an event where what the audience is getting up to is almost guaranteed to be more entertaining than what is happening on the screen. Perhaps the archetypal cult film.

> **'It's probably some kind of convention for rich weirdos.'**

ODD/SALIENT FACTS The film recreates Grant Wood's *American Gothic* in the opening scene with Richard O'Brien taking the place of the farmer. In the song 'Science Fiction Double Feature' there are references to several seminal B-movies: *The Day the Earth Stood Still* (1951), *When Worlds Collide* (1951), *Tarantula* (1955) and *The Forbidden Planet* (1956), as well as *King Kong* (1933). The latter inspires the climactic sequence in which Rocky carries Frank's body up the RKO tower. In this scene Magenta's hair is in the style of Elsa Lanchester's from *The Bride of Frankenstein* (1935). One of the film's unique boasts is that it features both Christopher Biggins and Koo Stark in supporting roles.

MEMORABLE MOMENTS Frank's entrance and performance of 'Sweet Transvestite'.

His arrival in Janet's bed disguised as Brad, and subsequent seduction of her, followed by his arrival in Brad's bed disguised as Janet, and subsequent seduction of him using the identical words.

KEY LINES

Brad to Janet, on arriving at Frank's castle: 'It's probably some kind of convention for rich weirdos.'

181

184

▲ *SALVATORE GIULIANO* *The white-jacketed Salvatore (far right) and his cohorts command the Sicilian high ground.*

over a dozen members of his gang in the dock, charged with participation in the May Day massacre. Giuliano's right-hand man, Pisciotta, admits to having betrayed and killed Giuliano under pressure from the Mafia and the *carabinieri*. He threatens to expose the links between politicians, the Mafia and the police, and after he and various associates are given life sentences, Pisciotta is poisoned in jail. In a 1960 postscript, the farmer who led the police to Pisciotta is killed by unknown assailants at a horse fair.

THE FILM Rosi came out of Italian neo-realism and shot this film on Sicilian locations using a largely non-professional cast. Gianni Di Venanzo's photography has a documentary feel in its hard-contrast monochrome and the positioning of the camera as a conscious observer, beginning with a scene in which a police spokesman addresses himself to the recording lens in describing the (as we later learn, highly dubious) scene of

the crime. But *Salvatore Giuliano* goes far beyond neo-realism. It is a Marxist take on *Citizen Kane*, in which a society is anatomized through a single individual. But Rosi isn't interested in Giuliano's individual psychology. The social bandit's mother grieves for him, he's revered as a local hero, but his public status is that of a social and political pawn at the disposal of the allied invaders during the war, the Mafia, the Sicilian aristocracy and the National government in Rome. There is no psychological 'Rosebud' to explain his actions In life, he's seen in the middle-distance wearing his regulation flat cap and white coat, a gun on his shoulder, or from behind observing his enemies through binoculars. In death he's a handsome corpse.

Salvatore Giuliano was the first of Rosi's complex political thrillers, followed by The Mattei Affair, Lucky Luciano, and Illustrious Corpses. It shaped the paranoid style in Hollywood pursued by John Frankenheimer (Seven Days in May) and Alan J. Pakula (The Parallax View, All the President's Men) and initiated a new kind of open-ended thriller. It was the springboard for the cycle of socially contextualized American Mafia movies that began a decade later with The Godfather.

ODD/SALIENT FACTS The discussion provoked by the film forced the Italian government to re-open the never-ending investigation of collusion between politicians and criminals in Sicily. Frank Wolff, who plays Pisciotta, was a Jewish American actor based in Rome; he later appeared in Spaghetti Westerns. The Marxist writer Franco Solinas went on to script Gillo Pontecorvo's cult classic The Battle of Algiers.

MEMORABLE MOMENTS The opening inventory of the dead Giuliano as if he's just been taken off the cross.

The later scene where his mother comes to identify his corpse on a slab as if she were the Virgin Mary.

The attack on the police headquarters at Castelventrato and the May 1947 communist rally; confused, chillingly violent assaults in which the assailants are not seen.

Shots of the mysteriously charismatic Giuliano leading his men into battle.

The courtroom confrontations between bemused judges on the bench and aggressive defendants behind bars.

KEY LINES

Narrator: 'Giuliano's rural kingdom, protected by a
    conspiracy of silence and terror.'

Conscript soldier, 1946: 'Who are they – bandits or
    partisans?'

Pisciotta's Defence Counsel: 'Nobody has realized the true
    nature of this tragic event. Because, Your Honour, to
    understand how a bandit can become a great political
    figure … one must have the courage to spotlight the sad
    life of misery, of ignorance, and feudal subjugations of
    so many poor people, the varied acts of political
    meddling and the nature of the Mafia. One must have
    the courage to pursue matters to the end.'

SEBASTIANE
UK, 1976, MEGALOVISION/CINEGATE/DISCTAC, 86 MINS
D DEREK JARMAN, PAUL HUMFRESS; **PR** HOWARD MALIN, JAMES WHALEY; **SC** JAMES WHALEY, DEREK JARMAN, LATIN BY JACK WELCH; **PH** (COL) PETER MIDDLETON; **M** BRIAN ENO; **ED** PAUL HUMFRESS
CAST LEONARDO TREVIGLIO (SEBASTIAN), BARNEY JAMES (SEVERUS), NEIL KENNEDY (MAXIMUS), RICHARD WARWICK (JUSTIN), DONALD DUNHAM (CLAUDIUS), KEN HICKS (ADRIAN), JANUSZ ROMANOV (ANTHONY), STEFFANO MASSARI (MARIUS), DAEVID FINBAR (JULIAN), GERALD INCANDELA (LEOPARD BOY), LINDSAY KEMP AND TROUPE (EMPEROR'S DANCE)

THE STORY Sebastian, captain of the palace guard and a favourite of the Emperor Diocletian, is dispatched to a distant garrison in a crack-down on the spread of Christianity. There he immerses himself in his spirituality as his comrades have fun in the sun. The centurion Severus is agonized in his unrequited love for Sebastian and becomes ever more vindictive towards him. The other men have contempt for Sebastian's self-absorption as they toss a frisbee, dance, fight, frolic in the surf, bathe and just sit around discussing sex and politics. After Sebastian mocks and humiliates Severus in a final rejection of his drunken sexual advances, Severus sentences him to death. Sebastian is taken on to a cliff-top, tied to a stake and shot repeatedly with arrows.

THE FILM Like Lawrence of Arabia (1962) this is an extended study of homosexual repression, frustration and extreme masochism in the desert. Jarman came to the project after a fruitful collaboration with Ken Russell, designing the sets for The Devils (1971) and Savage Messiah (1972). Jarman said: 'One of the things that most fascinates me about film-making, is its recreating the past in terms of the present.' The jarring, often humorous anachronism is a feature of his work, from the jokily modern references in Sebastiane to the time-travelling Elizabeth of Jubilee (1978). Jarman was an uncompromising film-maker, not so much or not only in his portrayal of homosexuality, which was central to his movies, but in his particular vision which often had him wilfully adhering to a vision of cheap, grainy, self-conscious artifice. His continuing devotion to Super 8 was unaccountable, perhaps symptomatic of a kind of nostalgia. Sebastiane is in many ways an impressive film, but its very serious ideas sit uneasily beside the Fire Island/Sardinian gay

KEY LINES

Tony: 'He may be a servant, but he's still a human being.'

Susan: 'What do you want from this house?'
Barrett: 'I'm a servant, miss.'

Tony: 'Do something about it, you're supposed to be the
   bloody servant.'

Tony: 'I don't know what I'd do without you.'
Barrett: 'So go and pour a glass of brandy. Don't just
   stand there.'

THE SET-UP

US, 1949, RKO, 72 MINS

D *ROBERT WISE;* **PR** *RICHARD GOLDSTONE;* **SC** *ART COHN
(BASED ON THE POEM BY JOSEPH MONCURE MARCH);* **PH** *(BW)
MILTON KRASNER;* **ED** *ROLAND GROSS*

CAST *ROBERT RYAN (BILL 'STOKER' THOMPSON); AUDREY TOTTER
(JULIE THOMPSON), GEORGE TOBIAS (TINY), PERCY HELTON (RED),
ALAN BAXTER ('LITTLE BOY'), WALLACE FORD (GUS), HAL
FIEBERLING ('TIGER' NELSON), DARRYL HICKMAN (SHANLEY),
KENNY O'MORRISON (MOORE), JAMES EDWARDS (LUTHER
HAWKINS), DAVID CLARKE ('GUNBOAT' JOHNSON), PHILIP PINE
(TONY SOUZA), EDWIN MAX (DANNY)*

THE STORY 9.05pm, a hot summer night in Paradise City.
Boxing fans are filing into the sleazy stadium. Across the street
at Hotel Cozy, the tired, punchy 35-year-old heavyweight Bill
'Stoker' Thompson is resting before his four-round bout with 23-
year-old 'Tiger' Nelson. Stoker's wife Julie wants him to quit, but
Stoker believes he might win and earn a better billing.
Meanwhile, his manager Tiny has taken fifty dollars from the
minor racketeer managing Nelson, for Stoker to take a dive in
the third round. Convinced Stoker will lose, Tiny doesn't tell him
about the set-up and squares Stoker's squalid second.

During three brutal rounds Stoker is more than holding his
own. Before the bell for the fourth round, Tiny reveals the set-
up, but a battered Stoker knocks out his opponent. Trying to
escape he's cornered in an alleyway by Little Boy and his
henchmen and is pinned down so that Little Boy can smash his
right fist to a pulp. He staggers out into the street where Julie

cradles him before the ambulance arrives. A clock shows the
time as 10.16pm

THE FILM *The Set-Up* is one of the great boxing movies, using
the game as a metaphor for the illusory nature of the American
Dream, with one of the screen's most realistic scraps, staged by
John Indrisano. In the symbolically named Paradise City,
Thompson and his wife stay at the sordid Hotel Cozy, and Julie
cradles her husband under the neon sign of the Dreamland
dance hall in the final scene. In the seedy dressing room Stoker
meets a range of boxers – a teenager making his debut, a
demented no-hoper going into the ring for the last time, a handsome black determined to box his way out of the ghetto. The
film is not an attack on boxing itself, and ultimately the doomed
Stoker snatches victory from his defeat.

The Set-Up was shot entirely in a studio and has a stylized,
expressionistic *noir* atmosphere. There is only source music from

▼ *THE SET-UP Typical 1940s production still shows Ryan's
Stoker Thompson standing stoic, isolated and alone.*

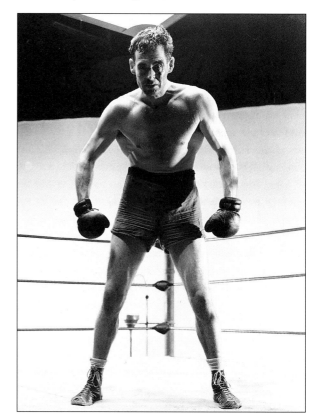

radios, bars and clubs. The film lasts exactly the 72 minutes from the opening to the closing shot (unlike *High Noon*, for instance, which is rather shorter than the time stated by the clocks).

Robert Wise edited *Citizen Kane* and *The Magnificent Ambersons* before he made his directorial debut with Val Lewton's low-budget horror movie unit at RKO and became a versatile genre director. *The Set-Up*, his ninth film, completed his RKO contract, after which he entered the big time, which ultimately led to such pictures as *West Side Story* and *The Sound of Music*.

ODD/SALIENT FACTS The film was based on a narrative poem published in 1928 by William Moncure March, who gave up his job as the first managing editor of *The New Yorker* to devote himself to writing. On the strength of it he went to Hollywood as a screenwriter, remaining there for a dozen years. In 1948 he volunteered to work on Wise's film of *The Set-Up* 'but they didn't want me around'. The rhythms and rhymes of his poem anticipate rap music and March was incensed that his black boxer Pansy Jones was changed into the white Stoker Thompson. Robert Ryan (1909–73) was a boxing champion while a student at the Ivy League college, Dartmouth.

MEMORABLE MOMENTS Tiny, the corrupt manager, striking a match across Stoker's name on the poster outside the stadium to relight the stub of his cigar.

The pained face of Stoker waking up in his shabby hotel.

Julie's walk through the garish, neon-lit urban hell of Paradise City.

Stoker's desperate glances from the ring at his wife's empty seat.

The shadow of a jazz band playing behind a barred window thrown on the alley wall as Little Boy advances to smash Stoker's hand.

KEY LINES

Tiny, on being told Stoker is resting: 'Doesn't that guy get enough shut-eye in the ring?'

Julie: 'I remember the first time you told me that. You were

just one punch away from the title shot. Don't you see Bill, you'll always be one punch away … What kind of a life is this, how many more beatings do you have to take?'

Little Boy: 'I paid for something tonight, Stoker. I didn't get it.'

Stoker: 'I won tonight.'

Julie: 'You won tonight. We both won tonight.'

189

SE7EN
US, 1995, NEW LINE CINEMA, 127 MINS

D DAVID FINCHER; **PR** ARNOLD KOPELSON, PHYLIS CARLYLE; **SC** ANDREW KEVIN WALKER; **PH** DARIUS KHONDJI; **PR DES** ARTHUR MAX; **M** HOWARD SHORE; **ED** RICHARD FRANCIS-BRUCE **CAST** MORGAN FREEMAN (SOMERSET), BRAD PITT (MILLS), KEVIN SPACEY (JOHN DOE), GWYNETH PALTROW (TRACY MILLS), RICHARD ROUNDTREE (TALBOT), R. LEE ERMEY (POLICE CAPTAIN), BOB MACK (GLUTTONY VICTIM), HAWTHORNE (GEORGE, LIBRARY GUARD), GENE BORKAN (ELI GOULD), JULIE ARASKOG (MRS GOULD), ALFONSO FREEMAN (FINGERPRINT FORENSIC MAN), MICHAEL REID MACKAY (VICTOR), MARTIN SERENE (WILD BILL), MICHAEL MASSEE (MAN IN MASSAGE PARLOUR BOOTH), CAT MUELLER (HOOKER), HEIDI SCHANZ (BEAUTIFUL WOMAN), RICHMOND ARQUETTE (DELIVERY MAN)

THE STORY The young Detective Mills, on his new assignment in a big city, and the soon-to-retire Detective Somerset investigate a series of murders based on the seven deadly sins. After Gluttony, Greed and Sloth, Somerset, who shares the killer's love of literature, tracks him down, but the man, John Doe, evades capture. Somerset and Mills search the killer's flat and find evidence of his connection to the crimes as well as 2,000 journals. After the bodies of a prostitute and model are found for the sins of Lust and Pride, Doe gives himself up to Mills and Somerset. He strikes a deal whereby he will sign a full confession on the condition that the detectives go with him to find the bodies of his final two victims. The three of them drive into the desert where a package is delivered to them. When he finds that it is the head of his pregnant wife, Mills shoots Doe repeatedly thus completing the themed killings with Envy and Wrath.

when John Cassavetes was appearing on a late-night radio chat show in New York and appealed to listeners to send in cash if they wanted to see him make a truly realistic picture dealing with racial issues in everyday life. The station received $2,000 in small sums. All the actors in the film used their own names for the characters they created. Anthony Ray, who played Tony, is the son of Nicholas Ray, director of *Rebel Without a Cause*, a film for which Cassavetes auditioned.

MEMORABLE MOMENTS Lelia walking down 42nd Street looking at the ads outside movie houses.

> 'We went out to have a ball. You pay the price. If you get beat up, you get beat up.'

Ben, Tom and Dennis in the Museum of Modern Art sculpture court where Tom rails against culture and mocks Dennis.

Tony and Lelia running away from David in Central Park.

Hugh and Rupert's long, conciliatory dialogue at Grand Central Station.

KEY LINES

Lelia: 'David's writing a new novel all about you Ben.'

Ben: 'It had better not be any of that Beat Generation jazz like the last one.'

Lelia, after losing her virginity: 'I didn't know it could be so awful … I thought being with you would be so important and that afterwards two people would be as close as it was possible to get, but instead we're just two strangers. It's over. I know that much about life.'

Tom: 'We went out to have a ball. You pay the price. If you get beat up, you get beat up.'

SHERLOCK JR

US, 1924, METRO PICTURES/BUSTER KEATON PRODUCTIONS, 45 MINS

D BUSTER KEATON; **PR** JOSEPH M. SCHENK;. **SC** CLYDE BRUCKMAN, JEAN HAVES AND JOSEPH MITCHELL; **PH** (BW) ELGIN LESSLEY, BRYON HOUCK; **ED** BUSTER KEATON

CAST BUSTER KEATON (THE PROJECTIONIST/SHERLOCK JR.), KATHRYN MCGUIRE (THE GIRL), WARD KRANE (THE RIVAL), JOSEPH KEATON (THE GIRL'S FATHER), HORACE MORGAN, JANE CONNELLY, ERWIN CONNELLY, FORD WEST, GEORGE DAVIS, JOHN PATRICK, RUTH HOLLEY

THE STORY A projectionist in a small town movie theatre dreams of becoming a detective. Short of money he buys his beloved a $1 box of chocolates. His rival, seeing the threat posed by the projectionist, steals the girl's father's watch, pawns it, buys a bigger box of chocolates with the proceeds and plants the pawn ticket in the projectionist's pocket. The projectionist briefly trails the cad before having to go to work in the projection booth where he falls asleep. Meanwhile the girl goes to the pawn shop and discovers the truth. As he sleeps, the projectionist's ghostly alter-ego leaves his body and enters the screen, first chaotically then suavely, as 'The World's most renowned crimebuster – Sherlock Jr.' Pursuing the cad who has kidnapped the girl, he rescues her and defeats the gang before waking up again in the projection booth. Inspired by events on the screen he kisses her. Fade to babies. The projectionist is left scratching his head.

THE FILM Like his great rival Chaplin, Keaton's most productive period had passed by the time sound had arrived. But while Chaplin continued to produce major films and his fortunes were improving, Keaton's luck changed and he faced poverty and alcoholism. By the late Forties the cult of the cinema's second great clown was reestablished and he found regular and lucrative work in films and on television and travelled the festival circuit. The film, originally titled *The Misfit* and made by an already established and independently creative star, came in the midst of Keaton's golden era which included *The Navigator* (1924), *Go West* (1925) and his great masterpiece *The General* (1927). He uses the opportunity to explore with wit and no pretentiousness the nature of film and film-making. This is one of cinema's first exercises in post-modernism, a brilliantly innovative and imaginative minor masterpiece which investigates and toys with the boundaries of the screen.

ODD/SALIENT FACTS Buster Keaton was famous for inventing and performing the stunts in his own films. In *Sherlock Jr* when he did the first take of the sequence in which he runs along the tops of the railway cars and grabs hold of the spout of the water tower, Keaton seriously underestimated the force of the gushing water. He was knocked to the ground but, with the bounce and spirit that, according to legend, had him nick-named 'Buster' as a kid by Houdini, he got straight back up and carried on with the work. Only in a medical examination many years later was it discovered that he had broken his neck in this fall. The scene in which Keaton escapes the gangsters by driving into the suitcase of ties his disguised accomplice is holding in front of his stomach, was accomplished without camera trickery. It was an old vaudeville gag which Keaton replicated for Ed Sullivan on his TV show *Toast of the Town* in 1957. Keaton employed his old pal Roscoe 'Fatty' Arbuckle to work as a co-director on the film at a time after his infamous murder/rape case when he could find no other work. Arbuckle was to be credited as William Goodrich, a pseudonym he used for his directorial work over the next decade, but was so irascible with the actors that Keaton removed him from the picture.

MEMORABLE MOMENTS Keaton shadowing his rival, matching him pace for pace as they walk down the pavement. The cad picks up a cigarette, takes three drags, tosses it over his shoulder where Keaton catches it and takes a drag himself before discarding it. The two trip up on the same paving stone and simultaneously swerve to avoid a passing car before entering a railway yard.

▼ *SHERLOCK JR The projectionist (Buster Keaton) is faced with the awful truth that his one dollar is not going to stretch to a three-dollar box of chocolates.*

Keaton's first moments in the film within the film when he finds himself tossed about in various jump-cutting scenes from the front of a house, to a garden bench, to the middle of a busy road, to the edge of a cliff, to between two lions, to a desert through which a train speeds, to a rock in the sea, to a snow-covered forest, and back to the garden.

Buster's escape from the gang's lair. His sidekick has supplied him with a hoop containing a concertinaed dress. This Buster places in the window frame before entering the house. The side wall is removed to reveal that the stunt is achieved without special effects. Having suddenly to flee, Buster dives out of the window, through the hoop and into the dress, in which he walks away, so when the gang rush straight out of the house, the only person they see is an innocent old lady.

KEY LINE
The card on Sherlock's performance in the fantasy film: 'His mind solved everything about the mystery except identifying the thieves and recovering the pearls.'

SHOCK CORRIDOR

US, 1963, FROMKESS-FIRKS/ALLIED ARTISTS, 110 MINS
D/PR/SC *SAMUEL FULLER;* **PH** *STANLEY CORTEZ;* **ED** *JEROME THOMS;* **M** *PAUL DUNLAP*
CAST *PETER BRECK (JOHNNY BARRETT), CONSTANCE TOWERS (CATHY), GENE EVANS (BODEN), JAMES BEST (STUART), HARI RHODES (TRENT), LARRY TUCKER (PAGLIACCI), WILLIAM ZUCCART ('SWANEE' SWANSON), PHILIP AHN (DR FONG), JOHN MATHEWS (DR CHRISTO), CHUCK ROBERSON (WILKES), JOHN CRAIG (LLOYD)*

THE STORY The film opens and closes with the title: Whom God wishes to destroy he first makes mad – Euripedes 425 BC. Reporter Johnny Barrett, ambitious to win a Pulitzer Prize, is coached by a psychiatrist and his editor to feign insanity so that he can be admitted to a state mental hospital and crack the unsolved murder of an inmate. Johnny's girlfriend Cathy, a stripper, pretends to be his sister and accuses him of attempted incest. He's admitted to the institution where he is under the supervision of Dr Christo and two male attendants, the caring Wilkes and the brutal Lloyd. Johnny identifies three psychotic witnesses to the murder and wins their confidence. Stuart, a Southern redneck who was brainwashed while a PoW in

193

196

▲ *SHOWGIRLS Elizabeth Berkley grapples with the greasy pole of success that is the world of Las Vegas glamour dancing.*

KEY LINES

Mr Karlman on Cristal (he says the same of Nomi after her debut as Goddess): 'She's dazzling! She's exciting! She's also very sexy.'

Al Torres, giving new girl Penny some career advice: 'If you wanna last longer than a week, give me a blow-job. First I get you used to the money, then I make you swallow.'

Nomi and James are getting steamy as they dance together, but when things go too far, Nomi cautions: 'It's my period.'
James, incredulous: 'Oh, right!'
Nomi: 'Check. [He checks.] See.'

James, to the departing Nomi: 'It's all right, I got towels.'
Al and Mama (Ms Bazoom) visit Nomi at the Stardust. Al suggests that maybe Nomi misses them.
Mama: 'She misses us like I miss that lump on my twat that I had taken off last week.'

—

SID AND NANCY

UK, 1986, ZENITH/INITIAL, 114 MINS

D ALEX COX; **PR** ERIC FELLNER; **SC** ALEX COX, ABBE WOOL; **PH** (COL) ROGER DEAKINS; **M** JOE STRUMMER, THE POGUES, PRAY FOR RAIN; **ED** DAVID MARTIN

CAST GARY OLDMAN (SID VICIOUS), CHLOE WEBB (NANCY SPUNGEN), DAVID HAYMAN (MALCOLM), DEBBY BISHOP (PHOEBE), ANDREW SCHOFIELD (JOHN), XANDER BERKELEY (BOWERY SNAX), PERRY BENSON (PAUL), TONY LONDON (STEVE), SANDY BARON (HOTELIER – USA), SY RICHARDSON (METHADONE WORKER), EDWARD TUDOR-POLE (HOTELIER – UK)

THE STORY In the aftermath of Nancy Spungen's death, Sid Vicious recalls their meeting and romantic life together. They meet at the flat of a mutual friend, a dominatrix, just after Sid joined the Sex Pistols. Nancy introduces Sid to heroin and hangs around during the group's brief spell in the limelight. The other members of the band resent Nancy's presence and the effects of drugs on Sid's abilities. Nancy, banned from coming along on the disastrous tour of America, stays in London and works as a prostitute. When Sid collapses on a plane, Nancy travels to New York to meet him and they spend time together in Paris where Sid does some recording. They move into the Chelsea Hotel in New York, and Nancy arranges a few gigs for Sid. They attend a methadone clinic, and spend a disastrous thanksgiving with Nancy's family. All the time their dependence on heroin becomes increasingly desperate. Having made a pact to go out together, Nancy dies from stab wounds, presumably inflicted by Sid. Sid is arrested, undergoes cold turkey in jail, and is released on bail. Sid is dancing with some kids on a wasteland outside a diner, when a cab pulls up. A smiling Nancy is sitting inside. Sid gets into the cab and it drives off.

THE FILM The working title for the film was *Love Kills*. It was not intended to be a film about music, a biopic of The Sex Pistols. It is a love story. Then why is there all that embarrassing stuff about punk that makes much of the first half of the film unwatchable, but unwatchable in a completely different way from the last section which is even harder to sit through. It has a lot to do with the writer/director. Cox began with the promising, flawed cult debut, *Repo Man* (1984), starring Harry Dean Stanton, a man of impeccable cult standing. By this, his second film, things were already starting to unravel and would go utterly pear-shaped in his disastrous third film, *Straight to Hell* (1986). Whatever the shortcomings of the film, and its lack of control, the central performances are remarkably raw, naked and courageously unsympathetic, and deserve to feature in some minor modern masterpiece rather than a fascinating cult failure.

ODD/SALIENT FACTS Thus far, Chloe Webb's post-Nancy career has featured only two notable roles, in Peter Greenaway's *The Belly of an Architect* (1987) and opposite Danny De Vito in *Twins* (1988). The role of Sid Vicious launched Gary Oldman as one of the Hollywood cult psycho character actors of the nineties, in *State of Grace* (1990), *JFK* (1991), Bram Stoker's *Dracula* (1992), and *True Romance* (1993). The film is the first in the new wave of cinematic heroin

chic, blazing the way for such distinguished druggy cult works as *Pulp Fiction* (1994), *Trainspotting* (1995) and *Fear and Loathing in Las Vegas* (1998). The supporting cast features: Kathy Burke, later to star in Oldman's grim, autobiographical debut as writer-director, *Nil by Mouth* (1997); Courtney Love who plays one of Nancy's friends and appeared in *Straight to Hell*, no stranger to the sex and drugs and rock 'n' roll lifestyle, and herself married to Kurt Cobain, a successor, if much more talented, to Sid Vicious's place in the 'live fast, die young and leave a pale body' stakes; and, as one of the prospective guests of the Chelsea Hotel put off by Sid and Nancy's antics, Iggy Pop, who must have been one of the models for the part of Rock-Head, the self-confessed 'Godfather of punk'.

MEMORABLE MOMENTS As their relationship collapses with their addiction to heroin, Sid and Nancy kiss on a New York

▼ *SID AND NANCY With vacant eyes and scars of self-mutilation, Gary Oldman in the performance that launched his career as Hollywood's favourite psychotic outsider.*

▲ *SOME LIKE IT HOT* Daphne (Jack Lemmon) is struck by something familiar about Sugar's (Marilyn Monroe) new friend Junior (Tony Curtis).

Joe, someone whom Sugar can rely on and confide in. Daphne is luckier and happier than Jerry could ever be. Even before the famous punchline, the romantic Daphne wants to go ahead with the wedding despite Joe's appealing to Jerry about the union's central hitch. At the heart of the film is Marilyn Monroe in one of her signature performances. Her husband Arthur Miller was a lot more impressed with her than the role: 'She had so assiduously worked on this small worthless part, and she couldn't get a part worth working on.' But this misses the point that the role defines Monroe's continuing cult status. She is a supremely gorgeous woman who should be unattainable to a sleaze-ball like Joe. But from the start she tells Josephine, the person whom she judges the most trustworthy, that Joe is precisely the kind of man she is attracted to, an unreliable saxophone-playing Lothario. Sugar and Joe don't meet until the final sequence, by which

stage he has been redeemed by being Josephine and by the innocence of Sugar's affection. Regardless of Curtis's famous comment that kissing Monroe was like 'kissing Hitler', their scenes together, in which both are lying but only Joe knows it, are truly romantic. Monroe was not invited to Billy Wilder's end-of-shoot party on 6 November 1958. The start of filming was delayed as Monroe was suffering from depression after a miscarriage. She had another miscarriage that began just hours after her final day of shooting. In marked contrast to the conditions under which it was made, *Some Like It Hot* remains one of the most joyous and strangest comedies to have come out of Hollywood.

ODD/SALIENT FACTS Billy Wilder initially acceded to the wishes of United Artists who wanted Frank Sinatra for the role of Joe. Director and prospective star made a positive start to negotiations but the deal fell through when Sinatra failed to show up for a subsequent meeting. The production was beset by delays, most of which were caused by Monroe. The scene in which the disconsolate Sugar goes into Josephine and Daphne's hotel room and asks 'Where's that bourbon' is said to have required 59 takes.

MEMORABLE MOMENTS The first appearance of Sugar at Chicago's railway station, carrying her ukulele and wiggling along in her tight skirt, being startled by a jet of steam. She moves, according to Jerry 'like jello on springs'.

Sugar's seduction of the 'frigid' Josephine on Osgood's yacht, in which her increasingly passionate kisses eventually steam up his glasses, intercut with Daphne and Osgood's tango.

KEY LINES

Joe's mantra as a 'brand new' girl: 'I'm a boy.'

Sugar to Josephine: 'I 'm tired of getting the fuzzy end of the lollipop.'

Joe/Josephine having kissed the crying Sugar: 'None of that, Sugar. No guy is worth it.'

Daphne's final reason why the proposed marriage can't go ahead: 'You don't understand, Osgood. [He removes his wig] I'm a man.'
Osgood: 'Well, nobody's perfect!'

SONS OF THE DESERT

US, 1933, MGM, 68 MINS

D WILLIAM A. SEITER; **PR** HAL ROACH; **SC** FRANK CRAVEN, BYRON MORGAN; **PH** KENNETH PEACH; **ED** BERT JORDAN

CAST STAN LAUREL (STAN LAUREL), OLIVER HARDY (OLIVER HARDY), CHARLEY CHASE (CHARLEY CHASE), MAE BUSCH (MRS LOTTIE CHASE HARDY), DOROTHY CHRISTIE (MRS BETTY LAUREL), LUCIEN LITTLEFIELD (DR HORACE MEDDICK), JOHN ELLIOT (EXALTED/EXHAUSTED RULER), CHARLEY YOUNG, JOHN MERTON, WILLIAM GILLESPIE, CHARLES McAVOY, ROBERT BURNS, AL THOMPSON, EDDIE BAKER, JIMMY AUBREY, CHET BRANDENBERG, DON BRODIE (SONS OF THE DESERT)

THE STORY Stan and Ollie make a solemn oath to travel to the annual convention of their fraternity, the 'Sons of the Desert', in Chicago the following week. When Ollie's wife refuses permission for him to go, he hatches a plan. He and Stanley hire a doctor to declare Ollie sick and recommend a break in Hawaii, and instead sneak off to Chicago. There they meet up with Charley Chase who turns out to be Ollie's brother-in-law. Betty and Lottie are distraught to learn that the boat on which their husbands were due to be travelling from Hawaii has sunk. Sneaking back to their neighbouring homes, Stan and Ollie hide out in the loft. When they finally confront their furious wives, Ollie is punished for inventing an elaborate cover story, while Stanley comes clean and is immediately forgiven and rewarded by Betty.

THE FILM Having been brought together by Max Roach in 1926, Laurel & Hardy established themselves as the most popular comedy double act in the history of cinema. Laurel was the creative force behind their films, devising many of their gags, constantly coming up with new ideas, and even working on the editing of the films. The pair always play childish, unsophisticated men struggling to get ahead, and striving to control the inevitable chaos that results from their schemes. They share an unspoken bond – they will always be friends and partners – and are perfectly matched. Stanley is utterly at sea in the world while Ollie is marginally less clueless, but always has his pride dented as a result of his and Stanley's mistakes and ends up suffering some kind of physical injury and indignity.

The duo had already used the basic plot of Sons of the Desert in Be Big (1930), in which Ollie feigns sickness in order that he and Stanley can avoid a trip to Atlantic City with their wives, and instead go to a club. Here as ever the women in their lives are ferocious creatures, stronger and smarter than their bumbling, ineffectual husbands. They manage to get away with their terribly executed plan, in which Stan hires a vet to confirm Ollie's illness, and then give the game away in an hilarious sequence. Betty and Lottie are trying to distract themselves from concern over their husbands' fate with a visit to the cinema. Just as they pray to see them one more time, there is a newsreel report from the Chicago convention. Stan and Ollie are in their Order's parade when they see the camera. Rather than hiding they approach the camera looking deliriously happy and carefree. It is the essence of the cinema's most enduringly loveable team.

ODD/SALIENT FACTS The film was released in Britain under the title Fraternally Yours. Oliver Hardy was a master mason in real life. Charley Chase, who plays Ollie's brother-in-law, was the brother of James Parrott, a seasoned director of comedy shorts who made several with Laurel & Hardy including their Oscar-winning The Music Box (1932). The film gave its name to the fan club started by the team's own biographer John McCabe, that to this day continues to celebrate Laurel & Hardy. He approached Stanley asking for his blessing for the enterprise and permission to use the title. As he recalls in The Comedy World of Stan Laurel: 'Stan made only one proviso. The group must, he insisted, maintain at all times a "half-assed dignity".'

▼ SONS OF THE DESERT Stan and Ollie trying to convince their wives they've indeed been to Hawaii.

SULLIVAN'S TRAVELS

US, 1941, PARAMOUNT, 91 MINS

D PRESTON STURGES; **SC** STURGES; **PH** (BW) JOHN F. SEITZ; **M** LEO SHUKMAN, CHARLES BRADSHAW; **ED** STUART GILMORE **CAST** JOEL MCCREA (JOHN L. SULLIVAN), VERONICA LAKE (THE GIRL), ROBERT WARWICK (MR LEBRAND, HEAD OF STUDIO), MR HADRIAN (PORTER HALL), MR JONES (WILLIAM DEMAREST), ERIC BLORE (SULLIVAN'S VALET), ROBERT GREIG (SULLIVAN'S BUTLER), MARGARET HAYES (SECRETARY)

THE STORY John L. Sullivan, ace Hollywood comedy director of such hits as *So Long Sarong*, *Hey Hey in the Hayloft* and *Ants In Your Pants* 1939, wants to confront the big issues of the time in a film of 'stark realism' called *O Brother, Where Art Thou?* Defying the studio bosses he goes on the road dressed as a tramp to gain authentic experience, and they send a back-up bus manned by PR men and a doctor to follow him. He gives them the slip, is briefly ensnared by an amorous widow and hitches a ride from a truckdriver who drops him back in Hollywood where a disenchanted actress (never identified by name) generously buys him breakfast. After discovering his identity, she accompanies him, disguised as a boy, when he dons a hobo outfit and goes on the road again, another unsatisfactory experience which he concludes, and offers to introduce the actress to Lubitsch. Sullivan then goes out for a third excursion, to distribute $5 bills to the poor. An old tramp mugs him, steals his money and the shoes that contain identification cards, and is then crushed by a train, leading to national press headlines like 'Strange Death of Hollywood Director'. Meanwhile the concussed Sullivan, stepping out of a freight car, reacts to a brutal railway policeman by hitting him with a rock and drawing a six-year sentence on a rural chain gang. After seeing a silent Mickey Mouse comedy, shown to an audience of convicts in a black baptist church, Sullivan secures his release, but determines to make more comedies rather than *O Brother, Where Art Thou?*

THE FILM This double-edged satire manages, like most of Sturges's comedies, to have it both ways, simultaneously attacking Hollywood's crassly commercial escapism and the patronizing left-wing artists who attempt to make politically relevant films (a parody of one such opens the movie). Sullivan is both pretentious and pathetic (like the aristocrat in J. M. Barrie's *The Admirable Crichton* he's far less smart than his butler). Technically interesting (1) for the long takes of dialogue scenes

▲ *SULLIVAN'S TRAVELS Rangy Joel McCrea and diminutive Veronica Lake hit the road in search of reality.*

and (2) for a couple of lengthy montage sequences where Sturges dispenses with speech and sound effects and there's only music on the soundtrack.

ODD/SALIENT FACTS The film that director Sullivan and his producers watch in the opening sequence is deliberately ambiguous: is this someone else's picture, a rough-cut of a proposed Sullivan film, or a fantasy created in their minds from the director's conference pitch? This is, like much else in the movies, post-modernism *avant la lettre*. Veronica Lake riding the rods as a hobo was almost certainly inspired by Louise Brooks's posing as a boy to accompany Richard Arlen on the road in William Wellman's early Depression film *Beggars of Life* (1928). In his posthumous autobiography (*Sturges on Sturges*, 1991), the director said: 'I wrote *Sullivan's Travels* to satisfy an urge to tell [my fellow-comedy directors] that they were getting too deep-dish; to leave the preaching to the preachers.' Joel McCrea (1905–90), an uneasily definable talent, competed with Gary Cooper and James Stewart in the middle-ground of American innocence, working thrice with Sturges, twice with Tourneur, once with Hitchcock, and finally with Sam Peckinpah in *Ride the High Country/Guns in the Afternoon* (1962) .

MEMORABLE MOMENTS Sullivan being instructed by his valet and butler on poverty. The luxurious studio back-up bus with short-wave and shower. Sullivan and the Girl suddenly facing a darker world and getting afflicted by fleas and lice in a hobo village. Sullivan, after his horrific days on a chain gang, laughing with fellow prisoners at a silent cartoon.

KEY LINES

The Girl: 'If you were a casting director I'd be staring into your bridgework saying "Yes Mr Smearcase".'

Sullivan: 'Wherever I start out I always end up back here in Hollywood.'

SWEET SWEETBACK'S BAAD ASSSSS SONG

US, 1971, A YEAH PRODUCTION, 97 MINS
D/PR/SC/ED/M *MELVIN VAN PEEBLES;* **PH** *(COL) BOB MAXWELL*
CAST *'STARRING THE BLACK COMMUNITY AND BRER SOUL'*

THE STORY Reared in an all-black brothel and given his nickname by its girls in awe of his sexual prowess, Sweet Sweetback is a prodigious stud who performs sexual acts for admiring black audiences in a Los Angeles underground circus. One night two white detectives providing protection to the establishment's owner ask if they can take someone into the police station for the night, just to show their boss they've collared a suspect. Sweetback goes along, but when they pick up and assault a young black radical, Sweetback beats them unconscious and goes on the run. The rest of the movie is a single chase in which Sweetback has sex with virtually every woman he meets, is arrested several times, kills some policemen in self-defence, and helps the young radical to escape. Meanwhile the white police and a pair of reluctant black cops are urged to bring in Sweetback, who becomes a revolutionary hero to the black community. Sweetback's friends and supporters are shot and tortured by the cops, though he is briefly helped by Hells Angels impressed by his courage and sexual successes. Eventually he staggers across the desert, tending his own wounds, and kills two police dogs in the Rio Grande as he crosses into Mexico.

THE FILM Melvin Van Peebles' rebarbative one-man-show, a low-budget film, is part crude exploitation skin-flick, part European art movie. It combines soft-core sex with slow-motion, speeded-up camerawork, jump cuts, shots in negative and a

total disregard for conventional narration. Born in 1932 in Chicago, Van Peebles is an authentic maverick, who was one of the first blacks given a commission in the US Air Force but refused to join the Establishment. After his military service he became a San Francisco trolley driver and writer, before relocating to Paris, where he was a local hero as journalist, actor and film-maker. His movie, *Story of a Three Day Pass*, brought an invitation to the 1969 San Francisco Film Festival and then a Hollywood contract to make him one of the first trio of black directors to work within the system, the others being Ossie Davies *(Cotton Comes to Harlem)* and *Life* photographer Gordon Parks *(The Learning Tree)*. Van Peebles's *The Watermelon Man*, a feeble tale about a complacent white middle-class professional waking up black, was a mild success, and he formed his own company and, using his own money, made the aggressive, transgressive *Sweet Sweetback*, which set out to offend both white society and respectable middle-class blacks. The film's long chase is a bitter poem of injustice in which the only sympathetic whites are fascistic bikers. Sweetback is neither a servile black like the characters in films of the 1930s and '40s, nor one of the saintly blacks of the 1950s and '60s. He's a stud who stands up for himself and is

▼ *SWEET SWEETBACK'S BAAD ASSSSS SONG Black activist Melvin Van Peebles reveals his superstud virility to a counter-cultural white chick.*

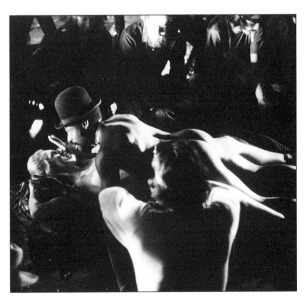

politicized by the brutality he sees. Black audiences responded to the picture's raw power, and it made a fortune but was excluded from normal distribution, and although Van Peebles was made modestly rich the movie was rarely seen outside the States. He refused to allow it to be shown in South Africa until 1994. *Sweet Sweetback* helped create the 'blaxploitation' movement of the 1970s, which Van Peebles believes turned his liberating movie on its head. It also gave a generation of African-American film-makers their vocation. Van Peebles subsequently worked in the theatre, but made no more movies.

ODD/SALIENT FACTS Van Peebles refused to submit the film for certification to what he called 'an all-white jury' and gave the film his own X-Certificate. The director's son Mario made his movie debut at the age of 13 in *Sweet Sweetback*. He later worked as a film-maker, directing his father in *Posse and Panther*. Melvin Van Peebles worked for a time in the 1980s on the New York Stock Exchange and wrote *Bold Money*, a bestselling book on investment.

MEMORABLE MOMENTS The erotic title sequence in which the teenage Sweetback is initiated into sex is a sly exercise in ethnic sexuality.

The second half is a sustained montage of pursuit, oppression and cruelty, accompanied by a choral commentary that anticipates rap music.

KEY LINES

The film's epigraph given in French and English: 'Sire these lines are not a homage to brutality that the artist has invented, but a hymn from the mouth of reality.'

Opening title: 'This film is dedicated to all the Brothers and Sisters who had enough of the man.'
Final title: 'Watch out – a baad assss nigger is coming back to collect some dues'.

TARGETS

US, 1967, PARAMOUNT, 100 MINS

D PETER BOGDANOVICH; **SC** BOGDANOVICH, FROM A STORY BY POLLY PLATT AND HIMSELF; **PH** LASZLO KOVACS
CAST BORIS KARLOFF (BYRON ORLOK), TIM O'KELLY (BOBBY THOMPSON), NANCY HSUEH (JENNY), PETER BOGDANOVICH (SAMMY MICHAELS)

THE STORY Ageing British horror movie star Byron Orlok decides that *The Terror*, his latest film for a minor Hollywood studio, will be his last because the gothic pictures with which he's associated are hopelessly old-fashioned in a world of random daily violence. 'I'm an antique, out of date, an anachronism', he says and refuses to read writer-director Sammy Michaels's latest script. But he reluctantly agrees to attend the premiere of *The Terror* at a drive-in in San Fernando Valley. Meanwhile Bobby Thompson, a seemingly well-adjusted insurance salesman married to a telephonist and living with his conformist, lower-middle-class parents, is turning the boot of his car into an arsenal. He's first seen holding the distant Orlok in the telescopic sights of a rifle he's buying at a gun-shop. The following day Bobby murders his wife, mother and a delivery boy, before taking up a position on a gas tank overlooking a freeway to pick off passing motorists. Fleeing from the police he takes refuge in the drive-in movie house where *The Terror* is to be shown. As dusk falls and the movie starts, Bobby returns to the rampage from a position high-up behind the movie screen, picking off isolated members of the audience in their cars and killing the projectionist. As panic reigns in the cinema, Orlok, immaculately dressed in a dinner jacket, walks intrepidly towards the screen. Despite being wounded he disarms the deranged Bobby.

THE FILM *Targets* is the first time a cinéaste critic comparable with the French New Wave directors was let loose on a Hollywood movie and the result is a minor masterpiece, a self-

▼ *TARGETS* Gun-crazy all-American boy Tim O'Kelly picks a target on the LA freeway.

conscious postmodernist work. There are allusions to Hitchcock, Welles and Preminger, and Orlok and Sammy watch Hawks's *The Criminal Code* (Karloff's first major film) on TV. The movie is about the thin line between art and reality, the relationship between life and film-making (e.g. the projectionist loading his projector parallels the assassin loading his rifle). It is also about the decline of values and banalization of American life by the media and how the availability of guns gives deadly expression to underlying frustration and anger. The ultimate postmodernist aspect of this astute picture is that clearly the script that Orlok refuses to read (i.e. the picture that will take his career in a new direction) is the movie written by Bogdanovich/Michaels in which he is appearing.

> **'All the best movies have been made.'**

ODD/SALIENT FACTS Producer Roger Corman gave his protégé Bogdanovich twenty minutes from his 1963 film *The Terror* (on which Monte Hellman and Francis Coppola did second-unit work), a twelve days' schedule and two days remaining from a contract with Boris Karloff who died in 1969 not long after it was released. Bogdanovich showed the draft of his screenplay to Samuel Fuller, who worked it over without credit. The film was inspired by an incident on 1 August 1966 in Austin, Texas, when honours student Charles J. Whitman, after murdering his wife and mother, locked himself in the University of Texas tower from which he shot 44 people, killing 14 of them, before himself being gunned down by the police. Roger Corman sold the movie to Paramount instead of releasing it via the AIP exploitation company, and following the assassinations of Martin Luther King and Bobby Kennedy, Paramount put out only six prints and prefaced the picture with a statement that it was a demand for gun control. Count Orlok was used for the central character of *Nosferatu*, FW Murnau's seminal 1922 version of Bram Stoker's *Dracula*. *Targets* has no written score, just source music, and the subtle soundtrack is credited to Verna Fields, who was to win an Oscar as editor on Spielberg's *Jaws* (1975) and the reputation (challenged by its director) of having salvaged the film.

MEMORABLE MOMENTS Karloff reciting Death's speech from Somerset Maugham's *Sheppey* about 'an appointment in Samarra'.

Bobby tidying up after his picnic while preparing to shoot passing drivers from his eyrie overlooking the freeway.

Bobby unable to distinguish between Byron Orlok on screen in *The Terror* and the real Orlok walking towards him.

KEY LINES

Sammy: 'All the best movies have been made.'

Orlok: 'God what an ugly town this has become.'

Orlok on the drive-in audience: 'Strange not hearing any reaction.'

Orlok on Bobby: 'Is *that* what I was afraid of?'

Bobby to police: 'I hardly ever missed, did I?'

TARZAN AND HIS MATE
US, 1934, MGM, 103 MINS

D CEDRIC GIBBONS, (UNCREDITED) JACK CONWAY; **PR** BERNARD K. HYMAN; **SC** JAMES KEVIN MCGUINNESS, **ADAPT** HOWARD EMMETT ROGERS AND LEON GORDON (BASED ON CHARACTERS CREATED BY EDGAR RICE BURROUGHS); **PH** CHARLES G. CLARKE, CLYDE DE VINNA; **M** (UNCREDITED); **ED** TOM HELD
CAST JOHNNY WEISSMULLER (TARZAN), MAUREEN O'SULLIVAN (JANE PARKER), NEIL HAMILTON (HARRY HOLT), PAUL CAVANAGH (MARTIN ARLINGTON), FORRESTER HARVEY (BEAMISH), NATHAN CURRY (SAIAI)

THE STORY In *Tarzan the Ape Man* (1932), Jane Parker comes to Africa to join her father, and his assistant, Harry Holt, in search of the ivory in a remote elephant's graveyard. When they're attacked by pygmies, Tarzan, a verbally challenged European reared by apes, comes to their rescue and following her father's death from battle wounds, Jane remains with Tarzan, and Harry, who's in love with her, returns to civilization. A year later, in *Tarzan and His Mate*, Harry recruits his British friend, the penniless, womanizing adventurer Martin Arlington, in a scheme to win back his fiancée with European perfumes and a modish wardrobe, and to get rich through the secret ivory hoard. On their journey, Harry and Martin's rival hunters are killed by ferocious tribesmen, and are saved from death by

Tarzan and Jane, whom they tempt with European clothes. When Tarzan refuses to help them find the elephants' grave-yard, Martin kills an elephant to make him take them there. He then shoots Tarzan, claiming the Ape Man died fighting a croc-odile. But Cheetah, Jane's personal monkey, comes to Tarzan's aide. Harry and Martin die when a native tribe calls on lions to kill them, and Tarzan, his elephants and his chimpanzees arrive in time to rescue Jane.

THE FILM Like *The Godfather Part II*, *Tarzan and His Mate* is that rare thing, a sequel that is superior to the original. Johnny Weissmuller was the best of all screen Tarzans and this was his best film. Its Africa is pure Hollywood, or European fantasy, and the ethos of a place populated by dangerous animals, reptiles and natives readily subjugated by the right white man is nowadays politically incorrect. The film-makers, however, underplay Edgar Rice Burroughs's racism by not insisting on Tarzan's aristocratic background. Their movie is violent, sexy, funny and fast-moving and much livelier than any Tarzan movies before or after. The rigid application of the Hollywood Production Code shortly after this picture was made ruled out from later pictures the sexual innuendo, the nudity and Jane's scanty clothing. Subsequent films make far less of her sexual attraction to Tarzan or of the way she is torn between the city and the jungle.

ODD/SALIENT FACTS This is the only film on which Cedric Gibbons, long-time head of MGM's design department, is cred-ited as director, but in fact much of it was directed by Jack Conway who took over from Gibbons. Johnny Weissmuller, who made ten Tarzan movies, was Olympic swimming cham-pion in 1924 and 1928, and in 1950 was voted the greatest swimmer of the first half of this century. A parallel series of Tarzan movies were produced by Sol Lesser and his son Julian, leading to one critic calling one of their films 'the evil of two Lessers'. The Irish-born Maureen O'Sullivan, who played Jane five times, was the mother of Mia Farrow, whose screen mother she played in Woody Allen's *Hannah and Her Sisters*.

MEMORABLE MOMENTS Tarzan saving Jane from a lion, a rhino, a leopard and a crocodile.

Harry and Martin's party battling with a gang of gorillas as they climb an escarpment.

Tarzan, Jane and Cheetah performing acrobatic feats as they swing through the jungle.

Harry and Martin looking at Jane's naked silhouette as

▲ *TARZAN AND HIS MATE Me Jane, you Tarzan, she Cheetah – the whole family until Tarzan Finds a Son (i.e. Johnny Sheffield).*

she changes in the tent into the European clothes they have brought her.

Tarzan puzzling out the workings of a gramophone.

KEY LINES

Martin Arlington: 'She's priceless – a woman who's learnt the abandon of a savage and yet would be at home in Mayfair.'

Arlington: 'It's the survival of the fittest.'
Harry Holt: 'Up here the fittest is Tarzan and he wouldn't let her go.'

Arlington: 'You're the first woman I've ever had to coax *into* a dress.'

Tarzan: 'Jane loves Tarzan – Tarzan loves Jane.'

The line 'Tarzan – Jane' (*not* 'Me Tarzan – you Jane') appears in *Tarzan the Apeman*.

THE TERMINATOR★

US, 1984, CINEMA '84/GREENBERG BROTHERS/PACIFIC WESTERN/EURO FILM FUNDING/ORION PICTURES, 107 MINS

D JAMES CAMERON; **PR** GALE ANNE HURD; **SC** JAMES CAMERON AND GALE ANNE HURD; **PH** (COL) ADAM GREENBERG; **M** BRAD FIEDEL; TERMINATOR CREATED BY STAN WINSTON; **ED** MARK GOLDBLATT

CAST ARNOLD SCHWARZENEGGER (TERMINATOR), MICHAEL BIEHN (KYLE REESE), LINDA HAMILTON (SARAH CONNOR), PAUL WINFIELD (TRAXLER), LANCE HENRIKSEN (VULOVICH), RICK ROSSOVICH (MATT), BESS MOTTA (GINGER), EARL BOEN (SILBERMAN), DICK MILLER (PAWN SHOP CLERK), SHAWN SCHEPPS (NANCY), FRANCO COLUMBU (FUTURE TERMINATOR), BILL PAXTON (PUNK LEADER)

THE STORY We cut from Los Angeles AD 2029 to LA in 1984. Two naked men arrive separately, each with a blinding flash of light, in the city at night, both in pursuit of Sarah Connor. The bigger man, the Terminator, steals an arsenal of hi-tech weaponry and kills the first Sarah Connor to be listed in the phone book. Meanwhile the real Sarah, a waitress, is freaked out by this first death but terrified when she learns that the second Sarah has also been killed. The Terminator kills Sarah's flatmate and the flatmate's boyfriend and tracks Sarah down to a nightclub. There, Sarah's life is saved by the other man, Reese, who explains that Sarah's unborn (unconceived) son will in the future save the planet from the machines that have taken over, that the machines have sent a Terminator back in time to kill her before she can produce her

'I'll be back.'

son, and that her grown-up son has in turn sent him, Reese, back in time to protect her, and as it turns out to father him, John. Pursued through the city, and then to a police station the couple at last seek refuge in the country. Having killed Sarah's mother, the Terminator finds them and in a final confrontation in some indeterminate automated factory, Reese is killed and the Terminator destroyed. Sarah, newly pregnant, heads off to Mexico assured of her own crucial role in the post-apocalyptic future.

THE FILM James Cameron came to *The Terminator* after the unpromising directorial debut with *Piranha II: The Spawning* (1981). His real preparation had been his degree in physics and early work in the art departments of films such as *Battle Beyond the Stars* (1980) and John Carpenter's *Escape From New York* (1981). What this culminated in was the film that launched the movie career of Arnold Schwarzenegger and is arguably the best, most imaginative and interesting action film of the last twenty years. Coming from the subsequently profligate Cameron, the most striking aspect of *The Terminator* is its budget – $8 million. It is the film's beautifully constructed plot and its surprisingness at the time, coming unheralded as it did, that lend it an enduring cult status. The effects are jerky and grainy, whereas the sequel, which ultimately negates the entire story of the first film, has slick, computerized liquid-metal effects which Cameron first exploited in *The Abyss* (1989). Never has Arnold Schwarzenegger been better used on screen, with an economical script requiring him to deliver fewer than 200 words.

ODD/SALIENT FACTS The central idea of the film, perhaps borrowed unconsciously from a comic strip, of two men travelling back in time to battle for the future, is brilliantly neat. But in this compact, roller-coaster script, the exploration of the notion of time travel is just one of three big ideas toyed with. The club in which Sarah takes refuge is called the Tech Noir, pointing at another of the main strands of the film. In his direction, as well as within his scripts, Cameron has consistently involved himself in technical developments and pushed the boundaries of computer effects. It is ironic that this technophile should achieve his first great success with one of the most obsessively technophobic films of all time. The film is an extended essay on the dangers of unrestricted technological advance. Reese explains: 'It was the machines, Sarah.' In *The Terminator*, everything bad that happens, does so because of some machine or other: answerphones, telephones, walkmans. The film also marks the beginning of perhaps the most consistent strand in Cameron's work – the centrality of women in the action film and the idea that women are ultimately tougher, better equipped to survive crises than men. Sarah's surface ordinariness (like the Arnie character in *True Lies*, 1994) masks her natural abilities, her innate strength. Within twenty-four hours of being informed of her awesome destiny, she is preparing field dressings, and showing herself as a motivator, a fighter and a survivor impervious to pain. Her character foreshadows the natural superwomen of *Aliens* (1986) and *The Abyss*.

MEMORABLE MOMENTS The Terminator performing eye surgery on himself.

shadows, sweeping crane shots, fast tracking movements, garish hotel rooms and sordid neon-lit streets, creating a mood that embodies the lives of the character. The tormented Quinlan, his wife murdered, himself crippled by a gangster's bullet, is a tragic figure, as complex as Kane, Macbeth or Falstaff. He is an evil man, yet he intuitively knows the guilty from the innocent, and he is destroyed by breaching his own twisted code. The movie is populated by grotesques like Grandi with his ill-fitting wig, the blind woman shopkeeper, the deranged motel clerk. Vargas is perhaps the only normal, untainted character, and he's the voice of decency, though dull and unimaginative.

Most of the cast are familiar faces from earlier Welles pictures. Notably there are four actors from *Kane* – the credited Ray Collins and Harry Shannon, the uncredited Joseph Cotten and Gus Schilling. *Kane* is evoked by Quinlan's cane. 'His cane. I forgot to give him his cane', Menzies shouts, and it is the cane left at the scene of Grandi's murder that does for Quinlan.

ODD/SALIENT FACTS The film was cut and scenes added after Welles left Hollywood, but it has since been restored in two versions. The sequence where Janet Leigh encounters a disturbed young night clerk at the motel where she's the only guest anticipates *Psycho*, which Hitchcock was to make two years later at the same studio. The veteran cinematographer Russell Metty did some of his best work on *Touch of Evil*. In 1960 Metty won an Oscar for *Spartacus*.

MEMORABLE MOMENTS The virtuoso three and a half-minute opening take from the priming of the bomb to its explosion off screen.

▼ *TOUCH OF EVIL* Good cop Charlton Heston goes eyeball to eyeball with bad cop Orson Welles.

Quinlan's first appearance, shot from ground level as he levers himself out of a police car with his cane.

The murder of Grandi, the only light source being a flashing neon sign from the street.

The final pursuit of Quinlan in a Mexican wasteland beneath oil derricks looking like creatures feeding in a primeval swamp.

KEY LINES

Quinlan: 'I'm no lawyer – all they think about is the law.'

Vargas: 'This isn't the real Mexico. All border towns bring out the worst in people.'

Vargas: 'A policeman's job is only easy in a police state.'

Schwartz: 'Hank was a great detective alright.'
Tanya: 'And a lousy cop.'

TWO-LANE BLACKTOP

US, 1971, UNIVERSAL, 102 MINS

D *MONTE HELLMAN;* **PR** *MICHAEL S. LAUGHLIN;* **SC** *RUDOLPH WURLITZER, WILLY CORRY;* **PH** *(TECHNICOLOR WIDESCREEN) JACK DEERSON;* **M SUP** *BILLY JAMES;* **ED** *MONTE HELLMAN*

CAST *WARREN OATES (GTO), JAMES TAYLOR (THE DRIVER), DENNIS WILSON (THE MECHANIC), LAURIE BIRD (THE GIRL), BILL KELLER (TEXAS HITCHHIKER), H. D. STANTON (OKLAHOMA HITCH-HIKER), KATHERINE SQUIRE (OLD WOMAN), MELISSA HELLMAN (CHILD)*

THE STORY The Driver and the Mechanic, both laconic, long-haired and in their twenties, win a Californian drag race in their souped-up Chevrolet and head east for more races. In Arizona they are passed by GTO, a middle-aged man in an orange Pontiac. At Flagstaff a young girl quits her psychedelic van and climbs into the back of their Chevy. In Santa Fe they beat a local driver, and the Girl sleeps with the Mechanic. GTO meets up with them at a filling station, they taunt each other, and agree to race to Washington DC, the winner taking the other's car. GTO adopts a different identity – war veteran, test pilot, TV producer – for everyone he meets. He and the boys alternately help and hinder each other as they race through Texas and Oklahoma. The Girl drives a wedge between the

▲ *TWO-LANE BLACKTOP Chameleon GTO warily sizes up the Driver, the Girl and the Mechanic.*

Mechanic and the Driver, before moving over to GTO's car and he offers to take her places after the race. Suddenly, however, she rides off with a young motorcyclist, and the race is abandoned. GTO takes two GIs aboard and spins them a yarn. The Driver and the Mechanic compete in a race but as the car is accelerating the film burns up in the projector.

THE FILM This is arguably the best, most austere of the pessimistic road movies of the late 1960s; pictures like Coppola's *The Rain People*, Hopper's *Easy Rider*, Spielberg's *Duel*, all reflecting the tensions of the divisive years of Nixon and the Vietnam War, when the counter-culture was pitted against the Establishment, the hip against the square.

The film's images are bleached out to prevent the West from looking romantic, the car races aren't exciting, the characters have no histories, and they work in the margins of a disturbed nomadic society, identifying themselves through their relationship with their cars. The Girl undermines their alliance. The relationship between the boys and GTO is illuminated by a passage in Tony Tanner's 1970 study of American fiction, *City of Words*:

In many recent American novels we will find the hero in quest of identity confronting a Protean figure whose quick metamorphoses seem to make him enviably well adapted to reality; but the hero seldom takes him for a model, no matter how he may learn from him, for that way lies chaos, the nightmare jelly, the ultimate dissolution of self.

217

camouflage his car. A pair of vicious gays attempt to steal the car. Super Soul, a blind black DJ, publicizes the chase and sends him helpful messages. But a gang of rednecks break into the station, beat up Super Soul and his engineer, and put out dangerous disinformation. A hippie biker and his girlfriend living in a Death Valley shack help him make it to the Californian border. Meanwhile a series of flashbacks and police information bulletins have revealed that Kowalski served in Vietnam, was wounded and won the Medal of Honor. Subsequently he worked with distinction as a cop before being discharged for attacking a colleague who had attempted to rape a female suspect. In 1966 his countercultural girlfriend died while surfing. The movie ends with a smiling Kowalski driving at top speed at the road block and his white Challenger going up in flames.

THE FILM *Vanishing Point* is a time-capsule film of the 1960s ethos, all the purer for being a British-financed production shot entirely on location in the United States. The hero, Kowalski, is obviously named for that embodiment of the positive, aggressive American spirit, Stanley Kowalski, protagonist/antagonist of Tennessee Williams's *A Streetcar Named Desire*. Like Wyatt and Billy in *Easy Rider* and the Driver and Mechanic in *Two-Lane*

Blacktop, the countercultural road movies that preceded and followed it, *Vanishing Point* has a central character embarked on a death trip. On his side are a drug-dealer, a blind DJ who acts as a Greek chorus, an elderly desert dweller, a hippie biker and his girlfriend. Against them are arraigned the police of four states, Colorado, Utah, Nevada and California. In between, listening on the airwaves, waiting for something to happen, are the citizens of anonymous towns. The young protagonists of *Easy Rider* and *Two-Lane Blacktop* are outside the system. The middle-aged GTO in *Two-Lane Blacktop* remains an enigmatic chameleon. Kowalski is presented as someone who has paid his dues as a soldier and cop, joined the counterculture, been disillusioned, has only death to face and elects to die on his own terms in a mad assault against the bulldozers in his path.

ODD/SALIENT FACTS Guillermo Cain, the film's credited screenwriter, is a pseudonym for one of the most gifted writers of the second half of the twentieth century, the Cuban critic and novelist G. Cabrera Infante. Also, Iain Quarrier, credited as

▼ *VANISHING POINT* Two venomous gay hitchhikers fail to faze death-seeking Barry Newman.

'Creative Associate', was a British protégé of Roman Polanski and had minor roles in *Cul-de-Sac* and *The Fearless Vampire Killers*. Cleavon Little found permanent cult fame as the black sheriff in Mel Brooks's *Blazing Saddles*.

MEMORABLE MOMENTS Aerial shots of Kowalski making patterns in the sand of Death Valley.

Kowalski discovering his girl's surfboard washed up on the beach.

The Prospector arriving to capture the rattlesnake that threatens Kowalski.

The rednecks (maybe disguised policemen) smashing the radio station.

KEY LINES

DJ Super Soul: 'There goes the Challenger being chased by the blue, blue meanies on wheels. The vicious traffic squad cars are after an unknown driver, the last American hero, the electric sitar, the super driver of the Gold West [...]You can beat the road, you can even beat the clock, you can't beat the desert, nobody can.'

Prospector: The best way to get away is to root right where you are.'

Super Soul: 'Big Brother's not so much watching as listening in.'

THE WANDERERS

US/NETHERLANDS, 1979, ARROW FILMS, 117 MINS

D PHILIP KAUFMAN; **PR** MARTIN RANSOHOFF; **SC** PHILIP KAUFMAN AND ROSE KAUFMAN, BASED ON THE NOVEL BY RICHARD PRICE; **PH** (COL) MICHAEL CHAPMAN; **M** VARIOUS; **ED** RONALD ROOSE, STUART H. PAPPÉ

CAST KEN WAHL (RICHIE), JOHN FRIEDRICH (JOEY), KAREN ALLEN (NINA), TONI KALEM (DESPIE GALASSO), ALAN ROSENBERG (TURKEY), JIM YOUNGS (BUDDY), TONY GANIOS (PERRY), LINDA MANZ (PEEWEE), WILLIAM ANDREWS (EMILIO), ERLAND VAN LIDTH DE JEUDE (TERROR), VAL AVERY (MR SHARP), DOLPH SWEET (CHUBBY GALASSO)

THE STORY The Bronx, 1963. Turkey, Joey, Richie and Buddy, members of the Italian New York gang the Wanderers, are

▲ THE WANDERERS *The gang try out their unsubtle collective chat-up technique on another unsuspecting young New Yorker.*

saved from a beating at the hands of rival gang, the Baldies, by new kid Perry. Joey's brutal father is having an affair with Perry's alcoholic mother. Richie is dating Despie, the daughter of a local gangster, Chubby Galasso. Turkey has shaved his head in the hope of joining the Baldies. A liberal high-school teacher's lesson in racial harmony leads to racial conflict in the classroom between the Wanderers and various black gangs. Richie meets and instantly falls for the middle-class Nina, but tries to set her up with Joey. He, Buddy, Perry and Joey follow her in their car, but get lost and wander into the territory of the sinister Ducky Boys. They just manage to escape with their lives. During a party at Despie's house, Richie and Nina are caught making out in a car. Turkey, now a member of the Baldies, stumbles into the Ducky Boys and is killed. The following day President Kennedy is assassinated, and Richie and Despie make up. She is pregnant by him and Richie is forced to marry her. The arrival of the Ducky Boys at a football game unites the Wanderers with the black gangs and the Wongs who together drive them away. At Joey's bachelor party the different gang members join together in harmony. Nina passes the restaurant. Richie runs after her but only stops and watches as she goes into a folk club. Joey and Perry drive out west as Richie returns to his party where everyone joins in singing 'The Wanderer'.

THE FILM This is an episodic film, a series of adventures marking a specific time of change in American life. It is partly a light-hearted coming-of-age film with comic-book escapades, partly a serious look at the politicization of the country and its popular music, and how America was transformed by the death of Kennedy. The sequence in which the Baldies are coerced into joining the Marines is a comic sketch waiting for a punch line. Instead they just drive off, a bunch of no-hopers on their way to Vietnam. In the climactic sequence, Richie follows Nina but realizes that their paths only crossed briefly. He watches longingly as she takes her seat in the folk club where Bob Dylan, perhaps too emblematically, sings 'The times, they are a'changin'' and he realizes he isn't part of this world. It is the strangest and darkest of the Seventies coming-of-age films.

ODD/SALIENT FACTS The film is the second, after *Bloodbrothers* (1978), to be adapted from a novel by Richard Price, who plays one of the bowling bankrollers. An authentic voice of New York street life, Price wrote the screenplay for *Sea of Love* (1989) and two for Scorsese, *The Color of Money* (1986) and the 'Life Lessons' segment from *New York Stories* (1989). *The Color of Money* is the belated sequel to *The Hustler* (1960), which is name-checked in the sequence in which Price appears. When Chubby Galasso gets his revenge on the bowling team that hustled Richie and his friends, he smashes the bowling hand of one of them in emulation of the famous scene in his favourite movie. When Walter Hill was accused of stealing from Kaufman in *The Long Riders* (1982), he quipped, referring to The Wanderers: 'If he can steal *The Warriors* from me then I can steal *The Great Northfield Minnesota* raid from him.'

MEMORABLE MOMENTS The Baldies, now including Turkey in their number, indulge in a game of 'cock 'n' roll' or 'cock and rock' with Richie and Joey. The two are taken to the park, and tied to a fence on a bridge over a stream. Each has one end of a length of twine tied around his penis, with the other tied around a hefty stone. Turkey throws the rock over the bridge, Joey and Richie scream until the rock, with plenty of twine to spare, hits the water.

The scene after Turkey's murder, where Joey wanders along the street. He sees a group of people, some weeping, staring into a shop window. As he gets closer he sees that it is a TV shop and they are watching the news of JFK's assassination.

KEY LINES

Turkey: 'Nobody fucks with the Baldies, man.'
Joey: 'Those guys look like pricks with ears.'

Galasso, on the racial divisions among high-school kids:
'It's a shame to see kids beating each other's brains out. Especially when there's no financial advantage.'

WHITE HEAT
US, 1949, WARNER BROS, 114 MINS

D RAOUL WALSH; **PR** LOUIS F. EDELMAN; **SC** IVAN GOOF, BEN ROBERTS; **PH** (BW) SID HICKOX; **M** MAX STEINER; **ED** OWEN MARKS

CAST JAMES CAGNEY (CODY JARRETT), VIRGINIA MAYO (VERNA JARRETT), EDMOND O'BRIEN (HANK FALLON/VIC PARDO), MARGARET WYCHERLEY (MA JARRETT), STEVE COCHRAN (BIG ED SOMMERS), JOHN ARCHER (PHILIP EVANS), WALLY CASSELL (COTTON VALETTI), FRED CLARK (TRADER), FORD RAINEY (ZUCKIE HOMMELL), FRED COBY (HAPPY TAYLOR), G. PAT COLLINS (READER), MICKEY KNOX (HET KOHLER), PAUL GUILFOYLE (ROY PARKER), ROBERT OSTERLOH (TOMMY RYLEY), IAN MACDONALD (BO CREEL), RAY MONTGOMERY (TRENT), MARSHALL BRADFORD (CHIEF OF POLICE)

THE STORY Cody Jarrett and his gang pull off a raid on a train in which four railway men are killed and one of his gang badly scalded. As the police are closing in, Jarrett gives himself up and confesses to a lesser crime committed at the same time as the train job. As Jarrett begins his two-year stretch, the Treasury Department send in their undercover specialist Hank Fallon to pose as Cody's cell mate, Vic Pardo, find out the truth about Jarrett's crimes and discover the identity of his money launderer. Pardo saves Jarrett's life and becomes a trusted friend. He helps comfort Jarrett when his beloved mother is killed for standing up to Big Ed, one of Jarrett's men taking advantage of his boss's absence. In fact Verna, Jarrett's wife, was having an affair with Ed and she shot Ma Jarrett in the back. Jarrett and Pardo escape from jail and Pardo becomes a gang member on Jarrett's next big job on a chemical plant. During the raid, Pardo is at last unmasked as a cop, but manages to escape. The police pick off the gang one by one until it is just Jarrett left. He makes his way to the top of a vast petrol tank. Fallon shoots Jarrett who in

▲ *WHITE HEAT* Cody Jarrett (James Cagney) goes out with a big bang and fulfils his promise: 'Made it, Ma. Top of the world.'

turn fires at the tank and disappears in a vast explosion.

THE FILM Cagney was on a bad box-office run during the late Forties when he chose this project to revive his fortunes. He reunited with Raoul Walsh, who had directed him in one of his best gangster films, *The Roaring Twenties* (1939). The project also marked his return to Warner Bros., the studio where he had had his early success and had become an icon (and had grown to loathe studio boss Jack). The writers based the action on the story of Ma Barker, and distilled all the brothers into one intense, violent, mother-fixated psychopath. It is at times a crude public information film showing off the cops' latest technology. We see their well-orchestrated, discreet pursuit of Ma Jarrett through the streets of a Californian town using three alternating

cars. They use spectrograph scans and fingerprints to establish a link between Jarrett and the train job. Later Fallon/Pardo improvises a radio which the cops use to track down the gang at the chemical plant.

At the same time it is a dark exploration of violent psychosis and betrayal. It is a study of an insane, unpredictable, vindictive cold-blooded killer. But the power of Cagney's personality makes him the magnetic force of the film. The audience roots for Jarrett and despises the anonymous, bland and deceitful cops. Jarrett is a brilliant crook, who is defeated not by his psychic flaws, but by the actions of others. On the first raid fellow gang members use his real name, tune in a radio, choose not to kill their badly wounded friend. His mother is spotted by the police while out buying strawberries for him. He is betrayed by Big Ed, Verna and finally by the only person he really trusted apart from his Ma, Pardo. As Jarrett, Cagney gives one of the great performances in the cinema. Orson Welles believed

KEY LINES

Damiel (to Cassiel): 'It's great to exist as the spirit, to testify, day after day and forever on the spiritual in people's minds. But I do get tired of my physical existence, of forever hovering above. I wish I could grow a weight which would bind me to the earth. I wish I could say at each step, at each gust of wind, "Now". Say "Now" and "Now" and no longer "Forever" and "For eternity" ... Every time we participated it was a pretence ... It would be rather nice to come home after a long day and feed the cat like Philip Marlowe, to have a fever, black on my fingers from reading a newspaper. For once to find excitement not in the mind but in a meal.'

Homer (while flicking through a book of photographs by August Sandor): 'If I do give up, mankind will lose its storyteller, and once mankind has lost its storyteller it will have lost its childhood.'

Damiel (after becoming human and meeting Marion): 'To know now what no angel knows.'

WITCHFINDER GENERAL (US TITLE: THE CONQUEROR WORM)

UK, 1968, TIGON BRITISH, 87 MINS

D MICHAEL REEVES; **PR** TONY TENSER, ARNOLD L. MILLER, LOUIS N. HAYWARD; **SC** MICHAEL REEVES, TOM BAKER (FROM THE NOVEL BY RONALD BASSETT); **PH** (EASTMAN COLOR) JOHNNY COQUILLON; **M** PAUL FERRIS; **ED** HOWARD LANNING

CAST VINCENT PRICE (MATTHEW HOPKINS), IAN OGILVY (RICHARD MARSHALL), HILARY DWYER (SARA), RUPERT DAVIES (JOHN LOWES), ROBERT RUSSELL (JOHN STEARNE), MICHAEL BEINT (CAPTAIN GORDON), NICKY HENSON (TROOPER SWALLOW), PATRICK WYMARK (OLIVER CROMWELL), WILFRID BRAMBELL (MASTER LOACH)

THE STORY England, 1645. Matthew Hopkins is travelling through a country torn by civil war with his brutal assistant John Stearne, lining his pockets and identifying and executing witches. He is invited to a small Suffolk town where peasants have denounced their priest, John Lowes. Sara, Lowes's niece, is betrothed to Richard Marshall, a farmer and officer in Cromwell's army. To save her uncle from torture she gives herself to the lecherous Hopkins. But after she has been raped by Stearne, the disgusted Hopkins proceeds to torture and hang Lowes. Marshall returns and vows vengeance on Hopkins and Stearne, who renew their alliance. Marshall hears that Hopkins is holding witchcraft trials in Lavenham, Suffolk. He is re-united with Sara only for them both to be arrested by Hopkins, charged with witchcraft and taken to the local castle. As Sara is being tortured, two of Marshall's comrades attack the castle. Marshall breaks free, blinds Stearne with his boot and is hacking Hopkins to death with an axe when Trooper Swallow breaks in to end the Witchfinder's life with a bullet. Sara lies on the torture table screaming, and the picture concludes with this freeze frame.

THE FILM This ferocious low-budget period horror movie, an exploitation version of Arthur Miller's *The Crucible*, is one of a small handful of pictures to touch on one of the major episodes of Western European history, the English Civil War and the Commonwealth. The film begins with a woman, protesting her innocence, being dragged to the gallows to be hanged as a witch. It ends with another woman, also accused of witchcraft, screaming on the block after her torturers have been killed. *Witchfinder General* is about a disturbed Puritan – part true believer, part opportunist – taking advantage of a divided, lawless nation to exercise his guilty licentiousness, greed and sadism under the guise of duty. His initially decent antagonist, Marshall, is corrupted by his instinct for revenge, his growing violence reflected in the increasingly demented way he gallops through the countryside. The film's exteriors are flat, open, more agoraphobic than idyllic; the interiors have the cold, precise tone of Van Dyck.

The great cult actor Vincent Price gives one of his most restrained performances as Matthew Hopkins, a historical figure who in reality lived to write his memoirs and died in his bed. The cult status of the film began with its original release when it was denounced for its sadism by most critics, and praised for its historical insight by a few. The most famous of the film's assailants was the playwright and former academic historian,

> 'Perhaps he had a motive. People have strange motives for the things they do.'

▲ *WITCHFINDER GENERAL Vincent Price and his sleazy accomplice Robert Russell go about their venal business.*

Alan Bennett (writing in *The Listener*); its foremost supporters were Tom Milne (*Monthly Film Bulletin*) and Robin Wood (*Movie*). Within weeks of the film's release, its 25-year-old director Michael Reeves died of a drug overdose, having directed three and a half movies, all in the exploitation horror genre, of which this is by some way his best.

ODD/SALIENT FACTS Michael Klinger and Tony Tenser, the owners of Tigon, the British exploitation company behind *Witchfinder General* and Reeves's *The Sorcercers*, had financed Polanski's first English-speaking films, the low-budget *Repulsion* (1965) and *Cul-de-Sac* (1966). Cinematographer John Coquillon went on to shoot four films for Sam Peckinpah, including *Straw Dogs* (1971) and *Pat Garrett and Billy the Kid* (1973). In the United States, *Witchfinder General* was released

as *The Conqueror Worm*, beginning with quotations from Edgar Allan Poe's macabre poem of that title, to give the impression that it was a continuation of Vincent Price's Poe series.

MEMORABLE MOMENTS Cutting from Marshall and Sara making love to Hopkins, dressed in black, riding through the countryside with his grim assistant.

The silhouette of Hopkins and his accomplices leading the captive Marshall and Sara up the hill to Lavenham Castle – a homage to Bergman's *The Seventh Seal*.

KEY LINES

The Revd. Lowes: 'It is not the King's armies which bring death this year. The lack of order in the land encourages strange ideas.'

Matthew Hopkins: 'Perhaps he had a motive. People have strange motives for the things they do.'

Matthew Hopkins: 'I intend to instigate a new method of execution, a fitting end to the foul ungodliness in womankind.'

Marshall to the soldier who shoots Hopkins to put him out of his misery: 'You took him from me! You took him from me!'

WITHNAIL AND I★

UK, 1986, HANDMADE FILMS, 107 MINS

D BRUCE ROBINSON; **PR** PAUL HELLIER; **SC** BRUCE ROBINSON;
PH PETER HANNAN; **M** DAVID DUNDAS, RICK WENTWORTH;
ED ALAN STRACHAN
CAST RICHARD E. GRANT (WITHNAIL), PAUL MCGANN (I),
RICHARD GRIFFITHS (MONTY), RALPH BROWN (DANNY), MICHAEL
ELPHICK (JAKE), DARAGH O'MALLEY (IRISHMAN), MICHAEL
WARDLE (ISACS PARKIN), UNA BRANDON-JONES (MRS PARKIN),
NOEL JOHNSON (GENERAL), IRENE SUTCLIFFE (WAITRESS),
LLEWELLYN REES (TEA SHOP PROPRIETOR), ROBERT OATES
(POLICEMAN ONE), ANTHONY WISE (POLICEMAN TWO), EDDIE
TAGOE (PRESUMING ED)

THE STORY Camden Town, London, 1969. It is nearly the end of 'the greatest decade in the history of mankind' and the two out-of-work actors are coming down off a 60-hour bender. Living in a seedy flat shared by rodents, resorting to embrocation for warmth, and lighter fluid for intoxication, they resolve to get out of the city for a few days to 'rejuvenate'. So they seek out Withnail's theatrical, camp Uncle Monty and persuade him to let them use his country retreat near Penrith. They travel there in a beaten-up Jaguar and have a boozy idyll, while struggling to stay warm and scavenge food. Petrified of Jake, the local poacher, they are joined by Monty, who has designs on I. Barely managing to resist Monty's amorous advances, I insists on returning to London having landed an acting role. There they face Danny, their drug dealer, squatting in their flat, an eviction notice and an acting job that will end their friendship.

THE FILM *Withnail and I* was relatively unsuccessful at the box office but grew, largely by word-of-mouth, into its current status as a modern cult classic. The casting is perfect, and in the film's central character, Withnail, the tragically failed actor, a neu-

rotically deranged, hysterical, hilarious, doomed figure, it provides one of the great characters in British cinema. It was Grant's first screen role, and launched his career. Bruce Robinson, having written the screenplay for *The Killing Fields*, decided to have as his directorial debut a film loosely based on his own experiences as a drama student in the Sixties. He revealed in the introduction to the 10th Anniversary edition of his screenplay that Withnail was based on his friend Vivian who, like his fictional incarnation, was brilliant at being himself. He and Viv apparently used to visit the wolves in London Zoo often, and according to Robinson, a self-confessed liar, the chief model for the character of Withnail, died of cancer (at an unspecified date).

ODD/SALIENT FACTS 'While My Guitar Gently Weeps', which is playing on the soundtrack as Withnail & I return to their flat after Penrith, was written by George Harrison, the film's executive producer. Richard Starkey MBE is credited as special production consultant. The adoration of fans for the film has extended beyond the standard quotation of the film's many memorable lines into more dangerous territory. The *Withnail and I* drinking game apparently requires players to match the film's characters drink for drink. To be played correctly this would demand the consumption of: lighter fluid (presumably optional),

'Warm up? We may as well sit around a cigarette.'

two large gins and a pint of cider, several swigs of sherry and a rhesus-negative bloody Mary, a couple of shots of whisky, an assortment of red wines, a few large scotches, at least two pints and two quadruple whiskies, more wine and finally, and expensively, a 1953 Château Margaux. Richard E. Grant is a teetotaller, allergic to alcohol. In early drafts of the script the Paul McGann character was called Marwood.

MEMORABLE MOMENTS The confrontation with the aggressive Irishman in the Mother Black Cap, a Camden Town pub recreated in West London. Withnail reveals himself as an inventive coward, pleading with the man: 'I have a heart condition. I have a heart condition. If you hit me it will be murder. My wife is having a baby.'

The trip to uncle Monty's in which Monty reminisces about his acting career and reveals his love of vegetables.

The rolling and smoking of the Camberwell Carrot, about which Danny explains: 'I invented it in Camberwell and it looks like a carrot.'

KEY LINES

Withnail: 'I feel as sick as a pike.'

Withnail, having spat on the floor: 'Jesus, look at that. Apart from a raw potato, that's the only solid to have passed my lips in the last 60 hours.'

Withnail, desperately: 'I must have some booze, I demand to have some booze.'

Withnail on his hangover: 'I feel like a pig shat in my head.'

Withnail having arrived in the cottage: 'Warm up? We may as well sit around a cigarette.'

Withnail to the farmer: 'We've gone on holiday by mistake.'

Withnail in the tea rooms: 'We want the finest wines available to humanity.'

THE YELLOW SUBMARINE
UK, 1968, UNITED ARTISTS, 87 MINS

D GEORGE DUNNING; **PR** AL BRODAX; **SC** LEE MINOFF, AL BRODAX, JACK MENDELSOHN, ERICH SEGAL; **ST** LEE MINOFF; **PH** (COL DELUXE) JOHN WILLIAMS; **DES** HEINZ EDELMAN, JOHN CRAMER, GORDON HARRISON; **M** THE BEATLES, GEORGE MARTIN; **ED** BRIAN J. BISHOP

VOICES JOHN CLIVE (JOHN), GEOFFREY HUGHES (PAUL), PAUL ANGELUS (RINGO/CHIEF BLUE MEANIE), DICK EMERY (LORD MAYOR/BOOB)

THE STORY In Pepperland all is well until the Blue Meanies and their Chief freeze the people, turn everything grey and rid the country of music. Fred, the leader of Sergeant Pepper's Lonely Hearts Club Band escapes in his yellow submarine and travels to Liverpool. There he recruits The Beatles to help him and together they go back to Pepperland, travelling through the Sea of Time, the Sea of Science, the Sea of Monsters, the Sea of Green, the Sea of Holes, on the way picking up the verbose polymath Nowhere Man, Boob. In Pepperland, the band find instruments, and defeat the Blue Meanies bringing music and colour and love back to the land.

THE FILM By 1968, The Beatles had long since stopped playing live. The previous year they had dazzled the world with the ground-breaking Sgt Pepper's Lonely Hearts Club Band album, which, while representing their greatest achievement, also saw evidence of the band splintering, with individual creations now clearly audible and Paul having decisively taken the reins of the group. All four had been experimenting with acid for some time and John was well on the way to a drug dependence that would remain with him for much of the remainder of his life. Yet *Yellow Submarine*, as dated as it clearly is, remains a joyous expression of all that was most optimistic of the flower generation. The animation, under the overall design control of Heinz Edelman, is crazy but wonderfully positive and clever, offering a witty collage of modern art from Beardsley to Dalí. The film's cultural references range from *Ulysses* through *Frankenstein* and *King Kong* to The Goons and the Hamlet cigar ads. The story is filled out with The Beatles' bespoke cheeky scouse humour with relentless painful puns along the lines of John's comment, having evaded the 'dreaded vacuum flask': 'So long, sucker.' Essentially a collection of ingenious animated pop videos, with a sweet cameo coda from The Beatles themselves, this remains a superb record of its time, with the unashamedly hippie message of the indomitability of music and love.

ODD/SALIENT FACTS The American release version of the film lacks one song sequence, but, unlike the British version, has film

▼ *THE YELLOW SUBMARINE* The animated Paul, John, Ringo and George bring music and colour back to Pepperland.

of the conversion of the Blue Meanies to the joys of Peace and Love and Music. One of the acts of the Blue Meanies was to subvert the positive image of Pepperland, destroying the vast colourful YESes that decorated the landscape. The word 'Yes' played a crucial role in the life or, according to Albert Goldman, the mythology, of The Beatles. When John visited Yoko Ono's exhibition in Mason's Yard on 7 November 1966, one exhibit was a step-ladder leading to a magnifying glass suspended from the ceiling. In *The Lives of John Lennon*, Goldman writes: 'Lennon anticipated that he would read the sort of phrase that he would have put at the end of the climb, something like "Tee-hee!" or "Fuck you!" He was surprised and pleased to read "Yes".'

MEMORABLE MOMENTS Having regressed to childhood, the band suddenly ages, growing long beards and singing 'When I'm 64'. The dazzling images are interrupted by the slogan 'Sixty-four years is 33, 661, 440 minutes and one minute is a long time … let us demonstrate.' We then see the numbers marking the next 64 seconds rendered as illuminations of the art nouveau and psychedelic periods.

KEY LINES

Peering through one of the doors in Ringo's elaborate house,
George: 'Yes, dey do look very nice, don't dey?'
Ringo: 'Yes, dey do.'
John: 'Dey do, dough, don't dey?'
George: 'Yes, dey do.'
Ringo: 'Don't dey, dough?'
George: 'Doh.'

ZOO IN BUDAPEST
US, 1933, FOX, 85 MINS

D ROWLAND V. LEE; **PR** JESSE L. LASKY; **SC** DAN TOTHEROH, LOUISE LONG, ROWLAND V. LEE (FROM A STORY BY MELVILLE BAKER AND JOHN KIRKLAND); **PH** (BW) LEE GARMES; **ED** HAROLD SCHUSTER; **M** LOUIS DE FRANCESCO
CAST LORETTA YOUNG (EVE), GENE RAYMOND (ZANI), O. P. HEGGIE (DR GRUNBAUM), WALLY ALBRIGHT (PAUL VANDOR), PAUL FIX (HEINIE), MURRAY KINNELL (GARBOSH), RUTH WARREN (KATRINA), ROY STUART (KARL), FRANCES RICH (ELSIE), NILES WELSH (MR VANDOR), LUCILLE WARD (MISS MURST), RUSS POWELL (TOSKI), DOROTHY LIBAIRE (ROSITA)

THE STORY The handsome, fair-haired Zani, works as an assistant in the Budapest Zoo and has a close rapport with the animals. He has spent his whole life there. His mother died the day he was born; his father, a head keeper, was killed by a tiger three years later. The saintly zoo director, Dr Grunbaum, protects him from Herr Garbosh, the zoo's rigid bureaucratic manager, who wants to hand Zani over to the police for stealing (and destroying) furs from rich visitors. Zani loves 18-year-old Eve, who comes to the zoo every week in a party from her orphanage. She is about to be sent away to work at a tannery, and her friends help her escape just as the zoo closes. At the same time Paul, an upper-class child, gives his nanny the slip and hides in the zoo. Meanwhile Zani has stolen a fur and is being sought by the police. Zani finds a sanctuary for Eve in the cave of an unused bear garden, where they're joined by little Paul. Zani's enemy, the lazy, vindictive guard, Heinie spots them. Zani intervenes when Heinie attempts to rape Eve, and Paul accidentally makes all the animals run amok. As Dr Grunbaum tries to restore order, Zani rescues the trapped Paul with the help of Rajah, the elephant, and is badly mauled by a tiger. Paul's father adopts Eve, appoints Zani to care for the animals on his country estate, and the couple marry and settle down to rural bliss.

THE FILM This enchanting fairy tale takes place over a single day and night. Like *King Kong*, made at the same time, it juxtaposes the natural world with a repressive, unnatural society to produce a complex fable about freedom and imprisonment and the effects of unleashing primitive forces. The zoo is at once a prison and an Eden, its expressionist jumble of cages resembles something by Piranese, but the vast ponds where birds live freely suggest a primeval world. The orphans Zani and Eve are like the prelapsarian Adam and Eve with the Dr Grunbaum as a benevolent God. The world outside, the distant, exotic Budapest, parallels Depression America with its uncaring rich and bullied orphans. But it is not only the rich who oppress the animals by taking their furs; the zoo's employees act callously – the officious Garbosh, the vicious Heinie, encouraging animosity between Rajah the elephant and Sultan the tiger. Zani, the naif hero who understands and communicates with the animals, is a forerunner of today's animal rights activists as he steals furs and thus becomes an enemy of society. The movie turns into melodrama, and the role of Paul is more a plot device than a contribution to the film's moral structure.

The picture is held together largely by the magical images of Lee Garmes, one of Hollywood's great cinematographers, who had made several films with Josef von Sternberg and went on to collaborate with Wyler, Hitchcock, Ophuls and Hawks.

ODD/SALIENT FACTS *Zoo in Budapest* was the first production at the Fox studio by Jesse L. Lasky, who the previous year had been ousted from Paramount, the company he had co-founded. In her final film, *Hoopla* (1933), Clara Bow, 'The It Girl', played a tough girl with a travelling carnival and swam in the nude in the pool left over from *Zoo in Budapest*. In 1959 Rowland V. Lee (as writer-producer) worked once more with Lee Garmes on the widescreen biblical epic *The Big Fisherman*.

MEMORABLE MOMENTS Rajah the elephant being encouraged to spray water over Sultan, the caged tiger.

Eve half-concealed by bushes changing from her orphan's uniform into the special dress she and her friends have made.

Zani carrying Eve across the mist-shrouded lake to the sanctuary of the deserted bear-garden.

KEY LINES

Rich visitor to his wife: 'You are an animal, I am an animal, so imagine how we must smell to the other animals.'

Garbosh: 'People come to the zoo to see wild animals, and they see Zani petting them as if they were house-guests.'

Zani: 'In the zoo at night it's peaceful – no people to make the animals nervous.'

▼ *ZOO IN BUDAPEST* Blonde orphan Loretta Young kneels beside idealistic Gene Raymond who has given his all to quell chaos in the zoo.

INDEX

PICTURE ACKNOWLEDGEMENTS

The publisher would like to thank the following for supplying images for this book. Every effort has been made to acknowledge all copyright holders. However, should any photographs not be correctly attributed, the publisher will undertake any appropriate changes in future editions of the book. The images listed below are protected by copyright.

Aquarius: 161, 197, 208.
Ronald Grant Archive: 29, 74, 167.
Kobal Collection: 98, 113, 137; 2, 23, 57, 72, 84, 138, 175, 225 Warner Bros; 42, 110, 129, 222 20th Century Fox; 21, 39, 45, 94, 97, 168 MGM; 17, 46-47, 115, 212, 216 Universal; 37, 89, 92, 106, 131, 155, 180 Columbia; 219 Orion; 24, 78, 122, 204, 206 Paramount; 27; Goskino; 34 Ladd Company/ Warner Bros; 35 Allied Pictures; 44 SNC/Raymond Cauchetier; 48, 66, 101, 104, 109, 128, 136, 150, 200, 203 United Artists; 50, 120, 146, 149, 160, 188, 214 RKO; 51 New World; 53 Columbia/Persky-Bright/Reno; 55, 68 Rank; 58 Bunuel-Dali; 63 Allarts/Erato; 65 Compton-Tekli; 69 Producers' Leasing Corporation; 77 Riama-Pathe; 81 Concord/Warner 82 AFI/Libra; 88 RAO; 91 Herzog/Filmverlage Der

Autoren/ZDF; 103 Columbia/Tri Star; 107 Warhol; 112 Memorial; 117 Wark Producing Company; 119, 194 Allied Artists; 124 Argos; 125 Films Du Carrosse/Sedif/Raymond Cauchetier; 133 Nero; 142 De Laurentiis Group; 143 AIP; 147 MTI/Orion; 152 Prana-Film GMBH, Berlin; 154 Two Cities; 158 Andre Paulve/Films DuPalais Royal; 162 Anglo Amalgamated; 165 British National/Anglo Amalgamated; 170 Embassy Pictures; 173 Republic; 174 Daiei Films; 178 Hammer/Columbia; 182, 184 Lux/Vides/Galatea; 186 Megalovision; 187 Associated British; 190 New Line Cinema; 191 Lion; 193 Metro; 196 MGM/UA; 201 Hal Roach/MGM; 205 Melvin Van Peebles; 211 Vortex-Henkel-Hooper/Bryanston,; 217 Universal/GTO; 223 PSO/POLYC International; 228 Svensk Filmindustri; 229 Road Movies/Argos Films/WDR; 231 Tigon; 235 Fox.
Pictorial Press Limited: 25, 32, 61, 171.
Subafilms 233.
Walt Disney Collection: 86.
Colour section: **Kobal** (in order): Warner Bros, Monty Python Films, Dreamland Productions, Live Entertainment, Zoetrope/UA, Warner Bros, Warner/Goodtime, Handmade Films, British Lion, 20th Century Fox, MGM, Universal, MGM, Columbia, Embassy, Orion, Universal, Warner Bros, 20th Century Fox, Paramount.